BODIES OUT OF BOUNDS

BODIES OUT

OF BOUNDS

Fatness and Transgression

Edited by
Jana Evans Braziel
and Kathleen LeBesco

University of California Press
Berkeley Los Angeles London

University of California Press
Berkeley and Los Angeles, California

University of California Press, Ltd.
London, England

Grateful acknowledgment is made for permission to use: "Fat Beauty" from *Eat Fat* by Richard Klein. Copyright © 1996 by Richard Klein. Reprinted by permission of Pantheon Books, a division of Random House, Inc. Sharon Mazer's " 'She's so fat . . . ' : Facing the Fat Lady at Coney Island's Sideshows by the Seashore" from *Theatre Annual: A Journal of Performance Studies* 47 (fall 1994), published by The College of William and Mary. Michael Moon and Eve Kosofsky Sedgwick's "Divinity: A Dossier, a Performance Piece, and a Little-Understood Emotion," from *Discourse* 13, no. 1 (winter–fall 1990–91); also in *Tendencies* by Eve Kosofsky Sedgwick (Duke University Press, 1993).

Library of Congress Cataloging-in-Publication Data

Bodies out of bounds : fatness and transgression / edited by Jana Evans Braziel and Kathleen LeBesco.

p. cm.

Includes bibliographical references and index.

ISBN 0-520-21746-2 (alk. paper)—ISBN 0-520-22585-6 (pbk. : alk. paper)

1. Obesity—Social aspects—Miscellanea. 2. Overweight women—Social aspects—Miscellanea. 3. Body image—Social aspects—Miscellanea. 4. Physical—Appearance-based bias—Miscellanea. 5. Discrimination against overweight persons—Miscellanea. I. Braziel, Jana Evans, 1967– II. LeBesco, Kathleen, 1970–

RC552.O25 B63 2001
616.3'98'0019—dc21

2001027446

Manufactured in the United States of America

10 09 08 07 06 05 04 03 02 01

10 9 8 7 6 5 4 3 2 1

The paper used in this publication meets the minimum requirements of ANSI / NISO Z39 0.48–1992 (R 1997) (Permanence of Paper).

Contents

Acknowledgments

We would like to thank the contributors for the diligence, patience, and intellectual acuity that made this anthology possible. We would like to thank Naomi Schneider, executive editor at the University of California Press, as well as her editorial assistants, Jeanne Park and Ellie Hickerson, project editor Sue Heinemann, copyeditor Alice Falk, and the director of design and production, Anthony Crouch, for facilitating its publication. We also value and appreciate the feedback provided by Sarah Banet-Weiser, Marcia Millman, and two anonymous reviewers for the Press. Their expertise made the final stages of this process easier and more expeditious, and for that we are deeply grateful.

We offer our sincerest appreciation to Peg Leahy of Troy, New York; Saila Poutiainen of Helsinki, Finland; Jennifer Rodgers in the Comparative Literature Department at the University of Massachusetts–Amherst; and Renee Wingertsman at the Office of Information Technology at the University of Massachusetts–Amherst for technological and administrative assistance.

To our families, to our friends, and to our colleagues at the University of Massachusetts–Amherst (especially, but not only, in the Departments of Communication and Comparative Literature), we express appreciation for your support and encouragement. Specifically, we would like to thank Lisa Henderson, whose graduate seminar, "The Politics of Sexual Representation," fostered our mutual interest in the "power and politics" of corpulence. Our doctoral committee members—Briankle Chang, Leda Cooks, Barbara Cruikshank, Lisa Henderson, David Lenson, Elizabeth Petroff, Catherine Portuges, and Robert Schwartzwald—have been a continued source of support and guidance. Thanks!

Several essays in this collection appeared first in other venues, and for the permission to reprint, we offer acknowledgment and gratitude. Richard Klein's "Fat Beauty" first appeared in *Eat Fat,* published in 1996 by Pantheon Books/Random House, and is reprinted here by their permission. Special thanks to both Richard Klein and Betty Graber, the permissions editor at Random House, for making this possible. Sharon Mazer's essay, " 'She's so fat . . .': Facing the Fat Lady at Coney Island's Sideshows by the Seashore," appeared first in *Theatre Annual: A Journal of Performance Studies* published by The College of William and Mary; the article is reprinted here with editorial permission of Richard H. Palmer. The collaborative essay by Michael Moon and Eve Kosofsky Sedgwick appeared first in *Discourse,* was reprinted in Sedgwick's book *Tendencies* (Duke University Press, 1993), and is reprinted again here with the authors' permission. The cartoon "I was a fat kid" is the work of Max Airborne, and it appears in this book with the artist's permission.

JANA'S PERSONAL ACKNOWLEDGMENTS

I would like to express love and gratitude to my family and close friends—especially my parents, Ronald and Judy Evans; my siblings, Julie Crawford, Dawn Evans Kyle, and Ron Evans; and my dearest of friends, Neil Hartlen, Annelie Klein, and Anita Mannur. I am deeply indebted to my children Jessi, Maddie, and Dylan, for teaching me about love; and of course, to Katie, for pragmatism and near-never-failing humor. For everything else, *and I do mean everything,* I owe this one to Jim.

KATHLEEN'S PERSONAL ACKNOWLEDGMENTS

Thanks to Kurt LeBesco for giving me a reason to fight for fat, and to Peg Leahy for showing me how to be proud; to the dozens of fat activists who have influenced my thinking and writing over the past three years, particularly members of the on-line fat community and the *FaT GiRL* Editorial Collective; to Ben and Jerry for sugary sustenance; to John Shields, Alissa Sklar, and Karen Wolf for unwavering support and friendship; and to Jana Evans Braziel for her strong sense of what we "might could" do if we put our minds to it.

Editors' Introduction

KATHLEEN LEBESCO AND JANA EVANS BRAZIEL

A central question in envisioning this anthology was how to reconceptualize and reconfigure corpulence. Others followed: How does the dominant American popular view of fatness, as bodily excess, diverge from other configurations of fatness? How has fatness been differently constructed in other cultures? in different historical contexts? How can we transcend the restrictive constructions of corpulence within discourses—medical, psychological, and capitalistic—that have accumulated around the site of the "fat body" (the singular denoting the sameness with which such bodies are reductively examined)? How are these discourses deployed in order to contain fat bodies, fat people? How do they simultaneously construct and erase the fat body, attempting to expel it from representation at the very moment that defines it? How can we begin to resist and deconstruct the discourses that place the "corpulent body" under erasure, even as they demarcate its discursive terrain?

One of our objectives, then, is unmasking the fat body, rendering it visible and present, rather than invisible and absent: seen, rather than unsightly. Clearly, this first objective demands a second: the unraveling of the discourses that have most intransigently defined and fixed fat bodies, nearly preventing the further interpretive analysis of and epistemological inquiry into corpulence and corpulent bodies.

Resisting the dominant discursive constructions of corpulence, the essays in this collection analyze the politics and power of corpulence and answer a variety of research questions related to the social representations of fatness: How do media representations of fat people erase and asexualize them? How do weight, body size, food consumption, and eating *dis*orders constitute the normative discourses of fatness? How are these discourses deployed in order to contain the fat body? Exploring this terrain, the contributors employ interdisciplinary approaches as they interrogate the constructs *corpulence* and *fat* (in media, cinema, literature, art, life) and call into question the dominant theoretical framings of fatness—that is, etiological, pathological, and psychological methods of exploring a medicalized conception of obesity.

UNMASKING FAT, UNRAVELING DISCOURSES

Since World War II, when the diet and fitness industries burgeoned and fostered a mass obsession with weight and body shape, *fat* has been a four-letter word. It has been vilified in ways ideologically loaded yet cleverly intertwined with concepts of nature, health, and beauty. As people in the 1990s increasingly recognized that language creates reality, we have made efforts to use language that promotes more equitable relations among people. As a result, terms deemed offensive to less powerful groups are frowned on. Racial and ethnic jokes are less frequently punctuated by laughter. Stories that denigrate women and physically challenged people are not well received. Still, there is something about fat that escapes this change. People openly, disparagingly refer to themselves and others as fat. Perhaps it is because fat is a subject-marking experience over which we are perceived to have some degree of control (unlike gender or race, which are commonly—though mistakenly—taken to be fixed, static identifiers) that fat continues to be so maligned.

What counts as fat and how it is valued is far from universal; indeed, these judgments are saturated with cultural, historical, political, and economic influences. Somehow, this fact escapes notice as we fear fat every day. Few stop to ask questions about the ideological ground on which our current conceptions of corpulence are built. We believe that such questioning will prompt the recognition of fatness as constructed, thereby problematizing the notion of *obesity* as inherently "abnormal" or pathological: within this reading, the *concept of obesity* (as currently understood) is historical, not ahistorical or universal.

The chapters in this book examine current perceptions of fat framed by different historical, cultural, and economic positions in order to illustrate the strangeness of Western vilification of fat. In a postmodern capitalist patriarchy such as the United States, fat is seen as repulsive, funny, ugly, unclean, obscene, and above all as something to lose (see Richard Klein's essay in this volume).[1] As recently as thirty years ago, this notion began to be actively challenged by radical fat activists who argued that our perception of fat is not natural—that it is a function of our historical and cultural positioning in a society that benefits from the marginalization of fat people.[2]

In our attempt to overturn a universalizing, ahistorical, and transcultural conception of fat and fatness—thereby creating political space for the subjectivity of people whose body size does not adhere to society's confining standards—we could look to the conceptions of fat held in premodern ages, survey a wide variety of perspectives on fat outside the United States in modernity and postmodernity, or even look at marginalized, alternative conceptions of fatness within twentieth-century America. African American, Chicano/a, and Latino/a subcultures offer internal sites of resistance to the dominant cultural assessment of corpulence in North America, but they remain marginalized societally and pathologized medically within the hegemonic conception. The richness and variety of meanings attributed to body size in other times and places demonstrate the inconsistency of our modern Western view of fat and lend support to the political project of fat activists who seek to illustrate its politically marginalizing social construction. Once we remove the blinders of late-twentieth-century America, we can see that fat is a malleable construct that has served dominant economic and cultural interests, to the detriment of *all* people.

Pejorative notions of fatness have been deployed with particular frequency within psychological discourses, which tend to analyze the corpulent body as an encoded surface that signifies the subtext of the psyche. Such discourses of corpulence posit the fat body as symptomatic (or, more precisely, "sympto-somatic"), bearing the bodily markings of an interior psychic struggle. Frequently the fat body is read as the corporeal presencing of other, presumably more intrinsic, incorporeal qualities or characteristics—the signifying of latency and lack. Fat equals reckless excess, prodigality, indulgence, lack of restraint, violation of order and space, transgression of boundary. One scholarly work in psychology, Stanley Schachter's *Emotion, Obesity, and Crime* (1971), even goes so far as to conflate fatness and criminality.[3] Stereotypes of obesity are both read and reinscribed in psychological discourses as manifestations of destructive behavior—literally enmassed upon the body—yet presumably driven by indulgence and lack of control; therefore, the fat body is interpreted and constructed as a body heedlessly embracing proscribed social mores.

Even those who believe themselves "sympathetic" toward fat people tend to perpetuate the trope of the symptomatic fat body. Certain behaviors (e.g., overeating or binge eating, anorexic starvation, bulimic purging) and the body presumably produced by such compulsive behaviors are ineluctably interpreted as corporeal, exterior displacements of incorporeal, interior disorders. Among the many books and tapes on the "psychology" and "self-help" shelves we find *You Can't Quit Until You Know What's Eating You; Starving in the Silences; The Famine Within;* and *Feeding the Hungry Heart.*[4] All these psychology-based works conceptualize the body as a blank slate onto which the psyche's contents are transcribed or written. In this paradigm, the fat body is the symptomatic body.

The insatiable *hunger within* creates the beastly fat that cannibalistically consumes and eats away the "healthy" body. Ironically, the relation of the consumer to that which is consumed seems perilously reversed in discourses of obesity and eating disorders: the fat or adipose tissue is regarded as a voracious parasite, an inessential and excisable mass, that suffocates and even consumes the "ideal" or essential body. The eating-disordered body resists being consumed either by starving the parasitic adipose cells or by initiating a bodily flux (binge-purge) that prevents the parasitic fat from taking root. All too often, eating disorders are explained as coping strategies for dealing with sexual abuse, domineering parents, or expectations of perfection. While these early traumatic experiences are certainly real and merit sensitive scholarly research, the tendency within psychological discourses has been to collapse the fat body into the traumatized body,[5] without sufficiently investigating other causes of obesity or, more radically, trying to understand corpulent bodies without seeking any internal causal agent.

Feminist scholars have been influential in reconceiving corpulence and the clinical treatment of obese patients. They have begun to redress the readings of obesity historically perpetuated in psychological discourses, subversively locating the basis of psychological struggles related to obesity not within the individual subjective psyche but within societal fat-phobia.[6] Several scholarly works by psychologists identify fat oppression and fat-phobia as responsible not only for feelings of debasement and low esteem in corpulent individuals but also for anorexia, bulimia, bulimarexia, and other appetite disorders. Both *Fear of Being Fat* and *When Food Is a Four-Letter Word* argue that eating disorders cannot be cured, unless the patient effectively transcends the societally imposed and self-interpolated phobia of corpulence.[7]

The psychoanalytic emphasis of the 1970s and 1980s eventually gave way in the late 1980s and 1990s to more medicalized discourses—encouraging the commodification of "cures" for what was now viewed as an anatomical disease. At the same time, new scientific theories were arguing for genetic causes of corpulence (i.e., the "fat" gene); pharmaceuticals for treating obesity were developed and then prescribed in massive quantities, despite severe, sometimes permanent, and even fatal side effects; and more sympathetic theories about "overweight" patients focused on the individual's metabolism and metabolic set-point (identifying, for example, the "yo-yo diet" syndrome). However, the current medicalized discourses of corpulence, asserted in the absolutist tones of Science, threaten to eradicate or erase all other discursive readings of corpulence, all divergent interpretations of fatness—more completely than the earlier hegemony of psychology had ever done.

An influential model of medical discourse is provided by the National Institutes of Heath (NIH), which reported in 1990 that 58 million people in the United States (roughly one out of three) were overweight—a label applied to men whose body fat exceeds 25 percent of their total weight and women whose body fat exceeds 30 percent. More than half of the people defined as "obese" are adult women, who number 32 million; 26 million adult men and 4.7 million youths (ages six to seventeen) are so classified.[8] The NIH also identifies obesity as a causal or contributing factor in other diseases, including hypertension, breast and colon cancer, cardiovascular disease, and gall bladder disease—but fails to consider how designating causes as "primary" or "secondary" relates to genetic predispositions or other risk factors. The labeling of obesity as a primary cause seems inextricably and discursively bound to a view of corpulence as a fatal but preventable disease, whereas the pathological conditions considered involuntary or unpreventable are termed secondary. This arbitrary distinction seems more financially than medically determined: the possibility of prevention suggests a potential market.

The expanding use of pharmaceuticals in the "battle of the bulge" has been mired in the market-driven politics of financial gains and losses, despite health risks to the patient. This form of medical therapy in some ways resembles the once-popular approach to eradicating obesity literally, by surgically excising fat. Whereas surgical treatments of obesity—such as biliopancreatic diversion (BPD), gastroplasty or gastric bariatric operations to reshape and excise portions of the stomach, and stomach banding and stapling—now are ostensibly restricted to cases of "morbid obesity" with severe co-morbidity factors of hypertension, breathing difficulties, and orthopedic diseases,[9] pharmaceutical treatments of obesity have, unfortunately, far fewer proscriptive and prescriptive restrictions. In the past few years, regulated (and frequently unregulated) doses of phentermine, fenfluramine, and selective serontin reuptake inhibitors (SSRIs) have been recklessly prescribed despite their potential to damage neurons and deplete serotonins, resulting in sleep and mood disorders. In 1997 reports of serious cardiovascular illness and severe hypertension led to the well-publicized removal from the market of phen/fen (a combination of phentermine and fenfluramine). Yet new drugs, regardless of their side effects and potential dangers, are sure to be enormously successful in a market driven by scorn for the huge.

Thus Glaxo Wellcome, a leading manufacturer of pharmaceuticals, affirms its commitment to obese patients by stating, "As the chronic nature of obesity [genetic] has become clear, clinicians have realized that a long-term commitment to obesity treatment is necessary."[10] Indubitably, "a long-term commitment to obesity treatment" is also profitable! The *Medical Sciences Bulletin*, published by Pharmaceutical Information Associates, acknowledges as much: "The pharmaceutical industry is finally waking up to the fact that obesity is a chronic medical condition that requires *lifelong* treatment, preferably with a pill, and that the market for such a pill is enormous."[11] Undeniably, what Prozac has been to psychological and chemical-neurological ailments in the last decade, these pharmaceuticals now seem to promise for obesity and other genetic or unexplained physiological disorders—the versatile panacea of the *fin de millénaire* in American popular culture (the acme of capital culture in the West).

Many sociological and cultural critics have incisively critiqued the power and politics underlying social and capitalistic constructions of anorexia, specifically interrogating the commodification of thinness and the thin body.[12] While such authors explicitly address the commodification of the anorexic body (waifs and heroin-chicsters alike), they have paid little critical attention to the power and politics underlying the social and capitalistic constructions of corpulence and the fat body. Whereas the "thin body" manifests the quintessential commodity in American culture—the pinup beauty marketed in glossy shots, calendar photographs, centerfolds, and advertisements for virtually all products—the "fat body" is the taboo, verboten site around which other commodities proliferate: Slim Fast, Dexatrim, and other appetite-suppressant drugs; Nutrasweet, Equal, Sweet'n Low, Diet Coke, Tab, Diet Pepsi, Crystal Lite, and myriad other sugar-free beverage products; fat-substitutes such as Simplesse, Avicel, and Olestra; and so on.

The fat body is simultaneously produced and abnegated through this very proliferation of commodities: each product alludes to the fat body as the marker of its capitalistic circulation, but also resists and erodes that marked body. These diet and dietary products—all synthetic objects to be consumed, yet all resisting storage as fat—are designed for the purpose of eliminating or preventing the very object that they signify, the fat body. (Olestra is exemplary in this regard, since it actually leaches the body of other nutrients, such as the fat-soluble vitamins A, D, K and E, as well as carotenoids, believed to help prevent cancer, according to the Center for Science in the Public Interest and medical researchers at the Harvard School of Public Health.)[13]

We could subject this commodity-based discourse to a pathologizing analysis similar to the one that has predominated in discourses of corpulence—in medical terms, obesity—in the last few decades in American popular culture; indeed, we might successfully interrogate the broader complicity between medical and capitalistic/corporate discourses during this period. Keeping in mind the normal cycle of food (consumption/ingestion ⇒ digestion ⇒ incorporation), a skeptical feminist analysis might point out that the contemporary U.S. economy proposes a synthetic eradication of "fatness," an artificial replacement of the corpulent body driven by consumerism and capitalism. As the synthetic dietary products are, in economic terms, *consumed* and *incorporated*—or, in the individual, *ingested* and *digested*—the organic composition of the corpulent body is supplanted by the synthetic chemical composition of the consumed product itself. Here again, note how deeply medical/pharmaceutical corporations are complicit in the production and marketing of diet aides. Unfortunately, as medical research into the harmful effects of obesity on health continues, few researchers investigate the possible deleterious side effects of these synthetically produced, aggressively marketed food substitutes (or perhaps we should call them "fat body" substitutes). Such research would not fuel the economy of body commodities. The essays in this volume thus take as their point of departure a critical shift away from these delimiting discourses.

OVERVIEW

By recognizing corpulence as a medical or social *problem,* traditional studies have failed to appreciate the ways in which corpulence is historically, politically, culturally, and economically constructed. Our anthology therefore sets out new avenues for research on *corpulence:* How do fat people understand and conceptualize their corporeal experiences? How are fat people (in literature, plastic art, television, or film) exposing their bodies, their sexuality, and their desire? How do self-definitions of corpulence by fat people resist the normative delimitations of social representation? To interrogate the social constructions of corpulence, the essays in *Bodies*

Out of Bounds analyze several thematic elements: first, the discursive production of fatness as a contested site overdetermined by contradictory discourses; second, the codification of the body in terms of the overlapping issues of containment and excessivity; and last, the proliferation of pathological discourses (which treat fatness as a disease) and psychosomatic discourses (which treat fatness as symptom of a psychological disorder), deployed to contain both the interpretations and the material presences of excessive bodies. These common elements run through the book, uniting the individual parts and suggesting other ways to read fatness. In short, all the essays address and analyze the politics and power of corpulence.

The American preoccupation with weight, exemplified by the glut of books published on "obesity" (framed unproblematically in accord with unquestioned standards of weight: e.g., *under*weight, *over*weight) is ironically paralleled by a disinterest in critically examining our assumptions about corpulence and the erasure of fat bodies. The current scholarship emphasizes medical studies of obesity and eating disorders and stresses psychological treatments of the fat body as symptomatic, without exploring more celebratory expressions of *corpulence.*

Faced with the current hostility toward fat, we must ask, why is this so? and how can we make it otherwise? Peter Stearns, in an interesting history of fat in America, suggests that, indeed, "hostility to fat is part of larger cultural shifts involving doctors and science, artistic standards, religious uncertainties, and, quite strikingly, an effort to establish a backhanded kind of ethical code in a period of rapidly changing values."[14] In *Bodies Out of Bounds,* we hope to begin unraveling the discourses of consumerism, medicine, and psychology that so permeate contemporary constructions of corpulence and fat.

The essays in this collection conspire to further unmask the social creation of these discourses and to suggest new ways of recognizing the power and politics of corpulence. Many of the chapters consider the gendered constructions of corpulence, analyzing conceptions of masculinity and femininity, size and the literal occupation of space, media representation as related to visibility and invisibility, and social oppression. All the contributors to *Bodies Out of Bounds* examine fat in spaces between subjectivity and subjection, all the essays are grounded in contemporary theory, and all propose to map potential trajectories for research in this largely uncharted territory. The essays are divided thematically into five groups.

Part I, "Revaluing Corpulence, Redefining Fat Subjectivities," offers a theorization of contemporary conceptions of fatness within a historical frame. It begins with Richard Klein's essay, "Fat Beauty," which outlines premodern perceptions of fatness; this is an appropriate first selection (a kind of hors d'oeuvre) both because of its content—Klein sets modern conceptions of fat and fatness in historical context through a sinuous and labyrinthine argument, at once etymological, ideological, and artistic, revealing that fat not only can be but has been regarded as beautiful—and because of its rich and disarming style. His words, dare we say, go down like melted butter. The section continues with Joyce L. Huff's essay, "A 'Horror of Corpulence': Interrogating Bantingism and Mid-Nineteenth-Century Fat-Phobia," which examines nineteenth-century precursors to our twentieth-century conceptions of fatness. Her careful analysis of the construction of the "proper" mid-Victorian body counters the widely held myth that corpulent bodies prior to the twentieth century were thought beautiful, and she argues that the refusal to question pre-twentieth-century representations of corpulence has prevented us from identifying some of the historical roots of fat-phobia. Cecilia Hartley's "Letting Ourselves Go: Making Room for the Fat Body in Feminist Scholarship" and Kathleen LeBesco's "Queering Fat Bodies/Politics" explore the ideological and epistemological valences of fatness within the contemporary identity politics of feminism and queerness, respectively.

Looking at the relationship of the body to feminism through the lens of "fatness," Hartley analyzes the myths surrounding fatness, thinness, and sexuality. Deconstructing the fashion-beauty myths as circulated in the media through an analysis of the "fertile" (i.e., the "full" or "fat" body) and the "sterile" (i.e., the "thin" or "waif" body), Hartley demonstrates that these ideals are contradictory and illusory, exposing the rhetoric of "sex" as related to media images of the female body. Through her subtle arguments, she cogently suggests that we need to make room for the fat body within feminist scholarship. LeBesco draws on queer theory (especially of Judith Butler and Elizabeth Grosz) to suggest how the theorization of fat bodies might be shifted from medical or scientific discourses of obesity to the field of cultural studies and critical theory. At stake is the ability of groups (constituted through action, not through essential identity) to create meaning and themselves as political subjects. Through performance, "we can begin to envision *fat play,* rather than *fat pathology.*"

Part II, "Representational Matrices of Power: Nationality, Gender, Sexuality, and Fatness," continues the analysis of fatness within the larger frames of identity politics—here, nationality, gender, and sexuality. Its selections further interrogate how fatness and contemporary conceptions of fatness overlap with sociocultural ideas about gender, sexuality, and even nationality, as Marcia Chamberlain's essay, "Oscar Zeta Acosta's

Autobiography of a Brown Buffalo: A Fat Man's Recipe for Chicano Revolution," so trenchantly reveals. Chamberlain shows how Acosta's deliberately controversial work exposes the hegemonic function of traditional American autobiography; insists that society's institutions and attitudes, never his own fat body, needed policing; and radically rewrites the popular corporeal paradigms of obesity circulating in the 1970s. Acosta turns notions of "spoiled identity" on their head as he carves out a place for Mexican American nationalism.

The collaborative essay by Antonia Losano and Brenda A. Risch, "Resisting Venus: Negotiating Corpulence in Exercise Videos," examines a particular instance of the politics of gender in relation to beauty and fatness, as first explored in Hartley's essay. By scrutinizing not only the content but also the filmic construction of aerobics videos, Losano and Risch reveal ideological contradictions in the standards of beauty and health presented in the videos and explore the implications of their ideologies for the construction of female identity. Similarly, in discussing the competing politics of gender, sexuality, and corpulence, Le'a Kent's "Fighting Abjection: Representing Fat Women" provides a specific articulation of ideas first explored in LeBesco's piece. Noting the mainstream denial of subjectivity to the fat body, Kent examines recent fat liberationist cultural productions to explore possibilities of "rewriting the fat body to challenge both abject images of the fat body and the horror of the body itself."

Part III, "Fat Perversities? Reconstructing Corpulent Sexualities," further theorizes the ambivalences surrounding sexuality and corpulence. In "Roscoe Arbuckle and the Scandal of Fatness," Neda Ulaby analyzes the rise and fall of the legendary "Fatty" Arbuckle, the silent film comedian whose great popularity did not survive a rape scandal in 1921. Examining how Arbuckle employed his fat as the performative point of departure to criticize and explore cultural inscriptions of fatness within a slapstick discourse, Ulaby argues that when imbricated with (and hyperbolized by) excessive gregariousness, histrionic infantilism, and raw licentiousness, as in Arbuckle's case, fat becomes scandal itself. Jerry Mosher's essay, "Setting Free the Bears: Refiguring Fat Men on Television," also examines male sexuality through the lenses of corpulence, comedy, and transgressiveness and challenges mainstream representations of corpulence. *Bear* is the gay term for large, hirsute men, and Mosher's analysis of various television stars, from Jackie Gleason to John Goodman, offers a gay-informed counterinterpretation to hegemonic conceptions of corpulent masculinity.

Part IV, "Deconstructing the Carnivalesque, Grotesque, and Other Configurations of Corpulence," considers the ambivalences of fatness, frequently configured as the "carnivalesque" (often drawing on Mikhail Bahktin) or the "grotesque" (often drawing on Mary Russo's writings).[15] In " 'It's not over until the fat lady sings': Comedy, the Carnivalesque, and Body Politics," Angela Stukator examines the possible subversiveness of corpulent women in film. She suggests that films that configure fatness as the carnivalesque can unsettle "the institutionalized hierarchies and conceptual categories by which social identities are ordered and defined." In "Devouring Women: Corporeality and Autonomy in Fiction by Women Since the 1960s," Sarah Shieff finds that in contemporary women's literature, the abjection of corpulence (i.e., the grotesque) is mediated and the cultural delimitations of corpulence are negotiated by writers who claim their own voice and autonomy. "Locating the mouth as the site of the body/world interface (taking things in, spitting things out)," Shieff explains, these writers "dramatize their own transition from the private and the domestic to the public."

In "Sex and Fat Chics: Deterritorializing the Fat Female Body," Jana Evans Braziel examines the cultural positioning of the fat female body between two poles—the asexuality of obesity and the extreme salaciousness (or hypersexuality) of *fat-femmes,* who threaten to devour all. Deconstructing these poles, Braziel suggests that because fatness has been seen through the history of Western thought as threatening to stability, order, and hierarchy, it needs to be tamed or delimited. Fat persists, however; and through its exaggerated and hyperbolic mimicry of the "masculinist" metaphysical economy, it threatens to subvert that economy, turning order into disorder.

Finally, part v, "Bodies in Motion: Corpulence and Performativity," redeploys fatness not as a fixed cultural construction but rather as a mobile category, capable of being revalued. The first essay, Sharon Mazer's " 'She's so fat . . .': Facing the Fat Lady at Coney Island's Sideshows by the Seashore," analyzes fatness, sexuality, corporeality, and identity as performed and performative, focusing on a sideshow Fat Lady as created and embodied by the performance artist Katy Dierlam. The Fat Lady is caught somewhere between emergent subject and abject object, and the ambivalence she evokes in the performer, writer, audience, and reader points to a subversive space for thinking differently about fatness. Petra Kuppers's "Fatties on Stage: Feminist Performances" also engages the performance of fatness, sexuality, and identity, but by two performers on the other side of the Atlantic, U.S. performance artist Nao Bustamante and English comedian Jo Brandt. Both demonstrate possibilities of performing fatness while neither being defined by nor denying their bodies.

We end this section and the volume with the nomadic and wonderful, if also sometimes abstruse and arduous, dialogue between Michael Moon and Eve Kosofsky Sedgwick, "Divinity: A Dossier, a Performance Piece, a Little-Understood Emotion," a wide-ranging exploration of the "divinity-effect"—the result of a certain combination of abjection and defiance—that pays particular attention to Divine and to the many John Waters films in which she starred. This critical and joyous intellectual exchange offers many readings and thus makes possible rereadings of the cultural positionings of fatness, as it relates to issues of gender, sexuality, class, and race in the United States. Indeed, the fertility of its ideas is reflected, in multiple and different ways, in the other essays in this volume. By closing the book with this productive dialogue, we hope to assist a discursive re-scattering of Moon and Sedgwick's ideas—into readers' thoughts, into societal conceptions of fatness, and elsewhere.

AND "ELSEWHERE"—

With *Bodies Out of Bounds,* we hope to initiate a critical discussion of corpulence and the roles that it plays in the popular cultural imaginary—whether as the maligned historical construction, located in the fissures between bodies and discourses, that Klein, Huff, LeBesco, and Losano and Risch discuss; as the *abject,* as Kent proposes; as the *carnivalesque,* explored differently by Stukator, Shieff, Braziel, and Mazer; as an unresolved problematic, painfully caught in the connections of race, nationality, and gender, which Hartley, Chamberlain, and Kuppers lucidly tease out; or as a transgressive and performative hyperbolization of American ambivalence toward bodies and queerness, as Mosher, Ulaby, and Moon and Sedgwick all indicate. Indeed, corpulence is a dense, polyvalent, and contradictory construction; it plays all these roles in the cultural imaginary, and more. Within the discourses of medicine, psychology, and capitalism, fat proliferates, and its cultural locations are complex, myriad, and varied.

However, *Bodies Out of Bounds* is only a first, critical beginning . . .

Other areas related to the social constructions of corpulence still await study. The intersections of race, class, gender, and sexuality—all examined to some degree by this collection—remain largely unnavigated territories. We hope that the essays in *Bodies Out of Bounds* will spur research into these uncharted domains. Many issues still need to be addressed: How are constructions of corpulence, particularly in medical discourses on obesity, affected by race and class? How do minority discourses on corpulence within North America (especially in African American, Latino/a, and

Asian American subcultures) diverge from the dominant popular cultural constructions? How are their differences labeled as "anomalous" or "pathological" within the dominant discursive frames? How do these divergent constructions mark cultural, racial, and class-based resistance to the hegemony of "American" (i.e., white middle-class) culture, whose imperialism is increasingly manifest on an international scale because of the United States' position within the global economy? What sorts of political alliances can be forged between feminism, queer theory, ethnic-based politics, and fat activism? These questions, and more, point the way to new terrains to be discovered, mapped, interrogated, and discussed.

NOTES

1. Ironically, as Hillel Schwartz argues in *Never Satisfied: A Cultural History of Diets, Fantasies, and Fat* (New York: Free Press, 1986), the desire for the loss of fat significantly contributes to capital's gains: "It is through the constant frustration of desire that Late Capitalism can prompt ever higher levels of consumption" (328); quoted in Richard Klein, *Eat Fat* (New York: Pantheon, 1996), 145.

2. For example, the work of the Fat Underground, the National Association to Advance Fat Acceptance (NAAFA), and Lisa Schoenfelder and Barb Wieser's 1983 anthology *Shadow on a Tightrope: Writings by Women on Fat Oppression* (Iowa City: Aunt Lute) sent small shock waves through a community whose members were unified primarily in their shame, replacing this identity with a rhetoric of "fat rights."

3. Stanley Schachter, *Emotion, Obesity, and Crime* (New York: Academic Press, 1971).

4. Donna LeBlanc, *You Can't Quit Until You Know What's Eating You: Overcoming Compulsive Eating* (Deerfield Beach, Fla.: Health Communications, 1990); Matra Robertson, *Starving in the Silences: An Exploration of Anorexia Nervosa* (Washington Square, N.Y.: New York University Press, 1992); Katherine Gilday, *The Famine Within*, Direct Cinema, Santa Monica, Calif., 1993, videocassette; Geneen Roth, *Feeding the Hungry Heart: The Experience of Compulsive Eating* (New York: New American Library, 1982).

5. Psychological works that collapse the fat body into the traumatized body include George L. Blackburn and Beatrice S. Kanders, *Obesity: Pathophysiology, Psychology, and Treatment* (New York: Chapman and Hall, 1994); Albert J. Stunkard and Thomas A. Wadden, eds., *Obesity: Theory and Therapy*, 2nd ed. (New York: Raven, 1993); J. Kevin Thompson, ed., *Body Image, Eating Disorders, and Obesity: An Integrative Guide for Assessment and Treatment* (Washington, D.C.: American Psychological Association, 1996); Kelly D. Brownell and Christopher G. Fairburn, eds., *Eating Disorders and Obesity: A Comprehensive Handbook* (New York: Guilford, 1995); and W. Stewart Agras, *Eating Disorders: Management of Obesity, Bulimia, and Anorexia Nervosa* (New York: Pergamon, 1987).

6. On fat-phobia, see the important work of Laura S. Brown and Esther D. Rothblum, eds., *Fat Oppression and Psychotherapy: A Feminist Perspective* (New York: Haworth, 1989).

7. C. Philip Wilson, ed., *Fear of Being Fat: The Treatment of Anorexia Nervosa and Bulimia* (New York: J. Aronson, 1983); Paul Haskew and Cynthia H. Adams,

eds., *When Food Is a Four-Letter Word: Programs for Recovery from Anorexia, Bulimia, Bulimarexia, Obesity, and Other Appetite Disorders* (Englewood Cliffs, N.J.: Prentice-Hall, 1984).

8. National Institutes of Health Home Page, 1997, <http://www.niddk.nih.gov/ObStats/Obstats.htm> (accessed July 1997).

9. Charlotte Kenton, ed., *Surgical Treatment of Morbid Obesity: January 1983 through February 1985, 216 Citations* (Bethesda, Md.: U.S. Department of Health and Human Services, Public Health Service, National Institutes of Health, 1985).

10. Glaxo Wellcome Home Page, 1997, <www.glaxwellcome.co.uk/health/odyssey/obesity> (accessed July 1997).

11. Pharmaceutical Information Associates, *Medical Sciences Bulletin: The Internet-Enhanced Journal of Pharmacology and Therapeutics*, 1996–97 <http://pharminfo.com/pubs/msb/msbmnu.html#msb-Contents> (accessed August 1997).

12. Exemplary works on the commodification of thinness are Susan Bordo, *Unbearable Weight: Feminism, Western Culture, and the Body* (Berkeley: University of California Press, 1993); Sharlene Hesse-Biber, *Am I Thin Enough Yet? The Cult of Thinness and the Commercialization of Identity* (New York: Oxford University Press, 1996); and Carole Spitzack, *Confessing Excess: Women and the Politics of Body Reduction* (Albany: State University of New York Press, 1990).

13. CSPI Home Page, January 17, 1996, <http://www.cspinet.org>; see also the Harvard School of Public Health Conference Home Page (accessed July 1997) <http://www.hsph.harvard.edu/Academics/nutr/olestra.html>.

14. Peter N. Stearns, *Fat History: Bodies and Beauty in the Modern West* (New York: New York University Press, 1997), xiii.

15. See Mikhail Bakhtin, *Rabelais and His World*, trans. Hélène Iswolsky (1968; reprint, Bloomington: Indiana University Press, 1984), and Mary Russo, *The Female Grotesque: Risk, Excess, and Modernity* (New York: Routledge, 1994).

REFERENCES

Agras, W. Stewart. *Eating Disorders: Management of Obesity, Bulimia, and Anorexia Nervosa*. New York: Pergamon, 1987.

Blackburn, George L., and Beatrice S. Kanders, eds. *Obesity: Pathophysiology, Psychology, and Treatment*. New York: Chapman and Hall, 1994.

Bordo, Susan. *Unbearable Weight: Feminism, Western Culture, and the Body*. Berkeley: University of California Press, 1993.

Brown, Laura S. and Esther D. Rothblum, eds. *Fat Oppression and Psychotherapy: A Feminist Perspective*. New York: Haworth, 1989.

Brownell, Kelly D., and Christopher G. Fairburn, eds. *Eating Disorders and Obesity: A Comprehensive Handbook*. New York: Guilford, 1995.

Gilday, Katherine. *The Famine Within*. Direct Cinema, Santa Monica, Calif., 1993. Videocassette.

Harvard School of Public Health Conference Homepage. January 17, 1996. <http://www.hsph.harvard.edu/Academics/nutr/olestra.html> (accessed July 1997).

Haskew, Paul, and Cynthia H. Adams, eds. *When Food Is a Four-Letter Word: Programs for Recovery from Anorexia, Bulimia, Bulimarexia, Obesity, and Other Appetite Disorders*. Englewood Cliffs, N.J.: Prentice-Hall, 1984.

Hesse-Biber, Sharlene. *Am I Thin Enough Yet? The Cult of Thinness and the Commercialization of Identity*. New York: Oxford University Press, 1996.

Kenton, Charlotte, ed. *Surgical Treatment of Morbid Obesity: January 1983 through February 1985, 216 Citations*. Bethesda, Md.: U.S. Department of Health and Human Services, Public Health Service, National Institutes of Health, 1985.

Klein, Richard. *Eat Fat*. New York: Pantheon, 1996.

LeBlanc, Donna. *You Can't Quit Until You Know What's Eating You: Overcoming Compulsive Eating*. Deerfield Beach, Fla.: Health Communications, 1990.

Robertson, Matra. *Starving in the Silences: An Exploration of Anorexia Nervosa*. New York: New York University Press, 1992.

Roth, Geneen. *Feeding the Hungry Heart: The Experience of Compulsive Eating*. New York: New American Library, 1982.

Russo, Mary. *The Female Grotesque: Risk, Excess, and Modernity*. New York: Routledge, 1994.

Schachter, Stanley. *Emotion, Obesity, and Crime*. New York: Academic Press, 1971.

Schoenfelder, Lisa, and Barb Wieser, eds. *Shadow on a Tightrope: Writings by Women on Fat Oppression*. Iowa City: Aunt Lute, 1983.

Spitzack, Carole. *Confessing Excess: Women and the Politics of Body Reduction*. Albany: State University of New York Press, 1990.

Stearns, Peter N. *Fat History: Bodies and Beauty in the Modern West*. New York: New York University Press, 1997.

Stunkard, Albert J., and Thomas A. Wadden, eds. *Obesity: Theory and Therapy*. 2nd ed. New York: Raven, 1993.

Thompson, J. Kevin, ed. *Body Image, Eating Disorders, and Obesity: An Integrative Guide for Assessment and Treatment*. Washington, D.C.: American Psychological Association, 1996.

Wilson, C. Philip, ed. *Fear of Being Fat: The Treatment of Anorexia Nervosa and Bulimia*. New York: J. Aronson, 1983.

PART I

Revaluing Corpulence, Redefining Fat Subjectivities

1 Fat Beauty

RICHARD KLEIN

Suppose you wanted to find reasons to think that the current fashion in thin is due for a change. In a much-disputed article, "Facing Food Scarcity," in a recent issue of *World Watch,*[1] Lester R. Brown, the journal's publisher, trumpeted scary news of an estimate recently formed by the World Agricultural Outlook Board in Washington: "Measured in days of global consumption, the world's estimated carryover stocks of grain for 1996 had fallen to 49 days—the lowest level ever."[2] Carryover grain stocks are the key indicator of the world's capacity to meet the growing need for food. This cushion against scarcity is diminishing at this very moment. For example, China, in two years, has gone from being a net grain exporter to being a major importer, the grain-importing needs of Indonesia, Iran, Pakistan, Egypt, Ethiopia, Nigeria, Mexico, Bangladesh, and India have exploded, the global fish catch has begun to level off, if not decline. These latest developments reinforce the article's conclusion, stated in tones of dramatic alarm: "Indeed, for the first time in history, humanity is facing the prospect of a steady decline in both seafood and grain consumption per person for as far as we can see into the future."[3]

Under the present circumstances, in a world grown increasingly vulnerable, a sudden spell of drought worldwide could precipitate a food emergency. Its first effect, paradoxically, would be a drastic increase in the supply of food—of meat. Farmers everywhere would slaughter their animals rather than bear the expense of fattening them up with feed grown rare and precious. The oversupply would encourage people to gorge on meat, because it would suddenly be both very cheap and about to disappear from the tables of all but the rich. Thus, the poor, already fatter than the rich, would at first become even more fat, as a result of eating lots of cheap meat. But then, as meat vanished from their diet and scarcity spread, many would become thin, painfully thin. The rich, however, having despised fat when the poor were fat, would likely find, when the poor got thin, that fat was actually beautiful. It might happen almost overnight that the general perception of what is beautiful would all of a sudden change. Anna Nicole Smith would abruptly appear on the cover of *Vogue*. Her generous forms have already made her the pinup model of a current generation of chubby chasers. But the future may be hers. She's shown she has a gift for timing, and I'd bet on her chances of being the next Betty Grable for the boys in Bosnia.

It wouldn't require a drastic lack of food—consider the oil shortage in the seventies—for the specter of scarcity to get our attention. Just the hint of a new global threat to the food supply might produce a decisive shift in the aesthetic appeal and nutritional value we attribute to fat. The first intimation of starvation on a worldwide scale might be enough to change the whole culture of food, heightening anxiety, investing fat with suddenly rediscovered benefits and unsuspected beauty.

There may be other reasons one could find to imagine that a change in taste will turn from thin to fat. But in truth no explanation may be possible or even necessary in order to understand what is bound to occur. Of one thing we can be sure: There will come a time, if civilization lasts, when fat again will be beautiful, and thin will be hated. Like most shifts in fashion, this one will dutifully obey the invisible, cyclical principle that seems to be at work in all history, but especially in the history of fashion. The only rule is this: What is out will be in, what's in out. The fashion principle commands—preprograms and guarantees—that over long periods of history the great pendulum swings between loving thin and loving fat.

I once rode in a car with Roland Barthes, the great French critic, from New Haven to Ithaca. I asked him in Binghamton what he thought it meant that the Beatles had made long hair suddenly fashionable. Was it a sign of the effeminization of men in the sixties, a culture shift toward a new androgyny? Was it a sign of a return to an earlier moment of Romanticism, when long hair was the unpruned expression of some higher, freer consciousness? I went on with possible interpretations of this drastic shift in taste. At the end, Barthes shrugged. He thought it wasn't any of these things. For him the shift was purely formal. Since short hair had been the rule before, in the fifties, the new rule required long hair in its place. The only significant meaning to be found here is the arbitrary one guaranteeing that short skirts will climb after long ones, that color will burst after beige and neutral tones, thin belts will thicken over time, and high heels follow pumps, as the moon does the sun. Fashion is not a natural thing, but it obeys its own inherent logic. Fashion follows its own law, so the shift to fat could happen for no reason, no good reason that anyone can tell. Maybe we'll just get tired of thin. Such a move will be resisted, of course, by the health-beauty-fitness industry; after all, it has a giant stake in thin. But when fat comes back, the industry will surely find other ways to make money out of people's anxieties. When fat returns commentators, will, after the fact, doubtless find compelling reasons to explain what occurred, why a sudden shift in taste. But the fashion swing, like a real one hung from a branch, obeys only the rule that says it must always swing in a direction opposite from where it's been.

To demonstrate this principle, I invite the reader on a quick little trip through the history of fat. Fat History is a subject that has only just begun to be written, although it has already produced two or three magnificent works. Hillel Schwartz and Roberta Reid, in particular, have enlarged our understanding of social attitudes in America toward fat—toward dieting and the regime of thin. I propose a more rapid and much more superficial survey of nothing less than the whole history of fat beauty, starting with cave women.

The first figures found that depict the human body are thought to be more than fifteen thousand years old; they are all female, all very round and bumpy, with erotic zones (tits, belly, ass) that protrude abundantly. These Venuses, for that's what archaeologists call these chubby little Stone Age statues—have been found in caves, especially in Germany and Italy but widely from France to Siberia.

The most famous of course is the Venus of Willendorf, a little figure four and half inches tall, endowed with the most extraordinary proportions. Twenty thousand years ago, more or less, this magnificently abundant woman was carved out of soapstone, her enormous proportions compressed within a tiny compass. Projected to a life-size scale, she's about the fattest woman one can imagine. Two enormous mountains for breasts, perfectly rounded, plumped-up mounds, tower above her vast taut belly. While the hips curve into an endless ass, the giant thighs taper to thin legs cut off at the ankles. At the focus of all these immense sweeping hills of flesh is a fat and beautifully fashioned vulva. In the center of it all is a navel, vast and dark and deep.

Venuses, we know, are goddesses of love, but archaeologists don't get it. With their professional bias in favor of use and usefulness, they assume these figures must be fertility fetishes, serving some ritual purposes—objects of prayer fashioned to foster conception and protect pregnancy. They make that assumption based on the further assumption that since all of these figures are fat—fat breasts and bellies and thighs—they must be pregnant. To be sure, there is some direct proportion between the amount of fat a woman bears and her capacity to bear children. Fat is fertile; we have already pointed that out. Certainly, we know that the obverse is even more likely to be the case: thin women are less fertile, less successful at bearing children. After a certain point of emaciation, menstruation stops altogether, and fertility vanishes. The advantages of fat were surely even more pressing to our ancestors in the cave; when famine lurked as a constant menace, a pregnant mother blessed her fat's insurance against the loss of her future child.

But the question remains. What certainty do we have that these are ritual objects, magical amulets, or voodoo dolls? How do we know that their shapes and form are intended to cause the condition they seem to represent? Why do they have to be useful? Scientists, who aren't supposed to take beauty into account, assume that cave people were not able to distinguish their love of what was beautiful from their desire to replenish the supply of human workers. But when you look at these amazing figures in three dimensions, in the very round, you see a lot of things sticking out on every side. Asses are no less the focus of artistic attention than breasts or vast, prominent bellies, and that's important. In humans who face each other in love, asses come to have to do more with pleasure than with reproduction, and one that sticks out behind, with the same assertive audacity as bubble breasts in front, is hot. A fat ass doesn't serve any reproductive function. Except that it's fat, and in general fat is fertile. A big beautiful ass on these figures is an object of admiration and a spur to dreaming, a sort of pillow on which our grottoed ancestors may well have fantasized fat, and in times of scarcity dreamt of its pleasures. In the dreams of the caveman, these goddesses gambol at play in fat fields and splash in lively streams, lovely ladies abounding in the lush landscapes that compose his visions of paradise.

Nothing prevents us from assuming that these statues were absolutely useless, were simply beautiful—like more recent Venuses, mere representations of ideal feminine beauty. I believe it when I look at another soapstone figure from the Balzi Rossi cave, in Ventimiglia, on the border of what is now France and Italy. Right there, at the heart of what we now know as the Riviera, they found this little figure of a Stone Age bathing beauty with Bardot proportions—with tits and ass that stir the mind like a swelling Ode to Joy or La Marseillaise. And in between, you notice, she has the flattest stomach, a flat expanse of firmed-up waist stretching between the ballooning boobs on top and the rest. This woman is not pregnant.

She has a waist. Since no other animal in nature has a waist, one could say that it distinguishes humans from animals. Humans alone are moved by the erotic power of the shapely curves that narrow at the waist and open to embrace the hips and breasts. Formally speaking, the waist lends to the shape of the body its dynamic asymmetry. It permits the body to be seen not as a single block but as a balanced arrangement of distinctly different blocks—the flat broad plain of the chest or the globes of breasts and the triangle between them are in a certain relation of symmetry or asymmetry with the oval of the stomach or the sturdy rectangle of a muscular torso. Since the ancient Greeks, sculptors have exploited the pose that consists of putting your weight on one foot. The French have a name for it, *déhanchement;* it means swinging, or twisting, or sticking out a hip. The vital, mobile beauty of Greek statues, compared to Egyptian ones, depends in part on the way the Greek pose breaks the straight-on symmetry of the body, and turns it into a moving architecture of thrusts and counterthrusts, concavities and convexities, which multiply the curves that the waist initiates.

The fact that the Balzi Rossi figure has a waist doesn't exclude, I suppose, the possibility that it represents fertility. But I think it's just as plausible to think it was primarily an object of erotic and sensual pleasure. Maybe the sculptor just loved the business of chiseling out of soft, yielding stone the voluminous bodies of beautiful fat women. Perhaps he enjoyed rubbing the curves of her breasts until the stone yielded the high gloss of the perfectly rounded forms. This may be the first example of the sort of art that today would arouse the wrath of censors—art designed with a view to exciting aroused attention. These objects may be pure pornography, lascivious shapes of the sculptor's erotic fantasy, made to be scoped and fondled, but only with one hand. Why shouldn't their fat be a sign of exuberant sex? After all, there are African tribes that seclude their brides before marriage, in order to fatten them up, and certain Polynesian tribes have great reverence for women who reach two hundred or three hundred pounds.[4]

But I rest my case on the Venus of Laussel, found in a cave in Dordogne. The proportions have acquired a degree of fat realism that's quite astonishing. This lady has no waist. But she has curves, rolls and rolls of multiplying layers of fat, ballooning into thighs and hips, and ample pendulous breasts. Delicate fingers are spread out across the belly, perhaps patting, perhaps pointing to the riches contained within and below. The head is turned as if to suck on what the lady in her other hand is holding, what art historians delicately call the horn of the bull. If there are times when a horn is only a horn, and not a phallus, this one should be considered a horn of plenty, the first cornucopia in art—an emblem of the profusion of nature and a sign for the generosity of women's bodies.

Throughout the Middle Ages, women, especially fat ones, have been identified with the figure of *copia,* with the idea of plentiful abundance. As we have seen, that overflowing abundance has also for a long time been associated with the propensity of women to talk excessively. Maybe that's why the Venus of Laussel, head turned to drink or blow, could just as well be seen, anachronistically, to be speaking on the horn.

If you look at the Venus of Laussel and compare her to Nefertiti, the fabulous beauty of ancient Egypt, you get some sense of the vast cycles of fat and thin that punctuate human history. Ten or fifteen thousand years after the Stone Age Venus, in the time of Anket-Amon, lived the most beautiful woman in antiquity, Nefertiti, the mother of Tutankhamen. Her son, despite having died young, is today the most famous pharaoh, lucky that his tomb was found immaculately untouched by grave robbers. Nefertiti's body bears only the most distant relation to the ideal of Stone Age beauty. The elegance of her lines, compared to the behemoth in soapstone, is still very far from suggesting anything like the bony angular thinness we have lately come to love. She is no Kate Moss. The breasts are beautiful but, in proportion to the hips, small. The belly is ample and only slightly protuberant, but the thighs are solid and embracing.

The famous head of Nefertiti displays the incomparable thinness and angular tilt of her neck, and the bare trace of a smile. The graceful elegance of the head is accentuated by the slender crown she wore, one that extends the line of the nape and resembles no other crown worn by Egyptian queens. Not only beautiful but chic, she knew what looks good. But what makes her face so immediately recognizable, the source of its extraordinary fascination, is the thin upbeat line of the smile that permanently seems to play at the corners of her exquisite lips. Those lips are more than features of her beauty; they hint at moods that on her face look witty, sharply intelligent, often amused. Nefertiti's beauty is often called immortal. What's immortal, it seems to me, is the slender elegance of her neck and the mystery of that smile. I still can't believe how perfectly her mouth resembles that of Claudia Schiffer, whose greatest charm, above the neck, abides in the gently upturned corners of her mouth that lend that face its breath-stopping look of sweet or sexy amusement. Cover her face, all but her mouth, and Claudia, like Nefertiti, is instantly recognizable.

Her facial resemblance to the queen of Egypt can't obscure the difference between their bodies. Compared to the Venus of Willendorf, both these ladies may be thought to be thin. But, comparing idealized statues and airbrushed photos, Claudia Schiffer, the modern model, is skinny compared to Nefertiti, despite having much larger breasts. (Skinny as she is, Claudia is often cited as one of the few voluptuous top models who don't look utterly anorexic.) The shape and widths of Claudia Schiffer's body correspond to the peculiar ideal of beauty invented in our century, the one that wants women to be (or seem to be) larger around the breasts than around the hips. Compare her to Nefertiti, whose hips and thighs swell from the waist, whose stomach protrudes in two gentle mounds. The stomach of Claudia Schiffer (you could almost call it an ab) is alarmingly flat. In the photos taken by Karl Lagerfeld of Claudia barely dressed, her stomach has the emaciated flatness of one that has been tightened and toned, stretched and loosened by years of exercise and yo-yo dieting—the price her beauty pays to the anorexic ideal of designers. Compared to the beauty of antiquity or classical times, the elongated shape of Claudia's body lacks the solid form and weighty movement that lend authority and dignity to a royal body.

Of course, too much fatness promotes stolid symmetry, at the expense of more fluid, plastic qualities permitted by thin: imbalance, precariousness, complication of line. It's hard to sculpt fat wrestlers, for example. Kenneth Clark, with his classical taste, understood that the beauty of the nude body required both symmetry and asymmetry in the right places, both fat and thin, neither wholly one nor entirely the other.

You mustn't be too thin or too fat, thought the ancient Greeks. In his book *The Nude*, Clark gives us a figured vase from the fifth century B.C., on which four men are drawn.[5] On one side of the jar are two hunky athletes, throwing the discus and javelin; they are muscular, solid, and lithe. On the other side, clearly separated from the action, is a fat young man seen in profile, with a big belly, turning his back to the games. Next to him is a skinny guy, facing the athletes but seeming to pull away as far as he can from the action. The moral of the jar seems unambiguous; both fat and thin are at odds with the Greek ideal of vigorous male beauty. Greeks, then as now, loved their fat. Homer is full of roasting meat. At the same time, we know that the Spartans exiled a citizen for being too fat. A fat body for the Greeks lacked the asymmetry of lithe, moving lines that belong to the restless energy of thin. But thin, similarly for them, lacked the noble thickness that lends dignity and a commanding air to those perfect bodies, to these embodiments of the very gods themselves.

The Greeks, as in all things, took a moderate position toward fat, and aspired to a golden mean. The only fat Greek statues are those of *sileni,* satyrs, half man and half goat, related to Bacchus, the god of wine and festivity. Greek women reputedly envied the wasp waist of Etruscan women, who, it was believed, "had found a magic potion that kept them slim."[6] Hippocrates, the father of Greek medicine, considered fat a disease. And Socrates danced every morning as a way of controlling his weight. Dancing every morning is a form of dieting little practiced in the world today, but one that ought perhaps to be revived. Philosophical dieting. Maybe Richard Simmons is right; the only way you can truly stay thin is by dancing every day, because if it doesn't work, it doesn't matter. You will have danced every day of your life. Unless you don't think that what Richard Simmons is doing is dancing.

Aphrodite by our standards is fat. If you take another look at the Venus de Milo, you have to be impressed by her girth. She's a chunk—immense round hips, great tits, this is a big girl! Her beauty lies in the proportions of her body, not in its slenderness. She's not chic like Nefertiti, she doesn't immediately arouse you with some mysterious electric spark—like what flies from the corner of Claudia's mouth, or from the jut of a bony hip, or from the racy elongated curves of these strange and exciting poses. But Venus de Milo is beautiful, with an antique beauty that touches a viewer more profoundly. Her thickness is "fruitful and robust," says Kenneth Clark and, compared to more conventional nudes, she rises up, he says "like an elm tree in a field of corn."[7] She is both vigorous and fat, with no skinny chest, but a vast expanse of her neck and shoulders and breasts. It is no wonder that less than one hundred years ago we admired the compelling spectacle of abundant jewels flashing around the neck of a beautiful woman dressed in a gown from which poured the full extent of her magnificent chest.

There are Etruscan tombs known as the Obesii, which depict the deceased male lying on top of his sarcophagus, half draped, resting on one arm, with his great big gut hanging out. The Romans used to make fun of the fat Etruscans, but the statues make you think that those stomachs had some sort of social significance, a sign of the departed's once substantial role in the city. Kenneth Clark thinks the Etruscan sculptors were just good realists, who were accurately depicting the look of middle-aged men, half naked, lying down.

In Roman times, the cult of the body was displaced by preoccupations with dress and adornment. Clothing concealed the body and lent it the dignity that Roman bodies might lack. The Romans weren't as athletic as the Greeks; their tastes went in more for banqueting. The *vomitorium* to which Romans retired in the midst of banquets was devised, it seems, less to prevent fat than to encourage more eating. Remember that Nero was fat.

To be sure, there is some evidence of the surgical removal of fat in Roman and Byzantine times. The fantasy of liposuction has roots that go very deep in our culture. Fat has always been conceived as a kind of cancerous growth, inessential to the body or its image, an excrescence, a corruption of the flesh whose removal left the body intact and in better shape. Fat is something that we wear; it is on the outside of our inside. It doesn't belong to us exactly, and it doesn't belong where we find it. We dream of its being removed from us, leaving our essential being not only unaffected and unchanged but more purely, because more thinly, itself. For the Greeks and Romans, fat in moderation was a principal source of pleasure and a major component of beauty.

Kenneth Clark, in *The Nude,* begins by observing that many civilizations have no art of the nude. Consider the Orient, where neither in Japan or China or elsewhere is there a long and ancient tradition of representing beautiful naked bodies. It is first in the West, and with the culture of the Greeks, that the naked body becomes a nude, the object of artistic contemplation and representation. The greatness of Clark's book, as a piece of art history, lies in the way he shows the two basic models of the body on which the whole art of the nude has been based. There's the classical nude and the Gothic. The difference, we might say, is a question of fat in the right or wrong places.

According to Kenneth Clark, with the triumph of Christianity over paganism, "the body ceased to be a mirror of divine perfection and became an object of humiliation and shame."[8] Whereas the Greeks wanted to celebrate the athlete's nobility in the gym, the earliest medieval statues of humans undressed represent the shame and humiliation of Adam and Eve. After the Fall, scales fell from their eyes and they perceived that they were not nude, but naked as peeled shrimp. The pious Christian ideal of beauty starts there, in the humiliation of the flesh. It bespeaks a hatred of every fleshy thing that prevents the soul from instantly achieving its spiritual destiny. Flesh was no longer the blessed stuff in which the gods became present among humans. The beauty of its forms was censored by Judeo-Christian taboos surrounding graven images, and its seductions were demonized by Christian morals. The landscape of the human body was no longer deemed to enact the mysteries of creation, proposing to the eye of the dazzled spectator an incomparable vision of tension and ease, force and yielding, strength and softness. In the Gothic period, the body was often angular, sharp, and mean. Its gauntness was evidence of the mortification of the flesh, punished for its power to entice the soul toward pleasure, away from grace. Whereas for the pagan Greeks the body was the place where physical pleasure and divine grace intermingled harmoniously, Judaism despised the body for its impurities and required its constant ritual purification. Christian teaching preached that pagan statues of Greek and Roman gods, under their beautiful guises, were actually devils, little demons that tempted thoughts away from the path of Christ. In early Christian times, one aspired not to the body of the athlete but to the anorexic skeleton of the anchorite, or hermit, who retreated from the material world, from all its delicious pleasures. For Christians, appetite is a lure that ensnares the soul and perverts its pious impulses. Finally, in Islam, the body becomes the site for harsh rituals of self-abnegation. Shiite Muslims parade through the streets on occasion flagellating themselves with cruel metal whips until blood flows.

Schiller, in *The Aesthetic Education*, argued that Greeks burned their dead because they aspired to what they lacked—a fully grasped understanding of the eternal infinite possessed by Judeo-Christianity. By contrast, Christians and Jews bury their dead, because they aspire to what the Greeks lack: a fully realized, pagan sense of the immediate, incarnated presence of divinity in the flesh.

Even today, one cannot help believing that the current fashion for thin is linked to an upsurge of pious belief. Fat, like a Greek god, has become a devil. Throughout most of human history, fat has been thought to be the best thing, the most beautiful and desirable stuff of all. But at certain moments, in periods of high religious sentiment, fat comes to be despised. For the early Christians, for the medieval Gothic period, during the period of Romanticism, fat was taken as the emblem of all the mortal weight of sin arising from temptations to which the flesh is given. The Gothic idea or ideal of the pious body was ethereal—gaunt, bony, and potbellied.

Why was the Gothic belly a pot? In the earliest representations of Eve, leaving the Garden of Eden, she is engraved with skinny legs, small breasts, a long curving stomach. It's probably too simple to assume that her fat belly was supposed to be seen to be the pregnant destiny of Christian womanhood. This young lady isn't pregnant yet, but the rounded curve of her belly means that babies are on her horizon.

Just as we've seen with the Stone Age figures, this pregnant interpretation of the Gothic belly may fail to account for what, after all, is simply a matter of taste. Compared to the classical ideal, Kenneth Clark calls the Gothic body rarefied, because of the way it flattens the thrusting arc of the hip. Central to the body of the Greek and Roman nude was the "sensuous arc" formed by the hip and waist, which resulted from the figure being posed with its weight unevenly distributed, resting heavily on one foot.[9] The sexy arc formed by the jutting hip and flaring torso has the power to move us in ways that aren't rarefied at all. In ways that may be biological.

Texas professor Devendra Singh, you remember, believes the secret of sex appeal lies at the waist—or, to be precise, the waist-hip ratio calculated by dividing the waist measurement by the hip size. The smaller the waist in relation to the hip, the more desirable a woman is seen to be. As a result of her recent study, she concludes, "The waist is one of the distinguishing human features, such as speech, making tools and a sense of humor." "No other primate has one. We developed it as a result of another unique feature—standing upright. We needed bigger buttock muscles for walking on two legs."[10] A fat ass makes us human.

The classical nude, both male and female, exploits the architectural and erotic possibilities of that breathtaking curve at buttocks and hips. But the Gothic nude tends to elongate the body, both male and female. In the Renaissance, the male body reasserts the classical prerogatives, only it looks thicker. Thick is fat, as in German, the word *dick* means both. Thickness in men around the chest and waist still exerts a powerful attraction on women, and other men. Here's one version of that:

> He was naked. He stood there, the hair over his cock and balls emphasized by my own lack of covering. I was overcome by the sight of him. The chest, the full muscled stomach, the arms promising such strength. Mr. Benson, my master, my man, the one for whom I would do anything.[11]

That's how John Preston's narrator, a submissive slave to S/M, describes the moment when he sees his master undressed. What rivets his attention to the body of the male master is the fullness and strength of the torso. Not the arc but the thickness of the chest and stomach—the density of the muscled flesh is what the naked slave loves. Just like Michelangelo. Look at the great allegorical statues of Day or Dawn, or consider the series called Captives, or think of some of the male figures in *The Last Judgment*, there you'll see Michelangelo thickening the stomachs on these heroic guys almost to the point of becoming obese and funny. But for him, the whole drama and pathos of what he was trying to express, in these heroic drawings and carvings in stone, writhed into life in the thick intensity of muscle and fat at the shoulder and chest and waist. It's true that Michelangelo liked lithe boys like his *David*—slim waisted, with bony ribs. But as he aged he painted more and more obsessively those thick waists on females as well as males. His late statues of women, sculpted for the pope's tomb, look like men lying down wearing oranges on their chest. But Michelangelo was less interested in the difference between male and female than in that between master and slave. He must have loved slaves dearly, because he made so many of them, but his slaves, powerful, rippling bodies, serve to represent the mystery of thick flesh—its humbling power to move us profoundly. The flesh to which we wish to submit is thick and heavy and tragic.

In France, in the sixteenth century, the first great attempts to represent naked beauty since the Dark Ages gave rise to the School of Fontainebleau. Mannerist artists brought from Italy to France by Francis I infused the moving, dynamic lines of the South with severe Gothic angularity to produce strangely disturbing, extravagantly elegant elongated nudes. Kenneth Clark observed that the legs of Cellini's *Nymph of Fontainebleau* are six times the length of her head, compared to the classical model, which dictated three. These figures, with their "somewhat ridiculous shape—feet and hands too fine for honest work, bodies too thin for childbearing, and heads too small to contain a single thought," says Clark, are the embodiment of chic. The beauty they embody is antinatural; they bear no relation to real women, but only to impossible ideas of women, whose illusion they created. Clark writes, "The goddess of mannerism is the eternal feminine of the fashion plate."[12] Top models, with their emaciated forms, vacant stares, and otherworldly airs are the latest embodiment of mannerist chic, the most persistent incarnation of the insubstantial Gothic ideal.

Clark is aware that this antinatural vision of chic has its victories in the history of art. It has triumphed in the twentieth century. But we should not be deluded, he tells us, into thinking that the beauty that's in fashion is the only form of it or the greatest. As he says, when we are in need of "greater nourishment," the lover of beauty cannot be satisfied with the amusing or provocative detours of chichi, the strange thin forms that unreal beauty takes. When a connoisseur of Venus *naturalis* wants to drink deeply of the springs of feminine beauty and consume with eyes the most substantial fruits of flesh, it is to Rubens he must turn. Clark writes, "The golden hair and swelling bosoms of his *Graces* are hymns of thanksgiving for abundance, and they are placed before us with the same unself-conscious piety as the sheaves of corn and piled-up pumpkins that decorate a village church at harvest festival."[13] These women are cornucopia, with bodies that swell and plump. The graces hold and squeeze each other's arms, as if even they cannot get enough of their exuberant fleshy beauty. Rubens was attracted by the twist and sweep, by the large arc of a hip, and "the shining expanse of . . . stomach."[14] He loves the comprehensiveness of these bodies, the way they sweep the eye around with arcs and twists, intriguing rolls and blushing dimples. The roundness of these fat women inspires in the onlooker an enormously powerful desire to embrace them, to be embraced in their enclosing perfumed thicket of flesh.

You have to love the sweetness of these faces, the transparent delicacy of the palest skin, and the way these ladies seem to float and dance like exuberant pillows, billowing flesh enchanting the viewer with a spectacle of boundless grace, when nature in its abundance seems perfectly attuned to fostering the happiness of humanity.

In the seventeenth century, at the dawn of classical rationality, one could still believe in the harmony of a rational natural order with a deeply felt divine plan. For Rubens, there was no contradiction between reason and faith. The world was good and God-given, and humanity through its own rational powers could understand nature and improve it. Clark repeatedly refers to the sweetness and generosity of Rubens's fat women—qualities very far removed from the hard, angular principles of chic.

Kenneth Clark likes painters who like fat girls. To be sure, he dismisses the Venus of Willendorf. She is fatness, he thinks, grown to be a mere symbol of fertility. He has little interest in the sexy mounds of the statuette, carved so softly in stone. It's enough that the fat be fertile to turn Sir Kenneth off. When it comes to really fat, he backs away from his otherwise acutely trained sense of the beauty of what is solid, substantial, what has density and aplomb—the quality of being well centered and perfectly balanced. For him, her fat is too fat.

But there are other forms of fat he defends indignantly. Kenneth Clark asks the reader and himself, "Why do we burn with indignation when we hear people who believe themselves to have good taste dismissing Rubens as a painter of fat naked women and even applying the epithet 'vulgar'?"[15] Why does he burn when he hears that? Because these people, who are supposed to have taste, are the most tasteless of all. These are people so concerned with chic that they cannot see beauty; they consider fat vulgar and thereby reveal the vulgarity of their taste. Clark, more refined than these vulgarians who think fat is vulgar, has taste, and appreciates the taste of fat. Fat makes Rubens's nude one of the highest summits of the art of the nude in all of history.

"Rubens," Clark says, "wished his figures to have weight. So did the men of the Renaissance, and they sought to achieve it by closed forms, which had the ideal solidity of the sphere or the cylinder."[16] The forms of fat women are closed forms, and they evoke the desire to enclose them, to comprehend their sweeping arms in the sweep of our arms. The women of Rubens give rise to the desire to sweep them up, to feel their weight and solidity, to give oneself the incredible sweetness of their all-embracing fate. Clark gives us in *The Nude* the picture of Rubens entitled *The Rape of the Two Daughters of Leukippos.* Rape may be understood here in its first sense, which is that of seizing hold of, from Latin *rapere,* grasping, comprehending. You could imagine this painting to be a sort of allegory of the classical period, in which male reason surrounds, seizes upon, grasps, and comprehends an idea of feminine solidity. The idea of the fat woman is both intellectual and erotic—an image of ideal beauty in which what is most sensual is linked to what is most comprehensive, universal—the ennobling mixture of voluminous flesh with a transcendent idea of immensity. A single, glistening cylinder of fat, this luscious fat girl stands for all that the rational mind and the love of beauty desire to possess, to surround and carry off—the whole weight and wealth of human nature. The body of a Rubens woman is, according to Clark, "plump and pearly."[17]

Rubens did for the female nude what Michelangelo had already done for the male. Both great artists discovered whole new levels of expressivity in the form of the human body by imagining it thick or plump. Michelangelo's figures suffer (or profit) from what Clark calls "the peculiar thickening of the torso (increase, even, in correction)."[18] This means that as Michelangelo worked and reworked his drawings of male nudes, he tended more and more to broaden the torso, to give it ever wider girth, more ample expanse of fat and muscle. Some figures, like the Christ of *The Last Judgment,* look almost misshapen, from the chest down. But they nevertheless attain, in Clark's eyes, "a Pheidian splendor." Like Pheidias, the greatest sculptor in ancient Greece, Michelangelo not only reproduces the beauty of gods, he infuses his heroic images with a palpable aura, a pearly sign of the presence of divinity in the flesh. Great artists find their gods incarnate, embodied in the beauty of amply proportioned fat.

With the Christian Middle Ages, moral attitudes toward flesh reversed the classical model of beauty. The body as the locus of pleasure and hence of sin was depreciated and emaciation became a sign of spiritual elevation—of turning away from the fleshpots of this world. Think of the Venus de Milo, then think of the poor bodies of those emaciated, saintly, self-denying women, mostly nuns, who have been called, by Rudolph Bell, "holy anorexics." The first nude figures one sees in medieval art are Adam and Eve, whose nakedness is an occasion, not for celebration, but for shame and self-concealment. The Gothic woman, as she is represented in statues and images, displays a body shape and structure fundamentally different from the female body admired in classical antiquity. Of the Gothic woman, Clark says, "Her pelvis is wider, her chest narrower, her waist higher; above all, there is the prominence given to her stomach."[19] The hint of fertility is the only exception permitted to the general thinning and elongation of the female form. The woman's body is no longer seen and loved for itself, as an object of sensual contemplation, but envisaged as a vessel devoted to reproduction. The thinness of these Gothic bodies, which have their own mannered charm, negotiates a compromise between the allure of flesh and the rigors of spirit. On the one hand, there's the old urge to look hard at the body in order to paint or sculpt it, and, on the other, the church's taboo on undressing flesh. Countering the pure, pagan pleasure of eyeing gorgeous flesh, the Gothic skinny is a philosophical decision and a moral judgment about the place of the body in the hierarchy of values.

The emaciated Gothic ideal was not generally shared by the lower classes in the Middle Ages and Renaissance. Kristoff Glamann, quoted in Mennell, argues that as far as they were concerned, eating made you handsome. A thin wife brought disgrace to a peasant, but of a plump one it was said that "a man will love her and not begrudge the food she eats" [Mennell 30] [*sic*]. Men, too, were supposed to be stout, to judge, say, from the painter Breughel's scenes of high life and low, where mostly everyone is tubby, afloat in rolling fat, while gluttony abounds.

In the sixteenth and seventeenth centuries, gluttony was widespread, even at the highest level of society. Catherine de Médicis was known for her enormous appetite and frequent dyspepsia. Henry VIII was gargantuan in his appetite. Gargantua, the royal giant invented by Rabelais, as an infant drank the milk of 17,913 cows, and counted eighteen adipose chins.[20] In the seventeenth century, at Versailles, Louis XIV consumed prodigious amounts of food and became lustrously, heroically fat. At his court, the Princess Palatine died from overeating.

The eighteenth century represented a movement away from overeating toward greater refinement of taste, as cuisines became more delicate and taste more subtle. But even thin was not so skinny back then, by our current standards: Madame de Pompadour—111 pounds and only 5'1" tall—complained of being emaciated. Louis XVI was the exception that confirmed the rule.[21] His morbid obesity became an emblem of an aristocratic class grown bloated with self-satisfaction, inert from conservatism, and, like Louis himself, hugely impotent. He was so fat, it is said, he could not see his penis. Louis was already a scandal on his wedding day, when he so incapacitated himself with food and drink, that his grandfather, Louis XV, then the king, expressed outrage and muttered foreboding about the future of his dynasty. On his way to the guillotine, Louis asked for a little something to eat.

The hollow decadence of the old regime is often diagnosed in the taste it displayed, at the end of the eighteenth century, for frivolous flesh that seems gratuitous, floating on buttocks and bosoms in paintings by Watteau and Boucher. Fat is dimpled, all pink and fluffy in Boucher, the eighteenth-century Rococo court painter. The creamy skin of those large dollops of pink women—ladies, really, with beautiful aristocratic faces, winsome, and proud—arouses hunger, quenches thirsts. They are at play on billowy couches, and the light suffusing their bodies illuminates the round pillows of downy linen and their satiny flesh, ballooning, effervescent, like bubbles of fat. They are dressed alluringly in the gauziest veils, which barely cover them—just enough to excite the wish to see what is plainly visible through the filmy, flimsy cloth. The most famous Boucher painting, in the Louvre, features a woman lying on her stomach with her ass in the air looking back in laughter at the painter. The gorgeous display of her colossal adiposity, her thundering, moonfaced, creviced posterior, evokes a vastly delicious, (sub)lunar landscape in which an explorer could lose himself in pleasure forever. O blessed fat!

The chunky butts on women in Boucher are full of fat. They remind us how beautifully it accumulates in places of particular erotic attention. The fat of a breast, the heft and weight of that fat that surrounds a beautifully formed nipple—the shape and roundness of that fat invites fondling. It calls out for touching. Butts lend themselves to be grabbed—that is, to be held in big handfuls and to be squeezed. Squeezing the fat on butts is for many people, men and women, the source of the most intense erotic pleasure. Only humans have fatty breasts. There are those like Desmond Morris who say that breasts are behinds, that in humans the breast is surrounded by fat to remind men of behinds, which they used to love when we went on all fours.

When a fat king is overthrown, the new republic loves thin. In the nineteenth century, postrevolutionary Europe was swept by the Romantic movement, a new conception of the relation of mind to body and with it an altered sense of what is beautiful—a new figure of fashion. Hamlet ceased to be played by fat actors; only those who were thin could look brooding and melancholic. The Romantic soul inhabits a slender body, one whose shape bespeaks a disinterested, ascetic relation to food and to the material world in general. The Romantic movement reinvented a Gothic ideal of thin, ethereal beauty, in order to evoke the idea of some edifying elevation beyond the flesh. Beauty, as it were, is removed from this world, freed from the inertia and impenetrability of this too too solid flesh. The world, in a Romantic perspective, is seen at a distance, as if from a rugged mountain top where bodies like spirits appear almost transparent—like clouds reflected in an Alpine lake. Being without the earth means to be un-fat. A sublime aesthetic, a taste for the sublime, replaced its eighteenth-century opposite, the frivolous excess, the ornamental abundance of Rococo. Between 1800 and 1850, for the first time in almost four hundred years the look of thin once more looked beautiful. The French writer, Théophile Gautier, recalled that, during this period, when he was young, he could not have "accepted as a lyric poet anyone weighing more than 99 pounds."[22] Roberta Seid also notes that it was in 1832, at the height of the Romantic movement in Europe, that ballerinas first began dancing on point. The aspiration of the human body to approximate the human soul took form and body in these altered ideals of femininity. Even when fashion changed, around the 1850s, when both men and women began reverting to a heavier model, fat was still associated, not with gravity but with bubbly buoyancy.

By the end of the century, as we have seen, the Gay Nineties had brought the industrial world unprecedented wealth, and all classes aspired to look and feel fat. Men cultivated their corporations, and women squeezed their flesh in the middle with whale bone and leather in order to produce at both ends cascading avoirdupois. The exuberance of fat, its imposing assertiveness, its unfolding promise of ever more abundance sweeps everything before it until the first decade of the twentieth century, when, as if overnight, thin looked sleek and modern.

Until this century no one has ever dreamed of living in a skinny land. Fat has always been the shape of Utopia. Now, of course, the prejudice against fat seems universal and eternal; and thin belongs to what is truly good and beautiful. Nevertheless, there are those, even today, who dream of a fat utopia, and have written earnestly and vigorously in its favor. None has done so more eloquently than Hillel Schwartz. As he modestly asserts, at the end of his great book *Never Satisfied:* "No single critic has launched such an attack on dieting as I have launched here."[23] In a chapter entitled "Fat and Happy," Schwartz describes the conditions that would thrive in "The Fat Society: A Utopia," in which fatness would be both admired and rewarded. Here are some of the rewards and pleasures that would accompany this utopia of fat:

1. Dinners would be "scrumptious, sociable, and warm."
2. Children would acquire no eating disorders because "feeding would be calm and loving, always sufficient, never forced."
3. Fat people would love their bodies and "dress expressively." Women, in particular, "would wear their weight with new conviction."
4. "A fat society would be a comforting society, less harried, more caring."
5. A fat society would be less harshly competitive, less devouring.[24]

Schwartz is one of the first, and certainly the most eloquent, to find in fat the emblem of Capitalism, a metaphor and index of our society's relation to consumption. We are all consumers, and the fat that we wear or the fat that we flee expresses a certain relation we have, as consumers, to the objects of our desire. Schwartz was one of those who has most carefully and thoroughly distinguished hunger from appetite. Hunger is a drive, a biological need motivated from within by the body's lack of what it needs; appetite is a desire, stimulated by the attraction or seduction of things outside the self that provoke an interest or inclination to eat. One's appetite can be stimulated, even if one is not hungry. Indeed, for some, that is the function of good cooking.

According to Schwartz, the logic of capitalism, particularly in its late stages, expresses itself in the novel forms of dieting. On the surface, he argues, it might seem paradoxical to identify dieting and capitalism. After all, the capitalist is a consumer, a seeker after the commodities that excite his appetite. Dieting would seem to imply the opposite of consuming, and hence a form of resistance to the capitalist mode. The paradox would be a real one, a true antinomy, if dieting in fact succeeded for the most part in accomplishing what it aims to achieve. But writing in 1986, Schwartz can already feel confident about asserting as fact what has become massively evident in the meantime: diets don't work. Never have; never will. And it is precisely that fact that makes dieting such a perfect vehicle for launching a critique of capitalism. Dieters in truth, argues Schwartz, consume not less but more. "The diet is the supreme form for manipulating desire precisely because it is so frustrating."[25] Since capitalism depends on consumers consuming, the more they diet the more they frustrate desire, thereby magnifying its imperious demands. More diet means more appetite, and more appetite means more consuming. "It is through the constant frustration of desire that Late Capitalism can prompt ever higher levels of consumption."[26] The fact that dieters end up being fatter after a while than they were before they began confirms the paradoxical logic that Schwartz uncovers.

"In such a society, sexism, racism, and class warfare would be unlikely."[27] Fat people are not hungry like imperialists, impatient like exploiters, intolerant or warlike. Schwartz concludes: "The most effective physiological method of making war impossible in future would be to organize a society for the universal diffusion of adipose."[28] If everyone were fat, the world would be fat and happy and peaceful, Schwartz thinks. Leanness is concomitant with meanness; fat brings peace and contentment to character.

NOTES

"Fat Beauty" first appeared in *Eat Fat* by Richard Klein (New York: Pantheon Books, 1996).

1. Lester R. Brown, "Facing Food Scarcity," *World Watch*, October–November 1995, 10–20.
2. Ibid., 10–11.
3. Ibid., 17.
4. Roberta Pollak Seid, *Never Too Thin: Why Women Are at War with Their Bodies* (New York: Prentice Hall, 1989), 45.
5. Kenneth Clark, *The Nude: A Study in Ideal Form* (Princeton: Princeton University Press, 1956). *Eds. note:* Klein refers to figure 17, "Attic, *early 5th century* B.C., Palestral scene" (p. 24).
6. Seid, *Never Too Thin*, 46.
7. Clark, *The Nude*, 89.
8. Ibid., 309.
9. Ibid., 315.
10. Devendra Singh, quoted in *Irish Times*, November 10, 1994.
11. John Preston, *Mr. Benson* (New York: Bad Boy Press, 1992), 91.
12. Clark, *The Nude*, 139.
13. Ibid., 140.
14. Ibid., 144.
15. Ibid., 139.
16. Ibid., 144.
17. Ibid., 148.
18. Ibid., 60.
19. Ibid., 317.
20. Hillel Schwartz, *Never Satisfied: A Cultural History of Diets, Fantasies, and Fat* (New York: Free Press, 1986), 9.
21. Seid, *Never Too Thin*, 56.
22. Ibid., 94.

23. Schwartz, *Never Satisfied*, 332.
24. Ibid.
25. Ibid., 328.
26. Ibid.
27. Ibid., 330.
28. Ibid., 331.

REFERENCES

Brown, Lester R. "Facing Food Scarcity." *World Watch*, October–November 1995, 10–20.

Clark, Kenneth. *The Nude: A Study in Ideal Form*. Princeton.: Princeton University Press, 1956.

Preston, John. *Mr. Benson*. New York: Bad Boy Press, 1992.

Schwartz, Hillel. *Never Satisfied: A Cultural History of Diets, Fantasies, and Fat*. New York: Free Press, 1986.

Seid, Roberta Pollak. *Never Too Thin: Why Women Are at War with Their Bodies*. New York: Prentice-Hall, 1989.

2 A "Horror of Corpulence"

Interrogating Bantingism and Mid-Nineteenth-Century Fat-Phobia

JOYCE L. HUFF

William Banting has long been a problematic figure for medical historians. Because Banting was a proponent of the reducing diet before slenderness became a norm, his writings on corpulence and health are difficult to integrate into either the canonical history of diet or the feminist history of the growing "tyranny of slenderness," both of which tend to date the rise of the "culture of slimming" to the beginning of the twentieth century.[1] When scholars refer to earlier attitudes toward corpulence, they generally assume that prior to the twentieth century corpulence was, if not preferred, then at least a culturally acceptable mode of embodiment. But this view does not do justice to the variety or the complexity of the pre-twentieth-century views. Banting's pamphlet, *A Letter on Corpulence,* first appeared in 1863 in England and was reprinted in Europe and America shortly thereafter. Despite supposedly predating the devaluation of the corpulent body in Western culture, Banting's letter represents corpulence as a stigmatized mode of being. And though it was written before the culture of slimming became institutionalized in the West, the letter's publication sparked a minor reducing craze in England that lasted for nearly a decade. As we will see, an interrogation of this pamphlet and the fad that it produced can shed light not only on mid-Victorian attitudes toward corpulence but also on the historical conditions that have led to the current demonization of the fat body in Western culture.

Banting's pamphlet laid forth a system of dietary regimen for the purpose of reducing corpulence, a system he did not invent but merely championed. At sixty-six years of age, he had begun to suffer from hearing loss. In the spring of 1862, when his regular aural surgeon was called out of town, Banting had turned to Dr. William Harvey, surgeon to the Royal Dispensary for Diseases of the Ear. In his summary of the Banting case,

Harvey explains that he came to believe that corpulence was responsible for Banting's hearing problems: "A dispensary patient, who consulted me for deafness, and who was enormously corpulent, I found to have no distinguishing disease of the ear. I therefore suspected that deafness arose from the great development of adipose matter in the throat, pressing upon and stopping up the eustachian tubes."[2] Harvey had recently attended a lecture in Paris given by Charles Bernard on the treatment of diabetes. Bernard's treatment relied on new discoveries regarding the production of glucose, discoveries that would eventually revolutionize thought on digestion in England. According to the old theories, body fat was formed directly from dietary fat; treatments for obesity-related health problems therefore involved limiting the intake of fats and practicing general "moderation" in diet. Bernard's diabetes diet excluded glucose-producing foods—starches and sugars—as well as fats. It was Harvey's contention that Bernard's principles could be applied to reduce corpulence, and he tested his theories on Banting.

Banting's role was to generalize and popularize what had originally been intended as a cure for a specific medical condition. Indeed, within a year of its first printing, the pamphlet had become so popular that Dr. Edward Smith, medical examiner for the Poor Law Board, saw it as a threat to the medical community's authority over the body: he publicly condemned the Banting system in an address on the state of the national diet given to the British Association at Bath.[3] The pamphlet went through five editions, which appeared in England, Europe, and overseas, and it sold over 63,000 copies. Numerous copycats appeared as well, including a book on how to "Bant" in India, where nutritional requirements were assumed to be different.[4] Banting received over 1,800 letters from his "corpulent brethren" (both male and female) who had tried the Banting system,[5] and he had a large selection of these letters printed as a testimonial to his plan's efficacy. Over the following decade, his name became synonymous with dieting. It was turned into both a verb—"Do you Bant?"—and a noun, *Bantingism.*

Of course, there had been numerous earlier tracts on "physical self-management."[6] In fact, Banting's pamphlet was frequently critiqued as unoriginal or derivative. However, there were some major differences between Banting's pamphlet and other contemporary books of advice on diet. First, Banting promoted dietary regulation not simply as a general principle of physical self-management but specifically as a means of combating fat. Second, he assumed that all corpulent people had a need to reduce, whereas previous works on corpulence tended to recommend reducing only when obesity explicitly interfered with health. Finally, Banting presents himself as a fellow sufferer rather than as a medical authority. He thus demonstrates a recognition and an endorsement of the stigmatization and demonization of fat within his culture absent from most other Victorian works of the subject. "Of all the parasites that affect humanity," the pamphlet begins, "I do not know of, nor can I imagine, any more distressing than that of obesity."[7] Banting further describes corpulence as a "lamentable disease" and a "crying evil," confessing that from his childhood, he had experienced "an inexpressible dread of such a calamity."[8]

But although Banting heartily agrees with and participates in his culture's devaluation of the corpulent body, he also expresses a somewhat guarded protest against the stigmatization of corpulent people in mid-Victorian society: "Any one [*sic*] so afflicted is often subject to public remark, and though in conscience he may care little about it, I am confident no man laboring under obesity can be quite insensible to the sneers and remarks of the cruel and injudicious in public assemblies . . . and therefore he naturally keeps away as much as possible from places where he is likely to be made the object of the taunts and remarks of others."[9] Surprisingly, Banting's lukewarm indictment of this treatment was one of the most controversial aspects of the pamphlet. William E. Aytoun, one of Banting's harshest critics, argues that Banting's complaints were "unreasonable" and that his discomfort with his body was a response not to any real social pressure experienced by corpulent individuals but to a personal "morbid horror of corpulence" and an "extreme dislike to be twitted on the subject of p[a]unchiness."[10] Current historians seem to have accepted this view and thus have pathologized Banting as fat-phobic. He has been treated as a medical curiosity or simply ignored in most accounts of the history of diet. But such pigeonholing fails to explain why so many people, in England and overseas, recognized themselves in Banting's descriptions of the afflicted and became proponents and practitioners of the Banting system. It is more useful to view Banting's pamphlet not as an interesting footnote to the history of diet but as a central document in the history of the social construction of the corpulent body. I believe that Banting's fear of corpulence was a response to the increasing cultural pressures to normalize that characterized mid-Victorian attitudes toward embodiment. Banting's pamphlet and its reception need to be reevaluated in this light.

I approach Banting's framing of the corpulent body by looking at the ways in which his text constructs its reader, drawing on Louis Althusser's notion of interpellation to do so. Althusser explains that power relationships are instilled in the individual through the process of subject formation: "Ideology 'acts' or 'functions' in such a way that it 'recruits' subjects among the individuals" through the process of "interpellation, or hailing."[11] Banting's text interpellates his reader as a fellow sufferer. In the process, Banting projects on his corpulent reader a high degree of corporeal dissatisfaction, manifested as a fear of corpulence and a desire to eliminate it. By stressing that corpulence is a mode of bodily trespass, Banting's pamphlet places the corpulent subject it addresses always already in the wrong vis-à-vis the dominant discourse. Banting's system thus embeds fat-phobia and the desire to normalize the body within the very identity of the corpulent subject. To answer the interpellating voice of Banting's pamphlet, to recognize—or to misrecognize—oneself as the corpulent subject whom Banting addresses, is to accept a stigmatized mode of identity and a marginalized position within a fat-phobic society. Banting then offers salvation through Bantingism, a system for framing bodies and incorporating identities that introduces fat-phobia into the process of subject formation, thereby inducing it within the identity of both the corpulent and noncorpulent subject.

It is important to remember, however, that in the nineteenth century corpulence was not defined by a single monologic voice. The mid-Victorian period saw a general increase in interest in bodily proportion and shape.[12] One of the most significant things to note about fat at this time is that it was singled out as an object of study. Banting's pamphlet thus participated in a more general cultural discourse. The idea of an ongoing conversation about fat, participated in by various discourses—social, political, medical, literary, and economic—may well seem familiar to the twenty-first-century reader, because we ourselves live in a time that is saturated with discourse on the subject. But today, the combined voices of the diet and fashion industries have achieved hegemony; they call out relentlessly from magazines and televisions. While the diet industry has not succeeded in erasing other voices, it has been able to manage and partially neutralize competing discourses, so that any position assumed by a corpulent person today involves negotiating the primary role offered to him or her within a prevailing narrative that seeks to define corpulent bodies as weak-willed, unhealthy, and out of control.

In the mid-Victorian era, no single voice had attained hegemony, and the position of the corpulent body was much more hotly contested than it is today. Body fat served as a focal point for competing attempts to define and control the meaning of the body at a time when the medical community and the capitalist free-enterprise system were attempting to consolidate their authority over the body. Banting's voice was only one among the many seeking to position the corpulent body within mid-nineteenth-century culture. It was a particularly effective one, however, because the type of body that Banting documented, addressed, and came himself to embody was particularly well-suited to the forms of disciplinary power that appeared in the nineteenth century. Banting's pamphlet presupposes a body adaptable to certain forms of power. This body, which I call the Banting body, had four basic characteristics: it was dynamic, calculable, reformable, and legible. These traits not only defined it but also positioned it within a nexus of hierarchically arranged power relationships. I therefore elaborate on each aspect of the Banting body separately.

THE DYNAMIC BODY

In mid-nineteenth-century England, the body was viewed as radically dynamic in nature. According to an 1861 article in *Cornhill Magazine,* which appeared just three years before Banting's pamphlet was published, the body is not a object but an "action": "[T]o think rightly of organic bodies, they should be regarded rather from the point of view of their *action* rather than of their substance; rather as processes than as things."[13] Edwin Lankester, in his guide to an exhibit on nutrition at the South Kensington Museum, echoes this theory, asserting that the chemical components that make up the human body do not remain in a stable relationship to each other. Instead, the body renews itself cyclically. "[W]e may be said," he explains, "to moult or cast away our old body and get a new one every forty days."[14] The German professor Niemeyer points to the dangers of the dynamic body in an article on Bantingism: "The organs and the tissues of which the body consists, are constantly being worn out and used up; and in order, therefore, to prevent the dissolution of the body, it is absolutely necessary that the loss which thus arises, should be constantly replaced by new material."[15] The mid-nineteenth-century body was thus never static; it was constantly engaged in a never-ending process of bodily decay and renewal. The nineteenth-century subject experienced this dynamic body not as a stable solid but as something unstable and permeable.

Within this dynamic framework, body fat functions as sediment. In Victorian medical discourses, body fat was assumed to accrue to the body as the residue of food not converted to energy. In fact, in the 1860s, at just the time when Banting was writing his letter, a series of experiments was conducted by the Poor Law Board on the utility of various foods; the research sought to determine which nutrients were most readily converted to useful energy and which were more likely to be sedimented or excreted by the body.[16] Food was weighed prior to ingestion, and both patients and stools were weighed after digestion; the goal was to achieve the highest ratio of food to work. In the dominant narrative, a body functioning at its full capacity would not accumulate excess fat. This model of digestion cast fat as the residue of certain inefficient or incorrect eating practices.

Banting's pamphlet constructs adipose tissue through this sedimentary metaphor. For Banting, fat is "like the parasite of barnacles on a ship[;] if it did not destroy the structure, it obstructed its fair comfortable progress in the path of life."[17] Fat is thus defined as something exterior to and appended onto the body, rather than something belonging to and incorporated within the body. In the physical economy of the dynamic body, fat was "out of place." Mary Douglas's work provides a useful framework for understanding the sedimentary model that informs Banting's construction of corpulence. Douglas describes the ways in which "matter out of place" functions within cultures as a form of "symbolic pollution."[18] Pollution, in Douglas's view, is a contingent concept, taking its meaning from context. It thus depends on the concepts of order and classification: it presupposes socially imposed ideas about the order and hierarchy of things in the universe. Symbolic pollution is anything that violates classificatory categories, bringing together things that the dominant classificatory order insists on keeping separate and corrupting the categories that organize and make meaning of experience. The nineteenth-century body, in dynamic interaction with the world, was vulnerable to such symbolic pollution. Boundaries between body and world were constantly challenged. Adipose tissue therefore represented an invasion of the body by the world.

As Douglas has noted, matter can be considered out of place only in a highly structured environment. In the Victorian era, rules for the aesthetic distribution of fat on the body were strictly defined. In today's society, by contrast, fat in and of itself has become an enemy. Body ideals have become increasingly slimmer, as body management practices have taken on the impossible goal of completely eliminating fat from the body. But in earlier years, not all fat was bad; Victorian beauty manuals frequently advised one on how to cultivate plumpness.[19] Such advice has led many scholars to assume that the Victorians were not concerned with physical self-management or were free from stereotyping and fat-phobia. In fact, the opposite is true: they were so obsessed with physical self-management that they developed a highly articulated set of physical strictures regarding the arrangement of fat on the body, standards that were class, age, and gender specific. The entire body was verbally dismantled and codified. Thus, Victorian body management was a matter not so much of maintaining a thin body as of maintaining a "properly" shaped body.

Although adipose tissue functioned as matter out of place within the body, entire bodies could also be made to feel out of place in 1860s England, because mass-production techniques had enabled the construction of an increasingly standardized physical environment. The fat body was singled out and stigmatized in an environment tailor-made for a hypothetically average body.[20] The corpulent body in particular was viewed as polluted and polluting because it was assumed to be more engaged with, and thus more vulnerable to, the world than the thin body was. The world had entered the corpulent body and remained within it. And the corpulent body was not simply a polluted body in and of itself; it also collapsed and thus corrupted the categories of self and world, which in the Victorian era were seen as essentially and necessarily separate. The corpulent body thus became a focal point for anxieties regarding the permeability of bodily boundaries and the mutability of bodily forms.[21]

THE CALCULABLE BODY

To inhabit the dynamic body was daily to confront anxieties about its maintenance, control, vulnerability, and boundaries. These anxieties were compounded because, as the article in *Cornhill* makes clear, it was believed that the process of embodiment had to occur "within fixed limits, and in a definite form" in order for health to be maintained.[22] The dynamic body interacted with a stable and static norm; the chemical processes of life, it seemed, could not be carried out efficiently while the body was in flux. Bodies that failed to interact properly with this norm risked falling victim to a natural tendency toward corporeal dissolution. Medical science thus began to concentrate on defining the norm that would make possible optimal control and stability.

As Michel Foucault has argued, the end of the eighteenth century and the beginning of the nineteenth century saw the emergence of the idea of the norm and, with it, a new type of coercive power—disciplinary power.[23] Foucault notes that beginning in this period, the body became subjected to a normalizing judgment that both homogenizes individuals, by proclaiming a universally applicable standard, and differentiates them, by ranking them according to their difference from an unattainable ideal. The most important feature of this normalization process is its coerciveness. The individual body is subjected to a culturally formed composite picture that reflects not so much an actual average as a cultural ideal. Difference from this ideal is perceived as a failure to achieve it. In this manner, quantifiable physical difference is transformed into aberration.[24]

The nineteenth-century interest in fat, both dietary and bodily, was symptomatic of a more general fascination with quantification. Foucault has asserted that there emerged in this period a new type of subject, which he calls the "calculable" individual.[25] Since body fat was a visible and, more important, measurable physical substance appended to the dynamic body, its presence or absence, its placement, amount, and weight, could be used as somatic barometers. The technology for weighing and measuring a body, developed in the eighteenth century, would by the mid–nineteenth century assume an important role in the somatic identity of the individual. It enabled the production of a calculable body, one that could be weighed, measured, and then ranked according to a table of differences. It is thus significant that by the 1860s, insurance companies had begun to devise height-and-weight charts that linked size to mortality, providing individuals with a standard for classifying bodies according to their measurements. Banting includes one chart in his pamphlet, along with tables recording his own monthly weight loss. Through the use of such charts and tables, the calculable individual could be differentiated and positioned within a hierarchy, according to its difference from a hypothetical average.

THE REFORMABLE BODY

Because the norm was defined in static and universal terms, its acceptance automatically placed the dynamic and individuated body of the mid-nineteenth-century subject in the wrong. Since mid-Victorian bodies were in a constant state of flux, the norm could never be finally and satisfactorily attained, even by a body whose parameters fell within those defined as average. The body had to be continually managed if one wished to maintain a state of normalcy. The mid-Victorians saw the active management of the body as a willed activity. Such a view implied that the body acted as the passive instrument of the will; it demanded the cultivation of a docile body, whose activity, and thus significance, could be controlled from moment to moment. The dynamic body of the mid–nineteenth century was a reformable body.

To ensure the maintenance of physical normalcy and to facilitate the body's interaction with the norm, mediating disciplines were needed. The discourses of health, hygiene, and sanitation converged on the body, recommending standards for the strict regulation of bodily habitus and the maintenance of body boundaries in accordance with the norm. By the nineteenth century, as the literary critic Catherine Gallagher has noted, "the body came to occupy the center of a social discourse obsessed with sanitation, with minimizing bodily contact and preventing the now alarmingly traversible boundaries of individual bodies from being penetrated by a host of foreign elements."[26] Because body fat could function as matter out of place and thus disturb boundaries, attention was focused on its regulation.

The discourses of health and sanitation justified the desire to manage body fat. Yet, as Mary Douglas has pointed out, the need to distribute matter in its proper place has more to do with maintaining the purity of classificatory categories than with health, contagion, or disease. We combat pollution even when it is not necessary to do so, because the elimination of dirt is a goal in itself.[27] In the twentieth century, the social historian Peter Stearns argues, interest in weight control and the elimination of fat surpassed medical concerns over corpulence and health.[28] A similar lag occurred in the nineteenth century, demonstrating that most Victorian and contemporary fat avoidance rituals reflect a desire for normalization more than health. Although medical discourse is frequently invoked to justify fat avoidance behaviors, recent medical research shows that fat has a much more complex relationship to health than is generally acknowledged. Current investigations call into question the general threat to health posed by body fat, demonstrating that though there are some specific health risks associated with corpulence, fat is by no means the universally unhealthy condition that it is usually represented to be.[29] Yet the desire to eliminate fat frequently motivates individuals whose body fat arguably puts them at little risk to engage in diet and exercise practices that have been proved to be unhealthy, often with the full knowledge of the harmfulness of their actions. Now, as in the mid–nineteenth century, fat avoidance is a goal in and of itself.

As the cultural historians Peter Stallybrass and Allon White have argued, the Victorian abhorrence of dirt and devotion to hygiene is related to policing and social control.[30] They point to the cooperation that existed between hygienic efforts and police efforts to contain the slums and manage the bodies of the poor. Sanitation thus prevented disease, but it also enforced power relations. And just as sanitation colluded with the social regulation of the bodies of the poor, so bodily reformation through dietary regimen functioned as a form of social control for the bourgeois. Physical reform was seen as a social obligation: to maintain social standards, one must maintain physical standards of both health and beauty. One journalist asserted,

> How much of the social unhappiness of men arises from deranged system or disordered brain, perhaps we shall never know until that paradise to which all such things were strangers is restored; but we know a large part of our social grievances has its root in nothing else. . . . Without going so far as the physician who maintained that a man's theological opinions depended on the state of his liver we yet know very well how our feelings vary with our bodily condition, how dismal the world looks during a fit of indigestion, and what a host of evils will disappear as the abused stomach regains its zone.[31]

That the responsibility for upholding social standards through body management was distributed unequally between the sexes is made clear by Richard Tomes, author of the infamous *Bazar Book of Decorum:* "Though we may not give full assent to Madame de Pompadour's dictum that the chief duty of woman is to be beautiful, we do not hesitate to confess the opinion that it is a social obligation not only of her sex, but that of the male, to make the best possible appearance. A code such as that of good manners, which recognizes as its main purpose to render us mutually agreeable, can hardly be complete if it does not contain rules for the proper management of the person."[32] As in moral discourses, it is the woman's duty to ensure that standards are maintained. These remarks demonstrate that the practice of dieting had a serious purpose for the Victorians, one that extended far beyond the realm of individual health and physical well-being and into the formation of the social body.

The corpulent body was seen as particularly resistant to normalization, because it was visibly individuated; it would not resolve itself into the supposedly universal body defined as average. In Banting's pamphlet, dietary regimen provides the erring corpulent body with its means of salvation and reintegration into the norm. The connection between bodily and moral reform is made explicit, because Banting constructs his experience through evangelical discourse. He chose to publish his tract in a format used not only by medical writers but also by Christian reform societies. He also employed terms borrowed from evangelical literature, framing his struggle with his wayward body as a moral conflict. Banting's pamphlet tells the very traditional story of a sinner redeemed, though here the only sin seems to be the existential one of being corpulent. Banting is careful to stress that he is not guilty of any behavioral nonconformity; it is the shape of his body, rather than his diet or exercise practices, that places him in the wrong. In his narrative, he experiences retribution (in this case, social ostracization), sees the light, reforms his body through dietary regulation, and returns to spread the truth. The reformation portrayed is a literal and material re-formation of the body. It replicates on a microcosmic level the great mid-nineteenth-century project of social reform. Thus, Banting offers not only a way to purge the individual body of corpulence but also a means of cleansing the social body of corpulent individuals. He promises his readers that he will continue to circulate his pamphlet "whilst a corpulent person exists."[33]

The solution that a dietary regimen offered the corpulence sufferer was the illusion of self-mastery. After having finally attained a "happy natural medium" weight, Banting declares, "I hold the reins of health and comfort in my own hands."[34] But the quest for the happy medium is unending, in part because self-discipline is an end in itself. As Foucault has argued, the goal of social control "would be an indefinite discipline[,] . . . a procedure that would be at the same time the permanent measure of a gap in relation to an inaccessible norm and the asymptotic movement that strives to meet in infinity."[35] The current ideal of thinness, for example, is pursued less to achieve thinness itself than to cultivate and continually reinscribe docility on the body.[36] But a perfectly docile body can only be approached, never actually attained, making the struggle for physical self-control an unending battle. Rather than engaging in a relentless pursuit of thinness, Victorians fought with equal determination to maintain the average, trying to stabilize the body within narrowly defined margins as the endpoint of this discipline, total bodily control, was ever receding.

THE LEGIBLE BODY

If the norm is taken to define a supposedly universal humanity, then belief in the norm can be sustained only through its consistent physical embodiment. Any failure to conform challenges belief in the accepted definition of the human. So, too, to maintain one's identification within a group that consolidates the identity of any segment of that humanity—as middle class, male, a civilized subject, and so on—one must visibly embody its norms. The body, in other words, must render its norms visible and function as a sign of something else: it must be legible.

In *Unbearable Weight,* Susan Bordo demonstrates that today, body size has come to function as "a symbol for the emotional, moral, or spiritual state of the individual." "The firm, developed body," she continues, "has become a symbol of correct *attitude;* it means that one 'cares' about oneself and how one appears to others, suggesting willpower, energy, control over infantile impulse, the ability to 'shape your life.'" Corpulent bodies have come to represent the opposite: a lack of these qualities, a personal failure;

thus "the 'relentless pursuit of excessive thinness' is an attempt to embody certain values, to create a body that will speak for the self in a meaningful and powerful way."[37] To the mid-Victorians, the sign of a correct attitude was not a toned body or even a slender one, but a body that was correctly arranged. Since the corpulent body deviated visibly from the norm, it could serve as a symbol of bodily incorrectness. The corpulent body was thus subjected to a normalizing and stigmatizing stare. "The stare," as Rosemarie Garland Thomson points out in her study of bodies and disability, "is the gaze intensified, framing [the body] as an icon of deviance."[38]

It has frequently been noted that the corpulent body was sometimes presented as desirable in nineteenth-century erotic painting and literature. But its presentation was framed in such a manner that even in its desirability, corpulence maintained a stigma. The fat body could not represent normative sexuality for the mid-Victorians. It must represent an excess that was taboo. The eroticizing gaze that the nineteenth century directed at the corpulent body was thus also an exoticizing one. In the famous scene in chapter 19 of Charlotte Brontë's *Villette* (1853) in which a fleshy portrait is extolled as sensual, it is significant that the portrait is titled *Cleopatra* and bedecked with the trappings of Orientalism. When fat is enticing, it is the lure of something out of bounds, the excitement of slumming among the marginal.

Body fat was not in and of itself a stigma in the mid–nineteenth century. Rather, it served to stigmatize a body if it appeared in places or amounts considered anomalous. And that supposed anomaly was felt to require an explanation. Fat, it was assumed, must mean something; there must be a reason for its presence, especially if it appeared in amounts considered excessive. The corpulent body thus generated a myriad of explanatory narratives that assigned it a history and a position within its society. The disciplinary stare to which the corpulent body was subjected reduced the body to its culturally relevant trait, its corpulence, transforming it into a legible text and inserting it into a narrative framework. These explanatory narratives thus served to render the corpulent body intelligible and to neutralize the threat that matter out of place posed to the established order of things—specifically, the challenge that adipose tissue posed to distinctions between self and world. Narratives can position a body within its society, minimizing its threat to the social order. They particularize the stigmatized body, providing a reason for its existence and also assigning and distributing blame. Thus fat-phobic ideology recoups the corpulent body, pathologizing it and supplying ready-made interpretations for the irregular presence of fat within the individual as well as the social corpus. The narratives generated around the fat body compete to define, and thus to contain, it.

Michael Moon and Eve Kosofsky Sedgwick's contribution to this collection provides a useful way to understand the narrativizing gaze to which the corpulent are subjected in a fat-phobic culture.[39] They argue that this form of gaze attributes a history of deviance to the corpulent body, particularly the body of the fat woman. The spectator ascribes to the fat woman a history that is both etiological, in that she "must" eat too much, and pathological, in that she "must" have an underlying psychological reason for that overeating. Then the spectator congratulates himself or herself on having "discovered" this history, disclosed by the fat woman's wayward flesh in spite of her efforts to keep her inner deviance hidden. The medical establishment colludes with this gaze, lending its authority to the spectator's narratives and thus "transforming difference into etiology." Medical authority, Moon and Sedgwick continue, "confers on this rudimentary behavioral hypothesis the prestige of a privileged narrative understanding of her will (she's addicted), her history (she's frustrated), her perception (she can't see herself as she really looks), her prognosis (she's killing herself)."[40]

In the era of industrial capitalism, an economic model has framed the narratives inscribed upon the corpulent body. Alimentary and material consumption, as Gail Turley Houston has observed in her study of Charles Dickens, were frequently conflated in Victorian representations of the body.[41] Within scientific discourses, a one-to-one correspondence between alimentary consumption and the formation of adipose tissue was assumed. Within social discourses, this correlation was reinscribed and intensified by the economic metaphor. Body fat was interpreted as the residue of aberrant acts of consumption. The corpulent body was thus made to stand in for rampant, unchecked consumerism and the abuses of laissez-faire capitalism. It served as a trope for excessive consumption, representing both waste and luxury. Indeed, as Moon and Sedgwick have noted, in Dickens's representations, "The gibbous flesh of [corpulent] women might be carved directly from the narrow shanks of smaller bodies—bodies of children, of the poor."[42] In other words, the corpulent body metaphorically consumed other bodies, according to a skewed logic which insisted that the corpulent subject was selfish, was consuming more than his or her share of the limited resources available within the British economic system. The corpulent body, and particularly the corpulent female body, thus bore the guilt of exploitative economic relations as a legible, stigmatic mark upon the body, freeing the average man and woman from not merely the vagaries of embodiment but also consumer guilt.

The narratives that frame the corpulent body for the spectator's gaze are self-validating: dominant narratives carry more authority than the individual voice, compelling the body to speak in ways that the individual is not always even aware of. These narratives thus recruit the body in support of dominant ideology, to perform what Moon and Sedgwick have called the "representational labor" of embodying specific forms of cultural otherness.[43] Banting was aware of the narratives that defined his body and sought to counter them: "Few have led a more active life—bodily or mentally—from a constitutional anxiety for regularity, precision, and order, during fifty years' business career, from which I have now retired, so that my corpulence and subsequent obesity was not through neglect of necessary bodily activity, nor from excessive eating drinking or self-indulgence of any kind."[44] His critics responded, however, by simply citing the dominant (and opposed) narrative and trusting to its authority. They projected on Banting a variety of failed practices of body management. "We feel assured," Aytoun insisted, "that he would have found the same measure of relief had he simply exercised some control over his appetite, given his stomach more time to digest by lessening the inordinate number of his meals, abstained altogether from beer, and resolutely steeled his heart against the manifold temptations of the pastrycook."[45] As Aytoun's comment shows, narratives of aberrant eating could attach themselves automatically to the corpulent body, which could thus be made to signify in spite of itself.

This stigmatization process serves to secure the boundaries of the normal; that is, the spectacle of the fat body confirms and consolidates the identity of the normal body. The abjected bodies constructed and labeled as fat are made to bear the burdens of embodiment—the uncertainties, flux, and grotesqueries of embodied existence. The "well-managed" body denies its own embodiment, assuming the role as ideal in opposition to the corpulent body. Corpulence thus enables and creates the "proper" body. Of course, connections between fat and thin are obscured by this logic. But because all bodies contain some fat, the boundaries of the norm are never quite secure. Each individual body harbors the potential for corpulence. Corpulence is thus a slippery stigma; the boundary between fat and thin is an anxious one. Today, for example, a diet industry continually redefines the norm and thus corpulence, so that more and more people are included in its interpellating hail. This redefinition positions an increasing number of individuals as consumers of diet products. The syndrome known as Body Image Distortion Syndrome describes those who assume the identity of corpulent person, even though their culture labels their bodies thin.[46]

BEYOND BANTINGISM

Bantingism is a system for in-corporating identities and embedding them within a preexisting set of power relationships. Banting's pamphlet constructs its readers by interpellating them into the Banting body, addressing them as bodies in the wrong, and projecting a desire for social salvation onto them. The properly interpellated Banting subject should experience a sense of shame and dissatisfaction with his or her body's position in relation to the norm and should willingly undertake a program of dietary regimen as a means of subduing the erring body and rendering it docile. The next step is to become self-monitoring and self-regulating, assuming responsibility for the power relationships in which he or she is caught up. In Foucauldian terms, the individual should become "the principle of his [or her] own subjection."[47]

But as Judith Butler has observed, one's interpellation into any ideological system is never fully or completely accomplished.[48] The body is a contested site, multiply interpellated; it assumes different subject positions within different discourses fluidly and sometimes simultaneously. Thus, no single voice can ever fully construct the subject it addresses. Butler's critique of Althusser suggests that he disregards "the range of disobedience that such an interpellating law might produce." By raising the possibility of misrecognition and disobedience, Butler reframes interpellation and recognition as performative gestures, open to a variety of parodic rearticulations: "Here the performative, the call by the law which seeks to produce a lawful subject, produces a set of consequences that exceed and confound what appears to be the disciplining intention motivating the law. Interpellation thus loses its status as a simple performative, an act of discourse with the power to create that to which it refers, and creates more than it ever meant to, signifying in excess of any intended referent."[49] This excess signification has the potential to destabilize the norm, opening it up to alternative, subversive, or incorrect citation and thus to resignification. "What," Butler asks, "would it mean to 'cite' the law to produce it differently, to 'cite' the law in order to reiterate and co-opt its power, to expose the heterosexual matrix and to displace the effect of its necessity?"[50] This question, it seems to me, could be reformulated to apply to Bantingism and corpulent identities. For while Bantingism aims to produce a fat-phobic response in its reader, it simultaneously allows for a range of potentially subversive and irreverent responses within the reader it addresses. Indeed, some of the mid-Victorian replies to Banting's pamphlet voiced such irreverence. Although no friend of the corpulent, William Aytoun remarks that not everyone would recognize themselves as Banting's fellow sufferer: "We are acquainted with many estimable persons of both sexes, turning considerably more than fifteen stone in the scales—a heavier weight than Mr. Banting has ever attained—whose health is unexceptionable, and who would laugh to scorn the idea of applying to a doctor for recipe or regimen which might have the effect of marring their developed comeliness."[51]

Laughter was certainly not a response that Banting's pamphlet anticipated or intended. But though his reply to Banting did signify in excess of Banting's intent, Aytoun's response was not necessarily a liberatory one, for it was intended to trivialize the pain that Banting had experienced at his social ostracization; it thus replicated the sneers and taunts that Banting himself had suffered as a corpulent individual. It is possible, however, to imagine a laugh less scornful and more celebratory, a subversive laughter that throws the negative representation of corpulence defiantly back into the face of the society that created it. Risibility and corpulence are in fact two of the defining characteristics of an alternative tradition that privileges bodies that defy categories and celebrates symbolic pollution, the tradition that M. M. Bakhtin labels the "carnivalesque" and that Donna Haraway has more recently refigured as the "cyborg aesthetic."[52] In the carnivalesque tradition, corpulent bodies joyously refuse to assimilate to the norm and thus serve to challenge the tyranny of the average. The twenty-first-century subject can look to such alternative traditions for potential ways to positively resignify corpulence, co-opting the discourse that defines him or her as other to the norm and refiguring deviance as a difference to be celebrated. In this, it seems to me, lies a possibility for resistance and self-affirmation.

NOTES

1. Kim Chernin first used "tyranny of slenderness" to describe women's current obsession with the cultivation of the slender body; see *The Obsession: Reflections on the Tyranny of Slenderness* (New York: Harper and Row, 1981). Some representative histories of diet and obesity include Hillel Schwartz, *Never Satisfied: A Cultural History of Diets, Fantasies, and Fat* (New York: Free Press, 1986); Peter N. Stearns, *Fat History: Bodies and Beauty in the Modern West* (New York: New York University Press, 1997); and Anne Scott Beller, *Fat and Thin: A Natural History of Obesity* (New York: Farrar, Straus, and Giroux, 1977). Feminist writings on the history of beauty and the development of the slenderness aesthetic are

numerous. Among the most influential are Roberta Pollack Seid, *Never Too Thin: Why Women Are at War with Their Bodies* (New York: Prentice Hall, 1989), and Susan Bordo, *Unbearable Weight: Feminism, Western Culture, and the Body* (Berkeley: University of California Press, 1993).

2. William Harvey, afterword to *Letter on Corpulence,* by William Banting, 4th American ed. (New York: Mohun, Ebbs, and Hough, 1865), 35.

3. Edward Smith, *The Present State of the Dietary Question* (London: Walton and Maberly, 1864).

4. Joshua Duke, *How to Get Thin, or Banting in India,* 2nd ed. (Calcutta: Thacker, 1878).

5. William Banting, *Letter on Corpulence,* 4th London ed. (London: Harrison, 1869) xi.

6. Other nineteenth-century writings on physical self-management include Jean Brillat-Savarin, *The Handbook of Dining or Corpulency and Leanness,* trans. L. F. Simpson (London: Longman, Greenman, and Longman, 1865); Thomas John Graham, *Sure Methods of Improving Health and Prolonging Life,* 1st American ed. (Philadelphia: Carey, Lea, and Carey, 1824); Alfred Moore, *Corpulency* (London: F. W. Ruston, 1857); William Wadd, *Comments on Corpulency* (London: John Ebers, 1829); and Sydney Whiting, *Memoirs of a Stomach,* 5th ed. (London: Chapman and Hall, 1859). Wadd, Graham, and Brillat-Savarin predate Banting but were still considered authorities in 1863. There were also reams of advice on diet in manuals of household management and domestic medicine.

7. William Banting, *Letter on Corpulence,* 3rd American ed. (New York: Mohun, Ebbs, Hough, 1864), 5; unless otherwise specified, all subsequent references are to this edition.

8. Ibid., 5, 14, 7–8.

9. Ibid., 9.

10. William E. Aytoun, "Banting on Corpulence," *Blackwood's Edinburgh Magazine* 96 (November 1864): 609.

11. Louis Althusser, "Ideology and Ideological State Apparatuses," trans. Ben Brewster, in *Contemporary Critical Theory,* ed. Dan Latimer (New York: Harcourt Brace Jovanovich, 1970), 95–96.

12. The mid–nineteenth century produced numerous studies on body fat, as well as on nutrition, most notably those conducted in state-run institutions. Dr. Edward Smith did a study on body weight and food consumption using the inmates of workhouses as guinea pigs while Sir William Guy completed a similar study on prisoners. See Edward Smith, *Dietaries for the Inmates of Workhouses* (London: Eyre and Spottiswode, 1866), 35, and William Guy, *On Sufficient and Insufficient Dietaries with Special Reference to the Dietaries of Prisoners* (London: Harrison and Sons, 1863), 260. The first patent cures for corpulence appeared at about this time also, as did the first mention of anorexia nervosa.

13. [James Hinton], "Health," *Cornhill Magazine* 3 (March 1861): 337.

14. Edwin Lankester, *Guide to the Food Collection in the South Kensington Museum* (London: Eyre and Spottiswode, 1859) 5.

15. Professor Niemeyer, afterword to Banting, *Letter on Corpulence* (1869 ed.), 107.

16. For the details of these experiments, see Smith, *Dietaries for the Inmates of Workhouses.*

17. Banting, *Letter on Corpulence,* 9.

18. Mary Douglas, *Purity and Danger* (London: Routledge, 1966), 36. For a similar discussion of physical disability as matter out of place, see Rosemarie Garland Thomson, *Extraordinary Bodies: Figuring Disability in American Literature*

and Culture (New York: Columbia University Press, 1997). My own argument is partially indebted to Thomson's work in this area.

19. See, for example, Richard Tomes, *Bazar Book of Decorum* (New York: Harper, 1875).

20. Thomson refers to this way of stigmatizing physical difference as the production of "social dirt" (*Extraordinary Bodies,* 33).

21. These anxieties about the body were complicated by medical theories on sex and gender. Women were considered to be generally more vulnerable to pollution than men were, because women's bodies were assumed to be more open to the world than men's and the boundaries of their bodies more readily traversible. For an excellent discussion of women's "open bodies," see Sally Shuttleworth, "Female Circulation: Medical Discourse and Popular Advertising in the Mid-Victorian Era," in *Body/Politics,* ed. Mary Jacobus, Evelyn Fox Keller, and Shuttleworth (New York: Routledge, 1990), 47–68.

22. Hinton, "Health," 337.

23. Michel Foucault, *Discipline and Punish: The Birth of the Prison,* trans. Alan Sheridan (New York: Vintage, 1977).

24. There is an obvious connection here between discourses on corpulence and those on other forms of physical difference, including disability and race. For a discussion of the conflation of racial difference with other types of physical difference in Victorian thought, see Sander L. Gilman's article on the Hottentot Venus, "Black Bodies, White Bodies: Toward an Iconography of Female Sexuality in Late Nineteenth-Century Art, Medicine, and Literature," in *"Race," Writing, and Difference,* ed. Henry Louis Gates, Jr. (Chicago: University of Chicago Press, 1985), 223–61.

25. Foucault, *Discipline and Punish,* 193.

26. Catherine Gallagher, "The Body versus the Social Body in the Works of Thomas Malthus and Henry Mayhew," in *The Making of the Modern Body: Sexuality and Society in the Nineteenth Century,* ed. Gallagher and Thomas Laqueur (Berkeley: University of California Press, 1987), 90.

27. Douglas, *Purity and Danger,* 70.

28. Stearns, *Fat History,* 25.

29. For a detailed discussion of some of these medical studies questioning the assumption that fat is unhealthy, see Shelley Bovey, *The Forbidden Body* (London: Pandora, 1989).

30. Peter Stallybrass and Allon White, *The Politics and Poetics of Transgression* (Ithaca, N.Y.: Cornell University Press, 1986).

31. Hinton, "Health," 332.

32. Tomes, *Bazar Book of Decorum,* 19.

33. Banting, *Letter on Corpulence,* 18.

34. Ibid., 21.

35. Foucault, *Discipline and Punish,* 227.

36. Bordo makes a similar argument in *Unbearable Weight* (130).

37. Ibid., 193, 195, 67.

38. Thomson, *Extraordinary Bodies,* 26.

39. My ideas in this section are indebted to Moon and Sedgwick's essay (see chapter 15, below). Citations are from Michael Moon and Eve Kosofsky Sedgwick, "Divinity: A Dossier, a Performance Piece, a Little-Understood Emotion," in *Tendencies,* by Sedgwick (Durham, N.C.: Duke University Press, 1993), 215–51.

40. Ibid., 229–30.

41. Gail Turley Houston, *Consuming Fictions: Gender, Class, and Hunger in Dickens's Novels* (Carbondale: Southern Illinois University Press, 1994).

42. Moon and Sedgwick, "Divinity," 223.

43. Ibid., 231.

44. Banting, *Letter on Corpulence,* 7.

45. Aytoun, "Banting on Corpulence," 617.

46. For a detailed discussion of Body Image Distortion Syndrome, see Bordo, *Unbearable Weight,* 54–60.

47. Foucault, *Discipline and Punish,* 203.

48. See Judith Butler, *Bodies That Matter: On the Discursive Limits of "Sex"* (New York: Routledge, 1993).

49. Ibid., 122.

50. Ibid., 15.

51. Aytoun, "Banting on Corpulence," 609.

52. See Mikhail Bakhtin, *Rabelais and His World,* trans. Hélène Iswolsky (1968; reprint, Bloomington: Indiana University Press, 1984), and Donna Haraway, "A Manifesto for Cyborgs: Science, Technology, and Socialist Feminism in the 1980s," in *Feminism/Postmodernism,* ed. Linda J. Nicholson (New York: Routledge, 1990), 190–233. I am indebted to Thomson (*Extraordinary Bodies,* 114–15) for this reading of Haraway's cyborg.

REFERENCES

Althusser, Louis. "Ideology and Ideological State Apparatuses," translated by Ben Brewster. In *Contemporary Critical Theory,* edited by Dan Latimer, 61–102. New York: Harcourt Brace Jovanovich, 1970.

Aytoun, William E. "Banting on Corpulence." *Blackwood's Edinburgh Magazine* 96 (November 1864): 607–17.

Bakhtin, Mikhail. *Rabelais and His World.* Translated by Hélène Iswolsky. 1968. Reprint, Bloomington: Indiana University Press, 1984.

Banting, William. *Letter on Corpulence.* 3rd American ed. New York: Mohun, Ebbs, and Hough, 1864.

———. *Letter on Corpulence.* 4th American ed. New York: Mohun, Ebbs, and Hough, 1865.

———. *Letter on Corpulence.* 4th London ed. London: Harrison and Sons, 1869.

Beller, Anne Scott. *Fat and Thin: A Natural History of Obesity.* New York: Farrar, Straus, and Giroux, 1977.

Bordo, Susan. *Unbearable Weight: Feminism, Western Culture, and the Body.* Berkeley: University of California Press, 1993.

Bovey, Shelley. *The Forbidden Body.* London: Pandora, 1989.

Brillat-Savarin, Jean. *The Handbook of Dining or Corpulency and Leanness.* Translated by L. F. Simpson. London: Longman, Greenman, and Longman, 1865.

Butler, Judith. *Bodies That Matter: On the Discursive Limits of "Sex."* New York: Routledge, 1993.

Chernin, Kim. *The Obsession: Reflections on the Tyranny of Slenderness.* New York: Harper and Row, 1981.

Douglas, Mary. *Purity and Danger.* London: Routledge, 1966.

Duke, Joshua. *How to Get Thin, or Banting in India.* 2nd ed. Calcutta: Thacker, 1878.

Foucault, Michel. *Discipline and Punish: The Birth of the Prison.* Translated by Alan Sheridan. New York: Vintage, 1977.

Gallagher, Catherine. "The Body versus the Social Body in the Works of Thomas Malthus and Henry Mayhew." In *The Making of the Modern Body: Sexuality and Society in the Nineteenth Century,* edited by Gallagher and Thomas Laqueur, 83–106. Berkeley: University of California Press, 1987.

Gilman, Sander L. "Black Bodies, White Bodies: Toward an Iconography of Female Sexuality in Late Nineteenth-Century Art, Medicine, and Literature." In *"Race," Writing, and Difference,* edited by Henry Louis Gates, Jr., 223–61. Chicago: University of Chicago Press, 1985.

Graham, Thomas John. *Sure Methods of Improving Health and Prolonging Life.* 1st American ed. Philadelphia: Carey, Lea and Carey, 1824.

Guy, William. *On Sufficient and Insufficient Dietaries with Special Reference to the Dietaries of Prisoners.* London: Harrison and Sons, 1863.

Haraway, Donna. "A Manifesto for Cyborgs: Science, Technology, and Socialist Feminism in the 1980s." In *Feminism/Postmodernism,* edited by Linda J. Nicholson, 190–233. New York: Routledge, 1990.

Harvey, William. Afterword to *Letter on Corpulence,* by William Banting, 34–36. 4th American ed. New York: Mohun, Ebbs, and Hough, 1865.

[Hinton, James]. "Health." *Cornhill Magazine* 3 (March 1861): 332–41.

Houston, Gail Turley. *Consuming Fictions: Gender, Class, and Hunger in Dickens's Novels.* Carbondale: Southern Illinois University Press, 1994.

Lankester, Edwin. *Guide to the Food Collection in the South Kensington Museum.* London: Eyre and Spottiswode, 1859.

Moon, Michael, and Eve Kosofsky Sedgwick. "Divinity: A Dossier, a Performance Piece, a Little-Understood Emotion." In *Tendencies,* by Sedgwick, 215–51. Durham, N.C: Duke University Press, 1993. [see chapter 15 of this volume]

Moore, Alfred. *Corpulency.* London: F. W. Ruston, 1857.

Niemeyer, Professor. Afterword to Banting, *Letter on Corpulence,* by William Banting, 101–16. 4th London ed. London: Harrison and Sons, 1869.

Schwartz, Hillel. *Never Satisfied: A Cultural History of Diets, Fantasies, and Fat.* New York: Free Press, 1986.

Seid, Roberta Pollak. *Never Too Thin: Why Women Are at War with Their Bodies.* New York: Prentice Hall, 1989.

Shuttleworth, Sally. "Female Circulation: Medical Discourse and Popular Advertising in the Mid-Victorian Era." In *Body/Politics,* edited by Mary Jacobus, Evelyn Fox Keller, and Shuttleworth, 47–68. New York: Routledge, 1990.

Smith, Edward. *Dietaries for the Inmates of Workhouses.* London: Eyre and Spottiswode, 1866.

———. *The Present State of the Dietary Question.* London: Walton and Maberly, 1864.

Stallybrass, Peter, and Allon White. *The Politics and Poetics of Transgression.* Ithaca, N.Y.: Cornell University Press, 1986.

Stearns, Peter N. *Fat History: Bodies and Beauty in the Modern West.* New York: New York University Press, 1997.

Thomson, Rosemarie Garland. *Extraordinary Bodies: Figuring Disability in American Literature and Culture.* New York: Columbia University Press, 1997.

Tomes, Richard. *The Bazar Book of Decorum.* New York: Harper, 1875.

Wadd, William. *Comments on Corpulency.* London: John Ebers, 1829.

Whiting, Sydney. *Memoirs of a Stomach.* 5th ed. London: Chapman and Hall, 1859.

3 Letting Ourselves Go

Making Room for the Fat Body in Feminist Scholarship

CECILIA HARTLEY

> *The body—what we eat, how we dress, the daily rituals through which we attend to the body—is a medium of culture. The body . . . is a powerful symbolic form, a surface on which the central rules, hierarchies, and even metaphysical commitments of a culture are inscribed and thus reinforced through the concrete language of the body.*
>
> **Susan Bordo,** *Unbearable Weight* (1993)

There is something wrong with the female body. Women learn early—increasingly, as early as five or six years old—that their bodies are fundamentally flawed. The restructuring process begins often as soon as a child is able to understand that there is a difference between the sexes. When that awareness reveals a female body, the realization soon follows that that body must be changed, molded, reconfigured into an ideal that will never be reached by "letting nature take its course."

Not surprisingly, self-hatred often becomes a part of a woman's body image. By the onset of puberty, a sense of body deficiency is very firmly in place, and that sense of deficiency is exacerbated as the body matures. According to one study, 53 percent of thirteen-year-old girls are dissatisfied with their bodies, and that number increases to 78 percent when the girls reach eighteen. Seventy-five percent of those over eighteen believe they are overweight, including 45 percent who are technically *underweight.*[1]

This "tyranny of slenderness" has created a culture in which as many as 60 percent of women experience some type of difficulty in eating and one in five teenage girls will develop an eating disorder such as anorexia or bulimia.[2] Feminist scholars such as Sandra Bartky,[3] Susan Bordo, Naomi Wolf, and others have rightly identified this epidemic as a feminist issue and have sought theoretical explanations for women's desire to starve themselves. The fact remains, however, that pacing the exponential rise in eating disorders in the last two decades has been the increase in the numbers of women who are, by modern standards, fat.[4] Susie Orbach reports that approximately 50 percent of American women are overweight by cultural standards; both Marcia Millman and Laura Brown put the figure at 25 percent.[5] Despite the prevalence of women who resist (or fail to resist) the tyranny of slenderness, the fat body has largely been ignored in feminist studies that attempt to theorize the female body.

How should these women be theorized? Are there similarities between what drives the starvation impulse and the feeding impulse? Is there a place in feminist scholarship for the fat body? I examine these questions in terms of the culture's production of docile female bodies, through which the ideal female form is constructed in some cases and rejected in others. I scrutinize the culture's embrace of those who achieve the ideal form (even when those bodies are literally starving) and its brutal rejection of those who do not, or cannot, meet that ideal. Finally, I identify the sexism inherent in sizism (which produces both the slender and the fat body) and look at the ways in which rejecting fat oppression can lead to a heightened feminist awareness.

THE FEMININE IDEAL AND THE PRODUCTION OF "DOCILE BODIES"

Modern American standards require that the ideal feminine body be small. A woman is taught early to contain herself, to keep arms and legs close to her body and take up as little space as possible. This model of femininity suggests that real women are thin, nearly invisible. The women idealized as perfect are these days little more than waifs. The average fashion model today weighs 23 percent less than the average woman; a generation ago the gap was only 8 percent.[6] Not surprisingly, those women who claim more than their share of territory are regarded with suspicion. Brown notes that "Fat oppression carries the less-than-subtle message that women are forbidden to take up space (by being large of body) or resources (by eating food ad libitum)."[7] In recent years, of course, there has been an increasing move toward fitness and bodybuilding for women, and some hope that a different ideal female body may be developing. There is reason to regard such a shift with suspicion, however. This new ideal still requires a complete restructuring of the female body, a removal of softness, and a rejection of any indication of fat tissue. It is still based on the notion that the large female body is inherently wrong. In addition, the most successful female bodybuilders, those who become large through muscle mass, are often seen as taking on masculine characteristics. A quick flip through *Vogue* demonstrates that the waif model still persists as feminine.

Men are under no such size restrictions and are allowed—often encouraged—to take up as much space as they can get away with. But when a woman's stature or girth approaches or exceeds that of a man's, she becomes something freakish. By becoming large, whether with fat tissue or muscle mass, she implicitly violates the sexual roles that place her in physical subordination to the man. As Naomi Wolf points out in *The Beauty Myth,* the focus on the smallness of the woman's body has increased in the United States at the same time that women have begun to gain a real measure of power. The male need to establish superiority, undermined by the relative success of the feminist movement, has reasserted itself by inscribing inferiority onto the female body. She declares, "A cultural fixation on female thinness is not an obsession about female beauty but an obsession about female obedience."[8]

Bartky agrees that cultural expectations have progressively shifted away from what a woman is allowed to *do* onto what a woman is allowed to *look like:* "Normative femininity is coming more and more to be centered on woman's body—not its duties and obligations or even its capacity to bear children, but its sexuality, more precisely, its presumed heterosexuality and appearance."[9] As women have claimed intellectual and economic power for themselves, culture has simply found new ways for them to be inferior. Brown calls the ideal feminine body a "manifestation of misogynist norms flowing from a culture where women are devalued and disempowered."[10] That is, because women themselves are seen as somehow less than men, their bodies must demonstrate that inferiority.

These "misogynist norms" are not simply inflicted on women from the outside. Such overt oppression would be relatively easy for women to identify and resist. As Michel Foucault notes, however, the success of a society's imposition of discipline upon bodies depends on those bodies learning *to regulate themselves.*[11] That is, women feel the need to construct female bodies that are demonstrably smaller and weaker than men's bodies in part because they have, in Brown's words, "internalized fat oppressive notions."[12] Because the male gaze is always present, even when it is physically absent, women must continually produce bodies that are acceptable to that gaze. Thus a woman's own gaze becomes a substitute for a man's gaze, and she evaluates her own body as ruthlessly as she expects it to be evaluated by him.

Bartky discusses this "state of conscious and permanent visibility" while examining the ways in which women participate in the construction of their own bodies as inferior. Referring to Foucault's account of how docile bodies are produced by internalizing society's codes and expectations, she asks an important question: "Where is the account of the disciplinary practices that engender the 'docile bodies' of women, bodies more docile than the bodies of men?"[13] But given the number of female bodies that have not proved their docility by producing smaller, quieter, more ornamental versions of male bodies, I suggest that there must also be a follow-up question: Where is the account of the ways self-regulation *fails to* engender the "docile bodies" of women? That is, how and why are unruly (ungovernable?) bodies of fat women constructed?

Bartky further identifies three categories of disciplinary practices that produce the recognizably feminine body:

- those that aim to produce a body of a certain size and general configuration
- those that bring forth from this body a specific repertoire of gestures, postures, and movements
- those directed toward the display of this body as an ornamental surface[14]

She does not, however, suggest what might happen when those disciplinary practices are not successfully instilled in women, implicitly raising another question: What processes go into constructing the body that is *not* recognizably feminine? The construction of the body is undoubtedly a social act insofar as gender (that is, the construction of a body that is recognizably masculine or feminine) is performed for the satisfaction of both performer and audience.[15] In characterizing femininity as "spectacle," something performed for a watcher, Bartky admits that "under the current 'tyranny of slenderness' women are forbidden to become large or massive. . . . The very contours a woman's body takes on as she matures—the fuller breasts and rounded hips—have become distasteful."[16] Yet she fails to link our culture's attempt to construct the small female body with its distaste for the bodies that refuse to be constructed to those ideals. Since women *do* become large, what can we say about culture's rejection of them?

Women who do not maintain rigid control over the boundaries of their bodies, allowing them to grow, to become large and "unfeminine," are treated with derision in our society, and that derision is tied inextricably to the personal freedom of women. Women who are fat are said to have "let themselves go." The very phrase connotes a loosening of restraints. Women in our society are bound. In generations past, the constriction was accomplished by corsets and girdles that cut into the skin and left welts, marks of discipline. The girdles are now, for the most part, gone, but they have been replaced by bindings even more rigid. Women today are bound by fears, by oppression, and by stereotypes that depict large women as ungainly, unfeminine, and unworthy of appreciation. Large chunks of time and energy that could be channeled into making real, substantive changes in society are being spent pursuing the ideal body image: weighing, measuring, preparing and portioning food, weighing and measuring the body, jogging, stair-stepping, crunching away any softness of belly, taking pills, seeing specialists, finding clothes that hide figure flaws. Women in particular are literally terrified of getting fat. In survey after survey, being fat is listed as a primary fear.[17]

The fear of missing the mark of ideal beauty has generated, or been generated by, solid economic realities. The $33 billion a year diet industry and $300 million cosmetic surgery industry[18] are founded on women's fears and attempts at bodily constraint. Mounting evidence shows the ineffectiveness of low-calorie diets and the dangers of cosmetic surgeries that have set women up for repeated personal failures in attempting to attain an ever-elusive ideal, but the oppressive social control made possible by fat-phobia grips women as tightly as ever. Above all, women must control themselves, must be careful, for to relax their vigilance might lead to the worst possible consequence: being fat.

FAT OPPRESSION AND AMERICAN CULTURE

In modern American culture, women are expected to be beautiful, and beautiful equals thin. Whether we are given waifs or athletes to view, we are constantly bombarded by media images of women with little or no breast tissue and slim, boyish hips. The almost impossible ideal is set before women as the mold in which to construct their bodies, molds which the vast majority of bodies simply will not fit. Virtually every woman learns to hate her body, regardless of her size, and so she learns to participate in her own oppression. As Brown notes, "data suggests that North American women of most cultures, and all body sizes and eating styles tend to have fat-oppressive and fat-negative attitudes towards their own bodies and, by inference, those of other women."[19]

The fat woman, Millman observes, is "stereotypically viewed as unfeminine, in flight from sexuality, antisocial, out of control, hostile, aggressive."[20] Because they do not construct bodies that conform to the feminine ideal, fat women are perceived as violating socially prescribed sexual roles, and that violation is a threat to existing power structures. Women may have made gains in intellectual and economic power, but there is a price to be paid. At all costs, a woman must not be allowed to maintain (or win) physical power as well. If she does, she is in rebellion, not only against male power structures but against all that is feminine.

It is no wonder that such fat-oppressive attitudes have been internalized. Fat women in American society are perpetually victimized by public ridicule. They are "weighed down . . . by the force of hatred, contempt and pity, amusement and revulsion. Fat bodies are invaded by comments, measured with hatred, pathologized by fear and diagnosed by ignorance."[21] Fat-phobia is one of the few acceptable forms of prejudice left in a society that at times goes to extremes to prove itself politically correct. One study indicates that fat girls have only one-third the chance of being admitted to prestigious colleges as slim girls with similar school records.[22] Fat jokes still abound. Women who get fat publicly (Elizabeth Taylor, Oprah Winfrey, Sarah Ferguson) are openly censured and scorned as if their bodies were public property. And when they lose weight, as all three of these women have, they are met with an approval that again marks their bodies as public property.

Of course, a woman does not have to be a public figure for her body to receive similar treatment. Fat has become a moral issue unlike any other type of deviation from what society considers normal. The fat woman is often dismissed as sloppy, careless, lazy, and self-indulgent. Large women know all too well that strangers often feel no compunction about stepping forward to criticize a woman's size with statements such as "Should you really be eating that?"; "I know a good doctor who could help you"; "You have such a pretty face, if you'd just lose some weight. . . ."

Why does American society have such a visceral reaction to fat? Some, like Brown, agree that "a fat woman by her presence violates primal norms of misogynist society that deny nurturance, space, power and visibility to women."[23] But Wolf and others have drawn an analogy between the view of fat in modern culture and the view of sex in Victorian times: "What hysteria was to the nineteenth-century fetish of the asexual woman locked in the home, anorexia is to the late-twentieth-century fetish of the hungry woman."[24] For the Victorian woman, sex was forbidden, dirty, and shameful, and her repression of her desires led to hysteria. For the modern woman, "fat" is forbidden, dirty, and shameful, and her strict control over and repression of her bodily needs are manifested once again in the body, not in hysteria but in eating disorders. Although many studies refute a simple correlation between weight gain and overeating, Susan Bordo notes that American culture still sees fat only in terms of self-indulgence: "Anorexia could thus be seen as an extreme development of the capacity for self-denial and repression of desire . . . ; obesity, as an extreme capacity to capitulate to desire."[25]

In "capitulating to desire," fat women are seen as standing in rebellion against the strictures of society. They are breaking the rules, and culture's immediate reaction is to punish them. Bordo sees this ostensible rebellion as the source of society's hostility toward fat women: "the obese—particularly those who claim to be happy although overweight—are perceived as not playing by the rules at all. If the rest of us are struggling to be acceptable and 'normal,' we cannot allow them to get away with it; they must be put in their place, be humiliated and defeated."[26]

The same society that valorizes the female body, making it a cultural icon for beauty, subtly undermines any sense of self-love a woman might have for her body—even those bodies that meet the ideal. The body is suspect, needy, always in danger of erupting into something that will grasp more than is allowed. The end result is that women, fat or thin, often develop an antagonistic relationship with their bodies. The size and shape those bodies take on become directly connected to a woman's self-esteem. As Bartky notes, "Overtly, the fashion-beauty complex seeks to glorify the female body and to provide opportunities for narcissistic indulgence. More important than this is its *covert* aim, which is to depreciate woman's body and deal a blow to her narcissism."[27] The fat body, then, comes to represent all that must be avoided and all that is denied to women in American society. Because it must be avoided so strenuously, those who do not, or cannot, avoid fatness are a source of public discomfort, outrage, or both. The fat body, Brown tells us, is a reminder of all that a woman cannot and should not be:

> Fat women are ugly, bad, and not valuable because they are in violation of so many of the rules. A fat woman is visible, and takes up space. A fat woman stands out. She occupies personal territory in ways that violate the rules for the sexual politics of body movement.
>
> . . . A fat woman has strong muscles from moving her weight around in the world. She clearly has fed herself. . . . Thus, for women to not break the rules, and for women to not be ugly, bad, and invaluable, women must fear fat, and hate it in themselves.[28]

The fat woman demonstrates by her very presence that she has not submitted to the rules that society has established for feminine behavior. Overtly, her body shape *may* be a result of a conscious rejection of societal and cultural norms. More insidiously, however, that body also may be a result of years of dieting and refeeding in attempts to achieve the ideal form. Her own body's rejection of starvation and its subsequent padding of itself in protection against future periods of deprivation serve as a subtle indictment of patriarchy's requirement that she be unnaturally thin.

The link to patriarchy here might well be questioned. My study has focused on the fat *female* body even though a large percentage of the fat population is male. As has been noted, however, it is only the female body that has been rigidly inscribed as *necessarily* thin, that thinness rendering a woman visibly smaller and weaker than the average male. The male gaze, characterized by Brown as a "patriarchal psychic tapeworm,"[29] serves as a continual reminder that the female body must be smaller than man's to be acceptable. Bartky notes that "insofar as the disciplinary practices of femininity produce 'subjected and practiced,' an inferiorized body, they must be understood as aspects of a far larger discipline, an oppressive and inegalitarian system of sexual subordination."[30] I would suggest that the emaciated female body stands as a symbol of woman's sexual subordination.

THE MALE GAZE AND THE SEXISM OF SIZISM

Biologically, women have more fat than men, 10 to 15 percent more body fat until the onset of puberty. At puberty, as evidence of maturity and fertility, women's fat-to-muscle ratio increases as the male's decreases, widening the gap even more.[31] Ironically, however, it is that fat, crucial to a woman's reproductive health, that renders her undesirable in a heterosexual relationship. Culturally, women face far stricter limits than men on what amount of body fat is acceptable. The intensity of public scorn of the fat female body drives many women to take extreme measures in order to meet those guidelines. There is evidence, however, that the male sexual gaze indicates the attitude toward corpulence more accurately than does the sex of the body being constructed. It is not only women who must conform to the male ideal of beauty. Recent research has shown that internalized fat-oppressive attitudes are more often present in persons of *either sex* who want to be found attractive by men and that they are less common in persons of either sex who wish to be found attractive by women.[32] Still, while men are at much higher risk from illness due to obesity, 80 to 90 percent of all weight loss surgery is performed on women, despite the grave risks and complications that have been linked to the procedures.[33] Between 90 to 95 percent of anorectics and bulimics are women.[34]

As Wolf reminds us, "the demonic characterizations of a simple body substance do not arise from its physical properties but from old-fashioned misogyny, for above all, fat is female."[35] That which distinguishes women outwardly from men—the curves of breast and hip—are primarily accumulations of adipose tissue, the same adipose tissue that is attacked with such ferocity and treated as the enemy of women. Brown adds, "Most of the ways in which women feel physically 'wrong' e.g., having womanly hips, bellies, breasts, and thighs, are manifestations of how their body is not that of a man."[36]

It is here that the construction of the sexual female body takes a curious turn. The states of anorexia and obesity, both extreme reactions to the sexism/sizism of American culture,[37] situate women as simultaneously asexual and hypersexual. In the anorexic state, the body is stripped of all excess fat tissue, feminine curves disappear, and the female body is rendered nearly prepubescent in form. The anorexic body changes internally as well. When body fat drops below a certain percentage, ovulation and menstruation cease. "Infertility and hormone imbalance are common among women whose fat-to-lean ratio falls below 22 percent," Wolf points out.[38] In essence, femaleness is rejected in favor of a state of asexuality. One woman refers to her bout with anorexia as "killing off the woman in me."[39]

While anorexia is in very physical and chemical ways an "absolute negation of the female state,"[40] it is the anorexic and nearly anorexic body that is glamorized on runways, on magazine covers, and in television shows and movies. In its asexuality, the thin female body becomes, ironically, hypersexualized, culturally "feminine" and admired, accepted in its very rejection of excess flesh. Anorexia in many ways reflects an ambivalence about femininity, a rebellion against feminization that manifests itself by means of the disease as both a rejection and an exaggeration of the feminine ideal.

The fat body also exists in a state of simultaneous asexuality and hypersexuality. Increased stores of fat exaggerate the outward sexuality of the female body; breasts and hips become fuller and more prominent. A fat woman's body is unmistakably, maturely female. Internally, the body experiences heightened sexuality as well. Fat cells store estrogen, and increases in fat increase levels of that hormone in the body. In addition, some studies suggest that fat women desire sex more often than do thin.[41] Yet even as the thin female body is perceived as hypersexual by culture, the fat female body is perceived as asexual. "In our society," Millman points out, "fat women are viewed as unfeminine, unattractive, masculine, out of the running. In a word, they are desexualized."[42]

In many ways, both of these groups of women are attempting to remove themselves from their bodies, to live from the neck up. Anorexia can be read as an attempt to deny physiology, to make the body itself disappear. While obesity may be characterized as the reverse, as celebrating or reveling in the body, the issue is more complex. Certainly many fat women have made a conscious decision to allow their bodies free rein. Many other women, however, perhaps the majority, become fat because they are disconnected from their bodies and have trouble learning to use and move them in productive ways. Millman links this inability to use the body in physical ways to the male gaze and cultural expectations of femininity: "Women are prone to disembodiment not only because they are constantly exposed to intrusive judgments about their bodies but also because they are taught to regard their bodies as passive objects others should admire. Unlike men who are raised to *express themselves* unself-consciously through physical activity and sports, women's bodies are employed to be looked at."[43] Either extreme, being fat or being anorexic, can therefore be seen as a rejection of the body as object of the male gaze. Thus a first step in reclaiming the female body might well be a loosening of the cultural restraints on it—an acknowledgment that the female body naturally contains more fat cells than a man's and a commitment to living *inside* the body. But such a step on the part of women is sure to be perceived as a threat as great as the suffrage movement of the nineteenth century or the women's liberation movement of the twentieth.

THE THREAT OF FEMALE FLESH

Women are still raised in our society to be nurturers. They are taught to tend first to the needs of others and only then to themselves. Nowhere is this more evident than in feeding patterns. Men are expected at every turn to eat more. The perception is that they are larger, that their bodies need more fuel, and that women are generally dieting anyway. This notion persists despite evidence that a woman's daily caloric needs are only 250 calories less than a man's.[44] The idea that a woman's body needs less fuel than a man's is evidently held to apply from birth. Orbach cites one study of mother-child interaction in which 99 percent of baby boys were breastfed, while only 66 percent of the girls were. In addition, the girls were weaned significantly earlier than the boys and spent 50 percent less time feeding.[45] This study suggests that females may be undernourished and undernurtured from the outset,[46] a pattern of undernourishment that may well be the root cause of both obesity and bulimia. Binge eating is more accurately classified by many eating disorder specialists as "refeeding," a term connoting that binge eating is a physical reaction to prolonged periods of nutritional deprivation.

Women's self-feeding represents a type of deviant behavior: it sets itself in opposition to what has been prescribed as "normal," and at the same time it promotes the construction of a body that is not culturally recognized as small and therefore feminine. Self-feeding in women is thus viewed with suspicion, seen perhaps rightly as a rejection of cultural codes that require women to remain quiescent and needy. Millman notes that "eating is sometimes used [by women] in the spirit of *asserting oneself* against an outside force or power (and therefore, asserting personal control)."[47] Orbach argues even more strongly that "[g]etting fat can . . . be understood as a definite and purposeful act; it is a directed, conscious or unconscious, challenge to sex-role stereotyping and culturally defined experience of womanhood."[48]

Once the fat woman has rejected those roles, she often finds unexpected benefits to refusing to construct the acceptably feminine body. Orbach declares: "For many women, compulsive eating and being fat have become one way to avoid being marketed or seen as the ideal woman: 'My fat says "screw you" to all who want me to be the perfect mom, sweetheart, maid and whore. Take me for who *I* am, not for who I'm supposed to be. If you are really interested in *me,* you can wade through the layers and find out who I am.' In this way, fat expresses a rebellion against the powerlessness of the woman."[49] As Brown notes, being fat is "is an ultimate form of female covert power."[50] It allows a woman to nurture herself, to reject sexually stereotyped roles, to deny society's demand that she be the perfect woman, and to stake a claim on the world, taking up space without having to demand it.

The fat body speaks its construction just as the thin body does. As Orbach reminds us, the mouth has two functions, to speak and to eat.[51] When the mouth is silent, whether it is closed against food or filled with food, the body speaks its needs to the world. The fat body is not merely lazy or self-indulgent: it is inscribed by culture, and it is a reflection of oppression as surely as is the body of the rail-thin anorectic. Just as we have come to realize that the thin ideal is not an innocent construction, so we can no longer afford to dismiss the fat body as making no particular response to the society that would construct it otherwise. We now recognize that the idealized female body has been culturally encoded to mark a woman as physically passive, taking up little space, and non-self-nurturing. To the extent that the fat body has been vilified as marking a woman who refuses to accept that prescribed construction, a place must be made in feminist scholarship for theorizing the fat body in ways that acknowledge the power of her refusal.

NOTES

1. Susan Bordo, *Unbearable Weight: Feminism, Western Culture, and the Body* (Berkeley: University of California Press, 1993), 185.
2. See Marcia Millman, *Such a Pretty Face: Being Fat in America* (New York: Norton, 1980); Susie Orbach, *Fat Is a Feminist Issue: The Anti-Diet Guide to Permanent Weight Loss* (1978; reprint, New York: Berkley, 1994); and Naomi Wolf, *The Beauty Myth: How Images of Beauty Are Used against Women* (New York: Anchor Books/Doubleday, 1992). On the "tyranny of slenderness," see Kim Chernin, *The Obsession: Reflections on the Tyranny of Slenderness* (New York: Harper and Row, 1981); the figure of 60 percent comes from Wolf, 183.
3. Sandra Lee Bartky, *Femininity and Domination: Studies in the Phenomenology of Oppression* (New York: Routledge, 1990).
4. Millman (*Such a Pretty Face*) and Laura S. Brown ("Fat-Oppressive Attitudes and the Feminist Therapist: Directions for Change," in *Fat Oppression and Psychotherapy: A Feminist Perspective*, ed. Brown and Esther D. Rothblum [New York: Haworth Press, 1989], 19–30) have explained why the term *fat* is preferable to terms such as *overweight* or *obese*. While *fat* is merely a descriptive term, *overweight* implies an ideal weight based upon weight tables, many of which have been proven obsolete, and *obese* is a clinical medical term based on similar principles. Both scholars argue that the word *fat* should be reclaimed until pejorative connotations have been removed and the word no longer has wince-value.
5. Orbach, *Fat Is a Feminist Issue*, 3; Laura S. Brown, "Women, Weight, and Power: Feminist Theoretical and Therapeutic Issues," *Women and Therapy* 4, no. 1 (1985): 61–71.
6. Wolf, *The Beauty Myth*, 183.
7. Brown, "Fat-Oppressive Attitudes," 20.
8. Wolf, *The Beauty Myth*, 187.
9. Bartky, *Femininity and Domination*, 80.
10. Brown, "Women, Weight, and Power," 63.
11. For complete discussion of the role of self-regulation in producing docile bodies, see Michel Foucault's *Discipline and Punish: The Birth of the Prison*, trans. Alan Sheridan (New York: Vintage, 1979), 135–228.
12. Brown, "Women, Weight, and Power," 68.
13. Bartky, *Femininity and Domination*, 65.
14. Ibid.
15. For a discussion of the ways in which gender can be read as a performative act, see Judith Butler's *Bodies That Matter: On the Discursive Limits of "Sex"* (New York: Routledge, 1993).
16. Bartky, *Femininity and Domination*, 73.
17. Millman, *Such a Pretty Face*, and Wolf, *The Beauty Myth*.
18. Wolf, *The Beauty Myth*, 17.

19. Brown, "Fat-Oppressive Attitudes," 20.
20. Millman, *Such a Pretty Face*, xi.
21. R. Bull, quoted in Susan Tenzer, "Fat Acceptance Therapy (F.A.T.): A Non-Dieting Group Approach to Physical Wellness, Insight, and Acceptance," in Brown and Rothblum, *Fat Oppression and Psychotherapy*, 47.
22. Millman, *Such a Pretty Face*, 90.
23. Brown, "Fat-Oppressive Attitudes," 26.
24. Wolf, *The Beauty Myth*, 198.
25. Bordo, *Unbearable Weight*, 201.
26. Ibid., 203.
27. Bartky, *Femininity and Domination*, 39–40.
28. Brown, "Women, Weight, and Power," 65.
29. Ibid., 63.
30. Bartky, *Femininity and Domination*, 75.
31. Wolf, *The Beauty Myth*, 192.
32. Brown, "Fat-Oppressive Attitudes," 25; Millman, *Such a Pretty Face*, 245.
33. Jaclyn Packer, "The Role of Stigmatization in Fat People's Avoidance of Physical Exercise," in Brown and Rothblum, *Fat Oppression and Psychotherapy*, 52.
34. Wolf, *The Beauty Myth*, 181.
35. Ibid., 92.
36. Brown, "Women, Weight, and Power," 85.
37. Studies indicate that dieting itself may cause both eating disorders and obesity; see Wolf, *The Beauty Myth;* Brown, "Fat-Oppressive Attitudes"; and Millman, *Such a Pretty Face.*
38. Wolf, *The Beauty Myth*, 192.
39. Millman, *Such a Pretty Face*, 125.
40. Wolf, *The Beauty Myth*, 184.
41. Ibid., 192.
42. Millman, *Such a Pretty Face*, 98.
43. Ibid., 202.
44. Wolf, *The Beauty Myth*, 192.
45. Orbach, *Fat Is a Feminist Issue*, 18.
46. See Millman, *Such a Pretty Face.*
47. Ibid., 43.
48. Orbach, *Fat Is a Feminist Issue*, 6.
49. Ibid., 9.
50. Brown, "Women, Weight, and Power," 66.
51. Orbach, *Fat Is a Feminist Issue*, 76.

REFERENCES

Bartky, Sandra Lee. *Femininity and Domination: Studies in the Phenomenology of Oppression*. New York: Routledge, 1990.

Bordo, Susan. *Unbearable Weight: Feminism, Western Culture, and the Body.* Berkeley: University of California Press, 1993.

Brown, Laura S. "Fat-Oppressive Attitudes and the Feminist Therapist: Directions for Change." In *Fat Oppression and Psychotherapy: A Feminist Perspective*, edited by Brown and Esther D. Rothblum, 19–30. New York: Haworth Press, 1989.

———. "Women, Weight, and Power: Feminist Theoretical and Therapeutic Issues." *Women and Therapy* 4, no. 1 (1985); 61–71.

Butler, Judith. *Bodies That Matter: On the Discursive Limits of "Sex."* New York: Routledge, 1993.

Chernin, Kim. *The Obsession: Reflections on the Tyranny of Slenderness*. New York: Harper and Row, 1981.

Foucault, Michel. *Discipline and Punish: The Birth of the Prison*. Translated by Alan Sheridan. New York: Vintage, 1979.

Lyons, Pat. "Fitness, Feminism and the Health of Fat Women." In *Fat Oppression and Psychotherapy: A Feminist Perspective,* edited by Laura S. Brown and Esther D. Rothblum, 65–77. New York: Haworth Press, 1989.

Millman, Marcia. *Such a Pretty Face: Being Fat in America*. New York: Norton, 1980.

Orbach, Susie. *Fat Is a Feminist Issue: The Anti-Diet Guide to Permanent Weight Loss*. 1978. Reprint, New York: Berkley, 1994.

Packer, Jaclyn. "The Role of Stigmatization in Fat People's Avoidance of Physical Exercise." In *Fat Oppression and Psychotherapy: A Feminist Perspective,* edited by Laura S. Brown and Esther D. Rothblum, 49–63. New York: Haworth Press, 1989.

Tenzer, Susan. "Fat Acceptance Therapy (F.A.T.): A Non-Dieting Group Approach to Physical Wellness, Insight and Acceptance." In *Fat Oppression and Psychotherapy: A Feminist Perspective,* edited by Laura S. Brown and Esther D. Rothblum, 39–47. New York: Haworth Press, 1989.

Wolf, Naomi. *The Beauty Myth: How Images of Beauty Are Used against Women*. New York: Anchor Books/Doubleday, 1992.

4 Queering Fat Bodies/Politics

KATHLEEN LEBESCO

Queens will not be pawns.

Derek Jarman

The body is a pliable entity whose determinable form is provided not simply by biology but through the interaction of modes of psychical and physical inscription and the provision of a set of limiting biological codes. . . . The body is not open to all the whims, wishes, and hopes of the subject: the human body, for example, cannot fly in the air. . . . On the other hand, while there must be some kinds of biological limit or constraint, these constraints are perpetually capable of being superseded, overcome, through the human body's capacity to open itself up to prosthetic synthesis, to transform or rewrite its environment, to continually augment its powers and capacities through the incorporation into the body's own spaces and modalities of objects that, while external, are internalized, added to, supplementing and supplemented by the "organic body" (or what culturally passes for it), surpassing the body, not "beyond" nature but in collusion with a "nature" that never really lived up to its name, that represents always the most blatant cultural anxieties and projections.

Elizabeth Grosz, *Volatile Bodies* (1994)

INTRODUCING FAT BODIES

Are fat bodies revolting? Popular culture would have us believe so, as would theorists who celebrate transgression writ large, though quite different rationales underpin these similar contentions. In the United States in the late 1990s, as in most Western countries with developed industrial economies since at least World War II, fat has a bad rap.[1] The medical establishment has proclaimed fat to be a scourge more far-reaching than the bubonic plague, a "national health crisis," with obesity "striking" nearly one-third of all adult Americans.[2] Aesthetically, fat is the antithesis of the beauty ideal of the day: tight, lean, and toned. Viewed, then, as both unhealthy and unattractive, fat people are widely represented in popular culture and in interpersonal interactions as revolting—they are agents of abhorrence and disgust.[3] But if we think of *revolting* in terms of overthrowing authority, rebelling, protesting, and rejecting, then corpulence carries a whole new weight as a subversive cultural practice that calls into question received notions about health, beauty, and nature. We can recognize fat as a condition not simply aesthetic or medical, but *political.*

In much of the West, fat is seen as disgusting/revolting and thus lurks on the cultural periphery. Given Judith Butler's contention that "all social systems are vulnerable at their margins, and . . . all margins are accordingly considered dangerous,"[4] fat people can tap into the resources of abjection[5] in the margin in order to strengthen their claim to the kinds of entitlement felt only by those bodies deemed natural, healthy, and beautiful. In this essay, I draw from the theoretical frames of Butler, Elizabeth Grosz, Eve Kosofsky Sedgwick, and others in order to queer fat bodies/politics, in hopes of propelling corpulent bodies to qualify as bodies that matter.

I hope ultimately to alter the discourses of fat subjectivity by moving inquiries about fat from medical and scientistic discourses to social and cultural ones, offering instead of self-help literature a different way of looking at, and living in, fat. My interest here stems from experiencing and imagining the possibilities of political relationships forged from affinities, from the performance of self and the recognition of other both as subject and subjected. According to the political theorist Patricia Mann, "if we assume the conjecture of multiple dimensions of both oppression and agency within concrete institutional settings, we can seek to construct a fluid micro-politics embracing diverse forms of intersectional agency and struggle."[6] Instead of simply venerating or denouncing fat subjects, my aim is to theorize fat embodiment in a way that alters the relational topography around body size and shape. This task calls for theorizing the simultaneous construction of fat people as choice-making, self-defining subjects who are also subjected to fat oppression in an attempt to understand the "diverse and conflicting practices, pressures, and possibilities that provide the context for political struggle and social transformation."[7] In so doing, this essay (and the larger project of retheorizing corpulence) guards against the propensity to long idealistically for the emancipation of innocent fat people from the bonds of subjection,[8] just as it suggests alternatives to helplessness in the face of overdetermined social relationships.

EMPOWERING DISCOURSE? LANGUAGE AND IDENTITY

> As we think about worlds that might one day become thinkable, sayable, legible, the opening up of the foreclosed and the saying of the unspeakable become part of the very "offense" that must be committed in order to expand the domain of linguistic survival. The resignification of speech requires opening new contexts, speaking in ways that have never yet been legitimated, and hence producing legitimation in new and future forms.
>
> Judith Butler, *Excitable Speech* (1997)

Language may be used to carry out the revolution that replaces the spoiled identity of fatness—an identity so powerful that even fat people roundly abhor their own bodies—with a more inhabitable subject position. Butler claims that "discourse becomes oppressive when it requires that the speaking subject, in order to speak, participate in the very terms of that oppression—that is, take for granted the speaking subject's own impossibility or unintelligibility."[9] Inarguably, current discourse surrounding body size and shape has worked to incorporate the protests of fat people against their own bodies; when civil rights are being demanded on the basis of the genetic subjection of fat people, the fat body is effectively rendered uninhabitable. This power of language isn't purely abstract, either; it enacts physical and material violence on bodies.[10]

Butler, following the work of Mary Douglas, suggests that a more important question than how a particular shitty/Othered identity is internalized is why the distinction between inner and outer is maintained. Whom does it serve in public discourse? When you think about it, only Others internalize things (such as oppression), thus rendering their *surfaces* invisible; that is how "a body figure[s] on its surface the very invisibility of its hidden depth."[11] My interest in transforming fatness from a spoiled, uninhabitable, invisible identity to a stronger subject position dissuades me from analyzing internalization, as it is a paradigm that further propels abjection.

Language, according to Monique Wittig, "is a set of acts, repeated over time, that produce reality-effects that are eventually misperceived as 'facts.'"[12] Thus, fat people (scholars, nonacademic intellectuals, activists, and lay people alike) can begin creating and regulating a new social reality through the use of words—spoken as well as written. Butler believes that language is capable of enacting material change "through locutionary acts, which, [when] repeated, become entrenched practices and, ultimately, institutions."[13] What I appreciate about this understanding of language is that it does not posit some truly representable reality on which language, like a tool, is used; instead, it speaks to the artificiality of the truths we think we know. Such a recognition of artificiality offers the possibility of generating new truths through language. Butler's work suggests to me that we just might be able to talk our way out of anything, even seemingly entrenched fat oppression, because speaking builds subjects.

However, the strategies for talking one's way into a subject position are a point of contention among fat activists today. They provide various rationales for preempting the position of the speaking subject: some want to be able to make claims on behalf of *all* fat people, to posit one specific notion of "the" fat experience; others want only to be able to speak for themselves, and frequently articulate concerns about the oppressive nature of fat community demands. Clearly, we need to examine more closely the range of terms used and reappropriated by fat people to redeploy and destabilize the dominant categories of the body and of fat identity. This task lies beyond my current scope, but by theorizing fat politics through queer politics, I hope to open a critical space for such an examination.

REINSCRIBING CORPULENCE, RESIGNIFYING FAT

Inasmuch as it aims to undermine what counts as normal, my theorization of fatness, my theoretical queering of fat politics, guards against the slip into relativistic evaluation of various transgressions. Butler writes that "The loss of the sense of 'the normal' . . . can be its own occasion for laughter, especially when 'the normal,' 'the original' is revealed to be a copy, and an inevitably failed one, an ideal that no one *can* embody."[14] However, we need some way of discerning which actions are truly disruptive of so-called normalcy, and which in fact help to maintain the status quo. We must therefore look at performances *in context* and ask: What performance in what context will help to destabilize naturalized identity categories?[15]

I argue that it is possible to theorize (or rather, to retheorize) the signs of fatness, rendering fat intelligible socially and culturally. Butler argues that "[i]f the rules governing signification not only restrict, but enable the assertion of alternative domains of cultural intelligibility . . . then it is only *within* the practices of repetitive signifying that a subversion of identity becomes possible,"[16] a claim vital for understanding that signification never equals determination, and thus that the reworkings (in specific language communities, in written and spoken discourses) provide very real promise. This is not a way *out* but a way *in,* a way to gain the upper hand in signification games—by gaining the ability to change the rules by which they are played. One who threatens and disrupts dominant significations is not doomed to a perpetually overshadowed pocket of resistance; instead, these actions are "a critical resource in the struggle to rearticulate the very terms of symbolic legitimacy and intelligibility."[17] Elizabeth Grosz concurs with Butler about the vitality of these disruptions: "Where one body . . . takes on the function of model or ideal, the human body, for all other types of body, its domination may be undermined through a defiant affirmation of a multiplicity, a field of differences, or other kinds of bodies and subjectivities."[18]

However, I am aware that the process of gaining the upper hand, or reconstituting fat identity to change its current status as spoiled, will in turn produce its own subset of unthinkable, unlivable, and abject bodies. Subjects are constituted by the processes of excluding and abjecting, so it is necessary to reflect on how these processes shape fat identity. While I examine strategies for transforming (widening) the fat body, I also consider the ways in which this transformation constitutes excluded and abjected Others. Butler's discussion of the possibilities of reworking abjection into political agency is illuminating here, as are Grosz's warnings against simply replacing the current standards of health and beauty with different models, while allowing the structure to remain intact.

In the domain of gender identity, Butler claims that "the public assertion of queerness enacts performativity as citationality for the purposes of resignifying the abjection of homosexuality into defiance and legitimacy."[19] Yet she asserts that one enters into public discourse not simply to get the advantage in the same old, tired dialectic but to attempt to "rewrite the history of the term, and to force it into a demanding resignification." This revision is crucial to making queer lives "legible, valuable, worthy of support, [lives] in which passion, injury, grief, aspiration become recognized without fixing the terms of that recognition in yet another conceptual order of lifelessness and rigid exclusion."[20] Though I recognize her goal of deviating from the citational chain "toward a more possible future to expand the very meaning of what counts as a valued and valuable body in the world"[21] as exceptionally worthwhile, for fat politics as well as for queer politics, I also realize that we're just not quite there yet. My theorization of corpulence takes one step toward its realization.

Like Butler, Grosz urges us to refuse "singular models, models which are based on one type of body as the norm by which all others are judged," instead favoring a field of body types "which, in being recognized in their specificity, cannot take on the coercive role of singular norm or ideals for all the others. Such plural models must be used to define the norms and ideals not only of health and fitness but also of beauty and desire."[22] We can appreciate this goal, without naively expecting a happy, separate-but-equal assessment of bodies, as the process of bringing into being the plural models is itself inevitably violent and disruptive. Ultimately, the question boils down to whether or not that process is *worthy*.

FAT IDENTITY POLITICS?

In revaluing bodies, we open up a space for revaluing fat bodies. An important related question concerns the foundation of fat identity. Can it be conceptualized as "the stylized repetition of acts through time, and not a seemingly seamless identity," as Butler defines gender identity?[23] What difference does the physical immanence of fat make, as compared with the usually-only-assumed physical presence of a specific set of genitals in gender identity? Fat, unlike gender, *is* written on the body for *all* to see; what kinds of dissonant and denaturalized performances are nevertheless possible in the assertion of fat identity? Like Butler on gender identity, I argue that the act of fat identity is "open to splittings, self-parody, self-criticism, and . . . hyperbolic exhibitions of 'the natural.' "[24] That claim leads to another question: Where do we see these happenings in fat-identified communities, and what are their consequences for the larger process of resignification?

The work of Elizabeth Grosz on identity and the body compels another line of questioning for the retheorization of fatness, fat bodies, and fat politics. Grosz maintains that identities, such as race, class, and sex, are not merely independent vectors that intersect with one another in the space of the person; rather, they mutually constitute one another. She urges us to attempt to understand the body through a range of disparate discourses, instead of confining our inquiries to scientistic and naturalistic modes of explanation.[25] In this essay, I thus begin to question how we can move the study of the fat body out of the natural and life sciences and into the realm of social and cultural criticism;[26] I hope that other scholars, activists, and members of the general public will follow suit in similarly rethinking fat bodies. Furthermore, Grosz contends that "bodies speak, without necessarily talking because they become coded with and as signs. . . . They become intextuated, narrativized; simultaneously, social codes, laws, norms, and ideals become incarnated";[27] it is therefore worth considering how these social codes, norms, ideals, and signs present themselves narratively on culturally invisible fat bodies.

New strategies for playing games of identity wherein pleasure can be taken by and in fat bodies need to be theorized.[28] Following Mann, we should consider the extent to which political struggle over the meaning of fat is "buil[t] upon the facts of cultural intersectionality."[29] We can now easily recognize that an actor is no more "simply fat" than she is "simply white" or "simply female." However, this lesson was learned the hard way after notable attempts by certain social and political groups to organize their membership by shared, irreducible, and unchanging essential, physical characteristics. Examining those recent identity-based political movements (e.g., Black Nationalism and second wave feminism) can help us better understand the genesis of fat identity politics. We must also consider the contributions of queer theory and activism to the strategies of fat politics, a connection documented by Michael Moon and Eve Kosofsky Sedgwick that demonstrates the possibilities of organizing around conflicted identities.[30] These histories should help illuminate an analysis of what it means to stake a claim to fat identity when the definition of acceptable subjectivity is very narrow. They may also begin to explain how political subjectivities are constituted by physical and sensual arrangements and experiences, as well as clarifying the role of the body's biocultural position in constructing subjectivity. In terms of identity, the lived experience of fatness inhabits the same space as, and yet diverges from, other influential subject-marking experiences, such as the embodiment of race and sexuality.

Judith Butler asks what the political stakes are in according naturalness to identity categories that are actually *effects* of multiple and diffuse discourses.[31] The same question needs to be asked about fat identity politics. Other questions are equally pertinent. Specifically, what political possibilities does a critique of identity categories open up? We must inquire into the political construction and regulation of fat identity, rather than trying to make shared identity a foundation for fat politics. Building on Butler's claim that the body is a discursive production, I explore how the semiotic is used as a source of subversion. This type of theoretical investigation will enable us to understand how a flexible, diffuse fat politics can locate its subjects more favorably within fields of power.

A related question concerns the ways in which categories of body size and shape are regulatory constructs. We need to theorize how these categories are deployed and to guard against their uncritical extension, which might unwittingly propel a regime of power/knowledge that subjugates fat people. Many other questions still need to be examined, and I suggest below a critical direction for such inquiries by examining fat bodies/politics through the lens of queer theory. For example, do categories of body size and shape provide fluid and denaturalized possibilities, once they are no longer linked to fixity and causality? How is it that categories of health and beauty are constantly invoked and, in turn, refused by those interested in recontextualizing the fat body? Is it possible to articulate the convergence of these multiple discourses at the site of fat identity, thereby making that "simple" category forevermore troubled?

AFFINITY POLITICS AND PLAYFUL SUBJECTIVITY

Judith Butler criticizes the underpinnings of identity politics, which "assume that an identity must first be in place in order for political interests to be elaborated and, subsequently, political action to be taken."[32] She argues instead that the doer is constructed in doing the deed/political act, not the other way around. Queer activists and theorists propose forms of political action that recognize individuals both as subjects with the capacity to act and as subjected to larger forces over which they have less control. The claim of queer theory, here voiced by Samuel Delany, that insistent and articulate "rhetoric can *control* discourse,"[33] is one of its more appealing and promising for the project of theorizing new spaces for fatness. What can it mean to speak publicly about practices and persuasions that are normatively inscribed with evil meanings, as many queer activists do when they describe their sexual proclivities and acts? Queer theorists contend that such public performance of "perversion" enables sexual subjects to play a role in how they are inscribed with meaning—to enter themselves into discourse, if you will. As Sarah Schulman warns, "we're wasting our lives being careful."[34]

One queer activist group that particularly exemplifies the potential benefits of the creative and polyvocal practice of cultural politics is the Lesbian Avengers, whose members play with their "selves" loudly and visibly in an attempt to work the meanings ascribed to them to their liking and to their best advantage. A joyful sense of the creatively outrageous is ever present in the Lesbian Avengers' fire-eating, baton-twirling direct action political organizing. They strive for innovation, "avoid[ing] old stale tactics at all costs."[35] Indeed, the authors of the Avenger handbook seem to have abandoned abstract theoretical discussion and false polarities, instead recognizing that their audience (other Avengers and Avenger wanna-bes) identify themselves diversely both inter- and intrapersonally.

They follow Gayle Rubin in a radical rhetoric of sex that "identif[ies], describe[s], explain[s], and denounce[s] erotic injustice and sexual oppression."[36] Still, the mention of "Lesbian" in the name of the group may raise a flag for some; does their exclusive recruitment of lesbians posit the sexual essentialism so common in identity politics? The Avengers steer clear of this problem by making no claims about the fundamental nature of lesbianism; instead, according to Schulman, Lesbian Avengers urge people to "imagine what your life could be." They challenge: "Aren't you ready to make it happen? WE ARE. If you don't want to take it anymore and are ready to strike, call us."[37] They leave it up to the callers, the potential activists, to decide what the "it" is that they're not willing to take anymore. They urge imagination and inventiveness in anti-essentialized political action. They encourage playing with one's multiple selves.

The persistence of the "Lesbian" label might be explained, Eve Sedgwick suggests, "not in the first place because of its meaningfulness to those whom it defines but because of its indispensableness to those who define themselves against it."[38] But why would a political group that seeks to dismantle false polarities willingly select a name that lends itself so easily to a lesbian/nonlesbian dichotomy? Are the Lesbian Avengers actually caught up in the same political arena as dangerously essentializing liberal and nationalist political projects?

The queer theorist Lisa Duggan might here emphasize a "new elasticity in the meanings of 'lesbian' and 'gay' " in which "the notion of a fixed sexual identity determined by a firmly gendered desire beg[ins] to slip away." The queer community of Lesbian Avengers can be viewed not as an identity group but as "no longer defined solely by the gender of its members' sexual partners. This new community is unified only by a shared dissent from the dominant organization of sex and gender." Duggan would recognize the Lesbian Avengers as having constituted through their dissent a new stance of queer opposition and would argue that their stress on constant innovation makes their "actual historical forms and positions . . . open, constantly subject to negotiation and renegotiation."[39]

Such queer affinity groups (organized by a desire to work or play together, rather than by a shared identity) suggest that individuals can inscribe themselves with meanings over against dominant inscriptions. By exuberantly saying what they do, affinity groups use rhetoric to enter themselves into discourse in significant ways, demonstrating that even small collective actions can make important differences. In a political climate in which the comfort of some is predicated on the silence of others, queer theory encourages us to play with our selves and to make a joyful noise in the doing.

Some might argue that while queer theory provides a kind of philosophical fuel for such play, it is queer *activists* who make action. So corpulence theory and fat politics must interact, as fat activists plan events that focus less on official policy and more on repositioning fat in the cultural imaginary. They borrow tactics from the Lesbian Avengers: we see scale smashings, ice cream eat-ins, and fat bikini swim meets, which aim to publicly present a fatness that is not the victim of bad genes or its own lack of will. Through this rubric, we can begin to envision *fat play*, rather than *fat pathology*.

PERFORMATIVITY: THE RESCUE OF IDENTITY

Underlying the project of retheorizing corpulence is an understanding of communication as the primary process by which identities are negotiated and narratives are constructed, such negotiation and construction both scrambling traditional views of what it means to be a political subject. I take my cue from interrogations of essentialism in queer theory and performance studies, which suggest that identities are never merely descriptive; rather, they are strategically performed. The queer theorist Cindy Patton treats identities as a series of rhetorical closures that connect and reconnect with political strategies and alliances to stage political claims; she urges us to reconsider identity to see how it is used in everyday life, where the struggle to control the rules of identity construction is played out.[40] Fat identity (like queer identity), however performative, will possibly and indeed probably be read as admitting to what current Western mainstream standards imagine as grotesque perversion. A consideration of the ways in which fat identities alter how politics is staged (rather than merely representing yet another aesthetic choice) highlights the importance of communication as political practice.[41]

Judith Butler claims that performativity must be understood "not as a singular or deliberate 'act,' but, rather, as the reiterative and citational practice by which discourse produces the effects that it names."[42] This frame opens a radical critical space for investigating not only isolated incidents symbolizing fat identity but also the ongoing, even technologically enabled, discursive negotiations that regulate and constrain the signification of fat bodies. Because these negotiations are ongoing and can be cited as (sometimes) productive for fat bodies, they enable a more livable resignification.

QUEERING FAT BODIES/POLITICS

The politics of fat identity is rooted in the kind of controversy over essentialized identity politics seen in queer theory, with important implications for corpulent bodies that matter. An essentialist position on fat identity can take a biological or sociocultural perspective; common to both is the theme that the condition of fatness is necessary, could not be otherwise, or has some essential (usually failure-related) cause. Whether they trace a biological path to bad genes or horrible hormones or a social path to traumatic childhood experience, those arguing for essentialist positions view fat identity as the unfortunately unavoidable outcome resulting from some original variable gone awry. Of course, not all essentialist positions are anti-fat; some prefer to focus on the present fact of fatness and the impossibility of changing it, using this resignation as a platform for civil rights size-acceptance movements.

In contrast, an anti-essentialist position on fat identity does not seek causal factors but focuses instead on the ability of human actors to participate in the creation of meaning (including the meaning of material bodies) through the discursive processes of communication and politics. Many examples of such fat activism and discursive negotiation exist and others are still emerging: members of NAAFA (the National Association to Advance Fat Acceptance); Roseanne Barr, who in March 1999 hosted the "Large and Luscious Beauty Contest" on her daytime syndicated show; other actors, such as Camryn Manheim, who won an Emmy for her work on *The Practice;* and, more important, individuals from varied sociopolitical, economic, and educational backgrounds who are all invested in projects of fat resignification.[43] I hope that scholars interested in corpulence will begin to work through questions of how essentialism renders political struggle more or less effective; we must explore how people understand themselves through their shifting, fabricated locations, tolerating their changes in identity as they cross borders to know and create themselves in acts of affirmation and resistance.[44]

This essay is intended to initiate a different theorization of fatness and fat politics. By *queering* corpulent bodies/politics, perhaps we can resist dominant discursive constructions of fatness, while at the same time opening new (and playful) sites for reconstructing fat bodies through a lens that examines the corporeal alongside the material, the racial, and the sexual as mutually constitutive elements.

NOTES

1. Other scholars point to different periods during the twentieth century as marked by cultural disdain for fat. Joan Jacobs Brumberg, for instance, contends that widespread contempt for fat came of age at the turn of the century, as newly

"liberated" Victorians refocused their surveillance on their bodies instead of their morals (*The Body Project: An Intimate History of American Girls* [New York: Random House, 1997]). Pinpointing an exact moment for the beginning of fat hatred (an impossible task, in any case) is less important than recognizing the prevalence of this belief, which was forcefully manifested at various key moments during the century. Following Elizabeth Grosz, I want to be careful here *not* to suggest a lumpy ol' body hanging around passively, waiting to be signified by culture, for it is *through* culture that bodies are constructed. Although I feel that Grosz's criticism misrepresents the social constructionist project, I am inclined to examine, as she recommends, how particular bodies are lived, "interwoven with and constitutive of systems of meaning, signification, and representation" (*Volatile Bodies: Toward a Corporeal Feminism* [Bloomington: Indiana University Press, 1994], 18).

2. Melinda Beck, "An Epidemic of Obesity," *Newsweek*, August 1, 1994, 62–63.

3. Some might think it odd that I do not examine fat hatred as specifically antiwoman, given my feminist framework and the historical (though viciously arbitrary) link between woman and the flesh. However, I want to be cautious about equating "fat" with "woman," as this connection is, at root, culturally constructed.

4. Judith Butler, *Gender Trouble: Feminism and the Subversion of Identity* (New York: Routledge, 1990), 132.

5. According to Judith Butler, "the abject designates those 'unlivable' and 'uninhabitable' zones of social life which are nevertheless densely populated by those who do not enjoy the status of the subject, but whose living under the sign of the 'unlivable' is required to circumscribe the domain of the subject" (*Bodies That Matter: On the Discursive Limits of "Sex"* [New York: Routledge, 1993], 3).

6. Patricia S. Mann, *Micro-Politics: Agency in a Postfeminist Era* (Minneapolis: University of Minnesota Press, 1994), 160.

7. Ibid.

8. Paralleling Butler's reading of Michel Foucault on sexed subjects, to say that fat subjects are innocent victims "is an illusory and complicitous conceit of emancipatory . . . politics" (*Bodies That Matter*, 97).

9. Butler, *Gender Trouble*, 116.

10. Ibid.

11. Ibid., 134. Butler builds on Mary Douglas's *Purity and Danger* (London: Routledge, 1966).

12. Monique Wittig, quoted in Butler, *Gender Trouble*, 115.

13. Butler, *Gender Trouble*, 116.

14. Ibid., 138–39.

15. Ibid., 139.

16. Ibid., 145.

17. Butler, *Bodies That Matter*, 3.

18. Grosz, *Volatile Bodies*, 19.

19. Butler, *Bodies That Matter*, 21.

20. Ibid.

21. Ibid.

22. Grosz, *Volatile Bodies*, 22.

23. Butler, *Gender Trouble*, 141.

24. Ibid., 146–47.

25. Grosz, *Volatile Bodies*, 19–20.

26. A recent Infotrac database search powered by the term *fat* found only a few popular press articles (usually centered on dieting) and a bevy of journal se-

lections on lipids. To find much of anything in scholarly literature that deals with fat *bodies* rather than fat *molecules,* one must search on *obesity,* already comfortably (but problematically) lodged in medical/scientific discourse.

27. Grosz, *Volatile Bodies,* 35.

28. Though it is tempting to focus specifically on *women's* fat bodies, the project of resignification of fatness is vital to (and is in part propelled by) men as well. Thus, my intentions are not gender-specific.

29. Mann, *Micro-Politics,* 159.

30. Michael Moon and Eve Kosofsky Sedgwick, "Divinity: A Dossier, a Performance Piece, a Little-Understood Emotion," in *Tendencies,* by Sedgwick (Durham, N.C.: Duke University Press, 1993) [see chapter 15 of this volume].

31. Butler, *Gender Trouble,* viii–ix.

32. Ibid., 142.

33. Samuel Delany, "Street Talk/Straight Talk," *Differences: A Journal of Feminist Cultural Studies* 3, no. 2 (1991): 21–38.

34. Sarah Schulman, *My American History: Lesbian and Gay Life during the Reagan/Bush Years* (New York: Routledge, 1994), 279.

35. Ibid., 298.

36. Gayle Rubin, "Thinking Sex: Notes for a Radical Theory of the Politics of Sexuality," in *Pleasure and Danger: Exploring Female Sexuality,* ed. Carole S. Vance (Boston: Routledge and Kegan Paul, 1984), 275.

37. Schulman, *My American History,* 279.

38. Eve Kosofsky Sedgwick, "The Epistemology of the Closet," in *The Lesbian and Gay Studies Reader,* ed. Henry Abelove, Michèle Barale, and David Halperin (New York: Routledge, 1993), 55.

39. Lisa Duggan, "Making It Perfectly Queer," *Socialist Review* 22, no. 1 (1992): 11–13, 20, 23.

40. Cindy Patton, "Tremble, Hetero Swine!" in *Fear of a Queer Planet: Queer Politics and Social Theory,* ed. Michael Warner (Minneapolis: University of Minnesota Press, 1993), 143–77.

41. For a further discussion of fat performativity, see part 5 of this volume.

42. Butler, *Bodies That Matter,* 2.

43. Particularly important for drawing in diverse individuals are on-line sites and electronic mailing lists dedicated to fatness. On pro-fat Internet sites, users create narratives steeped in both essentialist arguments and perspectives to suggest, instead, an understanding of their own subject position as the vortex constituted by a whirl of discourses. I address these issues in "Revolting Bodies? The On-Line Negotiation of Fat Subjectivity" (manuscript, 1998).

44. See Gloria Anzaldúa, *Borderlands/La Frontera: The New Mestiza* (San Francisco: Spinsters/Aunt Lute, 1987).

REFERENCES

Anzaldúa, Gloria. *Borderlands/La Frontera: The New Mestiza.* San Francisco: Spinsters/Aunt Lute, 1987.

Beck, Melinda. "An Epidemic of Obesity." *Newsweek,* August 1, 1994, 62–63.

Brumberg, Joan Jacobs. *The Body Project: An Intimate History of American Girls.* New York: Random House, 1997.

Butler, Judith. *Bodies That Matter: On the Discursive Limits of "Sex."* New York: Routledge, 1993.

———. *Excitable Speech: A Politics of the Performative.* New York: Routledge, 1997.

———. *Gender Trouble: Feminism and the Subversion of Identity.* New York: Routledge, 1990.

Delany, Samuel. "Street Talk/Straight Talk." *Differences: A Journal of Feminist Cultural Studies* 3, no. 2 (1991): 21–38.

Duggan, Lisa. "Making It Perfectly Queer." *Socialist Review* 22, no. 1 (1992): 11–31.

Grosz, Elizabeth. *Volatile Bodies: Toward a Corporeal Feminism.* Bloomington: Indiana University Press, 1994.

LeBesco, Kathleen. "Revolting Bodies? The On-Line Negotiation of Fat Subjectivity." Ph.D. dissertation. University of Massachusetts, Amherst, 1998.

Mann, Patricia S. *Micro-politics: Agency in a Postfeminist Era.* Minneapolis: University of Minnesota Press, 1994.

Moon, Michael, and Eve Kosofsky Sedgwick. "Divinity: A Dossier, a Performance Piece, a Little-Understood Emotion." In *Tendencies,* by Sedgwick, 215–51. Durham, N.C: Duke University Press, 1993. [see chapter 15 of this volume]

Patton, Cindy. "Tremble, Hetero Swine!" In *Fear of a Queer Planet: Queer Politics and Social Theory,* edited by Michael Warner, 143–77. Minneapolis: University of Minnesota Press, 1993.

Rubin, Gayle. "Thinking Sex: Notes for a Radical Theory of the Politics of Sexuality." In *Pleasure and Danger: Exploring Female Sexuality,* edited by Carole S. Vance, 267–319. Boston: Routledge and Kegan Paul, 1984.

Schulman, Sarah. *My American History: Lesbian and Gay Life during the Reagan/Bush Years.* New York: Routledge, 1994.

Sedgwick, Eve Kosofsky. "The Epistemology of the Closet." In *The Lesbian and Gay Studies Reader,* edited by Henry Abelove, Michèle Barale, and David Halperin, 45–61. New York: Routledge, 1993.

PART II

Representational Matrices of Power

Nationality, Gender, Sexuality, and Fatness

5 Oscar Zeta Acosta's *Autobiography of a Brown Buffalo*

A Fat Man's Recipe for Chicano Revolution

MARCIA CHAMBERLAIN

Face it: some recipes go over better than others. Susan Leonardi writes that "the root of recipe—the Latin *recipere*—implies an exchange" and that "like a story, a recipe needs a recommendation, a context, a point, a reason to be."[1] Unfortunately, Oscar Zeta Acosta's *Autobiography of a Brown Buffalo* contains such an unpopular American recipe that it landed itself outside most circles of exchange after its 1972 publication. Thanks to Hunter S. Thompson and Marco Federico Manuel Acosta, the book was given a second chance in 1989 when Vintage Books reissued it; but distaste for *Autobiography of a Brown Buffalo* remains strong. Although Vintage praises the autobiography in a back cover blurb as "a landmark of contemporary Hispanic-American literature," most Chicano/a studies scholars continue to ignore it.[2] And even though the book features in its leading role an overweight man who nicknames himself "Buffalo," scholars of fat never refer to it. In this essay, I argue that the book is avoided because it is about swallowing those stories that are told about both fat bodies and brown bodies. American scholars tend to stay away from Acosta's autobiography because it chews through these two unmixable ingredients and in the process spits out some very tough buffalo gristle. My goal is to think through the gristle, in the hope that other unpopular recipes for revolutionary change will be mixed, tested, exchanged, and circulated in the United States.

Like Acosta, I want to put three key concepts—fat, race, and nation—into conversation. In the first section, I discuss the close relationship between nationality and autobiography, arguing that until recently, historians failed to account for the pressure and the presence of the body in these related narratives. I claim that Oscar Zeta Acosta's *Autobiography of a Brown Buffalo* is a book that brings into sharp focus those issues which disrupt the exclusive definitions of nation that make him an outsider. The narrator combines a big brown body with a loud, nasty mouth. He is constantly jabbering away, cranking out his autobiography from toilet seats and bar stools, tampering and tinkering with the master plot and the well-known protagonists of the great American story. As Hunter S. Thompson noted, Acosta's crazy life story is a massive and humorous affront to anyone who actually believes "that bullshit about the American Dream."[3] A 300-pound modern-day buffalo, Acosta paradoxically pushes to the extreme what the dream is supposed to represent. His fat body is simultaneously the ultimate dream-come-true and the ultimate American nightmare, "a gross, physical salute to the fantastic *possibilities* of life in this country."[4]

In the second section, I propose that Acosta embraces, enacts, and performs the very categories that are meant to contain and limit him within the nation. I connect his deliberate and self-conscious use of social mimesis, including his adoption of the hungry brown buffalo as a personal and political symbol, with the important cultural task of national remembering. Acosta seems to share Benedict Anderson's desire to correct or at least to acknowledge historically "the amnesias of nationalism."[5] Given the unhappy and largely forgotten fate of the American buffalo, it is significant that Acosta calls himself a "historian . . . with a sour stomach" (18): Anglo stories about his Mexican and Indian past leave a bad taste in his mouth and ulcers in his stomach. Yet he refuses to slip into silence or unconsciousness. He thunders around the country and devours large meals like memories, because he recognizes that to deny himself certain foods is to cut himself off from the past. As the critic Marialisa Calta puts it, "Everyone's past is locked up in their recipes[,] . . . the past of an individual and the past of a nation as well."[6] Mimesis becomes a concrete and confrontational way for Acosta to unlock those pasts and keep them alive. His body and the large space it occupies become a perpetual, obnoxious reminder of just what the nation wants to forget. Eating and acting like a buffalo become Acosta's most effective cures for societal amnesia.

In the third section of the paper, I examine the ways in which medical and psychological discourses about fat bodies became important channels for the rhetoric of nationalism. Hillel Schwartz, Anne Beller, and other cultural historians have argued that doctors had a professional and economic stake in keeping bodies slim enough to pursue the American Dream. The stake was big enough by 1973 for Albert Stunkard to note that America's medicalized concern over obese persons had "grown from a mild concern to an overriding one" and that the country's obsession was assuming "the dimensions of a national neurosis."[7] Fat, according to the President's Council on Physical Fitness at the time, was distinctly un-American. And fat minorities were seen as a particularly cruel affront to a picture-perfect nation. I describe the ways in which the anti-fat and anti-brown rhetorics of the 1950s, '60s, and '70s shaped Acosta's earliest understandings of his big body and his small place within the nation. I contrast some of the popular corporeal paradigms of obesity circulating during these decades, including the idea of "spoiled identity," with Acosta's radical rewriting of them in his autobiography.[8] I argue that Acosta carves out a niche for the "spoiled" Mexican American person that puts a dangerous kink in the system of explanations that were being grafted onto his fat body.

In the final section, I juxtapose two different activist movements of the 1970s—Fat Power and Brown Power—to point out the positions available to Acosta within each of them. I argue that the desire of many fat activists to believe that the nation had dealt successfully with its ethnic and racial prejudices points to the racism that made many alliances among struggling groups of the 1970s impossible. Also, the care that fat activists took to present themselves as peaceful and nonrevolutionary discouraged the participation of more militant fat persons, especially those of color such as Acosta, who demanded a more oppositional politics of engagement and more radical self-representation. I conclude by offering some tools for reading the violent language directed against women, gay men and lesbians, Jews, and other marginalized groups in the autobiography. Certainly, Acosta's is a hard book for many readers to digest. He does not just pose difficult questions about fat, race, and the nation: he performs them. In doing so, he manages to offend almost everyone. I suggest ways to make the reading of *The Autobiography of a Brown Buffalo,* shocking though it is, productive.

NATIONALITY, AUTOBIOGRAPHY, AND THE FAT BODY

Despite French gastronome Jean Brillat-Savarin's interesting nineteenth-century correlation between a nation's destiny and its diet,[9] cultural historians in the United States have more often equated a nation's destiny with its literature. Both autobiographers and literary historians have generally assumed that national literature was the product of "the American mind," which was collapsed neatly into a container called "the American self." In the 1990s, such talk that loosely suggests the interchangeability of the two became less common. Feminist scholars in particular have come a long way in deconstructing the problematic equation between "self" and "mind" that used to dominate American literary history.[10] They have detailed the consequences of privileging the mind over the body, and they have brought into critical play previously ignored categories such as gender, class, and race. They have eschewed transcendence and focused more attention on bodies and the concrete ways in which they get constructed. By talking explicitly about supposedly nonliterary subjects such as food, fat, and bodily functions, feminists have introduced fresh vocabulary into the field of literary criticism and have ushered in alternative ways of writing about national history. In short, feminists have paved the way for a better understanding of the stories that are told, both knowingly and not, about bodies and American citizenship.

As feminists first began to untangle the complex relationship between story and nation, one of the places to which they turned their attention was the genre of autobiography, for it is here that, according to the literary critics Richard Ruland and Malcolm Bradbury, "the history of America begins."[11] It is not surprising that so many literary historians posit autobiographical narratives as one of the building blocks of the nation. After all, on the most basic level, nations and selves seem to be invested in a similar project: staking out their own space in the world by differentiating themselves from others and by proclaiming their own sovereignty and subjectivity. For this reason, many critics read the first coming-of-age stories published in this country as miniature versions of the grand coming-of-age story of America. They fail to acknowledge, however, that these stories also helped create and consolidate a narrow and exclusive sense of national identity and citizenship. Although the national identity was supposedly based on the mind and its abstract qualities, feminists critics demonstrated that all these stories of self were also rooted in the body. Autobiographies such as Acosta's remind us that membership and nonmembership in America have as much to do with the markings on one's body as with the contents of one's mind.

According to many literary historians, transplanted British colonists wrote the earliest American autobiographies, but the first well-publicized story of "an American self" came after the Revolution: Benjamin Franklin's *Autobiography,* published following the war for independence, first tapped into the myth of an individual, yet representative, national self. For this reason, it is an important starting point for my examination of Acosta's autobiography, which batters and shatters that myth. The commentator in the *Heath Anthology of American Literature* notes that Franklin's book is known by nations around the world as the quintessential text that "defines the American self."[12] Why? One reason is that the book presents a safe, unified picture of the nation—which is precisely why Franklin's famous *Autobiography* succeeds for America, and Acosta's infamous autobiography fails. The former charts the steady development of an "average" American boy into a disciplined, rational, successful man and so describes, by implication, the nation. The latter chronicles the zigzagging course of a *vato loco* whose chaotic life suggests the ups and downs of not only an individual but, by extension, a whole nation.

We should not be surprised that Acosta uses food, and the accompanying issues of weight gain and loss, as a key metaphor for his tortured relationship to the nation, nor that he makes visible the inconsequential "details" that disappear in Franklin's story. Whereas Franklin insists he learned as a child to take "no Notice . . . of what related to the Victuals on the Table" and that his "perfect Inattention to those Matters" freed him to focus on the one disembodied story that mattered—America's[13]—Acosta insists that the American poor cannot help but pay attention to their diet and to the politics that produce it. Beans for breakfast, lunch, and dinner are impossible to ignore. America's story, Acosta makes clear, concerns precisely those personal, bodily matters that Franklin wants to repress. Acosta tells us that paying attention to "Victuals," or what goes into and out of the body, amounts to paying attention to the condition of the nation. "How in the fuck can I be constipated when I have so much to offer?" is one of the first questions Acosta asks in his autobiography (12). To get to the bottom of that question means telling the national story from a different position than Franklin had in mind.

Critics rightly state that Franklin wanted his "own growth [to be] a pattern for the growth of the nation itself."[14] The problem with this formulation is that he associated growth with mental, emotional, and symbolic maturity, never with actual body size. Acosta's autobiography graphically reveals what it is like for a poor flesh-and-blood fat man to live in a society in which the word "growth" has such contradictory connotations attached to it. On the one hand, one chronicler of Fat Power points out, "the fat man . . . is an insult to the American philosophy of unlimited achievement. . . . [H]e has given the lie to the American Dream" by taking the idea of growth to an unacceptable extreme.[15] On the other hand, the fat man actually fulfills and embodies the promise of America because he achieves the unachievable—the dream of unlimited growth—and then displays it for all to see. In essence, Acosta suggests that the American fat man thinks about body fat exactly as he has been taught to think about his bank balance: bigger is better. By becoming, in Hunter Thompson's words, an "overweight . . . overindulged brown cannonball,"[16] Acosta takes the national desire for growth to a personal extreme. Then, in an odd twist, the nation that first encouraged his appetite suddenly labels him grotesque.

From the outset of his autobiography, it is obvious that Acosta feels betrayed and split by the American Dream in ways that Franklin could not have. While Franklin understood autobiography as a way to present to the world a coherent self and nation, Acosta had less faith in the ability of autobiographies to deliver this vision. By writing about the gross inconsistencies in the American story as well as the paradoxes of his own fractured story, Acosta necessarily subverts the very genre he adopts. For instance, Acosta never separates his fat, brown body from the multiple "America"s and autobiographical "I"s that he constructs. Everything—nation, race, fat—works in tandem, and Acosta seems to be aware of the precarious juggling act that this kind of storytelling entails. At one point, he writes poignantly about his childhood: "My heart sags with the overpowering weight of my belly. . . . I am nothing but an Indian with sweating body and faltering tits that sag at the sight of . . . thousands of pigtailed, blue-eyed girls from America" (94–95). Here thousands of Anglo girls make Acosta feel like "nothing," but later in the autobiography thousands of imaginary brown-eyed Chicanas make him feel like an American hero. Neither passage gets at the exact truth about what defines either the "real" America or the "real" Acosta; if anything, the two passages highlight the influence wielded by the gaze of others on Acosta's changing sense of "I" and the constant renegotiation of his place within the nation.

So why does Acosta bother to use the autobiographical form at all (and how can such use be a viable strategy for voicing minority concerns)? I think Acosta's answer to this question would have been to say that it was "becoming" rather than "being" fat and brown in America that convinced him that autobiographies are absolutely necessary as well as absolutely suspect. A fat brown kid moving about in a group of pig-tailed, blue-eyed American girls requires just as many complicated negotiations as a fat brown man moving about in a herd of Mexican buffaloes. A narrator such as Acosta, who knows that his position is always precarious, has a shifty-hoofed strength at his disposal. In this context, autobiography becomes an important temporary tool for empowerment and agency, a way for Acosta to put forth a contingent, conflicted "I" that demands recognition from and space in a contingent, conflicted nation.

MIMESIS, MEMORY, AND THE AMERICAN BUFFALO

According to Hunter Thompson's account of Dr. Gonzo (a.k.a. Acosta) in *Fear and Loathing in Las Vegas,* Acosta was one of those rare human beings willing to dive into "the Belly of the Great American Beast" and daring to report back all that he saw.[17] In his own autobiography, Acosta goes a step beyond reporting: he actually becomes the Great American Beast to make America see what he saw. He lets his body display in large print the signs of various societal forces at work; in a sense, he takes on the burden of representing or mirroring to society its own ills. Thus, he engages in what the cultural anthropologists Gunter Gebauer and Christoph Wulf describe as mimesis, a process of appropriation that involves the body and the "fluid boundaries among representation, illustration, rendering, and reproduction, but also deception, illusion, and appearance."[18] Acosta plays to the hilt many roles: he is lawyer, writer, mathematician, missionary, cook, philosopher, drunk, political activist, jazz musician, physical therapist, Air Force recruit, and clown all rolled into one. What most horrifies others, though, is his star-studded performance as that great American beast, the brown buffalo.

Before his disappearance and probable death off the coast of Mexico in 1974, Acosta created a stir by living every moment in the limelight.[19] He stubbornly refused to hide anything about himself: his radical political views, his bulging body, his bouts with vomiting, his outrageous drug use, his hybrid heritage. In his autobiography, he barrels and booms his way across America, forcing people to acknowledge his presence, unexpectedly crashing their parties, interrupting their stories, and, in general, taking up lots of space in a nation that wanted him to shrink into extinction as had the other brown buffalo before him. One of the things that the brown buffalo does on a larger-than-life scale throughout the book is eat—beans, tortillas, salsa, tamales, menudo, anything he can get his hands on. The critic Anne Goldman explains that "to write about food is to write about the self."[20] Certainly, Acosta sees large helpings of food as a route to subjectivity and history, and he becomes determined to leave a big mark on his world.

In the introduction to Acosta's reissued autobiography, Hunter Thompson puzzles over the tiny interest in and minimal scholarship about a man who had devoted his life to getting attention at any cost. In large part, his life and death went virtually unnoticed because Acosta is a pungent reminder of what the nation wants to bury, or at least to package nicely and compactly: a past of racism, classism, and genocide. Acosta's autobiography begins when he decides to leave his job as an antipoverty lawyer at the East Oakland Legal Aid Society. Fed up with the injustices of the justice system, Acosta hits the road in search of hope and a new American identity. His journey takes him back into his own past, his father's past, his people's past, and the nation's past. He visits and remembers El Paso, Riverbank, Los Angeles, San Francisco, Alpine, and Mexico. In these places, Acosta alternately flees and confronts his fatness and his roots; but wherever he goes he wrestles with his responsibilities among groups of people. At the end of the autobiography, Acosta is on a Greyhound bus headed for Los Angeles where he plans to join the Brown Berets, a radical Chicano group that promises to give his life a new sense of purpose and history. He wants to cover lots of ground in a big way, making public use of his body, spilling out of the American places that are supposed to hold him and to hold the past.

Spilling is a good way to describe what happens during Acosta's mimetic performances throughout the autobiography. As Gebauer and Wulf put it, "Mimesis necessarily exceeds the meaning of something being represented again."[21] Deliberate mimicking and even "bad" mirroring provide a way for Acosta to represent again, with a difference, the past that contains him: it becomes a means of "influence, appropriation, alteration, repetition," a way to offer "new interpretations of already existing worlds."[22] In the opening pages of the autobiography, for instance, as he looks at himself and flexes his flab, Acosta attempts to imitate the sculpted, muscular body of the 1920s bodybuilder Charles Atlas: "I stand naked before the mirror. Every morning of my life I have seen that brown belly from every angle. It has not changed that I can remember. I was always a fat kid. I suck it in and expand. . . . I tighten, suck at the air and recall . . . Charles Atlas" (11). Acosta's fat body in the mirror reminds readers of the story usually told by and about Atlas, but his brown body is also a reminder of a history that is often forgotten. Atlas was "brown" too, an Italian immigrant originally named Angelo Siciliano who moved to the United States in 1910 and then "changed" his racial heritage by choosing to rename himself Charles Atlas.

Given this first mirror scene, it is fitting that Acosta renames himself twice: Zeta, after a character in a Mexican movie, and Buffalo. In the autobiography, the second name becomes his personal pro-fat symbol and his political rallying call to remember a brown past. In the 1970s, "Buffalo" might have seemed a risky choice. After all, buffaloes are seen as beasts, dumb and smelly and brown, and Anglos often described Mexican Americans in identical derogatory terms. Both fat activists and race activists at that time were encouraging stigmatized minorities to look inside themselves and adopt positive nicknames that reflected an internal sense of self-esteem. They preached that an oppressed person "can only be free to the degree that he can grasp reality on his own—and not as the reflected image provided by society."[23] Some manuals even advised that obese people should avoid standing in front of mirrors because they might see themselves as they imagined society saw them: ugly and fat.[24] In contrast, Acosta purposefully looks directly at mirrors to show that he can manipulate images to his own advantage. His autobiography insists that we all live in a mirror world—it is one of the conditions of human existence. Therefore, minorities should learn to rework mirror images, not steer clear of them.

The image that Acosta most thoroughly reworks in his own autobiography is that of the buffalo. By calling himself "Buffalo," he deliberately connects himself to the Native American population whose disastrous fate was linked to the buffalo's. It is estimated that there were 30 million buffaloes in 1800, but these vast herds had been reduced to a mere thousand by 1889. Acosta's nickname conjures up a past of exploitation, contraction, and ultimately decimation. What kind of an image is that? A complicated one, Acosta admits. It recalls a brutal past but it also acknowledges what the Native Americans have to say about the dignity and strength of the animal. As a brown buffalo, Acosta embodies the contradictions that coexist in his own past and present. His autobiography forces America, the country that today thinks of the buffalo as "somewhere between being a national symbol and being a national pet,"[25] to look into the mirror and remember its own brutish history.

Although the sad history of the buffalo unfolded on the plains, Acosta's story begins and ends in the city. In *The Naturalistic Inner-City Novel in America: Encounters with the Fat Man,* James Giles traces the way in which the fat man of the late nineteenth century came to personify "the sordid social reality of the inner city, as well as the human capacity for grotesque and 'evil' actions."[26] He argues that the fat man had to reassert himself as a complex human character in the naturalistic ghetto novel and that one way he did so successfully was through mimesis. Yet according to Giles, inner-city naturalism and the fat man began to disappear from American literature in the 1960s and the 1970s because of "a retreat from mimesis . . . as well as a conservative impulse that rejected identification with the economically dispossessed."[27] Acosta's autobiographical text is an important exception to Giles's observation: not only does *The Autobiography of a Brown Buffalo* revive and revise the tradition of the inner-city naturalist novel, it is also a stunning salute to the power of mimesis as a bodily social practice performed by fat people of color.

DOCTORS, DIETS, AND DANGEROUS ACTIVITIES

In addition to shattering certain myths about nationality, autobiography, and fat brown subjectivity, Acosta challenges a very specific set of ideas about obesity being disseminated by medical and psychological authorities from the 1950s through the 1970s. According to the historian Harvey Levenstein, the American medical profession's social control over the meaning of fat reached a new peak in the 1950s, when doctors' attacks on fat were widely reported in the national media.[28] Ordinary men and women, such as Jean Nidetch, who founded Weight Watchers, also joined the battle against the bulge. But it was the scientific journals that most convincingly spread the message that with the help of expensive modern-day medicine, surgery, and therapy, the obese could be changed, corrected, transformed. Some physicians recognized that they were responsible for turning weight reduction into a national fetish and that underlying many of their "scientific" discoveries about obesity was the American imperative to reach for the dream of the perfect body, a body increasingly represented in ideal terms. But new height-and-weight charts continued to appear, and they pushed Acosta, an obese Mexican American, further and further outside the nation's boundaries of the acceptable.

By the 1970s it was common to refer to America as divided, polarized into "two separate nations—one thin, one fat."[29] Acosta's autobiography is about growing up in a nation where only "thin" stories were read. It is about deciding to valorize, whatever the social cost, a good "fat" story. But according to Richard B. Stuart's study of overeaters, conducted in 1967, reading was a potentially dangerous activity for fat people: "if the patient reads while he eats, he is most likely to want to eat while he reads" was the rationale behind many behaviorist-based therapies for the obese.[30] It was also typical to link the activity of writing with excessive eating. Elmer Wheeler, an anti-fat crusader and founder of the F.B.I. (Fat Boy's Institute), joked about this connection when he observed once that the verb "edit" is an appropriate anagram for the word "diet." Acosta's life debunks both Stuart's and Wheeler's theories. First, Acosta refuses to accept the label *patient* for himself; and second, he encourages fat people to engage wholeheartedly in the dangerous activities of eating, reading, and writing. In fact, his autobiography suggests that their lives may depend on these actions.

In addition to being split into thin and fat factions, the nation was also split radically by differences of color. Acosta's book is about coming to terms with his status as a multiply marked outsider whose stories are a double threat to the nation. From boyhood onward, Acosta's large body is the focal point of medical scrutiny and the source of much anxiety among both family members and doctors. The more interesting point to be made is that in the 1950s this medical concern about Acosta's size gets couched in nationalistic language because he is Mexican American. His mother, who "has been on a diet all [her] life" and "has a definite concern about people being overweight" (73), is the target of the message that the social and scientific reformers of the 1950s were pushing to Mexican American mothers. Not only is obesity a sickness, it reflects on one's citizenship. The right kinds of food in the right portions are the key to sound national identities. To promote better health, Americanization programs taught Mexican American mothers to substitute white bread for tortillas, green lettuce for frijoles, and boiled meat for fried meat.[31] But they also warned immigrants to choose "white" foods because, as one later critic noted, "eating un-American foods [i.e., spicy, exotic foods] could be interpreted as a protest."[32] Mainstream foods were less threatening as well as supposedly less fattening. Of course, the historian George Sánchez correctly points out that these "patriotic" American foods were also more expensive.[33] As Acosta sarcastically notes in his autobiography, Chicanos do not always have a choice about the foods they will eat. Even during times of national peace, his family had to plant backyard "victory gardens," because unlike more privileged Americans, they constantly lived with economic shortage (78).

Despite being treated for obesity as a child, Acosta notes that his body, having learned to survive on large helpings of cheap foods, "stayed fat" (73). By the time Acosta turns twenty-one, he has had six different doctors instructing him to go on various diets. He refuses: "What value is life without booze and Mexican food. . . . Shit, I couldn't be *bland* if my life depended on it" (12). The doctors read his choice of foods pathologically but he reads them culturally. Enchiladas, hot sauce, and cheap beer are part of his heritage; they give him strength and vitality, and they connect him to the larger Mexican community. As Schwartz succinctly puts it, "No diet comes without a larger social agenda."[34] Acosta understands that the prescription to cut hot, spicy foods from his diet contains a mythical as well as a medical component. Ever since the Puritans came to America, argues the Mexican poet Octavio Paz, they have been trying to "equate spices with dishonesty and deceit."[35] And dishonesty and deceit, according to the

Los Angeles sheriff's 1943 Departmental Report on Mexicans, are common characteristics of people such as Acosta with "Indian blood."[36]

Proud of his Indian heritage, Luis Valdez, a Chicano activist and contemporary of Acosta, impatiently proclaimed in his introduction to an anthology of Mexican American literature: "frijoles, tortillas, y chile are more American than the hamburger."[37] Indeed, an important moment in Acosta's autobiography occurs on the Fourth of July, popularly known as "national hamburger day." At the Independence Day picnic, Acosta ignores the traditional fare of hamburgers and hot dogs and instead drinks spiked Kool-Aid, eats drugged guacamole, and watches someone irreverently sew corn chips to the American flag. The guacamole-as-meal underscores his sense of difference on two levels. Normally, holidays provide a license to eat and to let go, but not for fat people, who are watched and policed even then. Acosta, for instance, imagines on this day that there are Texas Rangers hiding out in the refrigerator, challenging his right to eat, questioning his status in the country. He ignores the rangers, skips the apple pie, and swallows gobs of Mexican hot sauce, which, like guacamole, represents his ethnic history. In this way, he stages in exaggerated style the double lie of the holiday. His choice of picnic foods exposes the unspoken assumptions about race and fat inherent in a holiday that marks the birth of a nation with very exclusionary requirements of membership.

Again and again, Acosta's autobiography suggests that one of the hidden prerequisites for belonging to the country club called America is purity, a category that is used to distinguish good people from bad people as well as good food from bad food. In the 1970s these national anxieties about purity were apparent among medical professionals who treated fat ulcerous patients and declared that they had "spoiled identities." Their prescriptions put patients in an awkward place, because they implied that the obese could not be "real" national characters until they sported slim unspoiled identities. For instance, the psychiatrist to whom Acosta speaks so regularly in the autobiography treats him as if he has something rotten inside him. The psychiatrist implies that a spoiled identity is creating Acosta's acute stomach problems; he seems to think that Acosta is trapped in a sick cycle of overeating and vomiting in order to fill up an aching emotional void left by his mother's absence. Acosta rejects this explanation, insisting that the accumulation of acids and ulcers in his stomach is not a psychological reaction to an individual, troubled past, and proposes instead that it is a "normal" gag response to the nation's declared war on fat and its policing of bodies and borders.

Despite distaste for such social labels as "spoiled identity," Acosta milks them for all they are worth. In the autobiography, he acts like a big spoiled brat with a bad case of the stomach flu. He throws fits, and he throws up. The medical reports tag him as a nervous, obese man, and the doctors give him pills to relax him. But as the literary critic Susan Donaldson insightfully observes, tenseness and vomiting sometimes offer clues to "the dangers of consuming . . . [certain] stories."[38] Acosta makes clear that what he is regurgitating is never just spoiled pork tamales or bad feelings about his mother but the indifference, poverty, and oppression that have been forced down the throats of Mexican Americans. In fact, the narrator traces his stomach problems to a defining moment in high school when he is dragged away by police from his white girlfriend's house because her parents cannot accept his "Mexican" coloring. On that night, "the convulsions down under began" (119). Contrary to the theories of his doctors and psychiatrist, it was that moment of racial prejudice that produced the "wretched vomit, the gas laden belly" (120). Acosta's episodes of vomiting and the social explanations that he gives for them contradict the official medical diagnosis; they literally soil the story. Despite doctors and diets, Acosta stays fat and furious, a dangerous combination. He implicates the society around him in his supposedly personal problems by insisting that it is not his own fat body that needs help; rather it is society's "spoiled" institutions and attitudes that need to be treated, cured, adjusted.

RACE, FAT, AND REVOLUTION

The 1970s were a telling decade for fat activism and brown activism. Both the Fat Power and Brown Power movements drew on the strategies and rhetorics used by many African Americans who fought for civil rights during the 1960s, and each gained considerable followings—but neither one offered Acosta all that he was looking for. Bodies such as Acosta's seemed to create problems for activists because they raised visible questions about power and where it originated: was it in fat or in color? Neither movement seemed to be capable of dealing with issues simultaneously, of recognizing in Acosta an intersection of loyalties. Rather than seeing him as a potential dynamo, activists from both movements tended to see such bodies as potential liabilities; oddly enough, the two minority "powers"—fat and brown—canceled one another out. Acosta, whether he was completely aware of it or not, was squeezed from both sides.

In the 1970s many Chicanos wanted to represent themselves, symbolically and literally, as underconsumers, as people who had not yet gotten a piece of the American pie. Many historians locate the beginnings of the modern-day Chicano movement in the national 1966 boycott of California table grapes, a protest organized by the United Farm Workers Union. Through stories and pictures, the union tried to capture for the American public the miserable situation of Chicano farm laborers. Although many Chicanos worked twelve-hour days in the fields, they owned no land and they were starving. The fat, often grinning, figure of Acosta messed up this picture of oppression. As one activist put it, "The fat are ultra-conspicuous symbols of overconsumption in two vital areas: food and space."[39] Acosta's body, regardless of his politics, seemed to align him with the Anglo oppressor. It is not a complete coincidence that the major Chicano leaders of the 1970s were thin: Cesar Chávez, Luis Valdez, Gilbert Padilla, Corky Gonzalez, David Sanchez. Fat Chicanos, when they were depicted at all, often appeared in cartoons as *Tío Tacos*—the derogatory Spanish term for Uncle Toms, or those who sold out to the Anglos. Nor were members of the liberal left much help at the time. In the 1970s they were worried about the large, greedy food conglomerates that were threatening to wipe out smaller operations. Activists traveled the country to spread the message that "bigness produced inefficiency."[40] A liberal, Acosta probably agreed with this claim in principle, but it also left him, by extension, open to critique. As a large man, was he, too, greedy and inefficient?

Acosta did not always fit well into the pro-fat picture either. The movement, which made it clear during the 1970s that it was concerned with only one issue, implicitly demanded that he leave his skin color at the door. In fact, its members seemed convinced that fat-phobia was the most burning issue of the day, that they were being unfairly singled out for the most abuse. "Now that ethnic and racial prejudice are out of fashion, the public finds itself with nobody left to be bigoted about except the fat," wrote Llewellyn Louderback in *Fat Power*.[41] Anne Beller, the author of a history of obesity, also seemed to buy into the idea that the fat have it particularly hard: "The fact that obesity is supposed to be reversible, while skin color and national origins are not, may make the stigma all the harder to deal with."[42] Perhaps. But ranking oppressions created tough situations for people like Acosta whose "stigmas" could not be neatly separated out and judged on a scale of one to ten. It is interesting to note that just as fat people were absent from positions of leadership within the Chicano movement, so too the converse was true: most spokespersons for fat power during the 1970s were white. Apparently, Louderback, Beller, and many others failed to grasp that persons of color were confronted all too often with overt racism, a form of hate that showed few signs of being "out of fashion."

Acosta certainly did not have the luxury of ignoring the everyday world in which Mexican Americans suffered injustice on the streets and in the courts. He was seven years old when the violent Zoot Suit Riots shook Los Angeles in 1943. And although he was only a child during the 1950s, he experienced the impact and insult of the Internal Security Act, the Immigration and Nationality Act, and Operation Wetback. In California the growing national anti-Mexican sentiment peaked during the 1970–71 economic recession, when legals and illegals alike were blamed for stealing the jobs of white Americans. In the same year that *The Autobiography of a Brown Buffalo* was published, the Immigration and Naturalization Service began to enforce barrio sweeps throughout California, and the INS director called the Mexican situation a "national disaster." Some Chicanos decided that radical measures were needed to combat the full-scale domestic war being waged against them. The Brown Berets, started in 1968 by David Sanchez and mentioned in Acosta's autobiography, were one of many militant Chicano groups fashioned after the Black Panther Party. For many young activists and students, including Acosta, the Chicano reality demanded revolution.

Among fat activists, though, social revolution was not an option or a goal. Although they borrowed some of the strong language of the 1960s to talk about themselves, they were careful to define those words in ways that would make them seem safe and would make their movement seem harmless. For instance, three popular books of the 1970s were Abraham Friedman's *Fat Can Be Beautiful,* Marvin Grosswirth's *Fat Pride: A Survival Handbook,* and Louderback's *Fat Power.* The last title is the most provocative, which perhaps explains why Louderback goes to such great pains to qualify it. "The fat are, by nature, an eminently peaceful, unorganized lot," he writes, assuring the reader that "Fat Power . . . would be peaceful."[43] Grosswirth's book slips in the word *revolution* but drains it of any collective, social power. Thus William Fabrey, the president of the National Association to Advance Fat Acceptance, writes in the introduction to *Fat Pride* that Grosswirth's "basic premise—that a fat person has something to be proud of—is a revolutionary idea."[44] Accepting oneself with pride, though, is not the same as addressing the systemic factors that produce oppression. That kind of revolution was a dirty word in the 1970s to those on both "sides" of the fat issue. Even Weight Watchers' Jean Nidetch promises readers that her "crusade has . . . no political or revolutionary . . . overtones."[45]

Caught between these two groups, Acosta decides to yoke his body to the bigger and, at the time, more socially oriented cause: Brown Power.

But he keeps his fatness in prominent view. Between 1968 and 1972, Acosta publicly defended several Chicano groups and activists, including the Saint Basil 21 and Corky Gonzalez. His brash courtroom behavior landed him in jail on several occasions, and it also got his picture, forever fat and brown, into the L.A. newspapers. Valdez complained in 1972 that "the Anglo . . . accepts Mexican culture only to the extent that it has been Americanized, sanitized, sterilized, and made safe."[46] But Acosta often shocked Mexicans and Anglos alike because he refused to clean up, tone down, or change his act for either audience. As a brown buffalo with an enormous appetite for "tortillas[,] . . . refried beans[,] and . . . revolution" (199), Acosta constantly challenged even his "own" community's ability to assimilate him peacefully into its melting pot. In the eyes of some readers, this makes him a hero.

To others, Acosta will always be a conflicted man who secured his sense of self as fat and brown by injuring those who were marked still differently. Indeed, Acosta's autobiography disparages, with gusto, almost every minority group imaginable, including ones to which he belonged. Women, African Americans, Jews, gays and lesbians, Chinese, Mexicans—Acosta goes after them all. His narration is offensive, bigoted, and rude. In his daily life, paradoxically, Acosta believed strongly in forming coalitions among oppressed groups. For instance, when he ran for sheriff of Los Angeles in 1970, he called on "the People" to unite forces and fight for the rights of the poor and underrepresented, regardless of their color, sexual orientation, and gender. So why does his autobiography seem to undermine these views? Hectór Calderón cogently argues that Acosta decides to reduce "good taste to the level of absurdity" in part because he is writing a political satire, and he wants to test his readers:[47] will they hang in long enough to see through his posturing, through their own posturing? Calderón notes that one important aspect of a traditional satire is the *cena*, a dinner party where the thin veneers of civility and manners are stripped away and the underside of civilization is exposed. I think Acosta's entire autobiography can be read as a *cena*. The narrator asks us to join him at a common table, and then he turns around and serves us bad food. His vulgarities and obscenities provoke anger, but they are intended to provoke conversation, contemplation, and action, too.

Leonardi compares recipes to stories because they both depend on a dynamic, collective give-and-take. Acosta's book invites readers with differences to meet, eat, and engage in an exaggerated exchange. The result might be a rethinking of one's ideas or a new recipe for tamales, but in both cases the effort will be worth the trouble and time. And time, for Acosta, was precious. In a 1967 letter to his parents, Acosta describes himself as "in a hurry to taste as much of life as I am able to."[48] At the time, he had quit practicing law and had been hired to cook for $1.25 an hour in a Mexican restaurant in Aspen, Colorado. He was thirty-two, and he wanted to write in a way that would startle people, shock them out of their lethargy and indifference, move them toward revolution. Perhaps Acosta felt, with Flaubert, that the test of a great writer was to be able "to put people into the frying pan . . . and set them hopping about like chestnuts."[49] *The Autobiography of a Brown Buffalo,* written in typical gonzo frenzy, certainly accomplishes that.

NOTES

I would like to thank Jose Aranda and the Rice Writing Group for all their insights and suggestions.

1. Susan Leonardi, "Recipes for Reading: Summer Pasta, Lobster à la Riseholme, and Key Lime Pie," *PMLA* 104 (1989): 340–47; quotation, 340.

2. Oscar Zeta Acosta, *The Autobiography of a Brown Buffalo* (1972; reprint, New York: Vintage, 1989); this edition is hereafter cited parenthetically in the text. An important exception to the critical neglect of Acosta is provided by Ilan Stavans, who wrote a book titled *Bandido: Oscar "Zeta" Acosta and the Chicano Experience* (New York: IconEditions, 1995).

3. Hunter S. Thompson, *Fear and Loathing in Las Vegas* (New York: Random House, 1996), 20. The many personal and professional connections between Acosta and the journalist/writer Thompson are important to note. For more information on their friendship and their falling out, see Thompson's own account, "Fear and Loathing in the Graveyard of the Weird: The Banshee Screams for Buffalo Meat," *Rolling Stone,* December 15, 1977, 48–54, 57–58.

4. Thompson, *Fear and Loathing in Las Vegas,* 18.

5. Benedict Anderson, *Imagined Communities: Reflections on the Origin and Spread of Nationalism* (London: Verso, 1983), xv. Anderson's analyses of nationalism and amnesia are an important backdrop for my discussion, especially as they relate to the appearance and conventions of the modern autobiography.

6. Marialisa Calta is quoted in Anne Goldman, *Take My Word: Autobiographical Innovations of Ethnic American Working Women* (Berkeley: University of California Press, 1996), 8. Goldman's work on cooking, culture, and colonialism highlights many of the same issues that I deal with here.

7. Albert Stunkard, a psychiatrist, is quoted in Hillel Schwartz, *Never Satisfied: A Cultural History of Diets, Fantasies, and Fat* (New York: Free Press, 1986), 253. Schwartz provides an illuminating history of American ideas about food, fat, and race, including the tendency of Americans increasingly to associate "good" foods with "whiteness."

8. On "spoiled identity," see Erving Goffman, *Stigma: Notes on the Management of Spoiled Identity* (Englewood Cliffs, N.J.: Prentice-Hall, 1963). Beatrice Kalisch, a professor in the School of Nursing at the University of Mississippi, also

discusses the concept in "The Stigma of Obesity," *American Journal of Nursing* 72 (1972): 1124–27.

9. Jean Brillat-Savarin, *La Physiologie du Goût* (1825), translated by Anne Drayton as *The Philosopher in the Kitchen* (Harmondsworth: Penguin, 1970).

10. See, for example, Susan Bordo's treatment of the self/mind dichotomy in *Unbearable Weight: Feminism, Western Culture, and the Body* (Berkeley: University of California Press, 1993).

11. Richard Ruland and Malcolm Bradbury, *From Puritanism to Postmodernism: A History of American Literature* (New York: Viking Penguin, 1991), 17.

12. David Larsen, "Benjamin Franklin, 1706–1790," in *The Heath Anthology of American Literature,* ed. Paul Lauter, 2nd ed. (Lexington, Mass.: D. C. Heath, 1994), 2:711.

13. Benjamin Franklin, "*The Autobiography,* Part One," in ibid., 757.

14. Ruland and Bradbury, *From Puritanism to Postmodernism,* 42.

15. Llewellyn Louderback, *Fat Power: Whatever You Weigh Is Right* (New York: Hawthorn Books, 1970), 25.

16. Hunter S. Thompson, introduction to Acosta, *The Autobiography of a Brown Buffalo,* 5.

17. Thompson, *Fear and Loathing in Las Vegas,* vii. "Gonzo" refers to "gonzo journalism," a genre of writing invented by Acosta and Thompson. The goal is to write quickly and furiously and to incorporate personal viewpoints and observations in the process.

18. Gunter Gebauer and Christoph Wulf, *Mimesis: Culture—Art—Society,* trans. Don Reneau (Berkeley: University of California Press, 1995), 320.

19. Many theories still circulate about Acosta's disappearance in Mexico while on vacation. Some say that he was killed by CIA or FBI agents. Others believe that he was kidnapped and killed by drug runners or that he faked his own death in order to lay low for a few years and make plans for a Chicano revolution.

20. Goldman, *Take My Word,* 4.

21. Gebauer and Wulf, *Mimesis,* 66.

22. Ibid., 316.

23. Louderback, *Fat Power,* 14.

24. See, for example, Marvin Grosswirth's *Fat Pride: A Survival Handbook* (New York: Jarrow, 1971).

25. B. Hodgson, "Buffalo Back Home on the Range," *National Geographic,* May 1994, 87.

26. James Giles, *The Naturalistic Inner-City Novel in America: Encounters with the Fat Man* (Columbia: University of South Carolina Press, 1995), 4.

27. Ibid., 188.

28. Harvey Levenstein, *Paradox of Plenty: A Social History of Eating in Modern America* (New York: Oxford University Press, 1993).

29. Louderback, *Fat Power,* viii.

30. Richard B. Stuart, "Behavioral Control of Overeating," *Behavior Research and Therapy* 5 (1967): 357–65; quotation, 360.

31. George Sánchez, *Becoming Mexican American: Ethnicity, Culture, and Identity in Chicano Los Angeles, 1900–1945* (Oxford: Oxford University Press, 1993), 102.

32. Warren J. Belasco, "Ethnic Fast Foods: The Corporate Melting Pot," *Food and Foodways* 2 (1987): 1–30.

33. Sánchez, *Becoming Mexican American,* 102.

34. Schwartz, *Never Satisfied,* 37.

35. Octavio Paz, quoted in Belasco, "Ethnic Fast Foods," 19.

36. The sheriff's report is quoted in David Gutiérrez, *Walls and Mirrors: Mexican Americans, Mexican Immigrants, and the Politics of Ethnicity* (Berkeley: University of California Press, 1995), 125.

37. Luis Valdez, introduction to *Aztlan: Anthology of Mexican-American Literature,* ed. Valdez and Saul Steiner (New York: Knopf, 1972), xxxiii.

38. Susan Donaldson, "Consumption and Complicity in Sheila Bosworth's *Almost Innocent,*" *Southern Quarterly* 30, nos. 2–3 (1992): 113–22.

39. Louderback, *Fat Power,* 28.

40. Belasco, "Ethnic Fast Foods," 6.

41. Louderback, *Fat Power,* 17.

42. Anne Scott Beller, *Fat and Thin: A Natural History of Obesity* (New York: Farrar, Straus, and Giroux, 1977), 12.

43. Louderback, *Fat Power,* viii.

44. William Fabrey, introduction to Grosswirth, *Fat Pride,* 19.

45. Jean Nidetch, *The Story of Weight Watchers* (New York: Signet, 1970), 19.

46. Valdez, introduction, xxxiii.

47. Hectór Calderón, "To Read Chicano Narrative: Commentary and Metacommentary," *Mester* (1983): 8–9.

48. Oscar Zeta Acosta, letter of July 12, 1967, in the Oscar Zeta Acosta Letter Collection, California Ethnic and Multicultural Archives, University of California–Santa Barbara; quoted with permission.

49. Flaubert, quoted in Gebauer and Wulf, *Mimesis,* 241.

REFERENCES

Acosta, Oscar Zeta. *The Autobiography of a Brown Buffalo.* New York: Vintage, 1989.

Anderson, Benedict. *Imagined Communities: Reflections on the Origin and Spread of Nationalism.* London: Verso, 1983.

Belasco, Warren J. "Ethnic Fast Foods: The Corporate Melting Pot." *Food and Foodways* 2 (1987): 1–30.

Beller, Anne Scott. *Fat and Thin: A Natural History of Obesity.* New York: Farrar, Straus, and Giroux, 1977.

Bercovitch, Sacvan. "The Problem of Ideology in American Literary History." *Critical Inquiry* 12 (1986): 631–53.

Brillat-Savarin, Jean. *The Philosopher in the Kitchen.* Translated by Anne Drayton. Harmondsworth: Penguin, 1970.

Calderón, Hectór. "To Read Chicano Narrative: Commentary and Metacommentary." *Mester* (1983): 3–14.

Donaldson, Susan. "Consumption and Complicity in Sheila Bosworth's *Almost Innocent.*" *Southern Quarterly* 30, nos. 2–3 (1992): 113–22.

Ellmann, Maud. *The Hunger Artists: Starving, Writing, and Imprisonment.* Cambridge, Mass.: Harvard University Press, 1993.

Fabrey, William. Introduction to *Fat Pride: A Survival Handbook,* by Marvin Grosswirth, 11–15. New York: Jarrow, 1971.

Franklin, Benjamin. "*The Autobiography,* Part One." In *The Heath Anthology of American Literature,* edited by Paul Lauter, 2:711–89. 2nd ed. Lexington, Mass.: D. C. Heath, 1994.

Friedman, Abraham I. *Fat Can Be Beautiful: Stop Dieting, Start Living.* New York: Berkley, 1974.

Gebauer, Gunter, and Christoph Wulf. *Mimesis: Culture—Art—Society.* Translated by Don Reneau. Berkeley: University of California Press, 1995.

Giles, James R. *The Naturalistic Inner-City Novel in America: Encounters with the Fat Man.* Columbia: University of South Carolina Press, 1995.

Goffman, Erving. *Stigma: Notes on the Management of Spoiled Identity.* Englewood Cliffs, N.J.: Prentice-Hall, 1963.

Goldman, Anne E. *Take My Word: Autobiographical Innovations of Ethnic American Working Women.* Berkeley: University of California Press, 1996.

Grosswirth, Marvin. *Fat Pride: A Survival Handbook.* New York: Jarrow, 1971.

Gutiérrez, David G. *Walls and Mirrors: Mexican Americans, Mexican Immigrants, and the Politics of Ethnicity.* Berkeley: University of California Press, 1995.

Hartsock, Nancy. "Foucault on Power: A Theory for Women?" In *Feminism/Postmodernism,* edited by Linda Nicholson, 157–75. New York: Routledge, 1995.

Hodgson, B. "Buffalo Back Home on the Range." *National Geographic,* May 1994, 64–89.

Kalisch, Beatrice. "The Stigma of Obesity." *American Journal of Nursing* 72 (1972): 1124–27.

Larson, David. "Benjamin Franklin." In *The Heath Anthology of American Literature,* edited by Paul Lauter, 2:708–11. 2nd ed. Lexington, Mass.: D. C. Heath, 1994.

Leonardi, Susan. "Recipes for Reading: Summer Pasta, Lobster à la Riseholme, and Key Lime Pie." *PMLA* 104 (1989): 340–47.

Levenstein, Harvey. *Paradox of Plenty: A Social History of Eating in Modern America.* New York: Oxford University Press, 1993.

Louderback, Llewellyn. *Fat Power: Whatever You Weigh Is Right.* New York: Hawthorn, 1970.

Nidetch, Jean. *The Story of Weight Watchers.* New York: Signet, 1970.

Sánchez, George J. *Becoming Mexican American: Ethnicity, Culture, and Identity in Chicano Los Angeles, 1900–1945.* New York: Oxford University Press, 1993.

Schwartz, Hillel. *Never Satisfied: A Cultural History of Diets, Fantasies, and Fat.* New York: Free Press, 1986.

Stavans, Ilan. *Bandido: Oscar "Zeta" Acosta and the Chicano Experience.* New York: IconEditions, 1995.

Stuart, Richard B. "Behavioral Control of Overeating." *Behavior Research and Therapy* 5 (1967): 357–65.

Thompson, Hunter. *Fear and Loathing in Las Vegas.* New York: Random House, 1996.

———. "Fear and Loathing in the Graveyard of the Weird: The Banshee Screams for Buffalo Meat." *Rolling Stone,* December 15, 1977, 48–54, 57–58.

———. Introduction to *The Autobiography of a Brown Buffalo,* by Oscar Zeta Acosta, 5–7. New York: Vintage, 1989.

Valdez, Luis. Introduction to *Aztlan: Anthology of Mexican-American Literature,* edited by Valdez and Saul Steiner, xiii–xxxiv. New York: Knopf, 1972.

6 Resisting Venus

Negotiating Corpulence in Exercise Videos

ANTONIA LOSANO AND BRENDA A. RISCH

In this essay, we analyze exercise videos as visual cultural products. By scrutinizing the content and the filmic construction of exercise videos, we reveal contradictions in the cultural negotiation of female corpulence. In our first section, "Venus Doesn't Do Squats," we argue that the muscle-toning phenomenon necessitates conflicts in video discourse. The fundamental crisis brought about by encouraging women to build muscles and get "in shape" coalesces around issues of size and construction. Muscular women will be larger, more imposing; what, then, separates the large corpulent body from the large muscular body? Through an analysis of the murals of languid, fat Venuses in *The Firm* series, we expose contradictions in the appeal to feminine erotic passivity in an environment that insists on muscular strength. In our second section, "The Fat Woman in Back Wears Gray," we examine the marginalization and policing of the corpulent body within exercise videos. An analysis of the editing practices and spatial regime of the video environment shows how the specter of corpulence haunts their material as well as ideological space. Our third section, "Lost in Space," examines the artificial community of thinness constructed by the exercise instructors' discourse of direct address. Finally, in "Parts Is Parts," we comment on the radical dissection of the female body that exercise videos perform. The corpulent body in exercise videos must become a body in bits and pieces in order to be brought under their reconstructing aesthetic. In this final section we focus in particular on the female buttocks as a metonym for the presence of problematic corpulence in exercise videos.

VENUS DOESN'T DO SQUATS

Times have changed. "Rubenesque" is no longer a compliment. The bathing nudes of Renoir and the flying Europa of Titian are no longer models for feminine beauty. In her book *American Beauty,* Lois Banner outlines the culturally ideal body types for women from the nineteenth century to 1960, from the little-boy flappers to the maternal, homebound physique to the brittle-thin collarbones of Twiggy.[1] Continuing this analysis into the present may be imprudent, for it may be impossible to see the present cultural pressures clearly from within one's own decade; but if history has taught us that the cultural idealization, one way or another, of women's bodies leads only to the formation of oppressed or anguished female psyches (the Victorian invalid or hysteric, the modern anorectic, etc.), then it is imperative to evaluate the processes that structure the female body while they are still *in* process.

To this end, we propose to investigate the cultural negotiations of female corpulence through the burgeoning contemporary discourse of exercise videos. In the past, body fashions have relied frequently on clothing; restructuring the female body of the High Renaissance, for example, required a long, cylindrical corset and a floor-length skirt to give the illusion of a thick, elongated torso and longer-than-natural legs.[2] Women by the late twentieth century, however, were wearing very little compared to their historical counterparts. No bustles, no padded derrieres—even padded bras are out.[3] For the appearance of the *contemporary* female body to be altered, *the body itself* must be changed, and exercise videos promise to make this transformation possible.

In the 1970s and '80s, through the popularization of aerobic exercise and severe calorie restriction, the female body was actively altered. In the 1990s a new component was added to aerobic exercise: "body shaping" or "body sculpting," emphasizing the artistic component in this restructuring of the woman's form. Body shaping or sculpting involves exercise using resistance—weights or machines—to target specific muscle groups and restructure them. The image of the "sculpted" female body is relatively new; the fit body of the 1970s and '80s was merely slimmed via calorie restriction and the pure aerobic exercise programs of those decades, whereas the exercise discourse of the 1990s stressed specific bodily alteration—not just overall size reduction—through muscle toning with weights and repetitive calisthenics. "This is the exercise that gives you that sexy little curve at the bottom of your butt," says Cher in her video *New Attitude* (1991), emphasizing that it is no longer enough to be "just thin," and that the female body is rife with "trouble spots" that must be individually perfected.

Exercise videos—500 or more of them produced yearly[4]—are one of the most successful contemporary media for the production and transmission of the new ideals for female form. While they dictate and promise a restructuring of the female body, they must work at the same time to reconstruct older cultural models. To make this new, *muscled* female form acceptable and desirable as a cultural commodity, to facilitate its smooth acceptance into the mythos of ideal female beauty, exercise videos must perform complex maneuvers that particularly imbricate them in issues of corpulence. The fundamental ideological crisis in encouraging women to build muscles coalesces around issues of *size* and *constriction*. In the past, a tape measure and a scale provided all the evidence necessary to demonstrate success. Weight Watchers advertisements, for instance, consistently show women shouting with exultation while standing on a scale; the company's name itself offers insight into exactly what corporeal aspect of women comes under scrutiny. Or who can forget the scene in *Gone with the Wind* (1939) when Scarlett O'Hara, resplendent in a dress made from old curtains, urges her trusty maid to pull her stays tighter: "I've gotta have it nineteen inches," she cries. Slimness in these instances is purely a matter of (lower) numbers.

Weight-training videos for women (either pure muscle-toning videos or aerobic videos with a weight component) cannot rely on the validation of numerical *decrease*, for muscles take up space; they bulge; they grow in girth. Encouraging women to become stronger subverts the traditional association of women with softness, men with hardness. The videos pull female participants tentatively into the cultural space of the masculine: hard bodies, hard work, physical heroism, sweat and toil. They must therefore strictly protect gender stability by their overwhelmingly conservative discourse of exercise. The specter of masculine muscularity haunts their language; hence, women are exhorted to shape their bodies into a careful in-between space. The finished sculpture retains all the qualities of femininity yet is muscular; it does not transgress into the overly muscled, masculine state. *The Firm* video series exemplifies this difficult paradox by insisting, "The same exercises that make a man more manly also make a woman more womanly."[5]

Yet muscular women will be larger, more imposing, less frail and willowy. What, then, is to separate the large *muscled* body from the large *fat* body? Exercise videos must walk a fine ideological line when they discuss muscle building. To begin with, the very phrase "muscle building" is unacceptable: videos exclusively use the phrase "muscle sculpting," suggesting a paring down or carving away rather than an accretive enlargement. *The Firm* series of videos sells and justifies their program of combined "aerobic weight training" by insisting that "only 2 percent of women have the special muscle components needed to build big muscles, and then only with years of training using weights much larger than we use at *The Firm*."[6] *Big* muscles, *much larger* weights: the discourse here lives in fear of size. Kathy Smith echoes this earnest disavowal and assuagement when she says during the weight-training section of her *Step Workout* (1992), "we're not building big, bulky muscles here." Even Susan Powter (of bleached-white stubble cut *Stop the Insanity* fame), who includes several corpulent women in her video, still titles it *Lean, Strong, and Healthy* (1993). Exercise videos consistently attempt to gloss over the anatomical fact that weight-training exercises are building muscles in women: the concept of a woman growing *larger,* in any way, must be sanitized and eradicated at all costs.

Big muscles on a woman are suspect (even as they are encouraged) not only because of the homophobic associations of female bulk with "butchness"—unacceptable masculinity in the female—but also because it is all too easy to "let oneself go" and have those hard-won muscles slip into fat, leaving a woman with a culturally grotesque bulk. Thus the dangers that supposedly threaten the female body are two halves of an insidious cycle. Exercise might (even as the videos promise that it won't) result in bulky, masculine muscles; and the muscled body might transgress its boundaries and transform into fat. Even a formerly thin body might make the journey from thin to muscled to fat.

On one level, fatness is obviously *the* specter that exercise discourse and video production work to exo(e)rcize. After all, women work out to aerobics videos to keep themselves from being fat. But on another level, which is our concern here, the image of female fatness is a literal, material, and spatial backdrop for exercise videos. The layout of *The Firm* videos provides our first example.

The Firm series is at the forefront of the movement toward muscle conditioning for women. They are without a doubt the most opulent of the available exercise videos: the instructor teaches from a raised oval platform in front of a floor-to-ceiling mirror that extends the wall's full length and reflects, often confusingly, a well-dressed class of twenty or so perfectly-in-shape participants. The lighting is bright, the floors are bright, the weight sets sparkle. Directly behind the "class" are shining white copies of Greek and Roman statues, many of them recognizable—the statue of Augustus in military drag, the *Discobolus,* the *Antikythera Youth,* the *Venus de Milo,* and one that looks to us like a replica of the statue of a boy picking something out of his foot, except the breasts are quite prominent, so we can't decide the figure's sex. The side walls are completely covered in enormous murals reproducing famous artistic representations of women: Botticelli's *Birth of Venus* on the set of volume 1; the figure of Spring from his *Primavera* in volume 2; The Three Graces Dancing, also from *Primavera,* in volume 6; Ingres's *La Grande Odalisque* in volume 4 and in their subseries *The Tortoise* and *The Hare;* and Titian's *Venus of Urbino* in volume 5. The "Information Section" at the end of each of the tapes begins, "The Greeks have always known . . ." and then discusses the importance of muscle building for both men and women while the *Venus de Milo* revolves on the screen. Pictures of Victorian women in floor-length skirts exercising with batons appear. Everybody's doing it. Everybody's already done it. It won't make you look like a man—we promise.

The problem with this forthright appeal to an art-historical tradition is that the chosen icons in no way conform to the body configuration presented by instructors and participants in the videos (or the models in the accompanying *The Firm Believer's Catalogue*). The thick, rather undulating midsections, flaring hips, and hint of long thigh beneath the drapery that characterize the *Venus de Milo* are hardly what the creators of *The Firm* have in mind. They tout slim hips, broad shoulders, flat bellies, thighs that do not touch in the middle, and above all the bodybuilder pose (frequently seen in *The Firm* body images), which are much closer to the classical statues of men or boys. The S-curve posture and faint, phallic bulge visible in the cover image of the *Fall Fashion Preview, 1993,* one catalogue distributed by *The Firm,* find dramatic echoes in the classical form of *masculine* perfection. The cover image is flanked at midriff with a caption advertising the "New FIRM PARTS Video Series," the words ending just above the V-line cut of her bikini, suggestively pointing to the slightly protruding groin area of the female "bodybuilder."

The artworks reproduced as murals in *The Firm*'s studio offer startling contrasts to the activities performed within. Consider the exercise instructors in volume 1 of *The Firm* and *The Tortoise.* In one scene, the instructor performs a weighted plié move; behind her is the enlarged head of Botticelli's *Venus.* The head is all that is reproduced; the entire painting, as we know, tells a different story. In another scene, the instructor performs a one-legged squat and leg raise on *The Firm*'s "step-up box," standing before a reproduction of part of Ingres's *La Grande Odalisque;* but the entire painting presents an orientalizing female image, as the woman reclines on a bed with her fluid back and rounded buttocks turned to the viewer's eye, her head glancing back seductively, if passively. Neither Botticelli's Venus nor Ingres's odalisque is likely to perform anything so undignified, linguistically or physically, as a "squat." The odalisque in particular does not appear capable of any strenuous motion whatsoever—unless, perhaps, another invites some action. She is, as the Victorian matrons might say in a different context, "receiving."[7] And the Botticelli Venus's long, soft torso, thick rib cage, protruding belly, and overlapping thighs are a marked contrast to the instructor in *The Firm* video, who incidentally is repeating "Power up! Power down! Engage those buttocks!" each time she raises and lowers her body.

Similar contrasts occur in all segments of *The Firm* series, regularly forcing viewers into the cognitive dissonance of dual identification. On the one hand, we are asked to model ourselves on the instructor as the voice of authority and the contemporary template of feminine perfection; on the other hand, we are invited to view the murals of languid female forms—forms that are, by the standards promulgated by the videos, fat.

"No pictorial subject is more determined by a complex web of cultural interests than visual narration of the female body," writes Julia Kristeva.[8] Given the "complex web" that these dissimilar visual narratives of feminine beauty evoke, why use such classical murals at all? To appeal to classical and famous icons of female beauty, however different they may appear from contemporary forms, is the obvious answer; but its irony is never noted. *The Firm*'s attempt to create a new, powerful female body within a space dripping with reproductions of passive femininity and classical male dominance with which the female body is not aligned but rather contrasted (the reproductions of statues of men are stuck in alcoves along the far walls of the studio space, as far away as possible from the always-female instructors) serves only to deny the possibility of an unproblematic female bodily power. All the representations of women are goddesses or hypersexualized figures (Venus, Primavera, the Graces, odalisques), while those of men are emperors, athletes, "real."

Another possible reason for including multiple instances of reclining, dripping, languid goddesses or female figures is to reinstate feminine sexuality into the videos, albeit in a very problematic register. The antiseptic, rigidly controlled environment of *The Firm* videos carefully eradicates the erotic from the discourse and image of exercise. The participants do not smile, or sweat, or appear to derive enjoyment or pain from their endeavors. Women are never, in any exercise video we viewed, encouraged to derive pleasure from the bodies of other women. The instructors remain impassive, professional. But behind them lurks the specter of erotic pleasure, in the forbidden yet never-forgotten realm of the corpulent woman—forbidden because the corpulent female body is culturally associated with sexual deviance or asexuality.

The erotic exists *outside* the frame of exercise videos: on the margins, like the Fat Woman in Gray whom we discuss in the next section. Early videos focused much more on the pornographic; the first televised exercise routines on the *Today Show* in the early 1980s were short (ten–twenty minute) segments aimed primarily at male passive viewers rather than female active participants. These segments—such as "Sandahl Bergman's Body," which aired in 1985—were designed and marketed both as exercise for women and as mild erotica for men, as the title suggests. Now, however, exercise videos are neither grouped with pornography in video stores nor marked as erotic—their box covers are not particularly seductive but emphasize active, nonsensual, physical exercise. But rather than disappearing, the erotic has merely become a subtext. Videos do situate the female body in an explicitly sexualized position, even if it is not one designed to be immediately erotic for the viewer. The female body is reconstructed to be looked at, implicitly by male eyes. Just as the discourse of health only perfunctorily covers the discourse of appearance as a motivational factor, so too does the do-it-for-yourself theme fail to hide the do-it-for-men message. "Squeeze those buttocks," says instructor Victoria Johnson in her *Dance Step Formula* (1991), "or no one else will!" The corpulent Venuses on the back wall in *The Firm* videos serve as a marker for this erotic position, holding, as it were, a woman's place in bed until she can return to it, gleamingly fit from her workout.

The "fat" figure, then, is anatomized, deconstructed, and reconstructed to suit our eyes. This fat Venus is behind us as we exercise to a *Firm* tape—behind us spatially, ideologically, and figuratively. Fatness is the strangely lauded—because essential to the classical images offered as interior decoration—yet utterly negated wallpaper; fatness is also that which must be avoided at all costs, but is simultaneously ever-present as essential femininity. Venus *is* woman, yet Venus is, by *The Firm*'s standards, corpulent. A visual battle is waged between the instructor and the mural: the instructor may appear to win, but Venus is never erased.

A goddess image printed in *The Firm Believer's Catalogue* (1993) shows a seated female figure with her anatomical parts numbered and labeled according to "trouble spots," which are then enumerated and analyzed. This goddess figure is directly commodified, her naked body dissected and offered as a site in constant danger of the accumulation of excess.

Numbered from head to toe, this only slightly corpulent woman becomes a veritable mountain of flab as the text builds, each numbered comment pointing to unsightly dimples, jiggling arms, and other unacceptably formed body parts. The imaged figure holds her arm across her averted face. Who wouldn't look away in shame when bombarded with such a list of aesthetic defects? "The backs of your arms are loose and shake . . . your shoulders seem flat and shapeless . . . the top of your bra is covered with extra fat . . . your thighs are too big to fit in most of your pants . . ." and so on.

The female body, though now routinely encouraged to build muscle, has no easy access to the new idea of strength. The possibility of strength is undercut by the juxtaposed contrast of older, distinctly passive, and borderline corpulent (at least by the standards of *The Firm* series) icons—or by hetero-erotic mandates. So once again the male body becomes the norm for the "fit" body, leaving the female body marginalized, because of this ambivalence around the danger of historical corpulence and its erotic potential. For example, when the speaker in the "Information Section" of *The Firm* begins to discuss the location of specific muscles, she remarks, "Because the muscles are basically the same on both sexes, we'll use the male body"—this in a series whose instructors are female, whose videotaped class participants are 90 percent female, and whose viewers are presumably mostly female.

THE FAT WOMAN IN BACK WEARS GRAY

The Firm's literal backgrounding, spatially, of classical images of fat women is echoed in other videos by the positioning and treatment of larger women exercisers. A division of bodies is essential: in the majority of videos, those by Richard Simmons and Susan Powter excepted, the truly "grotesque" body—uncontained, running liquid, wild, lawless—is simply unacceptable, the evil and troublesome Other. There is, however, a middle ground, a *marginally* grotesque body. This is the Fat Woman in Gray—generally older, perfectly lovely, but, in contrast to the likes of Kathy Smith, imperfect because of her size. *This* grotesque body, heavier than others in the videos, is the targeted template for transformation.

The token "fat woman" generally wears matte gray exercise gear—in contrast to the bright, shiny, magenta Lycra costumes of other video participants—and she occupies a marginal position in the video environment, in the back or to one side (or both). Her costumes are rarely flattering to her figure and are cut more conservatively than those on other participants.

In Jane Fonda's *Lean Routine* (1991), for instance, the "low-impact lady" is dressed in matte gray tights and a conservative black leotard with low-cut legs, which together serve to make her look shorter and plumper than the others pictured—whose costumes range from Jane's see-through lace unitard to ultrashort denim cut-offs paired with a bikini top.

Any marginally grotesque female body is rarely focused on extensively; it is usually shown only to indicate "modifications" of the routine—lower impact or lighter weights. When we closely examine the presentation of these alternate routines, we see that in the vast majority of exercise videos, they are never demonstrated coherently enough for a video user to follow—despite a purported mission to provide exercise instructions for users at all levels of fitness. For example, the editing in both Kathy Smith's *Fat Burning Workout* (1988) and Jane Fonda's *Lean Routine* focuses resolutely on anything *but* the Fat Woman in Gray, who leads the low-impact sections. Interspersed throughout Smith's *Fat Burning Workout,* even during these sections, are cuts to Kathy's face and breasts lasting approximately six seconds, which is roughly the same amount of time as is spent on demonstrating aerobic steps new to the routine. Low-impact exercisers receive on average two-second shots. The shots of Kathy's face and body ostensibly emotionally motivate the user; however, the odd timing of the camera's lingering attention on Kathy's face and breasts suggests that viewers are to emulate her *body* rather than her choreography, achieving her ecstatic, emotional state during their quest to eradicate corpulence. Fonda's *Lean Routine* also has a strong tendency to focus on faces for emotive reasons. Even when she is not technically leading the class, Jane is the center of attention, using her provocative outfit (a lace unitard) and several "posing" movements disguised as exercises to draw attention to her body.

Richard Simmons's *Sweating to the Oldies* (1988) and Susan Powter's *Lean, Strong, and Healthy* also use close-ups on the instructor's and class members' faces both to motivate the physical efforts of the home user and to provoke her to identify with the people in the video. However, these videos include actual corpulent women—not just a token Fat Woman in Gray—and they do not use close-ups of the instructor's faces and bodies to visually erase the presence of corpulence. These videos, made by former fat people Simmons and Powter, exemplify the practical use of editing to facilitate the home user's view of aerobic routines, to motivate the user, and to maintain visual interest. *Sweating to the Oldies* is designed as an entirely low-impact routine focusing on fun, easy dance steps, while *Lean, Strong, and Healthy* is exceptionally careful to demonstrate three different levels of activity in virtually every shot. Whereas ideological biases against corpulence and bodily difference are expressed in the very construction (editing) of other exercise videos, those produced by Susan Powter and Richard Simmons refuse to altogether eradicate the presence of corpulence.

Such strenuously controlled segregation and fragmentation of the corpulent female body is necessary in the present cultural system (and hence in the world of exercise videos) because it is precisely the female body that resists control, and corpulence that is the most visible sign of a deviant body. The female body cannot approach the ideal classical symmetry of the male body, as displayed in the Greek statues and da Vinci's drawing *Vetruvian Man* reproduced so visibly on the set of *The Firm* workouts. The female body is notoriously unstable, even more so when corpulent: it goes through periodic transformations, monthly cycles, weight loss and gain, and pregnancy, during which the actual material body expands and contracts uncontrollably. "I return again and again . . . to a problematic, unstable female body that is either a version of or wholly different from a generally unproblematic, stable male body," writes Thomas Laqueur in his analysis of the modern body.[9] It is this "problematic, unstable female body"—the body of the fat woman in the world of exercise videos—that must be relegated to the back of the room. Given the impact of such marginalization and subtle degradation of those users who, according to mainstream culture, could benefit the most from gains in fitness (i.e., the overweight, beginner, and elderly users), it is the mock encouragement of the instructors in aerobics videos that appears intensely problematic.

LOST IN SPACE

The methods used by aerobics videos to address their audiences and their construction of space both attest to one of the videos' primary goals: to involve the viewer as much as possible in an artificially created community of fitness and thinness. Direct address is extremely common in workout videos, not only to give the viewer/participant the instructions they need but also to motivate them. Since part of what videos are selling to their audience is motivational effect, establishing rapport with their consumers is extremely important. Statements such as "Watch out for that coffee table . . ." or "Move around that couch, dining table, little kid . . ." significantly extend the instructor's directive discourse. Positioned oddly between the personal and the impersonal, such remarks aim at breaking down boundaries between the viewer and the video workout personnel. They reinforce the notion that the people in the video are "really there" with the user, while simultaneously reminding the user that she is at home alone.

The use of direct address helps create the power relations inherent in the video/viewer matrix. The instructor is an authority to whom the viewer submits; just as the beat dictates the pace, the instructor dictates both the movement and psychic energy of the participant. The user receives constant cues as to what is amusing, important, or challenging; and though the user can choose to ignore the instructor's priorities (by pressing the mute button) or actively disagree with them (by sitting down or fast-forwarding at will), to successfully identity with the community of thinness presented in the video she must accept the instructor's directive discourse. The viewer is encouraged to believe that "She knows how to make me beautiful, desirable, popular . . . her program can change my life forever."

Instructors consistently and almost universally imply that they can "see" the exerciser. This claim provides a disciplinary structure that works like the Panopticon:[10] there may be no one *actually* there to watch you, but the *possibility* of being seen is held before you constantly as a disciplinary incentive. In Michel Foucault's words, bodily discipline "requires enclosure, the specification of a place heterogeneous to all others and closed in upon itself. It is the protected place of disciplinary monotony."[11] The enclosure of an exercise video provides an excellent example of such a "protected place"—and because video users willingly work out to the same video again and again, the phrase "disciplinary monotony" is particularly apposite.

In another move to reinforce their directives, video aerobics instructors rarely refer to their body except as it represents the impersonal body. One male instructor talks about wanting to eat, but he projects his desire onto the user and her environment, the home.[12] The directive style of video instructors situates women in an authoritarian setting rather than a consensual or communal one, a choice that may explain why videos so often include a group behind the instructor. Ironically, the class format, like direct address, reinforces the instructor's authority as it pulls the home viewer into his or her disciplinary gaze. The filmed participants model submission to the directive voice, while projecting an image of being in the "fitness community." Users never see them grimace or complain, because such actions would subvert both aspects of the message they are sending.[13]

Any woman who deviates from the instructors' directives is threatened not only with injury, or failure to burn "enough" fat, but also with overarching guilt. In an average tape, the instructor validates only two possible identities for those not able or willing to do the whole routine: beginner or low-impact exerciser. Since both of these positions are marginalized as much as possible short of excluding them altogether, neither is truly acceptable for a user who wants to feel part of the community of thinness. Even workouts that claim to be designed to accommodate low-impact exercisers or beginners show subtle discrimination against them and favor high-impact movements when both techniques are shown.

The construction of space in exercise videos provides a another means of drawing the participant into an imaginary community of thinness. *The Firm* series, for example, first disconnects the user from her mundane setting by offering the spectacle of a lavish studio and then achieves the user's identification with that space by forcing her to focus intensely on it to make sense of its radical fragmentation. A mirror is set up behind the instructor, and the class is positioned in front of her (rather than behind her, as in most videos). The video is then shot largely facing the mirror (so we see the front and back of the instructor, plus the reflections of the participants), with alternate cuts of the class occasionally shot from the perspective of the instructor.

The result is visual confusion that hyperbolizes what other exercise videos attempt in their positioning of the instructor. The instructor stands before the viewer as a mirror—participants follow her movements and are expected to replicate her body. Analysts of exercise videos explain, "This mirror relationship inaugurates a dual space linking cultural representation with the body of the viewer. In this case, the reflection determines the real, rather than vice versa, for participants attempt to embody the image of a unifying ideal in the mirror."[14] The process inverts the normal order of mimesis and places the identity of the viewer in flux: we look for ourselves in the mirror but find only a vision of unattainable physical perfection. In Lacanian terms, what the viewer sees and desires to replicate is an illusion, just as what the infant sees in the mirror is an illusion of future mastery: "The fact is that the total form of the body by which the subject anticipates in a mirage the maturation of his power is given to him only as Gestalt, that is to say, in an exteriority in which this form is certainly more constituent than constituted, but in which it appears to him above all in a contrasting size . . . and in a symmetry that inverts it, in contrast with the turbulent movements that the subject feels are animating him."[15] The viewer's efforts are motivated by the hope of someday looking as "thin" and "fit" as the instructor;[16] as the videos play on the viewer's fantasy of demonstrating her mastery of her body.

But the unified self dancing in the mirror is an illusion, (almost) never attained, since the bodies modeled for the home viewer/participant are rarely, if ever, achieved through exercise alone. Also disturbing is the necessarily static appearance of the women in the exercise videos. The instructor remains perfect, but the token Fat Woman in Gray never changes. Every time we watch, there she is, in the back, performing her low-impact modifications. Exercise videos, for all their apparent motion and emphasis on radical alterations of the body, are of course necessarily static. Hence, the very body most encouraged to alter is precisely the one that never changes, sending an unsettling message to the corpulent exerciser. Even those videos produced in series oddly don't use the same personnel in the "class," thus passing up what seems to be an obvious opportunity to demonstrate the efficacy of their workout system.

PARTS IS PARTS

Videos regularly use editing techniques to dissect the body into pieces that can then be "managed," with the overall goal of disciplining the body into a prescribed shape. Close-ups of body segments (legs, torso, neck, and face) are used to *suggest* rather than to actually demonstrate the exercises; cuts in most videos occur as often as every three seconds, creating a breathless display of seemingly free-floating body parts. But videos also dissect the body more literally, by presenting sequences within the workout designed to address individual muscle sets. The overall effect is remarkably similar to that achieved in the courtly love tradition of the blazon, whereby an ideal woman is simultaneously de- and reconstructed out of the ideal component parts.[17] Indeed, exercise videos are often titled according to the body parts they "work" (Kathy Smith's *Great Buns and Thighs Workout* [1993], Karen Voight's *Firm Arms and Abs* [1991], *Buns of Steel 2000* [1993], etc.), or they include separate sections within the workout focusing on women's "trouble spots"—abdominals, arms, thighs, buttocks—which in fact constitute the entire body, except the head, feet, and hands (which are targeted by other marketers). These body-sculpting segments involve repeated movements, such as the simple sit-up, which progressively "overload" the muscle involved and bring it to "exhaustion."

During the sculpting portions of each video, the female body is reduced to bits and pieces; each piece is then perfected through exercise. As the four women in Cher's *Body Confidence* (1991) video perform inner thigh lifts, Cher cries, "These horrible little presses mean beautiful legs!" The linguistic distance between exercise and body part is consistently this close:

exercise *means* beautiful legs, arms, whatever. *The Firm* video series speaks of certain exercises being "for" certain body parts, as if they were machines in gyms. The squat is "for" the gluteal muscles, the military press is "for" the deltoids—the body is partitioned, and to each part is connected an exercise promising to reconstruct that part as desired. The image from *The Firm* catalogue discussed above, of the seated female figure with her "trouble spots" numbered, is a perfect example of this type of discourse.

The unstable female body must thus be broken down and reconfigured before it can be considered culturally acceptable. Its "natural" asymmetry and variation must be overcome. Hardship and sweat and pain ("Go for the burn," says Jane Fonda, cheerfully) must be endured: the language of exercise videos is the language of work. "Tight, strong, control," grunts the leader of volume 3 of *The Firm*. "We look like the drill team from hell," remarks Cher in *Body Confidence*. Exercise is posited explicitly as labor, rewriting the biblical injunction of the role of women. The Rubenesque or Titianesque body spoke of leisure—white, soft, languid—a woman kept, or too rich to work. *The Firm*-ly muscled slim form of a woman "in shape" speaks again of leisure—but the leisure is now filled with a simulacrum of work, the "workout." An enthusiastic video user is quoted in *The Firm Believer's Catalogue:* "As a mother of three, a wife, a professional, and a full-time nursing student, the time I spend with *The Firm* is *my time*."[18] Women's leisure time has been restructured to include exercise; a woman's work in the home is spent no longer on the traditional cooking or cleaning but on reshaping herself. This labor, however, is explicitly participative. Exercise as labor is not coded by the videos as overly alienating (though it certainly may prove to be oppressive to women). Woman is not separated from her labor; she is not a spectator at her work(out). Conversely, as the cultural historian Susan Willis writes, "In the context of women's labor history, the nautilus machine is a capitalist wish-fulfillment. It gives a woman access to the machine but denies access to production. It requires energy and negates the experience of labor."[19] We do see changes in the body as the visible results of labor, which remain, technically, in the possession of the (productive) worker. But these results are for the benefit of others as well, and in that regard the work of exercise is alienating. To be thin is to be culturally acceptable, whereas fat people are trained to feel guilty and apologetic about their weight. They are often portrayed in popular culture as "imposing" their weight on others, often in a quite literal, spatial manner. One typical example is the scene in the 1987 film *Planes, Trains, and Automobiles* in which John Candy is shown literally spilling over his airplane seat, to the massive annoyance of Steve Martin, seated next to him.

All the issues that we have raised concerning exercise videos—the ruthless dismemberment of the body, the fear of size and the advocacy of constriction, the ambiguous relation to labor—coalesce around the one body part that so annoys Steve Martin: the human buttocks. The buttocks are traditionally considered the prime example of what Peter Stallybrass and Allon White call the "lower bodily stratum," which has been a historical site of cultural contestation. This lower bodily stratum stands in tension with the "classical body"—visible in *The Firm* videos as Greek statues or Renaissance paintings—which is elevated, static, and pristine.[20]

One of the central goals of exercise videos is precisely to *make classical* the traditionally grotesque female body, and doing so involves conquering the buttocks as the largest and most visible element of the grotesque body. The buttocks as a body part are inherently feminized, as the sociologist Pierre Bourdieu observes: "The opposition between the sexes can also be organized on the basis of the opposition, which is used intensively in gestural and verbal insults, between the front [of the body], the site of sexual difference, and the behind, which is sexually undifferentiated, feminine, and submissive."[21]

The buttocks—this space of feminine submission—along with the inner and upper thighs, are the most targeted muscle group in the majority of exercise videos. The primary reason is physiological: the gluteals, hamstrings, and quadriceps are large muscle groups, and activating them repeatedly is what makes aerobics aerobic. But there is an obsession with these muscle groups, especially the "glutes," that goes beyond the physiological. The *Buns of Steel* series is a case in point: twenty-nine videos (and counting) explicitly designed to improve the female ass. Remarkable. But *steel?* Why on earth would anyone want a metallic ass? Through these videos, a traditionally "soft" part of the female anatomy is technologized, concretized, hardened, and forced into a regimented, contained, secure pattern. Furthermore, that the series is called *Buns of Steel* rather than, say, *Biceps of Steel* (which could at least contribute to a woman's physical safety or functional effectiveness) suggests that the female backside is reconstructed purely for the (male) gaze.

In the same vein, *The Firm* markets their "step-up box" (a smaller version of the step) as a "revolutionary new technique which radically reshapes your hips and thighs like those of a racehorse."[22] Tail and all? Again, why is this considered a successful marketing technique? Does a woman want a horse's ass? The connection is disturbing; it reinforces the identification of the female backside as a place of degradation, excess, animalistic sexuality, and submission to authority. Thus it must be contained—even as it is explicitly animalized, it is controlled. A racehorse: not just a horse, but a horse *trained to perform and to submit to authority.*

This control of female corporeality bizarrely penetrates *inside* the body as well: several videos now feature sequences—generally placed just after the buttocks exercises—designed to strengthen the pelvic floor muscles, in order "to improve sexual response and prevent incontinence."[23] It is incredibly strange to watch—a room full of women in exercise clothes lying on the floor *not moving,* their faces blank, with their hands making and relaxing fists to symbolize the invisible muscle contractions within their bodies. Significantly, this exercise itself produces pleasurable sensations—the PC (pubococcygeal) muscle is one muscle that contracts during female orgasm, and these Kegel exercises are designed to mimic that motion. Essentially, we are watching a room full of women simulating orgasm on video, yet the erotic never makes it to the surface—it is killed by the lights and the bright floors and the sound of the calm, professional, rigid voice of the instructor. Pleasure here becomes *work,* and women are restructured, right down to their most private parts.

It is not our contention that women should cease to perform exercise videos, which can be valuable tools in an exercise program. However, the female body is standardized through such commodified forms, a process that we must recognize and theorize if health regimens that are not oppressive are to be made available for women of any size. In the words of the political and legal theorist Catharine MacKinnon, "For women, when we have engaged in sport, we have had to gain a relation to our bodies *as if they are our own.* . . . [I]t is our bodies as acting rather than acted upon. It is our bodies as being and presence, our bodies that *we* do things with, that we in fact are and identify with as ourselves, rather than bodies as things to be looked at or for us to look at in preparation for the crucialness of how we will appear."[24]

NOTES

1. Lois W. Banner, *American Beauty* (Chicago: University of Chicago Press, 1983).

2. This millinarily created body is then reproduced in the nude painting of the time. Anne Hollander, in her fascinating book *Seeing Through Clothes* (New York: Viking, 1978), details how clothing fashions through the eras contributed to artistic representations of the naked body. Nudes therefore had big bellies when empire

waists were in fashion, and tiny, tapered waists when tight V-front dresses made the waist appear negligible.

3. Since we first drafted this essay, the padded bra has made its reappearance, in the guise of the Miracle Bra popularized by Victoria's Secret. And thus we begin the fashion cycle yet again . . .

4. Jill Ross, marketing director of Collage Video, a leading exercise video catalogue; interview by authors, November 15, 1993.

5. In "Twenty Questions about Fitness," an information segment appended to early *Firm* tapes.

6. Ibid.

7. Body posture is gendered in *The Firm* landscape: to recline is feminine, to appear erect is masculine. In *The Firm* videos we see the reproduction of this cultural model: the statues in the background are of men, standing up tall. The portraits on the walls are of reclining women—Venus in particular—women in soft, S-shaped, contrapuntal stances.

8. Julia Kristeva, quoted in Susan Suleiman, introduction to *The Female Body in Western Culture,* ed. Suleiman (Cambridge, Mass.: Harvard University Press, 1986), 12.

9. Thomas Laqueur, "Orgasm, Generation, and the Politics of Reproductive Biology," in *The Making of the Modern Body: Sexuality and Society in the Nineteenth Century,* ed. Catherine Gallagher and Laqueur (Berkeley: University of California Press, 1987), 22.

10. The Panopticon—first designed by Jeremy Bentham in 1791—subjected prisoners to a constant but unseen disciplinary gaze, thereby providing an institutional structure of totalizing visual control. Michel Foucault suggests that this structure becomes internalized, making a formerly scopic regime the personal norm and subjects into self-regulating prisoners; see *Discipline and Punish: The Birth of the Prison,* trans. Alan Sheridan (New York: Vintage, 1979), 195–228.

11. Ibid., 141.

12. As part of the audience address that accompanies his routine on the *CIA 2001* (1991) video, Andre Houle says: "Try to use your whole living room, or whatever room you're in, hopefully not the kitchen, that's where I go to eat all the time. . . . After this we're going to have to go eat . . . Huh gang!" It is ironic that this remark occurs in the one series of tapes we examined that are marketed directly to aerobics instructors. It is a kind of meta–directive discourse projecting its desires onto those who go out to train the masses.

13. A few participants in *The Firm* videos do disobey the instructor's directive voice: the macho men, when they are lifting weights, display a curious inability to follow directions from women. Their insistence on using their own individual style points to the gendered nature of the message of submission to the patriarchy. Those men literally embody the patriarchy, so they need not pay close attention to the female mouthpiece of patriarchal law.

14. Elizabeth Kagan and Margaret Morse, "The Body Electronic: Aerobic Exercise on Video: Women's Search for Empowerment and Self-Transformation," *Drama Review* 32, no. 4 (1988): 169.

15. Jacques Lacan, *Freud's Papers on Technique, 1953–54,* ed. Jacques-Alain Miller, trans. John Forrester (New York: Norton, 1988), 2.

16. Indeed, all of the videos we viewed used ultrafit people as the instructors. While some rely on the instructor's former fame as a model, actress, or athlete (Kathy Smith, Jane Fonda), others attain similar credibility through the personal testimonials they have made public (Richard Simmons and Susan Powter). Interestingly, both Simmons and Powter, former corpulent people, incorporate a

segment in their exercise videos in which they introduce members of the class to the viewer, telling their names and how much weight and inches the person has lost. The amounts run between 40 and 210 pounds.

17. See Nancy Vickers's essay on the blazon, "This Heraldry in Lucrece's Face," *Poetics Today* 6 (1985): 171–84.

18. The Firm, *The Firm Believer's Catalogue* (Charlotte, N.C.: The Firm, 1993), 4.

19. Susan Willis, "Work(ing) Out," *Cultural Studies* 4, no. 1 (1990): 9.

20. For a discussion of the complex relations between the classical body and the lower body, see Peter Stallybrass and Allon White, *The Politics and Poetics of Transgression* (Ithaca, N.Y.: Cornell University Press, 1986), 21–22, 43, 186–87. Apparently, this role has not changed.

21. Pierre Bourdieu, *The Logic of Practice,* trans. Richard Nice (Stanford: Stanford University Press, 1990), 70. Yet how can the rear be both undifferentiated and feminine at the same time? And why is the rear submissive? If he means sexual submission—presenting the rear so that it might be penetrated with little active participation on the part of the one penetrated—only a masculine libidinal system would consider "taking it" to be submissive and assume that the pleasure and force belong solely to the one who stands behind. A feminine system might posit enclosure as a position of power—or at least a position of equal pleasure. But such arguments with the cultural construction are beyond the scope of our essay; here, we agree with the notion that the backside is (culturally considered) a feminine, often disparaged, and passive space.

22. *The Firm,* vol. 3, introduction.

23. The Firm, *The Firm Believer's Catalogue,* 34.

24. Catharine MacKinnon, *Feminism Unmodified: Discourse on Life and Law* (Cambridge, Mass.: Harvard University Press, 1987), 121.

REFERENCES

Banner, Lois W. *American Beauty*. Chicago: University of Chicago Press, 1983.

Bourdieu, Pierre. *The Logic of Practice*. Translated by Richard Nice. Stanford: Stanford University Press, 1990.

The Firm. *The Firm Believers' Catalogue.* Charlotte, N.C.: The Firm, 1993.

Foucault, Michel. *Discipline and Punish: The Birth of the Prison.* Translated by Alan Sheridan. New York: Vintage, 1979.

Hollander, Anne. *Seeing Through Clothes.* New York: Viking, 1978.

Kagan, Elizabeth, and Margaret Morse. "The Body Electronic: Aerobic Exercise on Video: Women's Search for Empowerment and Self-Transformation." *Drama Review* 32, no. 4 (1988): 164–78.

Lacan, Jacques. *Freud's Papers on Technique, 1953–54.* Edited by Jacques-Alain Miller. Translated by John Forrester. New York: Norton, 1988.

Laqueur, Thomas. *Making Sex: Body and Gender from the Greeks to Freud.* Cambridge, Mass.: Harvard University Press, 1990.

———. "Orgasm, Generation, and the Politics of Reproductive Biology." In *The Making of the Modern Body: Sexuality and Society in the Nineteenth Century,* ed. Catherine Gallagher and Laqueur, 20–41. Berkeley: University of California Press, 1987.

MacKinnon, Catharine. *Feminism Unmodified: Discourse on Life and Law.* Cambridge, Mass.: Harvard University Press, 1987.
Modleski, Tania. *Loving with a Vengeance: Mass-Produced Fantasies for Women.* London: Methuen, 1982.
Stallybrass, Peter, and Allon White. *The Politics and Poetics of Transgression.* Ithaca, N.Y.: Cornell University Press, 1986.
Suleiman, Susan R. Introduction to *The Female Body in Western Culture,* edited by Suleiman, 3–24. Cambridge, Mass.: Harvard University Press, 1986.
Vickers, Nancy. "This Heraldry in Lucrece's Face." *Poetics Today* 6 (1985): 171–84.
Willis, Susan. "Work(ing) Out." *Cultural Studies* 4, no. 1 (1990): 1–18.

VIDEOGRAPHY

Anderson, Kari. *Sweat Express.* Pro-Robics, 1991.
———. *Two the Max.* Pro-Robics, 1992.
Buns of Steel 2000. Maier Group, 1993.
Cher. *Body Confidence.* Cher Fitness, 1991.
———. *New Attitude.* Cher Fitness, 1991.
CIA 2001. Creative Instructors Aerobic, 1991.
The Firm. 6 vols. Meridian Films, 1987–92.
The Firm: The Hare. Meridian Films, 1994.
The Firm: The Tortoise. Meridian Films, 1994.
Fonda, Jane. *Lean Routine.* Fitness Quest, 1991.
———. *Step Aerobics.* Fitness Quest, 1992.
———. *Workout.* Fitness Quest, 1988.
Johnson, Victoria. *Victoria's Dance Step Formula.* Metro Fitness, 1991.
Powter, Susan. *Lean, Strong, and Healthy with Susan Powter.* Avision Entertainment, 1993.
Simmons, Richard. *Richard Simmons Sweating to the Oldies.* Good Times Videos, 1988.
Smith, Kathy. *Great Buns and Thighs Workout.* Media Home Entertainment, 1994.
———. *Kathy Smith's Fat Burning Workout.* Media of Heron Communications, 1988.
———. *Step Workout.* Media Home Entertainment, 1992.
———. *Weightloss Workout.* Media of Heron Communications, 1989.
Voight, Karen. *Firm Arms and Abs.* Voight Video, 1991.

7 Fighting Abjection

Representing Fat Women

LE'A KENT

"I was a fat kid." From *FaT GiRL*, no. 1 (1994): 8. (Courtesy Max Airborne)

Fat is Beautiful. Or, as the name of one fat girl's publication puts it, *I Am So Fucking Beautiful.*[1] What are the effects when fat women begin to say such things? More important, how do they manage to say such things? Beginning to publish and circulate images valuing the fat female body (or even beginning to value one's own fat female body) in what Eve Kosofsky Sedgwick has called a "fat abhorring world of images," a world in which fat women are charged with "concentrating and representing 'a general sense of the body's offensiveness,' "[2] requires radical confrontation with the representational status quo. It requires undermining the process of abjection that makes fat women's bodies synonymous with the offensive, horrible, or deadly aspects of embodiment. It requires finding a way of representing the self that is not body-neutral or disembodied (and therefore presumptively thin), but intimately connected with the body in a new vision of embodiment that no longer disdains the flesh. This vision of embodiment doesn't obsessively seek the good, thin body (a body good only because it is marked by the self's repeated discipline), but instead redefines the good body and also the good self. By insisting that the body's desires should mark the self as well and that the good self is the self so marked, this new vision of embodiment shifts the relationship between self and body. Shifting the relations of embodiment gives fat women a way to stop living their bodies as the "before" picture and to begin to have a body thought valuable in the present.

My interest in these questions is not, of course, strictly academic. Growing up with a miserably fat mother (or perhaps merely a miserably dieting mother), maturing into an eating-disordered teenager, and ultimately ending up in a body most fat activists would place on the small end of "fat" (fat enough to suffer street harassment, but thin enough not to suffer medical harassment—fat enough to have to shop in special stores, but thin enough that those stores can still be found in shopping malls), I've gone across borders my teenage self could not imagine. I got fat, but somehow I still exist. "The worst" has happened, and it's not that bad.[3] I'm "imprisoned" in a fat body, yet somehow, as the fat activist writer Marjory Nelson would say, "I'm home free." During my dieting days, I endlessly told myself and was endlessly told that becoming fat would mean being drowned in flesh—that once I was fat, no one would be able to see (or love, or want, or respect) me. And yet, it hasn't happened. With the help of fat feminist friends, with the help of books such as Kim Chernin's *The Obsession* and the fat activist anthology *Shadow on a Tightrope,* I found a way to think and live my fat body in the present. According to all cultural "wisdom" (and just watch what happens to self-valuing fat women on talk shows if you don't believe me), I must be deluded—I am impossible, I am living in a state of denial, and I must sooner or later come to my senses and resume loathing my body, if only for my "health."

My impossibility is different from the impossibilities of fat women who were fat children, and different again, in its white-middle-class-ness, from the impossibilities of fat women of color, but no less impossible for all that.[4] The narrative I have told, of moving from self-loathing and body obsession to a gradual acceptance of a fat female body, is common if not banal. Fat women who were fat as children seem to bear a different set of scars, inflicted by medical institutions and critical families.[5] Fat women of color often tell of simultaneously encountering racism and fat oppression after growing up in more fat-affirmative home cultures.[6] Nevertheless, in mainstream conceptions of the self and the body, as Max Airborne's cartoon at the start of this essay makes clear, the self, the person who one *is*, is presumptively thin—and the hard-won realization that one can live as a fat subject is nothing short of transformative. With the realization that the girl inside "ain't skinny," the young Max is transformed into the superhero Fat Girl, the savior of all fat women, who gives her name to a new magazine "for fat dykes and the women who want them."

The transformation from dieting teenager to Fat Girl is difficult. So difficult, in fact, that one woman I spoke to at a reading for the book *Women En Large: Images of Fat Nudes* said she was working on a manual for how to live as a fat woman. It's a good idea. A manual is necessary first of all as a counterweight to shelves and shelves of diet books, and second as a means of scraping together the cultural resources needed to live as a fat woman. Little in late-twentieth-century U.S. culture has given any inkling that it might be possible to *live* as a fat woman. Die as a fat woman, yes. Die *because* you're a fat woman, unquestionably. It is all too easy to find images of fat shot through with warnings about one's impending death—images of revulsion, images in which fat bodies are fragmented, medicalized, pathologized, and transformed into abject visions of the horror of flesh itself. In contemporary culture, the fat body generally becomes visible only at the margins, if at all, and only when written into a pathologizing narrative in which fat is a cause of ill health and a symptom of poor behavior. This narrative creates fatness as a "spoiled identity,"[7] an identity that can communicate only its own failure, an identity for which all other narratives are impossible. The fat body is never portrayed as effective, as powerful, or as sexual. Recent fat liberationist cultural production defies these limits, rewriting the fat body to challenge both abject images of the fat body and the horror of the body itself.

EVERYWHERE AND NOWHERE: ABJECT REPRESENTATION, 1994–95

To understand how contemporary fat women's representations combat prevailing visions of the fat body, it is necessary to understand something about how prevailing representations work. Unfortunately, one can choose from many recent examples. The presentation of fat bodies as pathological began a distinct resurgence in late 1994, spurred on by two events. The first was the widely reported discovery of the "obesity gene." That the gene discovered was not a human gene but a mouse gene and that the gene accounts for only a fraction of severe obesity even among mice were technicalities, less widely reported.[8] Among endless reports suggesting that soon fat people could be wiped out by a genetically engineered pill or shot, these details were overlooked. The second event was former surgeon general C. Everett Koop's "Shape Up America" plan, given pseudo-governmental legitimacy both by Koop's prominence and by the concurrent publication of an NIH "study" (in fact a selective review of already-existing research, done by a committee stacked with interested parties from the weight loss industry) endorsing yo-yo dieting. Weight loss programs Jenny Craig and Nutri System were reportedly among the concerns funding Koop's venture.[9] *Time* magazine heralded Koop's initiative with a cover headline, "Girth of a Nation." For fat people, the allusion to D. W. Griffith's film *Birth of a Nation* was perhaps sickeningly appropriate. Just as his white actors in blackface enacted a white fantasy of freed slaves, so in this article people not fat were photographed in lurid colors, and with distorting fisheye lenses, gulping down Doritos, Budweiser, and ice cream while sprawled before the television. In a single photograph, *Time* encapsulates the fat-abhorring narrative: fat people are freakish slobs who have no self-control (and they're driving up our health care costs).[10]

The February 1995 issue of *Life* magazine offers perhaps the most paradoxical example of this eruption of concern about fatness, if only because, despite its headline ("Twenty-eight Questions about Fat"), and despite the fact that "Fat" is the single largest word on the cover, the article within contains very few photographs of fat people. The cover features a thin woman pinching significantly less than an inch of her well-tanned abdominal fat; the question "Do men and women gain weight differently?" refers to a photograph of the boxer George Foreman and the ballerina Margaret Tracey; and another photo captioned "Fat Floats" pictures thin women doing aquarobics.[11] Fat is incessantly referred to, and just as incessantly erased.

Literal erasure and extreme fragmentation characterize the few representations of fat people in the magazine. The chin of a liposuction patient protrudes from the surgical draping. Some fat calves appear to be exercising in an institutional-looking gym. A fat man is captured in the background, overwhelmed by the foregrounded presence of the Duke University Rice Diet Program's sign.[12] All of these photographs are small, less than one inch by two inches, making the fat man (the only full-body photograph of a fat person in the entire magazine) less than half an inch tall as he walks past the sign of his own erasure. Other representations of fat in the article include a cross-section of a clogged artery, presumably from a fat person, although the source is not pictured. The lead-in to the caption reads "Fatty Tubes"; according to text below, "a 1993 study based on autopsies of 1,532 teenagers and young adults found that all of them had fatty patches in their aortas."[13] Thus fat is a contamination threatening everyone: yet the placement and caption of the photograph imply that arterial fat is always a consequence of body fat, a conclusion that the study itself does not support.

In an issue supposedly devoted to fat, the largest photograph of an actual fat person is a two-by-three-inch thermogram of a fat woman next to the story description in the table of contents. This thermogram, a visual representation of the temperature of various parts of the body—ranging from a purplish blue at the coolest parts, through greens and yellows, to a deep red and white in the warmest parts—is, in effect, a brightly colored pseudoscientific, psychedelic blob. Evidently, "What do fat people actually look like?" is not one of the twenty-eight questions considered. Yet the thermogram is significant as an example of the fat body as sign, and always sign of the same thing—lack of self-control, leading to disease. The medicalizing filter shaping that representation makes it difficult to read this body any other way. The depiction certainly undermines the subjectivity of this particular fat woman, who is erased to the point that the narrative of illness is the only narrative the thermogram can support.

Many other examples of the paucity of and prejudice in representations of fat people could be drawn from television, magazines, newspapers, and movies. This pattern has been noted by scholars and fat activists alike. When *FaT GiRL* surveyed members of its editorial collective about fat representation, the consensus was that fat women are invisible to mainstream media. Replies included "There are no fat reporters on TV news"; "I don't think we're represented at all, except in Jenny Craig ads, where you'll notice there are no fat people really"; and "Invisible." Other interviewees cited portrayals of fat women "as fools and objects of disgust"; "as out of control"; "as undesirable and unnecessary"; "As pathetic, helpless slobs. Tragic, ugly, lazy characters with no self control"; and "as sick, lazy, and slobs."[14]

To these observations, I would add the significant genre of the "before" picture in weight loss advertisements, both print and televised. The before-and-after sequence gets to the heart of mainstream fat representation and the resulting paradoxes and impossibilities of fat identity. Here the fat person, usually a fat woman, is represented not as a person but as something encasing a person, something from which a person must escape, something that a person must cast off. The fat body is once again caught up in a narrative of erasure. Typical of this genre is an advertisement for

"Medical Weight Control" that appeared in the *Los Angeles Weekly* in late 1994.[15] In this drawing, the before and after pictures are collapsed into one, with a rather manic-looking thin woman clad in aerobics gear emerging triumphant from the body of a fat woman, like a butterfly emerging from its cocoon. (A radically fat-affirmative reading might note the similarity between this image and the science fiction standby of the alien bursting forth from its human host.) The fat body is stiff, stationary, dressed in an unbelievably frumpy gingham dress, and has no head. "Imprisoned in every fat man," after all, "a thin one is wildly signaling to be let out."[16] In this scenario the self, the person, is presumptively thin, and cruelly jailed in a fat body. The self is never fat. To put it bluntly, there is no such thing as a fat *person.* The before-and-after scenario both consigns the fat body to an eternal past and makes it bear the full horror of embodiment, situating it as that which must be cast aside for the self to truly come into being.

In short, in the public sphere, fat bodies, and fat women's bodies in particular, are represented as a kind of abject: that which must be expelled to make all other bodily representations and functions, even life itself, possible. I borrow this idea of the abject from the feminist psychoanalyst Julia Kristeva. In *Powers of Horror,* she explains that the process of abjection is the act of primal repression that founds subjectivity and begins a sedimentation of identity around the newly forming self. The abject sets up the categories of self and not-self, but it is an expulsion of something internal to the self. In this process, according to Kristeva, "I expel myself, I spit myself out, I abject myself within the same motion through which 'I' claim to establish myself." In this way, "the one haunted by abjection is set literally beside himself." The abject is "what life withstands . . . on the part of death."[17] The abject is that revolting physicality, that repellent fluidity, those seepages and discharges that are inevitably attached to the body and necessary for life, but just as necessarily opposed to a sense of self. Kristeva also argues that in this psychological expulsion, the abject is consigned to a repeatedly retrieved past, placed in a representational "land of oblivion" that is nonetheless "constantly remembered."[18] Abjection is thus characterized by revulsion, fear of contamination, association with the deathly aspects of the body, a repeated expulsion that marks the self's borders, consignment to the past, and constant reevocation. Within mainstream representations of the body, the fat body functions as the abject: it takes up the burden of representing *the horror of the body itself* for the culture at large.

The fat body represents the corporeality and inevitable death of all bodies—a condition that, like plaque in the arteries, is universal but must be fought constantly and repeatedly, and is projected onto fat bodies.[19] The fat body is linked with death, and allowing fat into the body is thought to inevitably court death (the increasing concern about dietary fat in recent years may thus be read both as a displacement and as an intensification of the abjection of the fat body). The subject of the before and after pictures literally stands beside her abjected fat self, or drags herself out of it. Through the normative practice of dieting, millions enact the abjection of their fat bodies. The parallel between Kristeva's abject subject and the vomiting bulimic is too obvious to dwell on. The fat body rings the margins of the good self, haunting them as it helps create them. The fat body must be repeatedly evoked at the margins, drawn in and then expelled, in order to continue taking the weight of corporeality off thin bodies—playing much the same role as that taken by the female body in relation to the male, according to Elizabeth Grosz's analysis in *Volatile Bodies*. Because the fat body is the abject that makes possible the consolidation of the good body and the good self, it remains in a marginal state even when, as in *Life*, it is allegedly the focus of attention. As in the before and after pictures, the fat body is endlessly present in its representation as *past*. It is drawn back, recalled, referred to again and again, only to be cast out again; and through that casting out, it forms the margins defining the good body, the thin body that bears the mark of the self's discipline. In the article discussed, the fat body is evoked by the captions in order to be displaced by the photographs, invoked by the title in order to be displaced in the body of the text, or invoked under the sign of its own erasure (whether through dieting or through death).

STRATEGIES FOR THE ABJECT: *FaT GiRL* AND *WOMEN EN LARGE*

Clearly, the cultural process of abjection outlined above makes the idea of a *fat person* almost unthinkable. Fat is culturally and psychologically opposed to the self, not part of the self. To represent and affirm themselves as fat women, to put a self in the fat body, to envision their own existence, fat women producing fat liberationist culture must counteract the effects and the dynamics of abject representation. If the process of abjection means that the fat body is pushed to the margins, placed in the past, linked with death, envisioned as a crypt in which the (presumptively thin) self is in danger of withering away, and made to bear the horror of corporeality, then the process of fat-affirmative representation must counter or undermine these moves. Because the process of fat abjection is so central to ideas of proper selfhood in our culture, fat-affirmative representation often must create new modes of self and new ways of seeing and being in the body. At the very least, the fat body can no longer function solely as a symptom of the weakened self. It must be written out of this narrative and into others. The ultimate goal is to reunite the self and the body, as the self within is implicated in the fat body's desires. For this reunion to occur, the body hatred at the heart of the mind-body split must be set aside, and the body no longer abjected from the self.

FaT GiRL and *Women En Large,* the two examples of fat-affirmative cultural production I discuss, are among the latest ventures in a tradition of fat activism that is over twenty years old. In a foreword to the 1983 anthology *Shadow on a Tightrope: Writings by Women on Fat Oppression,* Vivian Mayer dates the feminist fat liberation movement, and therefore its body of cultural production, to the 1973 founding of the Fat Underground.[20] According to Mayer and to a recent interview with Judy Freespirit, an early member, the Fat Underground was founded as a radical alternative to the National Association to Advance Fat Acceptance, whose position on civil rights for fat people Freespirit characterizes as "do[ing] volunteer work for the Cerebral Palsy Association to show fat people were nice."[21] The Fat Underground had ties to feminist, lesbian, and leftist journals and published feminist analyses of fat oppression in *off our backs, Sister, Issues in Radical Therapy, Plexus, Hagborn, Conditions 6, Commonwoman,* and *Out and About.*[22] Fat liberation pieces were published by Fat Liberator Publications, a private photocopy press run by various members of the Fat Underground, through 1980.[23] *Shadow on a Tightrope* itself, probably one of the best-known and most enduring fat liberationist texts, includes pieces written between 1972 and 1982 and is something of a touchstone for the editors of both *FaT GiRL* and *Women En Large*—several writers in the first two issues of *FaT GiRL* mention reading *Shadow* when they were younger.

Earlier in this essay, I noted that late 1994 was marked by a resurgence of anti-fat discourses in the popular press. Not entirely coincidentally, late 1994 also witnessed a burgeoning of fat-positive publications featuring women, among them the first issue of *FaT GiRL: The Zine for Fat Dykes and the Women Who Want Them* and a book titled *Women En Large: Images of Fat Nudes.*[24] Although they differ considerably, both publications set forth a vision of fat women explicitly opposed to mainstream (non)portrayals.

Many of the authors in *Shadow on a Tightrope* are lesbians, and many were involved in various incarnations of lesbian feminism. The connections between lesbian activism, feminist activism, and fat activism continue to the present day, inspiring publications such as *FaT GiRL*, a quarterly magazine dedicated to political, erotic, and creative portrayals of fat dykes. *FaT GiRL* lists "angry," "feminist," and "political" as some of its founding adjectives (along with "fleshy," and, of course, "found next to your vibrator"),[25] and the interview with Judy Freespirit is included in its first issue. On the zine's masthead, the publishers proclaim: "Submit your daily experiences getting from here to there; your fictional explorations; your whimsical reminiscences; your sarcastic diatribes; your songs of laughter and tears of anger and pain; your non-linear meanderings; your artistic endeavors: wood cuts, drawings, photos, rubber stamps, cartoons; your hard-hitting investigative journalism; your hot sexual forays from the perverse to the sublime, your tales of gender play; news; reviews; announcements; letters; gossip and encouragement."[26] Such a publication clearly draws on a mixed heritage as it responds to earlier feminist fat liberationist texts and to the proliferation of lesbian pornography, magazines, and zines of the 1980s and early 1990s.[27]

In contrast with *FaT GiRL*'s deliberate avoidance of a slick style, *Women En Large* is a glossy book of photographs of fat nude women, with essays and poetry by and about them. Laurie Toby Edison, a photographer, and Debbie Notkin, a writer and activist, formed their own press, Books in Focus, to publish it.[28] Notkin's roots are in feminist and fat activism and in the science fiction community, but not specifically in lesbian politics (although several of the women pictured are lesbians and one, April Miller, is also on the editorial collective of *FaT GiRL*). The essays in *Women En Large* concentrate mainly on substantiating the phenomenon of discrimination against fat people, as well as asserting and proving that fatness is largely genetically determined, and therefore a phenomenon and identity just as stable and valid as any other. While *FaT GiRL* can be characterized as a radical approach to fat liberation ("we're here, we're fat, get used to it"), *Women En Large* is a more liberal, identity-based document, seeking a justification for fatness in the individual's genetic code, the biological bedrock of contemporary visions of identity ("fatness is genetic, so stop discriminating against us"). That *Women En Large* is willing to argue with anti-fat assertions and to justify fatness, while *FaT GiRL* refuses to argue those points, affects how the two publications combat mainstream representations of fat women.[29]

Women En Large includes forty-one "images of fat nudes" bracketed between a brief foreword and two concluding essays. The photographs and essay topics chosen were determined by a need to contradict mainstream images at the level of content. Because fat women are usually pushed to the margins or not represented, they are here at the center. Because fat women are often thought to be essentially "the same," Edison and Notkin strongly emphasize diversity, especially with respect to age, size, race, and abledness. Because fat women are thought to eat all the time and to never exercise, food is never shown or mentioned in the book and women are shown stretching and dancing. Because fat bodies are thought to be inherently perverse, the photos are "not intended to be erotic."[30] Because fatness is often thought to arise from laziness, bad eating habits, or other such culpable behavior, Notkin argues at some length in the first essay, "Enlarging: Politics and Society," that fatness arises from each individual's genetic makeup, and is thus out of her control.[31]

In the text and in a talk accompanying a slide show of photographs from the book,[32] Edison and Notkin emphasize the realness, the factuality of fat women and of Edison's photographs of the women. Every photographic decision is justified by their priorities of accurate representation—showing the women as they really are, showing them in their real variety, showing them as human. The women are photographed in their homes so we can see that they have lives. The women are photographed exercising because fat women do exercise. The women are photographed with musical instruments because they play them. These representational choices also attempt to work against mainstream stereotypes of fat people as slovenly, sedentary, or stupid.[33] The fat body in *Women En Large* is definitely not an uninhabited shell, nor a prison, nor perverse.

The essays in *Women En Large* concentrate on constructing a solid identity for fat women: an inevitable identity for which they are not to blame, for it is based on genetic immutability. Notkin sees medicalizing discourses as the major enemy of fat subjectivity, but she also relies on them, marshaling scientific citations to debunk the assertion that fat people are inherently unhealthy. What is inherently unhealthy, she argues, is yo-yo dieting and the inhumane stresses that a prejudiced world inflicts on fat people.[34] However, in engaging so extensively with the medical model, in rewriting the fat body using genetics as an identity technology, Notkin, like purveyors of mainstream representations, treats the fat body as a symptom—not of sloth and gluttony, but of a genetic difference. While this argument is a distinct improvement on mainstream discourse, by contributing to a sense that the fat body needs extensive explanation in a way that other bodies do not it sets itself at odds with the photographs' assertions of value and beauty.

The text of *Women En Large* directly and effectively counteracts images of abjection that constitute the mainstream representation of fat, both by simply representing fat women and by contradicting the medicalized linkage of fat with death, but it does not take issue with the fundamental split between body and self. The fat body is presented as beautiful, but apparently with the hope that it will become irrelevant, that the reader, guided by the homey interiors of the photographs, will ultimately come to realize that "we're all the same underneath" and stop unjustly punishing fat people for a benign genetic difference. Thus, although the fat body is no longer positioned as the abject, the body itself is still severed from identity. Who these women "really" are resides not in their embodiment, not in the flow of desire issuing from the fat body, but in their musical instruments, their house plants, their hobbies, or their poetry. The text downplays the fat body made visible in the photographs, in effect maintaining the mind/body split, maintaining the presentation of fat as symptom, and maintaining some of the mainstream erasure of the fat body.

In some of its more parodic or enigmatic photographs, *Women En Large* does attack the dynamic of abjection as well as the content of mainstream representation. One photograph in particular—that of Cynthia McQuillen cradling a human skull in front of her crotch—asks the question, "Is this what this body really is?"[35] Rather than writing fat in from the abject margins by asserting a sameness (as do most of the other photographs in the book), it overtly performs abjection, parodying the usual terms of fat representation and challenging the dynamic itself. Here McQuillen appears, like the woman pictured in *Life* magazine's thermogram, behind the sign of death; but she looks from beyond it, locking eyes with the viewer to confront and unsettle the process of abjection. Clearly, the self is in this body, alive and very much affronted by the juxtaposition. The alienness of the bony skull next to her rounded flesh and the life in her look expose the falseness and the violence of normatively abjected representations of fat women.

Such counterabjection characterizes much of *FaT GiRL*, which humorously emphasizes fat as an assertion of the physical, reclaiming the fat body to make it into a comedic weapon. But *FaT GiRL* isn't just about comedy. It's also about, as the cover of the second issue declares, "stories, reviews, smut, comics, resources, and more!!!" By relying on a parodic strategy of counterabjection, by rewriting the fat body as particularly powerful, and by eroticizing the fat body, *FaT GiRL* acts against mainstream abjection, undercutting both the dynamic of abjection and the denigration of the body in the mind/body split.

Rather than simply *not* subjecting the fat body to abjection, *FaT GiRL*'s representations often destabilize the process of abjection through recipes for counterabjection—political acts in which the fat girl performs a literal abjection in order to make fun of mainstream culture's obsession with abjecting fat bodies. In counterabjection, the abjected substance is not shamefully denied but proudly displayed, in order to affront the culture at large. This is an abjection with a difference. A prime example is the recipe for a "Fat Girl Revenge Cocktail":

> ingredients:
> one quart brightly-colored kefir (yogurt drink)
> one teaspoon syrup of Ipecac (vomiting agent)
> Drink the kefir. Upon approaching desired target (diet centers are good places), swallow the syrup of Ipecac. Position your mouth so it's facing your target. When your stomach begins to heave, aim quickly, and fire. Most effective if done in broad daylight.[36]

Rather than being the agent of abjection, here the diet center becomes the target of a literal abjection. Rather than assert reasonably, as *Women En Large* does, that dieting is unhealthy, here *FaT GiRL* does to the diet center what the diet center would do to fat girls (or would have fat girls do to themselves). Rather than abjecting her own fat body, the Ipecac-taking fat girl is abjecting diet culture. In this public abjection (best done in broad daylight, as opposed to the secretive vomiting induced by fear of fat) the diet center and not the fat girl is made to bear the mark of revulsion. In the revenge cocktail, a performance of a literal sick-making, the analytic point and its embodiment in the body of a fat woman are fused.

Through its expelling force, the fat body is a direct political agent. The fat body is similarly empowered and written as agent rather than symptom throughout *FaT GiRL*. A second political action tip suggests that when harassed "about being fat or looking pregnant" (an assertion of fat as symptom if there ever was one—based on the assumption that heterosexual reproduction is the only excuse for the fat body), the fat girl should perform the symptom to excess and act out a monstrous birth:

> Turn your back and look downward (giving them the misleading impression that they've made you feel humiliated and horrible about yourself), and stuff whatever you might be carrying into your clothing. Then, turn the tables on your unsuspecting victim(s) by clutching your bulging, padded gut and stumbling towards him/her with an arm outstretched, moaning and grunting: "Help me! I'm going to have my baby!" . . . The piece-de-resistance comes when you squat and grunt and give birth to whatever you were able to stash away under

> your clothes. Best results if you can pull it out from between your legs—especially if you pre-plan the action and have a bloody barbie [*sic*] doll, used tampon. . . . And remember, the more the merrier! (Friends having multiple simultaneous births makes for a more blessed event.)[37]

Distracting the harasser with a false performance of fat shame, the fat girl then enacts a parodic abject birth. The appearance of shame here functions not to entrap the fat girl but to snare her audience; and in giving birth to the bloodied Barbie doll, she expels and degrades one significant artifact of fat-hating beauty culture.

A slightly different, but no less assertive, mode of fat physicality is expressed in the lyrics to the *FaT GiRL*–theme polka (itself a dance associated with rotundity): the superhero Fat Girl threatens, "Shut up or I'll sit on you!"[38] In addition to affirming the unashamed fat body, this last manifestation also recuperates the common childhood taunt, "What are you going to do? Sit on me?" *FaT GiRL* attributes lack of power not to the fat body itself but to the shame that the fat person is made to feel. When fatness is performed without the shame, the taunt—an accusation of powerlessness that writes the fat body as unable to defend itself—becomes a threat. In imagining this powerful and unashamed body, *FaT GiRL* writes the self back into the fat body as a *fat self*—as a person particularly shaped and empowered by fat; a self whose body is effective, defining, and pleasurable; a self whose body is not a symptom but a weapon. The narrative of abjection is replaced by a narrative of attack.

It is also significant that in its rewriting a fat embodiment, *FaT GiRL* is frankly erotic, whereas *Women En Large* attempts (or at least claims) to avoid eroticism.[39] In its concern with counteracting myths about fat women at the level of content, *Women En Large* avoids representations of sexuality or of eating, fearing that it will reinforce those myths. *FaT GiRL,* on the other hand, revels in writing the fat body into forbidden sexual scripts. In picturing fat women feeding pastries, grapes, and ice cream to each other in its premiere issue, the zine enacts an erotic spectacle unimaginable in mainstream representation or in *Women En Large.*[40] The photos of eating accompany a discussion feature called "Fat Girl Round Table," but the zine also features erotic pictorials. In presenting fat bodies in sexual acts, fat women actively desiring other fat women, fat women in S/M scenarios, *FaT GiRL* appropriates sex as a joyous way of rewriting the fat body. It uses the erotic to envision a good, pleasurable body in which there is an interplay between the body's desires and the self's expressions—the good body is rewritten as the body that can tell the self its desires, act on its desire, provide pleasures. Suddenly the disciplined body, the dieting body, the subject of "self-control," seems empty and impoverished.

Several of the erotic short stories in the magazine focus on S/M, presenting the sexual scene as a story in which the top rewrites the previously loathed fat body into pleasure and desirability. These stories typically involve a scenario in which the fat woman is the bottom; by giving up control to the top she provides an opportunity for the top to convince the bottom that her body is an object not of loathing but of beauty, pleasure, and lesbian desire. One particularly clear example of this pedagogic scenario is "Thank You Note to a Top," by Drew:

> "You've got a beautiful body," she says and I don't believe her. I let the whip that's slicing across my back drown her out. I don't want to hear this right now. . . .
>
> I was having such a good time before she started talking about my body. . . .
>
> "Don't you believe me, baby? This is some sweet stuff you got. . . . You better believe me. You better believe every word I tell you." I can't tell if she's angry or not and I don't have a safeword tonight. "You've got a beautiful body," she repeats, testing me.
>
> "Yeah, well, I grew it myself," I spit, thinking how much I hate it when Tops lie.
>
> She pauses, looking into my tear-blurred eyes, and repeats slowly, "You grew it yourself. You learned how to love yourself enough to eat and sleep and work and play and give pleasure to yourself and other women, didn't you? And that's what you're doing now, you know." She's got four fingers in me now, pumping slowly in time with her words. I know the whip is still there, but I can't really feel it anymore. My mind is trained on her words.
>
> "This is a body for loving women with, isn't it, and you're giving it to me, aren't you, baby? Aren't you?" . . .
>
> Months later we are making out like teenagers in her truck and I remember to thank her for giving me my body back that night. When I bottom, I give my Top access to my pain, even the pain she didn't cause. And in that vulnerable state, my child-self exposed, I can finally hear those good truths: You're so good. You're beautiful. I'm proud of you. I want you.[41]

In this story, Drew clearly intends the S/M scene to rewrite the negative messages of childhood. In childhood, the narrator was involuntarily powerless and the messages of body hatred were written into her before she could know to reject them. Now, by voluntarily becoming powerless again, she can allow the top to rewrite these messages, using the pleasures and intensities of the body to reinforce them.

The non-S/M eroticism in *FaT GiRL* is just as crucial for rewriting the body and the self. Repeatedly, fat women are shown in the throes of sexual and sensual pleasure—eating, laughing, dancing, masturbating, sunbathing, and having sex. Here, unlike in *Women En Large,* all the pleasures in the catalogue of activities are mediated through the body. The fat body is not just an indifferent vehicle for the self, but a sensual surface with different potentials for different bodies.

This fat body is not marginal or coincidental, but central. It is also highly visible. The *FaT GiRL*–theme polka likens Fat Girl the superhero to Superman, only

> Fat Girl can't live out no clark kent lies
> girdles, corsets, vertical stripes, there is no disguise
> she's omnipresent she's an omnivore
> you know you can't hide from Fat Girl.[42]

Identity and selfhood are thematized in light of this omnipresent visibility as well: "Just as we see gender and race before we see an individual, we see FAT. Oh my God it's a FAAAAAAAAAT dyke! How people react to your identity is wrapped up in your physical presentation. . . . When you claim your dykehood you are demanding a public sexual persona. Fat women have a sexuality? Hard bodies only. Are you Height/Weight Proportionate? . . . Do you fit? How wide are your hips? Where do you fit in? How do you fit in relation to me; what does that say about my identity?"[43] While seeming to maintain the opposition between "physical presentation" and "an individual," Max Airborne also suggests the troubling power of the fat woman: by claiming a sexual identity for herself, she inevitably introduces questions about others' identities. When the abjection of the fat body within mainstream representation is what founds the good body and solidifies identity for the thin self, it is not surprising that when the fat body refuses to stay at the margins, other identities will be disturbed as well.

Simply by representing fat women, both *Women En Large* and *FaT GiRL* trouble the usual construction of embodiment, in which the self is presumptively thin and the fat body is made to stand in for the abjectness of flesh itself. While *Women En Large* attempts to counteract representations of fat women as the abject by correcting the medical and cultural assumptions that anchor them, it ends up reinstating the fat body as symptom. Moreover, by avoiding potentially negative images the book fails to write the fat body out of the narrative of medical symptom and into a narrative of sexual pleasure. *FaT GiRL*'s strategies make it possible to rewrite the fat body as a site of sexual pleasure, after first reiterating and parodying the conventions of mainstream representation. *Women En Large*'s content-based strategy results in splitting the body from the self, though the fat body is no more opposed to the self than is any other body. In *FaT GiRL*, by contrast, the fat body is rewritten as being particularly useful—a weapon, a site of political comedy, and an erotic object all in one. *FaT GiRL* thus not only puts a fat self in the fat body but begins to combat the denigration of the body itself. Once the girl within can be either fat or thin, the presumptively thin self of fat abjection will be displaced in favor of a diversely embodied subjectivity that can no longer afford to disdain the flesh.

NOTES

1. *I Am So Fucking Beautiful* is a zine that was produced in the mid-1990s, by Nomy Lamm of Olympia, Washington. It is dedicated to the exploration and affirmation of being a young, fat, feminist woman.

2. Michael Moon and Eve Kosofsky Sedgwick, "Divinity: A Dossier, a Performance Piece, a Little-Understood Emotion," in *Tendencies*, by Sedgwick (Durham, N.C.: Duke University Press, 1993), 217 [see chapter 15 of this volume].

3. I was overjoyed when I first read Marjory Nelson's formulation of this sentiment in "Fat and Old: Old and Fat," her contribution to *Shadow on a Tightrope:* "I realize that the 'worst' has happened to me. All that I've been warned about and worried about has occurred. The knowledge frees me. I know who I am. I'm fat and I'm old, and I'm home free" (in *Shadow on a Tightrope: Writings by Women on Fat Oppression*, ed. Lisa Schoenfielder and Barb Wieser [Iowa City: Aunt Lute, 1983], 236).

4. For discussions of differences between being a fat woman in a white community and being a fat woman in an African American community, see especially Chupoo Alafonte's and April Miller's remarks by Debbie Notkin in "Enlarging: Politics and Society," in *Women En Large: Images of Fat Nudes*, ed. Laurie Toby Edison and Notkin (San Francisco: Books in Focus, 1994), 94, 103. Fat African American women published in fat liberationist sources generally seem to agree that while fat women are more accepted and are found more attractive in African American communities, the anti-fat discourse of white culture is very difficult to avoid. In "Oh My God It's Big Mama!" (*FaT GiRL*, no. 1 [1994]: 14–20), Elizabeth Hong Brassil discusses the fact that although she is Vietnamese, with recognizably "Asian" facial features and an olive complexion, people often assume she is white because contemporary American images of Asian women fetishize their slimness. Fat liberationist women of color seem to bring to the fat liberationist project considerable strengths in the differences of their home cultures' ways of viewing the body; the project of examining fat liberationist cultural production as a site where these differing ideas of embodiment do battle with white mainstream representation is critical and yet to be done.

5. For accounts of fat women who were fat as children, see Lynn Mabel-Lois, "We'll Worry about That When You're Thin"; Terre Poppe, "Fat Memories from

My Life"; and Lynn Levy, "Outrages," in Schoenfielder and Wieser, *Shadow on a Tightrope,* 62–66, 67–70, 79–81, as well as Max Airborne, "My Life as a Fat Child," *FaT GiRL,* no. 2 (1995): 48–49.

6. See in particular Queen T'hisha's and Chupoo Alafonte's remarks in Notkin, "Enlarging," 106, 94.

7. Michael Moon uses this phrase when he asserts, in a discussion with Eve Sedgwick, that "at a certain active level of human creativity, it may be true that the management of spoiled identity simply is where experimental identities, which is to say any consequential ones, come from" (Moon and Sedgwick, "Divinity," 225). While Moon's insight is acute, I would also like to point out that Moon is certainly not the first to use the concept of spoiled identity to describe fat identity. The phrase was used in 1983 as part of a section title in *Shadow on a Tightrope* ("A Spoiled Identity: Fat women as survivors . . .").

8. See *Food for Thought: Networking Newsletter for the Size Rights and Anti-diet Community,* February 1995, and the January/February 1995 issue of *Rump Parliament* for further discussion of the anti-fat campaigns. One example of the media come-on surrounding the mouse gene discovery was provided by the ABC network. Advertisements for a story run on the program *20/20* on February 3, 1995, asked, "Could the discovery of the obesity gene mean a cure?" and contained video of a fat person getting a shot in the arm, implying that the program would address how the discovery of an obesity gene (in mice?) could lead to a "cure" for fatness. In fact, the bulk of the segment focused on a new "therapy" combining two previously known appetite suppressants, which sometimes resulted in the less-than-revolutionary loss of 10 to 15 percent of body mass. This was the ill-fated phen/fen combination, pulled from the market in 1997 because of its serious side effects.

9. K. and R. Stimson, "Countdown to International No Diet Day," *Food for Thought,* February 1995, 2, and Lee Martindale, "U.S. Gears Up for International No Diet Day" (press release issued by *Rump Parliament Magazine*), February 1995.

10. Philip Elmer-Dewitt, "Fat Times," *Time,* January 16, 1995, 59–61; see the photograph by Chip Simons, 58–59.

11. Bob Adelman, "The Boxer and the Ballerina: George Foreman and Margaret Tracey" (photograph), *Life,* February 1995, 63; Gerd Ludwig/Woodfin Camp & Associates, "Fat Floats" (photograph), *Life,* February 1995, 68.

12. J. Bolivar/Custom Medical Stock, "No Miracle" (photograph), *Life,* February 1995, 64; Nina Berman/SIPA Press, "A Leg Up" and "Let Them Eat Rice" (photographs), *Life,* February 1995, 62, 70.

13. Lisa Grunwald, Anne Hollister, and Miriam Bensimhon, "Do I Look Fat to You?" *Life,* February 1995, 60.

14. "Chew on This!" *FaT GiRL,* no. 1 (1994): 2.

15. "Medical Weight Control" (advertisement), *Los Angeles Weekly,* December 30, 1994–January 5, 1995, 50.

16. Cyril Connolly, quoted in Grunwald, Hollister, and Bensimhon, "Do I Look Fat to You?" 64.

17. Julia Kristeva, *Powers of Horror: An Essay on Abjection,* trans. Leon J. Roudiez and Alice Jardine (New York: Columbia University Press, 1982) 3, 1, 3.

18. Ibid., 8.

19. In this respect, fat is like the body fluids (fluid bodies?) usually assigned the role of the abject. Like body fluids, whose "control is a matter of vigilance, never guaranteed" (Elizabeth Grosz, *Volatile Bodies: Toward a Corporeal Feminism* [Bloomington: Indiana University Press, 1994], 194), fat is envisioned as that

which inevitably contaminates everyone (even the apparently healthy adolescents), but must nevertheless be the object of an eternal struggle.

20. Vivian Mayer, foreword to Schoenfielder and Wieser, *Shadow on a Tightrope,* x.

21. A. Hernandez, "Judy Freespirit: A. Hernandez Talks to One of the Foremothers of Fat Activism," *FaT GiRL,* no. 1 (1994): 6.

22. Lisa Schoenfielder and Barb Wieser, bibliography in Schoenfielder and Wieser, *Shadow on a Tightrope,* 241–43.

23. Lisa Schoenfielder and Barb Wieser, preface to Schoenfielder and Wieser, *Shadow on a Tightrope,* xviii–xxi.

24. See Lee Martindale's editorial (p. 1) in the January/February 1995 issue of *Rump Parliament* for further discussion of the connections between the two. It is Martindale's contention that the growth of fat and anti-diet activism, combined with the Federal Trade Commission's recent crackdown on misleading diet advertising, spurred the diet industries to design and fund former surgeon general Koop's "Shape Up America" plan.

25. "*Fat Girl* Is:," *FaT GiRL,* no. 1 (1994): overleaf of cover.

26. "*Fat Girl* Is a Political Act," *FaT GiRL,* no. 1 (1994): 1.

27. The combined heritages of *Shadow on a Tightrope* and *FaT GiRL* suggest a connection between gay and lesbian activism and fat activism, if perhaps not, as Michael Moon declares, "a profound and unacknowledged historical debt" (Moon and Sedgwick, "Divinity," 234). Moon's assertion that fat liberation is "a movement much younger than gay/lesbian liberation" (making the historical debt longstanding) is open to debate.

Though I take issue with the claim that the debt is unacknowledged (especially if the current blossoming of fat liberation is considered), it seems clear that there are tactical debts, as well as tactical similarities, between the two movements and commonalities in the situations that gave rise to each. Recent lesbian theorists in particular have described the position of the gay or lesbian person within the heterosexual symbolic order as one of abjection. Diana Fuss argues that gays and lesbians are an "indispensable interior exclusion" in such an order ("Inside/Out: Introduction," in *Inside/Out: Lesbian Theories, Gay Theories,* ed. Fuss [New York: Routledge, 1991], 3), and Lynda Hart uses this analysis to launch her own discussion of "the invention and circulation of 'lesbians' as a haunting secret" (*Fatal Women: Lesbian Sexuality and the Mark of Aggression* [Princeton: Princeton University Press, 1994], ix). Judith Butler's theorization of the abject is perhaps most resonant with an account of fatness as abjection. For Butler, "The abject designates . . . precisely those 'unlivable' and 'uninhabitable' zones of social life which are nevertheless densely populated by those who do not enjoy the status of the subject, but whose living under the sign of the 'unlivable' is required to circumscribe the domain of the subject" (*Bodies That Matter: On the Discursive Limits of "Sex"* [New York: Routledge, 1993], 3).

The connections Butler makes between abjection and a sense of uninhabitability, as well as her connections between abjection and repetition, apply well to the fat body and to the repetitive, yet never fully successful, process of dieting.

28. Notkin, "Enlarging," 112. That Edison and Notkin had to form their own press to get *Women En Large* published speaks to a certain level of fat-phobia.

29. In "Divinity," Moon and Sedgwick discuss the distinction between ontogenic and anti-ontogenic stances, which Shane Phelan examined earlier in *Identity Politics: Lesbian Feminism and the Limits of Community* (Philadelphia: Temple University Press, 1989). In both cases, the argument for an anti-ontogenic stance (one that does not begin by positing an origin or explanation for difference) grows

out of gay and lesbian political movements and holds that succumbing to the impulse to explain implies that one has accepted a nonprivileged status—things that are seen as normal, natural, and right never need explanation. The analysis of Phelan and others is explicitly Foucauldian, as they note that "explanations" usually involve submitting oneself to disciplinary apparatuses such as psychiatry or medicine.

30. Cookie Andrews-Hunt and Tara Hughes, "New Book, *Women En Large,* Shows Beauty of Fat Women," *Seattle Gay News,* January 27, 1995, 10.

31. Notkin, "Enlarging," 92–101.

32. Debbie Notkin and Laurie Toby Edison, lecture, Elliott Bay Books, Seattle, December 10, 1994.

33. Notkin, "Enlarging," 91.

34. Ibid., 92–101.

35. Laurie Toby Edison, photograph in Notkin and Edison, *Women En Large,* 61.

36. "Recipes: Fat Girl Revenge Cocktail," *FaT GiRL,* no. 1 (1994): 25.

37. "Helpful Hint: Hysterical Pregnancy and Insta-Birthing," *FaT GiRL,* no. 1 (1994): 40.

38. Max Airborne, "*Fat Girl:* A Polka by Max Airborne," *FaT GiRL* 1, no. (1994): 41.

39. Laurie Toby Edison, quoted in Andrews-Hunt and Hughes, "New Book, *Women En Large,* Shows Beauty of Fat Women," 10.

40. "Fat Girl Roundtable," *Fat Girl,* no. 1 (1994): 33–40.

41. Drew, "Thank You Note to a Top," *FaT GiRL,* no. 1 (1994): 26–27.

42. Airborne, "*Fat Girl:* A Polka," 41.

43. "Will I Sit on You and Squash You?" *FaT GiRL,* no. 1 (1994): 14.

REFERENCES

Adelman, Bob. "The Boxer and the Ballerina: George Foreman and Margaret Tracey" (photograph). *Life,* February 1995, 63.

Airborne, Max. "*Fat Girl:* A Polka by Max Airborne." *FaT GiRL,* no. 1 (1994): 41.

———. "I Was a Fat Kid" (cartoon). *FaT GiRL,* no. 1 (1994): 8.

———. "My Life as a Fat Child." *FaT GiRL,* no. 2 (1995): 48–49.

Andrews-Hunt, Cookie, and Tara Hughes. "New Book, *Women En Large,* Shows Beauty of Fat Women." *Seattle Gay News,* January 27, 1995, 10.

Berman, Nina, and SIPA Press. "A Leg Up" (photograph). *Life,* February 1995, 62.

———. "Let Them Eat Rice" (photograph). *Life,* February 1995, 70.

Bolivar, J., and Custom Medical Stock. "No Miracle" (photograph). *Life,* February 1995, 64.

Brassil, Elizabeth Hong. "Oh My God It's Big Mama!" *FaT GiRL,* no. 1 (1994): 14–20.

Brassil, Elizabeth Hong, and Max Airborne. "Two Fat Dykes." *FaT GiRL,* no. 1 (1994): 31–32.

Butler, Judith. *Bodies That Matter: On the Discursive Limits of "Sex."* New York: Routledge, 1993.

"Chew on This!" *FaT GiRL,* no. 1 (1994): 2.

Drew. "Thank You Note to a Top." *FaT GiRL*, no. 1 (1994): 26–27.

Edison, Laura T., and Deborah Notkin. *Women En Large: Images of Fat Nudes.* San Francisco: Books in Focus, 1994.

Elmer-Dewitt, Philip. "Fat Times." *Time*, January 16, 1995, 59–61.

"*Fat Girl* Is:." *FaT GiRL*, no. 1 (1994): overleaf of cover.

"*Fat Girl* Is a Political Act." *FaT GiRL*, no. 1 (1994): 1.

"Fat Girl Roundtable." *FaT GiRL*, no. 1 (1994): 33–40.

Fuss, Diana. "Inside/Out: Introduction." In *Inside/Out: Lesbian Theories, Gay Theories*, ed. Fuss, 1–10. New York: Routledge, 1991.

Grosz, Elizabeth. *Volatile Bodies: Toward a Corporeal Feminism.* Bloomington: Indiana University Press, 1994.

Grunwald, Lisa, Anne Hollister, and Miriam Bensimhon. "Do I Look Fat to You?" *Life*, February 1995, 60.

Hart, Lynda. *Fatal Women: Lesbian Sexuality and the Mark of Aggression.* Princeton: Princeton University Press, 1994.

"Helpful Hint: Hysterical Pregnancy and Insta-birthing." *FaT GiRL*, no. 1 (1994): 40.

Hernandez, A. "Judy Freespirit: A. Hernandez Talks to One of the Foremothers of Fat Activism." *FaT GiRL*, no. 1 (1994): 6.

Kristeva, Julia. *Powers of Horror: An Essay on Abjection.* Translated by Leon J. Roudiez and Alice Jardine. New York: Columbia University Press, 1982.

Levy, Lynn. "Outrages." In *Shadow on a Tightrope: Writings by Women on Fat Oppression*, edited by Lisa Schoenfielder and Barb Wieser, 79–81. Iowa City: Aunt Lute, 1983.

Ludwig, Gerd, and Woodfin Camp and Associates. "Fat Floats" (photograph). *Life*, February 1995, 68.

Mabel-Lois, Lynn. "We'll Worry about That When You're Thin." In *Shadow on a Tightrope: Writings by Women on Fat Oppression*, edited by Lisa Schoenfielder and Barb Wieser, 62–66. Iowa City: Aunt Lute, 1983.

Martindale, Lee. Editorial. *Rump Parliament*, January/February 1995, 1.

Mayer, Vivian F. Foreword to *Shadow on a Tightrope: Writings by Women on Fat Oppression*, edited by Lisa Schoenfielder and Barb Wieser, ix–xvii. Iowa City: Aunt Lute, 1983.

Moon, Michael, and Eve Kosofsky Sedgwick. "Divinity: A Dossier, a Performance Piece, a Little-Understood Emotion." In *Tendencies*, by Sedgwick, 215–51. Durham, N.C.: Duke University Press, 1993. [see chapter 15 of this volume]

Nelson, Marjory. "Fat and Old: Old and Fat." In *Shadow on a Tightrope: Writings by Women on Fat Oppression*, edited by Lisa Schoenfielder and Barb Wieser, 228–36. Iowa City: Aunt Lute, 1983.

Phelan, Shane. *Identity Politics: Lesbian Feminism and the Limits of Community.* Philadelphia: Temple University Press, 1989.

Poppe, Terre. "Fat Memories from My Life." In *Shadow on a Tightrope: Writings by Women on Fat Oppression*, edited by Lisa Schoenfielder and Barb Wieser, 67–70. Iowa City: Aunt Lute, 1983.

"Recipes: Fat Girl Revenge Cocktail." *FaT GiRL*, no. 1 (1994): 25.

Schoenfielder, Lisa, and Barb Wieser. Preface to *Shadow on a Tightrope: Writings by Women on Fat Oppression*, edited by Schoenfielder and Wieser, xviii–xxi. Iowa City: Aunt Lute, 1983.

———, eds. *Shadow on a Tightrope: Writings by Women on Fat Oppression.* Iowa City: Aunt Lute, 1983.

Stimson, K., and R. Stimson. "Countdown to International No Diet Day." *Food for Thought: Networking Newsletter for the Size Rights and Anti-diet Community,* February 1995, 2.

"Will I Sit on You and Squash You?" *FaT GiRL,* no. 1 (1994): 14.

PART III

Fat Perversities?

Reconstructing Corpulent Sexualities

8 Roscoe Arbuckle and the Scandal of Fatness

NEDA ULABY

In September 1921, one of America's most beloved silent film comedians was arrested for the murder of a young starlet. The prosecution held that Roscoe "Fatty" Arbuckle had ruptured Virginia Rappe's bladder as he raped her during a hotel party, an injury that led to peritonitis and her death four days later. This story was subsequently elaborated in the media. Two accounts especially took hold in the collective consciousness: rumors that Arbuckle squashed the woman under the weight of his body and that the attack employed a bottle (the latter obviously implying impotence).

Arbuckle was declared innocent in July 1922 after his third trial. Two previous juries were unable to render a verdict, stymied by the media circus. The over-the-top theatrics of Arbuckle's films were reproduced in the trial coverage and even played out in the behavior of the Women's Vigilante Committee and other prosecution-based interests determined to scapegoat him. The proliferation of sordid details surrounding the young starlet's death seemed to fulfill the burgeoning expectations regarding Hollywood and scandals. Arbuckle's body became not just an emblem of but a locus for contradictions, taking on a doubly outlawed trope: a sexualized fat person and a rapist.

Most current critical and historical treatments of Arbuckle agree—on the basis of convincing evidence—that Arbuckle was in fact guiltless.[1] My concern, however, is with Roscoe Arbuckle's project of representation rather than the question of his culpability. Like the figure of the giant described by cultural critics, Arbuckle had always been "a mixed category; a violator of boundary and rule; an overabundance of the natural and hence an affront to cultural systems."[2] Arbuckle's excess managed to absorb disparate American notions of aesthetic subjectivity, class status, male sexuality, and performance. The ways that Arbuckle performed his fat were primarily responsible both for Arbuckle's ascension to the heights of celebrity and for the subsequent public conviction that he had gone too far, resulting in his blacklisting and Hollywood disgrace. Many film historians today believe that the Hays Office was instituted in direct response to the Arbuckle case.[3]

Today, when Arbuckle's contemporaries Charlie Chaplin and Buster Keaton are endlessly valorized for their streamlined cinematic genius, we seem to have forgotten Arbuckle's own expansive effect on silent film comedy, the positive play of Fatty on screen. As an aesthetic subject, Arbuckle is relegated to the margins of Hollywood figures. It's almost as if we're inadvertently and endlessly collaborating with the architects of the Hays Code—and echoing the anti-fat presumptions that informed popular perceptions of Fatty the comic and of Arbuckle the rapist.

Complicating America's reaction was the figure of Arbuckle himself: on screen, he deploys the ambivalence of his fatness as he traverses age, gender, and sexual boundaries. This essay examines Fatty Arbuckle's ambivalent performance of corpulence on screen and how his corpulence ultimately framed him juridically and socially during his trial and after.

FATNESS ON SCREEN

Before Arbuckle, the fatness of performers contained limited meanings. Fat men on stage and screen were represented as bloated, degenerated temples to their own consumption. Arbuckle dominated through appropriating and fetishizing the attribute that most clearly identified him, his fat. As the literary and social critic Lauren Berlant argues, "Like a proper name, fat is always fundamentally a thing, a thing of excess. But as a thing that denotes an unquantified substance, its very fixity accrues to itself more stability of identity than one might have imagined."[4] Arbuckle's fat was so deeply entrenched in his persona that it erupted into his proper name. Yet it was by being fixed to and named through his role as fat that Arbuckle was able to consistently subvert audience expectations. Through theatrical transvestitism and comically violent routines, Arbuckle undermined conventional polarities (male/female, beautiful/ugly, good/bad), revolted against homogeneity, and challenged cultural norms. Arbuckle's nonconformist agency as he negotiated between fatness and concupiscence was not only paradoxical but somehow inscrutable. Such inscrutability displaced the abjectness of the subject, making his fat contours encompass a defamiliarized mobility. Rather than simply allowing his fat to limit him, Arbuckle ameliorated the tension provoked by the taboo image of his body.

As subject he employed his fat as the performative point of departure, criticizing and analyzing cultural inscriptions of fatness within a slapstick discourse.

Generally speaking, the authority of fat is undercut by the condemnation of fat on aesthetic grounds and by the collective social sense that it is inherently suspect. But the large body is capable of eliciting reactions of delight; it may resonate with a bygone ideal, the notion of pleasurable indulgence, and, in Fatty's case, a certain nostalgia for chubby childhood, when the body's extra weight may indicate its potential for fascinating mutability. Adult fat, however, carries the taint of destabilization, undisciplined "difference," and too much visibility.

While one might naturally assume that a little extra visibility would be an asset in Hollywood, Arbuckle had to struggle for the creative autonomy that propelled him to stardom, simultaneously resisting and embracing paradigms of fatness as understood and promulgated by the entertainment industry. Arbuckle's subtle characterizations, portraying neither libertine nor sluggard, bewildered most of his early producers and directors—those, that is, who were not utterly antagonized by his visions of mobile, sexy fat. The Keystone mogul Mack Sennett referred to Arbuckle unfailingly and dismissively as "that fat boy." "The Fat Boy," coincidentally, was how Arbuckle was addressed on hundreds of fan letters that poured into the studio before he became a name player, and these very letters helped him achieve celebrity status.[5]

Arbuckle functioned in the world of slapstick, which derived much of its humor from the broad comedy of music halls and frequently relied on stereotypes to communicate jokes. With his seraphic baby face and surprisingly athletic 275-pound body, Arbuckle was his own best sight gag. Although he used his bulk as a comedic propellant, the actual narratives of his comedies rarely revolved around his weight. Instead, they featured Fatty as mischievous schoolboy, wayward employee, spoiled little girl, imposing matron, or determined beau. A large stomach or rear was not only a fabulous sight gag in and of itself, but it could also be strategically employed to bump obstreperous colleagues out of the way. And we should note that Arbuckle was careful about his self-representation. Even when his character was employed in what we might anachronistically call food service, as was often the case (*The Waiter's Picnic*, 1913; *The Waiter's Ball*, 1916; *The Butcher Boy*, 1917), he was never seen overeating on screen. Drinking was another matter (*Wine*, 1913; *His Favorite Pastime*, 1914; *The Rounders*, 1914), but droll enactments of inebriation in slapstick films were hardly limited to physically large players.

Although Arbuckle performed notions of fat that accorded with dominant ideology—displaying laziness, lack of discipline, and unwillingness to conform—he refused to be limited by these expectations. Arbuckle exceeded the freaky potential of his fat. Difference for Arbuckle became a consistent and creatively interpreted strength, particularly in his own infantilization, transvestism, and voyeuristic spectacle (addressed in the following sections).

FATTY'S INFANTILIZATION

Using his body to infantilize his persona, Arbuckle capitalized on his fat to enter the realm of the neutral child. The fatness of Arbuckle's body miniaturized and obscured his genitalia, blurring his sexual identity and providing him access to a gleefully ironicized perversion. He contained and represented the innocent and the erotic, the enormous and the little, the adult and the baby. Fatty's regressive appeal was inextricably connected to his fantastic mobility and agility, his ability to occupy various positions of desire without fixing on one. Arbuckle's syncretization of fatness and infantilism was a crucial element in his insistent addressing of gender and sexuality. Freud's concept of the "pregenital phase" is unself-consciously performed throughout Arbuckle's films, as Fatty's ability to avoid fully demarcating the "masculine" and "feminine" add to his mobile appeal. In this phase, according to Freud, when the organization of and subordination to the reproductive function are still absent, the child displays polymorphous perversity, a chaotic, roaming sexuality that is excited by sensory surfaces such as the skin.[6] The Freudian notion of the infant's nongenital sexuality is integrated into this adult actor's representation of himself.

Arbuckle's characters emphasized the infant's craving, instinctual mouth and regularly stressed oral pleasure. Arbuckle constantly licks his lips, gestures to his mouth, sticks out his tongue, or spits incredible amounts of liquid on people in an excessive display of what the film historian Judith Mayne, in another context, calls an "obvious link between orality and sexuality."[7] The assault of fatness on notions of what constitutes a clean and proper body is abetted by the pleasures of orality, which throughout Arbuckle's work consistently unsettle the rules of erotic decorum. Displacement of fluids that should be inside the body (saliva/milk/semen/vaginal fluids) is both eroticized and situated within a comic discourse.

The impact of Arbuckle's self-infantilization should not be underestimated. Obviously aware of it himself, Arbuckle appeared in several films as the androgynous character "Baby Fatty," brandishing outsized rattles and dolls. Babies persistently represent a site of transformation; indeed, they are a *hypersite* of potential transformation. For a particular kind of individual, self-infantilizing becomes the quintessential means of expressing potential. Not only is Arbuckle's body seen as constantly expansive, but his self is constantly expanding and taking on new roles. Fatty manages to retain an element from his infancy, linking his sexuality with its polymorphous pleasures. The economies of desire in this case are portrayed as spontaneous, innocent, and vulnerable, belying the obvious overtones of grotesquerie.[8]

FATTY IN DRAG: TRANSSEXUAL DESIRE

Fatty assumed multiple roles not only in playing children but in drag as well, as he refused to be pinned down to any particular set of rules or appeals to the moment. His theatrical relationship to food and to infantilization—at once metamorphic, comic, and burlesque—carried over to his cinematic evocations, or caricatures, of womanhood.

Mabel Normand and a host of ingenues aided Arbuckle in establishing heterosexuality as a platform for theatrical disruption. Conventional stagings of romance were being revised in Arbuckle's comedies at just the time that the athletic Gibson Girl replaced the voluptuous Lillian Russell ideal. The slim sex symbol exemplified by Normand and the Sennett Bathing Beauties emphasized an intertwining of innocence and sexuality. Play, rather than mastery, infused and answered erotic demands in Arbuckle's films. Undoubtedly part of his general appeal to female spectators was his association with likable young actresses. Mabel and Fatty, for instance, never seem to question their proportional discrepancies or judge their appearances against a normative standard of beauty. Ignoring the unwritten prohibition against a fat boy being represented seriously as leading man, they constructed a cinematic space in which appearance matters less than bravery and loyalty do. Together, they mapped out alternative sexual—and spectatorial—modalities.[9] The ingenue worked well in conjunction with Arbuckle's deliberate alignment with the infant and both the boy- and girl-child. He frequently appeared in exaggerated copies of children's clothes: short pants and funny hats, or sailor dresses. As a little boy, Arbuckle tapped into the contemporary valorization of American male children, exhibiting bluster, playfulness, and aggression. As little girl, Arbuckle's status as playmate heightened the comic eroticization of the childlike qualities of his female costars.

Part of his enormous appeal was his ability to be child, woman, and man at once. He propagated a sort of utopian vision of the sexual appeal of difference. When Fatty shares the clothing of fat women, the erotics of difference intensify. In drag, Fatty doubles and parodies the stock matron figure. Arbuckle's performances in drag can be read as linking him to the "other" of female desire, a mysterious force that constantly threatens to erupt and challenge the patriarchal order. The logic of attraction is subverted when Arbuckle dominates the screen in the form of a fat woman asserting "her" sexuality, as the images of a fat woman being pursued and loved proliferate. Berlant points out that "a cross-margin identification with another corporally-marked person can disrupt the authority of public norms and rules of erotic decorum";[10] though she isn't commenting specifically about Arbuckle, his films repeatedly bear out such analysis.

SHIFTING GAZES—FATTY AS VOYEURISTIC, EROTIC SPECTACLE

The erotic object as presented by Arbuckle escapes overdetermination because of his sheer weight. By insisting on multiple points of view and by manipulating ingrained cultural notions, Arbuckle troubled the idea of a unified subject position. The mechanisms of role reversal are thrown into disarray as his body is mapped out as a possible site for erotic exchange, a destabilization that in turn influences the workings of the greater social body. In her study of spectatorship in silent film, Miriam Hansen notes: "The star not only promotes a dissociation of scopic and narrative registers but also complicates the imaginary self-identity of the viewing subject. . . . [The films] undermine the notion of a unified position of scopic mastery by foregrounding the reciprocity and ambivalence of the gaze as erotic medium, a gaze that fascinates precisely because it transcends the socially imposed subject-object hierarchy of sexual difference."[11] Arbuckle's method of offering himself to be viewed was to take over the spectacle. By feminizing himself, exploding expectations, and looking back at the camera, he shared and parodied the viewer's gaze. For example, a number of Arbuckle's films can be read as intertextual parodies of Sennett comedies: they adopt Sennett's fetishistic obsession with policemen and their accouterments and transform authority figures into scopophilic objects, which serve occasionally to distract the gaze from Fatty's own body. Ten dripping wet policemen (*Coney Island*, 1917), seven dripping wet policemen (*The Knockout*, 1914), or even two dripping wet policemen (*Fatty and Mabel at the San Diego Exposition*, 1915) compete with the fat for visual interest on screen and give Arbuckle another surface off which to play his identity-challenging performances. By making the viewer look at the soaked policemen in their uniforms, Arbuckle forced audience participation in the spectacle of social anarchy. Through standard slapstick spoofing of authority, such stereotypes as the fat figure, the matron, or the ingenue are deliberately, if temporarily, released from a controlling, voyeuristic gaze.

Even when they are subjected to that gaze, in Arbuckle's films these figures can look back. Arbuckle plays opposite his first wife, Minta Durfee, in *The Knockout,* a film in which Durfee is always watching Arbuckle. After Fatty rescues her from a gang of toughs, Durfee's point of view is privileged as he beats them all up. Reaction shots show her fascination with and approval of his big body. Later, in order to watch Arbuckle box, she dons men's clothing and hides herself among the male spectators.

Nonconformist interest in the masculine contours of Arbuckle's body is assumed and even (cautiously) sexually exploited. In both *The Rounders* and *Coney Island,* Arbuckle is beginning to undress when he notices the camera on him in a medium shot. Shyly smiling as he unfastens his trousers, he requests through gestures that the camera's gaze move upward, cutting out his lower body. The camera obeys, stopping when Fatty tells it to. While quoting codes of decency and shame, this scene contains a certain compulsion stemming from the director's playfully expressed faith in himself as a being worthy of sexual interest. Arbuckle problematizes the notion of erotic spectacle through a sustained blend of titillation and critique.

Fatty is searching for Mabel Normand on a busy thoroughfare when his attention is caught by a sign announcing a performance by the Royal Hawaiian Hula Dancers (*Fatty and Mabel at the San Diego Exposition*). He is entranced by the spectacle of authentic native women shimmying before him. Although other members of the audience respond somewhat apathetically to the dancers, who do not conform to Western hegemonic standards of beauty, Fatty applauds them wildly and salaciously. These women are not what American society wants to look at or look like; heavy, dark-skinned, and exotic, they present what the "correct" beauty ideal is defined against. Yet Mabel, a former Gibson Girl, must veil herself and mimic the dancers' routine—performing otherness—to recapture Fatty's attention. The hierarchy of the look thus is determined by Fatty: he insists not only on creating his own socially transgressive standards but on sharing them with the audience.

Like Rudolph Valentino, whose ethnic/exotic otherness informed conceptions of his masculinity, when Arbuckle enters the discourse he binds pleasure and power with his own set of polymorphous perversities. His relation to female viewers, Hansen points out, can also be understood as suggesting "an alternate organization of erotic relations as well as relations of cinematic representation and reception."[12] Through his ability to invite the on-screen gaze of both male and female actors, whose appreciative attention to Fatty provides a model for the audience, Arbuckle not only relaxed the roles imposed on the spectators but also rendered the traditional, scopophilic male gaze as ultimately grotesque—or, at the very least, inefficacious. Fatty's adoration by his female fans was no hysterical worship of the Valentino variety, but rather was organized around a certain intimacy. Like his female viewers, whose bodies were scrutinized because of their gender, Fatty attracted attention because of his body. No matter what kind of body he performed, Fatty projected a desire to be viewed with longing, illustrating that the capacity to attract and hold such a look is as frequently a gender-neutral source of power as a gendered target of male exploitation. He used his fatness to align himself with the feminine as well as the grotesque, ironicizing their perceived intersection and creating what Michael Moon calls an "alternative body-identity fantasy,"[13] or, more precisely, a number of different body-identity fantasies.

THE SCANDAL OF FAT MAN AS LOVER

It was when Arbuckle attempted to assert himself as a "real" man that the lovable buffoon became threatening. In "Love Confessions of a Fat Man," a *Photoplay* interview of September 1921, Arbuckle announced that "the fat man as lover is going to be the best seller on the market for the next few years."[14] This comment, hardly serious in intention, foreshadowed the tribulations to come.

The fat whose erotic mobility had made Arbuckle a star immobilized him when translated into the courtroom. Ultimately, the meaning of Fatty's sexuality would be reduced to rape, and he would be trapped in the role of an irresponsible adult. The compulsive, tantalizing attraction that Arbuckle usually drew was blocked when he was inserted into a judicial space where he could be read in only one way. The fat that first lifted him to the peak of his career turned into a millstone that dragged him to his death. Once the rhetoric of Arbuckle's fat was moved from the carnivalesque screen to the bureaucratic court, it ceased to empower him. The fat that once armored Arbuckle in resilience was unable to transfer to a new discourse without fixing him in traditional stereotypes. The "scandal" associated with fat eroded support of Arbuckle, reducing his image almost completely to that of a vilified libertine. Society's suspicion that fatness results from a failure to regulate and manage one's body seemed to be articulated in Fatty's on-screen violence, disorders, disasters, and bizarre behaviors and to be confirmed in the news of Arbuckle's commission of "rape" and "murder." Weight connotes unrestrained eating, which here was seen as mirroring a voracious sexual appetite that consumes and destroys the object of desire. Fatness was taken as signifying Arbuckle's uncontrollable desire to consume not only food but starlets as well. Both Clarence Darrow and Earl Rodgers refused to defend the star, the latter remarking: "Arbuckle's weight will damn him. . . . He will no longer be the good-natured fat man that everybody loved. He will become a monster. If he were an ordinary man, his own spotless reputation, his clean pictures would save him. They'll never convict him, but this will ruin him and maybe motion pictures for some time."[15]

Arbuckle was not an ordinary man. As a producer of "culture" who affronted cultural systems, he wore his overabundance on his body. He represented a corporeal extreme linked with uncontrollable desire. Since he had made the possibility of personal excess and sexual mobility an on-screen reality, Arbuckle was condemned to carry these notions into the courtroom. An unseen act translated his body from the screen to the courts. Crossing the intangible barrier from one public sphere to another reconstituted Arbuckle's body, changing it from that of a large baby to that of a rapist.

It was acceptable for Fatty to embody collective hungers and cravings, with his spitting and his cross-dressing and skirt-chasing. The fat of his body smoothed out suspicions of deviance, even allowing his films to be categorized as wholesome juvenilia. But when the fantasized urge for pleasure and drive for satisfaction coincided with allegations of off-screen perversions, Arbuckle's fat became dangerous and demeaning even to look at. The mass media encouraged the reexamination of Arbuckle and informed the public that what he had chosen to conceal below his fat was a monster.

The frames of reference for judging Arbuckle here changed abruptly and radically. Moving from the fiction of the screen (which attracted a plebeian and commercial public) to the juridical/reformist/moralistic discourse of censorship (the bourgeois public sphere), Arbuckle became criminalized. As his films were yanked from the screens of American movie theaters, his body was made genital and phallic in the space of the public sphere. The judicial context into which he was forced would not allow him to maneuver; he was caught, fixed at last.

Church and civic coalitions, predominantly female and touched by the spirit of Progressive reform, appropriated Arbuckle as an emblem of the vices swarming beneath Hollywood's glittering facade. Their anger was probably colored by a sense of betrayal; Arbuckle's ideally de-sexualized but amorphously erotic space had been stripped away and was now reconstructed as a lie. Far from being a mischievous challenger of the gender hierarchy in the social order, Arbuckle was regarded by the public as the perpetrator of the ultimate patriarchal crime—a violent rape—identifying him singularly with his male genital sex. Because of his previous self-creation/fetishization as a perverse child, he became an appropriate target for disciplinary action. Once the body was moved outside the limits of film, beyond the parameters of ambiguity set by Arbuckle as actor/director and the boundaries set by the screen, social tensions flared.

THE "UNRULY CHILD" AND THE HAYS OFFICE

In the courtroom, Arbuckle's portrayals of immaturity harmed him as much as his embodiment as fat. Adolph Zukor, the head of Paramount, had referred to Arbuckle as an "uncooperative and ungrateful child,"[16] and the studio system collaborated with the civic leaders and the courts to decide Arbuckle's fate. Who is big enough to chaperone the fat man? Only another personality in whom strong social forces converged. The interests of Hollywood and American public morality came together in the person of Will Hays. Whereas Arbuckle was ambiguous, chaotic, and corporeal, Hays was rigid, corporate, and corrupt. In April 1922, as his first ultimatum as "guardian of public morals for motion pictures," Hays banned Arbuckle's movies from American theaters and encouraged America to forget Fatty Arbuckle. America did its best to comply.

In his study of the scandal, Sam Stoloff points out that Hays's involvement marks a pivotal moment during Hollywood's shift from an earlier period of competitive proprietary capitalism to large-scale corporate production, helping to mask increasing consolidation of control.[17] Intensifying pressure put on the industry by various state and local attempts at censorship resulted in the formation of the Motion Picture Producers and Distributors of America, a "self-regulating" association with Hays as "czar." Censorship was only one concern; studio executives were displeased with the new economic mobility of their actors, and some of Arbuckle's biographers identify Zukor as the power behind the decision to blacklist Arbuckle.

As one of the highest-salaried actors in Hollywood, Arbuckle's wealth gave him the same kind of unregulated freedom he performed in his films. But what had previously produced class and professional status for Arbuckle ended up undermining him. Hansen notes the tenuousness of his position: "As a commodity whose value turned on his or her ability to touch an experiential nerve in people's lives, the star came to function as a linchpin between immediate market interests and long-term ideological structures, and often embodied the contradictions that erupted in the tensions between the two."[18] To quote Stoloff, Arbuckle's portrayal in the media as a "vindictive eunuch" can be interpreted as a strategic corporate move to wrest power from the actors who were beginning to double as their own trademarks.[19] The paradoxical representation as rapist/eunuch was necessary to control a figure already proven capable of changing his body unlawfully and willfully. And at the moment when corporate systems began to swell, the localized, personal expansiveness of an individual was called into question. In the abstract, the gigantic can be seen as symbolizing power, as conveying authority through scale. When displaced to the individual body, this authority of size became problematic. The massive system could not permit unregulated individual massiveness: the individual had to fit, neatly and thinly, into a regulated slot.

NOTES

1. See Andy Edmonds, *Frame-Up! The Shocking Scandal That Destroyed Hollywood's Biggest Star* (New York: Avon, 1991); Stuart Oderman, *Roscoe "Fatty" Arbuckle: A Biography of the Silent Film Comedian, 1887–1933* (Jefferson, N.C.: McFarland, 1994); Craig Saper, "Scandalography: From Fatty's Demise to Lacan's Rise," from *The Abject America*, special issue of *Lusitania* 1, no. 4 (1994); Sam Stoloff, "Fatty Arbuckle and the Black Sox: Stars and Scandals, 1919–1921" (Ph.D. diss. draft, Cornell University, 1994); and Robert Young, Jr., *Roscoe "Fatty" Arbuckle: A Bio-Bibliography* (Westport, Conn.: Greenwood, 1994).

2. Susan Stewart, *On Longing* (Durham, N.C.: Duke University Press, 1993), 73.

3. The "Hays Office" was administered by former postmaster-general Will Hays (whose professional achievements included serving in Warren G. Harding's cabinet, segregating the post office, and involving himself in the Teapot Dome scandal); its primary obligations were to bust unions and stringently regulate the morality of Hollywood pictures. Its official name was the Motion Picture Producers and Distributors of America (MPPDA).

4. Lauren Berlant, *The Queen of America Goes to Washington City: Essays on Sex and Citizenship* (Durham, N.C.: Duke University Press, 1997), 91.

5. Edmonds, *Frame-Up!*, 46.

6. Sigmund Freud, "Infantine Sexuality," in *Three Essays on the Theory of Sexuality*, trans. James Strachey (New York: Basic Books, 1975), 49.

7. Judith Mayne, "Mistresses of Discrepancy," in *The Woman at the Keyhole: Feminism and Women's Cinema* (Bloomington: Indiana University Press, 1990), 133.

8. The attractions of fat children were not an innovation of film. To offer just one example, in the 1840s and '50s, P. T. Barnum regularly exhibited such

curiosities as the "Highland Mammoth Boys," Vantil Mack (a seven-year-old weighing in at 275 pounds), and "The World's Fattest Baby" in his American Museum in New York.

9. Normand directed a number of the hugely popular "Fatty and Mabel" films; according to several biographers, Arbuckle's first wife, Minta Durfee, noted that Normand was one of the few Keystone players who routinely referred to him as "Roscoe" rather than "Fatty."

10. Berlant, *The Queen of America Goes to Washington City*, 95.

11. Miriam Hansen, *Babel and Babylon: Spectatorship in American Silent Film* (Cambridge, Mass.: Harvard University Press, 1991), 281.

12. Ibid., 294.

13. Michael Moon and Eve Kosofsky Sedgwick, "Divinity: A Dossier, a Performance Piece, a Little-Understood Emotion," in *Tendencies*, by Sedgwick (Durham, N.C.: Duke University Press, 1993), 216 [see chapter 15 of this volume].

14. "Love Confessions of a Fat Man," *Photoplay*, September 1921, 13. Ironically, this article appeared in the same month of Arbuckle's infamous Labor Day party, during which the alleged rape occurred.

15. Earl Rodgers, quoted in Edmonds, *Frame-Up!*, 180.

16. Adolph Zukor, quoted in ibid., 120.

17. Stoloff, "Fatty Arbuckle and the Black Sox," 2.

18. Hansen, *Babel and Babylon*, 248.

19. Stoloff, "Fatty Arbuckle and the Black Sox," 10.

REFERENCES

Banner, Lois W. *American Beauty*. New York: Knopf, 1983.

Berlant, Lauren. *The Queen of America Goes to Washington City: Essays on Sex and Citizenship*. Durham, N.C: Duke University Press, 1997.

Bordo, Susan. *Unbearable Weight: Feminism, Western Culture, and the Body*. Berkeley: University of California Press, 1993.

Butler, Judith. *Gender Trouble: Feminism and the Subversion of Identity*. New York: Routledge, 1990.

Edmonds, Andy, *Frame-Up! The Shocking Scandal That Destroyed Hollywood's Biggest Star*. New York: Avon, 1991.

Fowler, Gene. *Father Goose: The Story of Mack Sennett*. New York: Covici-Friede, 1934.

Freud, Sigmund. *Three Essays on the Theory of Sexuality*. Translated by James Strachey. New York: Basic Books, 1975.

Fussell, Betty Harper. *Mabel: Hollywood's First I-Don't-Care Girl*. New York: Limelight Editions, 1992.

Garber, Marjorie. *Vested Interests: Cross-Dressing and Cultural Anxiety*. New York: HarperPerennial, 1993.

Hansen, Miriam, *Babel and Babylon: Spectatorship in American Silent Film*. Cambridge, Mass.: Harvard University Press, 1991.

Kipnis, Laura. *Bound and Gagged: Pornography and the Politics of Fantasy in America*. New York: Grove, 1996.

Kunhardt, Philip B., Philip Kunhardt, Jr., and Peter W. Kunhardt. *P. T. Barnum: America's Greatest Showman*. New York: Knopf, 1995.

Mayne, Judith. *The Woman at the Keyhole: Feminism and Women's Cinema.* Bloomington: Indiana University Press, 1990.

Moon, Michael, and Eve Kosofsky Sedgwick. "Divinity: A Dossier, A Performance Piece, A Little-Understood Emotion." In *Tendencies*, by Sedgwick, 215–51. Durham, N.C: Duke University Press, 1993. [see chapter 15 of this volume]

Oderman, Stuart. *Roscoe "Fatty" Arbuckle: A Biography of the Silent Film Comedian, 1887–1933.* Jefferson, N.C.: McFarland, 1994.

Saper, Craig. "Scandalography: From Fatty's Demise to Lacan's Rise." From *The Abject America.* Special issue of *Lusitania* 1, no. 4 (1994).

Stewart, Susan. *On Longing: Narratives of the Miniature, the Gigantic, the Souvenir, the Collection.* Durham, N.C.: Duke University Press, 1993.

Stoloff, Sam. "Fatty Arbuckle and the Black Sox: Stars and Scandals, 1919–1921." Ph.D. diss. draft. Cornell University, 1994.

Young, Robert, Jr. *Roscoe "Fatty" Arbuckle: A Bio-Bibliography.* Westport, Conn.: Greenwood, 1994.

9 Setting Free the Bears

Refiguring Fat Men on Television

JERRY MOSHER

Robert De Niro made headlines in 1980 when he gained sixty pounds to play boxer Jake La Motta in *Raging Bull,* a virtuoso performance of bodily sacrifice that earned him an Academy Award. Over the course of the film, De Niro's lean, compact features expanded into a bloated mass, conveying La Motta's decline in a spectacle of corporeal dissolution. By the time he accepted his award De Niro had lost the weight, itself an extraordinary achievement that went largely unheralded.

Around the same time, 5-foot-10, 260-pound George Wendt was auditioning for a television situation comedy that would take place in a Boston bar called Cheers. The show's producers, impressed by Wendt's size and self-effacing demeanor, gave him the part of Norm Peterson, a hapless itinerant accountant who spends most of his time on a barstool drowning his sorrows in beer. Wendt did not have to gain any weight for the part; instead, he was encouraged to maintain that weight—in spite of his publicized attempts to diet—for eleven years.[1]

I do not offer these anecdotes to compare the respective talents of De Niro and Wendt, but rather to illustrate the very different physical demands of film and television performance. The film medium's ability to spectacularize even the most mundane characteristics works against actors with excessive bodies, whose appearance on the big screen may overwhelm a scene; fat actors in film are thus usually relegated to playing clowns, grotesques, "heavies," and minor character roles. Television's small screen, on the other hand, is friendlier to fat, making it appear more ordinary. A given show is transmitted into households over months and perhaps years; television's seriality allows for a slower development of physical nuance and encourages viewers to regard its characters as "real people," creating a verisimilitude that contributes to the fusion of actor and role.[2] The au-

thenticity inherent in this conflation renders fat television actors as iconic, deviant, and yet ordinary, positioning them as highly visible models of the often contradictory forces that figure fat men in America.

Since the 1950s both film and television have privileged method acting, a characteristically American practice that emphasizes a character's individual traits and minimizes his or her social and political dimensions. Method acting conflates actor and character by requiring the actor to construct a realistic psychological condition for the character, and thus to make his or her body deny the character's textuality. This attention to the psychological construction of the self positions Wendt's excessive body as a physical symptom of the individual, a character defect that facilitates the easy identification of "Norm" among the many characters of *Cheers'* ensemble cast. But because such a psychological reading overlooks the social and political dimensions of the body, it suppresses fat's capacity for social articulation.

The conflation of fat actor and character naturalizes the fat body's performativity and elides the expectations and narratives associated with fat—narratives that often reduce corporeal difference to the symptomatic and invite speculation on how fat people got that way. For the fat person who faces such narratives on a daily basis, fat performativity is a matter not of choosing which body one will inhabit each day but rather, in Judith Butler's words, of "reiterating or repeating the norms by which one is constituted." Such norms cannot be willfully ignored; they animate and contain the embodied subject, but they are also "the resources from which resistance, subversion, and displacement are to be forged."[3] The name of Wendt's character on *Cheers* thus takes on particular significance, for it establishes the character's political iconicity and the performativity expected from him: though marginalized for his corporeal deviance, the name *Norm* positions him as average, in the realm of the ordinary and mundane. Within this contradictory schema lies the potential for comedy that *Cheers* and Wendt so successfully realized.

Because women's fat is measured against a hegemonic ideal of beauty so powerful that any variation from it is considered a personal deficiency or aggressive act, the fat man's depiction as "ordinary" suggests that fat men are held to a standard less severe and more forgiving. Nevertheless, American men are increasingly succumbing to eating disorders and the use of cosmetic surgery to correct corporeal deviations, and they have never been immune to the persuasions of the multi-billion-dollar diet and beauty industries. The damage these industries have inflicted on women's bodies and self-image continues to be documented and resisted, and fat, as

Susie Orbach's 1978 book proclaimed, remains a potent feminist issue.[4] But fat is a men's issue, too, and its role in the changing constructs of men's bodies and patriarchal privilege is worthy of further study.

By examining the televisual representations and performativities of fat actors and characters in prime time—the three hours between 8 and 11 P.M. when the television industry's financial and artistic risks are greatest—I hope to uncover some of the norms and narratives that figure the fat male body in America. After a brief look at the historical precedents and cultural contexts for fat men on television, I examine four shows spanning the last thirty years—*Cannon* (1971–76), *What's Happening!!* (1976–79), *Cheers* (1982–93), and *Roseanne* (1988–97)—to illustrate their distinct strategies of constructing and containing the fat man. Finally, I explore how television viewers' interpretations and cultural productions can circumvent these containment strategies, creating spaces of reception in which the multivalency of fat men's televisual representations is emphasized.

HISTORICAL PRECEDENTS

The contemporary adage that in a society of abundance only the privileged can afford to be thin is amply demonstrated by American television series' representations of fat men. From bus driver Ralph Kramden in *The Honeymooners* (1952–57) to construction worker and mechanic Dan Conner in *Roseanne* (1988–97), fat men on television have tended to be working class.[5] Even when the fat men are detectives (Frank Cannon, Nero Wolfe) or white-collar employees (Norm Peterson, Drew Carey), they often are rumpled and disheveled, existing on the margins of corporate culture.

Fat men usually appear in the situation comedy, which provides the narrative space for plenty of fat jokes but also positions the home as a refuge from an increasingly fragmented culture, flattening social contradictions into everyday personal experience. The fat man's retreat to the domestic sphere is reflected in the surnames of Ralph Kramden (crammed in) and Archie Bunker, self-proclaimed kings of their castles whose layers of fat buffered them from the world and assimilated social turmoil into the more visual and understandable realm of individual corporeal deviance. Kramden, a figure of blue-collar alienation in an increasingly corporate culture, had by 1952 established the fat white male body as a televisual symbol of downward mobility.[6] By the time Archie Bunker appeared in *All in the Family* (1971–79) amid civil rights struggles and the growing feminist movement, the distended paunch had taken on the considerable

A figure of blue-collar alienation in an increasingly corporate culture, *The Honeymooners'* Ralph Kramden (Jackie Gleason) in the early 1950s established the fat white male body as a televisual symbol of downward mobility. *The Honeymooners,* publicity still. (Courtesy CBS Inc.)

burden of embodying the growing alienation of white men in general. (Though *All in the Family*'s creators, Norman Lear and Bud Yorkin, soon offered the similarly proportioned Fred Sanford as Archie's cantankerous African American counterpart in *Sanford and Son* [1972–77], the Sanfords' ghetto junkyard offered little mobility in any direction.) In Bunker's paunch—a corporeal display of deviance easily translatable to the small screen—fat was established as a televisual symbol of white heterosexual masculinity losing its definition, rendered soft and impotent.[7]

Unlike the lean, well-ordered patriarchs of 1950s–70s situation comedies such as *Father Knows Best, Leave It to Beaver, The Donna Reed Show, My Three Sons,* and *The Brady Bunch,* Kramden and Bunker found it increasingly difficult to exercise patriarchal control within the home. The "managerial patriarchs" had demonstrated how the middle-class WASP family could be successfully governed with proper corporate managerial skills[8]—skills that the blue-collar Kramden and Bunker, who could not even manage their own bodies, did not possess. Moreover, women's increasing presence in the workplace had already begun to challenge any patriarchal claims to rule in the home, as men could no longer assume special domestic rights and privileges based on their unique economic contributions. If a man was no longer a breadwinner for his family, these men asked, then what was a man?

This "crisis of masculinity," of course, is not a recent phenomenon, though its historical precedents have been suppressed in order to cast hysteria as strictly feminine. But there is a new development: the male body has supplanted the home as the site in which patriarchy is being contested. Studies of the male nude in art have demonstrated how patriarchy has maintained its power over the centuries by hiding the literal penis, thereby empowering the symbolic phallus and the imaginary ideal of masculinity.[9] Today, media representations of the "phallic male," most popularly manifested in the cinematic hard-bodied action hero, reveal a body under siege, more an object of punishment than of strength.

While the hiding of the penis privileges and empowers men, it also alienates them from their own bodies. Alienation is particularly acute in the fat male, whose penis is reduced in proportion to his body size, or is rendered invisible by his protruding belly. One fat man attests in *The Secret Lives of Fat People,* "All my life I've felt that my penis was too small. Having five children hasn't helped—and I guess that's part of the reason I wanted a lot of children. My stomach is just too big. Even when I have an erection, I can't see my penis."[10]

The two "poles" that characterize so many representations of masculinity and the male body are, as the film historian Peter Lehman notes, "the awesome phallic spectacle of power" and the "vulnerable and frequently comic image of its failed opposite"—in other words, the hard and the soft.[11] As hard-bodied cowboys and private eyes, following the managerial patriarchs, began to fade from television programming in the 1970s, increasing numbers of soft-bodied males came to populate the airwaves: henpecked husbands, beleaguered dads, couch potatoes, slackers. The fat and flaccid male body proved to be a handy visual metaphor for the impotence of patriarchal power and masculinity under siege: large and vulnerable, the fat male body became a recognizable symbol of insecure male performativity, its phallic potential buried under folds of flesh.

The impulse to exploit fat's visibility while hiding its raw appearance invests it with a pornographic signification that fat actors are forced to suppress, limiting their range of acceptable performativity. (Because fat television actors are rarely seen with their shirts off, the exposure of their flesh retains a shock value that is usually used toward humorous ends.) Efforts to contain the fat male body and its sexuality derive from the fear that the sexualization of fat people turns them into grotesques; often well-intentioned, these containment strategies pretend to protect fat people from the possibility of degradation or exploitation.[12] Ultimately, however, they serve only to return fat—and fat desire—to the closet. Invisibility is the performativity most expected from fat; the fat actor is thus saddled with the daunting task of playing both elephant and magician—a huge, docile animal that must make itself disappear.

Stereotypes offer the path of least resistance for such expectations, restricting fat actors to a narrow range of roles that thwart full expression of human vitality. These include the bumbling oaf (Kramden, Bunker, Sanford, Norm Peterson, Drew Carey, the Skipper on *Gilligan's Island,* Hoss Cartwright on *Bonanza,* Rerun on *What's Happening!!*), the effete servant (Mr. French on *Family Affair, Mr. Belvedere*), and the discriminating gourmet (*Cannon, Nero Wolfe*). Identifying such stereotypes, the cultural critics Ellen Shohat and Robert Stam note, reveals oppressive patterns of representation and demonstrates that they are "not an error of perception, but rather a form of social control."[13] To insist on only "positive" images of fat men, however, overlooks the fact that they can at times be as pernicious as overtly degrading images, providing a facade to veil paternalism. Characters are not unitary essences to be measured by their fidelity to an imaginary ideal, such as the positive or the realistic. Rather, they are fictive-discursive constructs; an exaggerated faith in realism ignores the fact that television shows are inevitably fabrications shaped by multiple socio-ideological discourses.

More important than the mimetic image, Shohat and Stam argue in their study of multiculturalism and the media, is "the actual or figural social voice or discourse speaking 'through' the image."[14] As several decades of historical precedents have demonstrated, getting significant screen time does not always guarantee the fat character an empowered position of enunciation. And even when a show's ostensible goal is to portray the struggle and dignity of fat experience, the lighting, sound, camera placement, point of view, and other elements of the mise-en-scène can unwittingly suture the viewer into a "sizist" perspective. My analysis therefore encompasses not only narrative structure and genre conventions but also televisual style, to consider how television translates mediations of social power into registers of mise-en-scène that figure the fat male body's potential for social articulation.

CANNON: A MATTER OF COMPETENCE

Because he shunned the situation comedy, William Conrad—one of the earliest fat actors to star in a television drama—proved especially challenging to strategies of televisual containment. Conrad's earnest, workmanlike performance as private detective Frank Cannon on *Cannon* (1971–76) clearly set out to overturn two decades' worth of bumbling, incompetent fat male television characters. Working outside the situation comedy gave Conrad the freedom to play a fat man who was more than an object of derision; Cannon had serious duties to perform and he accomplished them with a gruff, matter-of-fact dignity. Though Cannon always solved the crime, the show nevertheless suffered from the confused, contradictory impulses of television producers who sought to market the novelty of a fat private eye while trying to suppress his body and sexuality.

The television private eye genre had already grown stale by the late 1960s, and producers attempted to inject life into the genre with new angles, introducing unlikely detectives such as the blind Longstreet (1971–72), the paraplegic Ironside (1967–75), and the priest Sarge (1971–72). The gimmick in the latter two shows served to restrict the bodies of their large leading men, Raymond Burr and George Kennedy. Conrad was another improbable choice to play a television sleuth. He had become well known as the deep, authoritative voice of Marshal Matt Dillon on the radio version of *Gunsmoke* (1952–61), but when the series moved to television Conrad was deemed too fat to play Dillon. James Arness thus went on to star in the longest-running television series of all time (1955–75). As radio plays disappeared, Conrad found few jobs in the new televisual medium: "For 15 years before *Cannon* I couldn't get much work as an actor because I was too fat and unattractive. I'm 53 years old, 5-foot-9 inches tall, look like an overfed walrus, and I'm bald to boot. Producers took one look at me and ran."[15]

Cannon's typical plots positioned the fat detective's own body as the largest obstacle in his pursuit of criminals, and built suspense around the ingenious ways Cannon managed to do the work of hard-bodied action

William Conrad in *Cannon*. The show's containment of Conrad's body depends on frequent camera shots from the neck up. *Cannon*, publicity still. (Courtesy Viacom)

heroes despite his physical disadvantage. Explanations for Cannon's size and his avoidance of romance were established at the show's outset: he was a gourmet chef who charged his clients high fees in order to indulge his own expensive tastes in food, and he was a widower, still grieving for his wife and infant son years after an auto accident had claimed their lives. Promotional spots focused on Conrad's size: "Bigger than life. That's William Conrad. As private eye Cannon. Big excitement every week."[16] Conrad himself reasoned that adult viewers watched Cannon because they "see him as one of their own kind making it, not some stereotyped Hollywood god but the guy they get into the sack with every night,"[17] an equation of male fat with the plebian everyman established by characters such as Ralph Kramden and Archie Bunker.

Just as it was once common to see fat used to symbolize an excess of wealth and power (as in the greedy patriarchs of Depression-era films), today it is not uncommon to see it employed in the body of the discriminating, educated gourmet to symbolize an excess of knowledge. Cannon, a veritable warehouse of information, is revealed to be more than merely competent; he is an *expert* at detective work, as well as cooking, billiards, shooting, and driving. Cannon spends a large amount of time in his car—not a sleek sports car but a huge Lincoln Continental—and his driving skills are showcased in nearly every show. The car not only enables Cannon to perform the obligatory chase scenes so difficult for him to do on foot; it also provides a protective hard body to encase his soft flesh, and keeps his large belly out of sight.[18]

The containment of Conrad's body and sexuality is evident even in *Cannon*'s title sequence. Its graphics and music are similar to that of *Mannix* (1968–75), a traditional private eye show that starred former football player Mike Connors. Whereas *Mannix*'s title sequence shows the star leaping off a balcony to tackle a suspect, running across a bridge, and embracing a woman, *Cannon*'s titles reveal only Conrad's face within a round, static frame. This visual is consistent with Cannon's reputation as a "thinking person's detective," the cerebral sleuth whose uncanny powers of deduction must compensate for his lack of speed and agility.

The show's containment of Conrad's excessive body depends on the frequent employment of shots from the neck up, suggesting a mind/body dichotomy typical of the common representations and experience of fat in which the body is regarded, according to Marcia Millman, as "an unwanted appendage of the head-self." In *Such a Pretty Face,* Millman notes that fat people often focus on the face because it possesses a "high degree of synthesis and unity" and is usually the last part of the body to be affected by weight gain.[19] This disembodiment is extended to the show's reliance on Conrad's deep, powerful voice to compensate for the weakness of his soft flesh—an unusual strategy in the action genre, which tends to privilege body over voice. Indeed, suggests the film historian Yvonne Tasker, the action genre is often characterized as literally and figuratively "dumb": narrative frequently is accomplished by enacting spectacle rather than by speaking dialogue.[20] Cannon's deep and frequent utterances thus serve to further establish the primacy of his intellect and the repression of his body.

Cannon nonetheless proved to be the most physical performance of Conrad's career. Though the show quickly established that the fat detective could keep up with hard-bodied criminals, extratextual speculation about Conrad's weight and his ability to perform the role continued throughout its six-year run. Typical was this anecdote from *TV Guide:* "Just before the series made its debut in 1971, Bill had a healthy and glowing 230 pounds neatly distributed on his 5-foot-9 frame. . . . Now, however, with almost two full seasons behind him, Conrad seems to have ballooned up to the 260- or 270-pound class—depending on whether you catch him before or after dinner."[21] The conflation of fat actor and character served to promote the show: unlike Raymond Burr (paraplegic detective Ironside) and James Franciscus (blind detective Longstreet), whose disabilities were only fictional, Conrad's real-life struggles with his weight added another dimension of drama to *Cannon*, which cracked the Nielsen Top Ten in the 1973–74 season. Conrad never lost the weight, and he went on to play another fat television detective: the bookish and reclusive Nero Wolfe (1981), who hired assistants to do the chasing for him. Conrad's final television series, airing from 1987 to 1990, erased any doubts about the performativity producers expected from him: it was called *Jake and the Fatman*.

WHAT'S HAPPENING!!: TUNNEL VISION

By the late 1970s, the political edge displayed in the Norman Lear–Bud Yorkin situation comedy *All in the Family* had been blunted in weaker spinoffs such as *Maude* (1972–78), *Good Times* (1974–79), and *The Jeffersons* (1975–85). To get their brand of racial humor across to family-oriented prime-time audiences, Lear and Yorkin continued to rely on the "crusty but benign" central character: outspoken, irascible, but ultimately harmless.[22] Fat provided a convenient, visible "softening" of such characters, as evidenced in the girth of Archie Bunker (Carroll O'Connor), Fred Sanford (Redd Foxx), Maude Findlay (Bea Arthur), and Florida Evans (Esther Rolle). In this infantilizing strategy, the fat body served to contain excessive orality, implying that such characters were not threatening but rather were "all mouth," and thus incapable of action.

When applied to African American characters, the approach drew particular criticism for relying on the stereotypes of minstrelsy, such as the buffoonish coon and the fat mammy. Such was the case with the Yorkin-produced *What's Happening!!* (1976–79), a feckless situation comedy about lower-middle-class urban blacks that featured no fewer than three fat characters: the clownish underachiever Rerun (Fred Berry), the surly waitress Shirley (Shirley Hemphill), and the sensible "Mama," Mrs. Thomas (Mabel King). Though it drew more viewers than the African American sitcoms *Good Times* and *The Jeffersons*, the show was critically panned as "Amos 'n' Andy for kids and teenyboppers" and a "dreary search for jokes about fat blacks."[23]

In its "color blind" approach to comedy,[24] *What's Happening!!*'s frequent use of fat jokes offers an instructive example of how Hollywood employs one marginalized group to unwittingly oppress another. Such a practice is not uncommon; as the film historian Charles Ramírez Berg has noted, Hollywood social problem films dealing with the "building up" of a particular ethnic or racial group similarly tend to "partake in a strange kind of Other tunnelvision, losing sight in the process of their insensitive

What's Happening!! affords Rerun (Fred Berry) plenty of opportunities to dance, allowing him to break out of its oppressive sizist narratives into a space in which his body is not excessive, but graceful and precisely controlled. *What's Happening!!* publicity still. (Courtesy ABC Inc.)

stereotyping of any but the focused-upon ethnic or racial group."[25] By frequently succumbing to the easy fat joke, *What's Happening!!*'s tunnel vision ignored the fact that being fat in America may be as great a social and economic liability as being black.

Described by *Variety* as a "fantasy world created by whites and peopled by benign, friendly 'darkies,'" *What's Happening!!* was roundly condemned for failing to address issues of race.[26] But because the show's critics viewed fat simply as an object of derision, they failed to consider fat's social implications and cultural specificity. African American culture has traditionally been accommodating to fat; as recent rap groups like the Fat Boys and as Sir Mix-A-Lot's hit single "Baby Got Back" (1992) attest, fat does not have to be a source of shame: it can be claimed and asserted as a positive sign of cultural difference. In this light, dieting may be viewed skeptically as an assimilationist attempt to conform to white culture's restrictive corporeal ideals. Though the fat characters on *What's Happening!!* are given little social articulation, their occasional swapping of fat jokes suggests that fat should not be dismissed as merely a function of class or ignorance—in this context, fat carries its own cultural currency and self-identifying specificity.

Despite being the target of most of *What's Happening!!*'s fat jokes, Fred Berry quickly established Rerun as the star of the show, suggesting an appeal that went beyond mere buffoonery. Rerun continually fails high school courses (and hence must "rerun" them), but he is an extremely agile dancer who often gets the girl, beating out his skinnier and less charismatic friends Raj and Dwayne. The show affords Rerun plenty of opportunities to dance, allowing him to break out of its often oppressive sizist narratives into a space in which his body is not excessive but precisely controlled. Attempts to discredit these performances as merely coonish minstrelsy are not unfounded; nevertheless, they seem reductive, for they adhere to a narrow conception of "positive images" that does not account for the body's capacity for articulation. Indeed, Berry's pre-Rerun career as a professional dancer (including stints on *Soul Train* and in the Los Angeles dance group the Lockers) suggests he is more than an ethnic dupe; he is one of the few televisual fat men whose dancing skills are frequently and seriously expended to express physical grace.

CHEERS: THE CLASSICAL AND THE GROTESQUE

The fat body's capacity for grotesquerie offers the potential of subversion, as demonstrated in the work of Mikhail Bakhtin, who positions the grotesque body—soft, oral, always in the act of becoming—within the subversive pleasures of the carnival.[27] This is unapologetic fat: fat that exaggerates, rather than conceals, the bulges and orifices of the vulgar lower strata, site of sex and defecation. The grotesque body's inversion of the hard, closed classical body's spiritual upper strata is the stuff of comedy, in which the clown—frequently fat—reconfigures the threatening forces of the cosmos and death within the physicality of his own body. As the film and television historian Virginia Wright Wexman notes, the clown "conquers fear by incorporating it."[28]

Because of their association with bodily functions and especially reproduction, grotesque bodies often come in pairs, as evidenced by comedy teams like Laurel and Hardy.[29] Offering its own pair of grotesques—accountant Norm Peterson and postal carrier Cliff Claven, the "boys at the end of the bar"—*Cheers* (1982–93) is one of the few television series to have exploited the comedic potential of opposing classical and grotesque bodies. Though other ensemble comedies have cast actors and actresses of

As a member of *Cheers'* "Greek chorus," beleaguered accountant Norm Peterson (George Wendt) exposes the pretensions of the lean, athletic bartenders and provides a source of identification for the viewing audience. *Cheers,* publicity still. (Courtesy Paramount)

varying body types, *Cheers'* setting in a bar—a place of oral pleasure and sexual rendezvous—emphasizes the characters' relation to drinking, eating, and sex, thereby staking out the body as a place where these pleasures are either encouraged or denied. Its casting strategy can thus be seen as pitting endomorphs versus ectomorphs, the grotesque versus the classical.

From its outset, the show's creators (MTM veterans Jim Burrows and Glen and Les Charles) conceptualized Norm and Cliff as *Cheers'* "Greek chorus," an audience for the activities of the employees.[30] Offering a stark contrast to the lean, classical bodies of bartenders Sam and Diane, the grotesque pair of Norm and Cliff continually expose the bartenders' pretensions and provide a source of identification and pleasure for the viewing audience. Though Norm is a frequent object of fat jokes, his positioning within this chorus gives his size a social dimension capable of inverting normative conceptions of the body: when he is in top form, fat becomes "the norm" and the lean, classical body is rendered deviant and marginal. Characteristic of the carnival's celebration of vitality, the 260-pound Norm enjoys making a public display of his eating and drinking.[31] Like other televisual fat men, however, his sexual appetite is contained: he is married to a woman whom viewers never see, an absence that provides a convenient way to avoid the visualization of Norm's (hetero)sexual life, as well as an excuse for him to avoid the few women who approach him.

In Cheers' spatial arrangement, the rectangular bar at center stage acts as symbolic social barrier, keeping Norm's and Cliff's grotesque bodies at the margin while centering the classical bodies of Sam and Diane. Norm and Cliff usually assume regular positions on the same stools; if Norm, Cliff, or both are not sitting at the bar at stage right when the show begins, viewers can expect they will be entering from stage left at any moment. When Norm enters the bar, the patrons, employees, and even some audience members yell "Norm!," a recurring motif of the place "where everybody knows your name." Cheers has other regular patrons, but this ritual is extended only to Norm, who, as his name suggests, stands in for everyman. As Norm saunters to his stool, an employee or patron usually asks how he's doing. Norm's response is routinely self-deprecating, invoking his life, his wife, or his need for a beer. So ritualized is Norm's entrance that some *Cheers* fans maintain lists of these "Normisms."[32]

When *Cheers* began its eleven-year run in 1982, notions of what constituted the working-class job were shifting from blue-collar factory work and physical labor to nonunion service industry and information age "McJobs"—usually low-paying sedentary work that has contributed to the increasing obesity of Americans. As an itinerant accountant, Norm signifies an important change in the sitcom's representation of fat men's occupational roles: Ralph Kramden's bus driver and Archie Bunker's loading dock worker—both holding union jobs that require a measure of physical strength—have given way to Norm's hapless information-age worker, a glorified data entry clerk stuck in a padded office cubicle.[33] With the demise of skilled labor positions, notes the critic Richard Dyer, "the values of masculine physicality are harder to maintain straightfacedly and unproblematically,"[34] frequently resulting in desolate alienation or tongue-in-cheek self-deprecation—such as the Normism.

Whereas the excessive bodies of erudite gourmets such as Frank Cannon and Nero Wolfe symbolized the storage of wisdom, Norm's body reflects what Jean Baudrillard calls the "age of empty inflation," emblematic of the bloat of information systems storing useless data.[35] Though Norm's excessive body carries the subversive potential of the premodern carnival, his dull information-age job continually enforces the well-ordered classical ideal. He turns for solace to Cheers, where his grotesquerie can be unleashed amid an ample supply of food and drink. Dulling his subversive potential, however, is his role first and foremost as *consumer,* the average guy who serves as the norm for the consuming audience.[36]

Since the 1930s, theories of addictive eating have linked it to nostalgia; fat people hope to return to a past in which food was satisfying and comforting.[37] The song lyrics and Victorian imagery of *Cheers'* title sequence emphasize its function as a place of nostalgic escape, and the bar provides typical sitcom shelter from a fragmented, incoherent culture. Norm and Cliff's retreat to Cheers from their emasculating jobs and troubled relationships can be seen as a search for the primeval banquet, which is simply another term for Bakhtin's carnival—a premodern celebration of vitality. Today, for an increasingly fat population alienated by a culture of slimness, a communal banquet "where everybody knows your name" may be just as enticing.

ROSEANNE: LOVIN' LARGE

Roseanne (1988–97) eschews any notions of escape, revealing the hardships of being fat and working class in corporate America. The show is frequently linked to *The Honeymooners* and *All in the Family* as a milestone in sitcom representations of the working class, with its class consciousness embodied in the excessive paunches of another pair of grotesques: blue-collar couple Roseanne and Dan Conner. To the show's credit, issues of class do not stop there but permeate every aspect of the Conners' existence. Significantly, this warts-and-all approach does not spare Roseanne's and Dan's sexualities, which are treated—like everything else on the show—both comedically and poignantly.

Created around the considerable talents of former stand-up comedian Roseanne Barr, the show overthrows any pretense of patriarchal privilege in the home: Roseanne has inherited the throne as beleaguered king of the castle, her sister and sidekick Jackie playing Ed Norton to Roseanne's Ralph Kramden. Drawing on Bakhtin, critics have noted how Roseanne's role as "unruly woman" and "domestic goddess" depends on the use of her excessive body as spectacle to subvert patriarchal control.[38] The over-the-top grotesquerie of the early seasons, however, evolved into a performance tempered by wit and intelligence. Roseanne's unruliness was reined in by her duties as a mother of three, which she took seriously and endured with a good-natured sarcasm.

Roseanne's exceeding charisma and intelligence (as well as her many controversies and makeovers) tend to overshadow the work of John Good-

Roseanne and Dan Conner (Roseanne and John Goodman) rub their large bodies against each other while passing through the living room or dealing with a family crisis in the kitchen, revealing a tactile sensitivity rarely seen in televisual couples. *Roseanne,* publicity still. (Courtesy Capital Cities/ABC Inc.)

man, who within the constraints of the situation comedy has created a sensitive and complex portrayal of a working-class father who is neither know-it-all nor buffoon. (Appropriately, Goodman describes his college theatrical training as "Stanislavsky and Pabst Blue Ribbon.")[39] Dan Conner is not only knowing in the ways of youth culture and motorcycles; he is a fat man whom viewers actually see at work, forging an identity outside the home. Though he often is seen eating and drinking, Goodman and the show's writers must have realized that there was not enough room on the show for two unruly grotesques, so he does not overexaggerate the rowdy aspect of his character. (Goodman's film characters have leaned more toward the grotesques and "heavies" typical of fat men's big screen roles. Television's small screen, in contrast, has allowed him to explore the nuances of fat performativity: the expressive use of his jowls, the emphatic waving of his bearlike paws, the suggestive movements of his girth.) Nor does Goodman play the callow, henpecked husband so familiar to sitcom viewers for decades. Playing self-acknowledged second fiddle to Roseanne allows Goodman the freedom to explore the intricacies of fatherhood and work without carrying the burden of political iconicity, as was the case with Kramden and especially Archie Bunker.[40] Indeed, Goodman has likened his role to that of Alice Kramden, who frequently got off the best lines while enduring a domineering spouse.[41]

The physical grace Goodman brings to his performance as Dan Conner is quickly dismissed by the actor, who begrudgingly discusses his weight but fears that such talk minimizes his acting talents. Goodman is aware of the invisibility expected of fat performativity, which he views in terms of the social experience of trying to fit in: "A fat guy that moves around like that doesn't think of himself as primarily a fat guy moving around like that. He's just a guy trying to find the groove like anyone else."[42] The self-deprecating humor and depressive streak Goodman brings to Dan Conner, the film critic Lewis Cole notes, reveals the fine line Goodman walks between acting "big," which makes Dan heroic, and acting "fat," which makes Dan tragic. Indeed, Dan's weight "buoys him when he's happy and sinks him when he's sad."[43] Dan's sensitivity may be relative to and accentuated by his wife's exaggerated vulgarity, and his girth and willing subordinance to Roseanne certainly link him to earlier televisual representations of masculinity in crisis. Indeed, Dan suffered his own crisis in the show's last season, as he temporarily separated from Roseanne and then suffered a heart attack. Nevertheless, he is a fully realized fat man, both hard and soft, secure enough in his masculinity to openly fret about his relationships with his mother, children, and employees while letting Roseanne run the house, and willing to acknowledge a libido that frequently finds fulfillment in the Conner bedroom.

Much has been made of *Roseanne*'s straightforward portrayals of its gay and lesbian characters; its representations of fat desire, however, may be even more extraordinary. Roseanne and Dan Conner are a couple who have been married for twenty years but still find the time to have sex, no matter where the kids are or how much money is (or isn't) in the bank. They understand that the fat body is not immune to the sense of touch: they use their excessive bodies to rub against one another while passing through the living room, or to reach around one another in the midst of a family crisis in the kitchen, revealing a tactile sensitivity rarely seen in televisual couples. Sex in the Conners' marriage is not the irritant or source of neurosis it is for most sitcom couples; though the show is usually associated with other dysfunctional television families such as the Simpsons and the Bundys, on *Roseanne*, Cole observes, "the family is healthy; it's the judgments of the society around them that create discord and chaos."[44] Dan and Roseanne are not immune to these judgments and occasionally make attempts to diet (e.g., "I'm Hungry," February 13, 1990), but for the most part they use their bodies unapologetically, to engage in pleasures both subversive and sensuous. Their sexuality is not unthinkable; rather, they are unthinkable without it.

FAT RECEPTION AND THE PRODUCTION OF MEANING

"Who would you rather sit next to on the subway?" reads the heading above a still photo from *Seinfeld* depicting Jerry on the subway, sitting across from a naked fat man (*Seinfeld,* "The Subway," January 8, 1992). "If you said Jerry Seinfeld, then this might not be the page for you. If you said Ernie Sabella, then you have great taste in men[;] . . . if you don't find men of the flesh attractive, I suggest you move on. As for me, I worship every square inch of them."[45]

So begins one of the hundreds of home pages on the World Wide Web dedicated to admiration of the fat male, an electronic outgrowth of established hard-copy publications such as *Bulk Male, Bear,* and *American Bear.* Enthusiasts of fat men come in many sexualities and many shapes and sizes. A few websites are produced by women who admire fat men,[46] but most are maintained by men, assembled around three general categories: chubs and chubby chasers (fat men and their admirers), bears (large men with beards, body hair, or both) and their admirers, and gainers and encouragers (men seeking to become larger and their encouragers). Aside from an active disregard for normative discourses of beauty and health that seek to contain and eradicate fat, what is remarkable about a number of these sites is how they appropriate and recontextualize media representations—often televisual representations—of the fat male, presenting them as icons of fat desire that validate chub or bear culture and illustrate their classification schemes of body types and preferences.[47] The sites reveal the limitations of network television's attempts to suppress fat sexuality and desire, attempts that deny viewers' ability to produce meaning and, in the words of the cultural critic Henry Jenkins, "transform the experience of watching television into a rich and complex participatory culture."[48]

Television viewers typically operate from a position of marginality, lacking direct access to the means of cultural production; attempts to castigate fans of television shows as losers, social misfits, and mindless consumers, however, overlook the imagination and intelligence they incorporate into the viewing experience to produce pleasure. To conceptualize the pleasurable processes of television viewership, the media critic John Fiske draws

on Roland Barthes's twofold notion of pleasure—*plaisir* and *jouissance*.[49] Both are opposed to ideological control, but *plaisir* is a mundane pleasure particularly confirming of one's own identity (and an everyday pleasure more typical of television viewership), whereas *jouissance* is a more bodily pleasure—the pleasure of bliss, ecstasy, or orgasm. For fat admirers, watching Norm Peterson challenge the pretensions of *Cheers'* bartenders might provide a source of *plaisir*. The episode in which Norm must strip after losing a bet ("Bar Wars VII: The Naked Prey," March 18, 1993), on the other hand, might provide *jouissance;* indeed, the sexual desire the scene generates for fat admirers is noted on several websites.[50] As Fiske notes, "Sexual orgasm is the moment when the body escapes culture, or, at least, makes that escape seem possible."[51] The appropriation of the *Cheers* scene into a context of fat desire produces bodily pleasure while escaping the oppressive normative discourse that seeks to eradicate it. The polysemic potential of *Cheers'* text is thus multiplied by its many intertextual relations.

One of the earliest uses of *fan* to denote a devotion to commercial entertainment referenced women theatergoers, or "Matinee Girls," who, according to male critics, had "come to admire the actors rather than the plays."[52] A century later, fat admirers are hunting the airwaves with similar intent, "poaching" among the shows featuring their favorite fat icons. A male admirer of David Anthony Higgins, who played Ellen DeGeneres's fat sidekick Joe Farrell on *Ellen* (1994–98), stated: "I don't find her that funny, so he's the only reason I tune that show in. I love all the sexual innuendos he uses, and hope they will show him at least shirtless soon."[53]

Assuming that such male sexual responses to the male body are limited to homosexual or bisexual viewers would of course be misguided. Indeed, John Goodman's appearance on mainstream magazines' lists of "America's sexiest men" and on chubby chasers' top-ten lists suggests an appeal that produces a wide range of sexual responses. One *New York Times* writer noted Goodman's attraction for heterosexual men, explaining that Goodman is "the best friend we've always wanted, a guy who'll keep the bullies at bay, [and] make us feel manlier just by association."[54]

At the same time, most network shows' rigidity of gender roles and emphasis on desiring the opposite sex do leave an enormous space for queer reception and cultural production. As the queer theorist Alexander Doty notes, it is deviance from the demands of strict heterosexual paradigms that most often defines viewers' sexualized or gendered pleasures.[55] An awareness of this dynamic may account for the many television episodes that do encourage nonnormative sexualized or gendered responses and pleasures in straight viewers, such as the highly publicized kiss between Roseanne and another woman in a lesbian bar (*Roseanne,* "Don't Ask, Don't Tell," March 1, 1994). Among fat male characters, a notable episode involves Archie Bunker claiming to be a hero after giving mouth-to-mouth resuscitation to a woman in his cab, and then learning that she is a transvestite (*All in the Family,* "Archie the Hero," September 29, 1975); another involves Norm Peterson pretending to be gay in order to get an interior decorating job with some wealthy clients (*Cheers,* "Norm, Is That You?" December 8, 1988). Such episodes invite heterosexual viewers to consider the gender and sexuality of seemingly straight fat male characters as destabilized and fluid, and to formulate new responses that may or may not include pleasure.

Despite *Roseanne*'s groundbreaking portrayals, on television fat desire, like homosexuality, is still marginalized as deviant behavior, even when the fat desire involves straight heterosexual sex. The Conners' active mutual attraction can be easily rationalized because they *both* are fat (and hence can't do any better). Sex between thin and fat characters, however, is usually "explained" by the thin character's confusion, lack of self-esteem, or some other psychological condition or perversion that is ultimately cured or contained before consummation or the episode's end. For fat men on television, even straight sex is still taboo: a viewer is as likely to see an episode in which a seemingly heterosexual fat man is perceived to be homosexual as an episode that suggests he actually has sex with his wife or girlfriend.

Given the dearth of televisual fat males experiencing active sex lives, fat admirers sometimes feel compelled to construct imaginary erotic scenarios for them, a cultural production not uncommon among devoted fans.[56] "Slash," which designates the same-sex genre of these fan stories, frequently arouses controversy among fans and television producers, some of whom argue for maintaining characters' sexual orientation as given in the narrative. That orientation, however, is often unclear; and the assumption that *all* of their sexual activity would be heterosexual is culturally constructed, not inherent in their screen behavior.

Indeed, it does not require much of a stretch for viewers to envision a sexual relationship between, for example, the hulking Skipper and his "little buddy" on *Gilligan's Island.* In the case of *Cheers,* the producers' conception of Norm and Cliff as a "Greek chorus" and "the boys at the end of the bar" suggests a relationship that does not exclude the possibility of sexual intimacy. By bringing that possibility closer to reality, typical slash fiction, Jenkins notes, extends male homosocial desire "to a direct expression of homoerotic passion" and positions homosexuality in a larger social context.[57] In addition, it explores alternatives to a masculinity made normative in both heterosexual and homosexual cultures.

Many fat men are disappointed to find that fat-phobia is even more evident in gay culture than in heterosexual culture. A man thin by straight standards may be considered fat in gay culture, and dieting is common among gay men when they first come out.[58] The stereotype of the "thin homosexual" is so prevalent that it has even been spoofed on *Seinfeld* (1990–98), television's highest rated show in the 1990s, as Jerry's parents and friends occasionally question his sexuality because he is a thin, single man (see especially "The Outing," February 11, 1993). The identification of a singular gay male body type, thin and effeminate, proves to be just as reductive as are hard-bodied notions of heterosexual masculinity. Seinfeld's fears about his body image are thus rendered even more ironic by the website caption ("Who would you rather sit next to on the subway?"), for it positions the fat man, Ernie Sabella, as the more alluring object of desire.

The political activism of bear culture, as the bear historian Les Wright has documented, operates on three levels of identity formation: that of males, of homosexuals, and of self-identifying masculine gay men.[59] Bear culture's increasing visibility seeks to challenge not only heterosexist containment of male homosocial desire but more specifically gay male culture's privileging of the "twink"—the thin, smooth, buff young man—as an ideal of male beauty. Just as critics have proved the polarities of hard and soft inadequate to define fluid, dynamic notions of heterosexual masculinity, so bear activists hope to break down long-standing polarizations of gay male performativity that have historically separated into masculine/feminine dichotomies such as wolves and fairies, leathermen and queens. Because the term *bear* has many meanings and connotations even within bear culture, it is considered to be more of an attitude than a definable male type. Refusing to be reduced to mere fetishists, members of bear culture recognize the multivalent signification of fat men and their televisual representations.

Television's need to employ male fat as a visual shorthand for the "crisis of masculinity" as it simultaneously contains fat's performativities reveals the ambivalence and hypocrisy of American society's attitudes toward fat men. Television's depiction of male fat as novelty, as grotesquerie, or as deviance is often at odds with its positioning of the fat man, in an increasingly fat society, as ordinary, as everyman, as the norm. The frequent employment of the soft, fat male to represent the impotence of patriarchal power invests male fat with an effeminacy (or "sensitivity") for which the heterosexual masculine ideal has little tolerance. Representations of fat men thus are broadly drawn from contradictory impulses: they are rendered ordinary but deviant, average but grotesque, male but not masculine. While such reasoning may appear contrary or confused, it reflects the successful strategy of the multi-billion-dollar diet and beauty industries. Their continually new and improved technologies to eradicate fat guarantee its presence—and profits—as long as an estimated one-half of the adult population identifies itself as overweight.

Television producers' desire to induce humor with occasional sojourns into "deviance" does provide glimpses of fat subversive pleasure (such as Norm's grotesquerie or Roseanne and Dan's fat love), but the need to hide fat's raw appearance invests it with a pornographic signification that television must suppress. Hard-core fat pornography obliterates these restrictions and, as Laura Kipnis has demonstrated in her writings on contemporary pornography, performs a "social service" by revealing America's hypocrisy toward fat, commending bodies that defy social norms, and soliciting "an erotic identification with bodies that are unresponsive to social control."[60] Still, the tendency to relegate fat pornography, straight or otherwise, to the "fetish" section suggests again that fat sex and desire cannot be "ordinary," even if fat people are.

Because it must cater to both popular tastes and popular moralities, television provides a more visible battleground for the daily discourses that figure male fat and masculinity. While audiences may produce any number of readings, television is an exclusionary industry that tightly controls its channels of distribution. Producers and consumers remain discrete and widely separated categories, an imbalance of power that enables television shows to persuasively pull audiences into their ideological projects and ultimately contain the fat male body. Television viewers' openness to circumventing the medium's containment strategies can thus be seen, like fat pornography, as performing a social service. Their alternate readings express a sense of comfort with men's masculinity and bodies that is not subservient to the vogues of male attractiveness so prevalent in mainstream gay and heterosexual culture. As independent cultural productions, such readings complement the shows and reveal the space in which fat admiration and desire are welcome.

NOTES

I wish to extend my sincere thanks to Vivian Sobchack, Marc Siegel, and Daniel Hendrickson for their careful readings and helpful suggestions on earlier drafts of this essay.

1. *TV Guide* predicted in June 1988, "You'll be seeing less of George Wendt next season," but the weight loss was hardly discernible (Paul Francis, "On the Grapevine: Weight Watchers," *TV Guide*, June 18, 1988, A-2). *Entertainment Weekly* reported that during one season Wendt gained seventy-five pounds, "lost it during hiatus, then gained it back during the next season" (Entertainment Weekly, *The 100 Greatest Shows of All Time* [New York: Entertainment Weekly Books, 1998], 14).

2. David Marc and Virginia Wright Wexman have commented on Jackie Gleason's exceptional modes of performance, which established him as more than merely ordinary and distanced him from the plebian character Ralph Kramden. In his "presentational" mode, Gleason addressed the audience of his variety show as "himself" and demonstrated his considerable talents as showman and dancer; in his "documentary" mode, he cultivated his extratextual, "real-life" image as playboy and sportsman. However, most television actors identified with a highly recognizable character find it difficult to avoid typecasting within the medium's more limited range of roles; not surprisingly, after *Cheers* Wendt would go on to play bumbling oafs in *The George Wendt Show* (1995) and *The Naked Truth* (1997). See David Marc, *Demographic Vistas: Television in American Culture* (Philadelphia: University of Pennsylvania Press, 1984), 99–102, and Virginia Wright Wexman, "Returning from the Moon: Jackie Gleason, the Carnivalesque, and Television Comedy," *Journal of Film and Video* 42, no. 4 (1990): 20–32.

3. Judith Butler, "Critically Queer," *GLQ* 1, no. 1 (1993): 22.

4. Susie Orbach, *Fat Is a Feminist Issue: The Anti-Diet Guide to Permanent Weight Loss* (New York: Berkley, 1978).

5. Representations of fat bankers (such as Theodore Mooney on *The Lucy Show*, 1962–68) are throwbacks to the greedy, avaricious patriarchs of Depression-era films; today they have given way to the lean, mean corporate raider as memorably portrayed in the film *Wall Street* (1987) by Michael Douglas, who appropriated the suspenders from the older model but no longer needed them to hold up his trousers.

6. Studies have shown that fat people have less chance of being hired or promoted in the appearance-conscious service sector. Appearance is so important, one recent study concluded, "that businessmen sacrifice $1,000 in salary for every pound they are overweight" (Gina Kolata, "The Burdens of Being Overweight: Mistreatment and Misconceptions," *New York Times*, November 22, 1992, A1).

7. Dieting is such an institution in the United States that most American sitcoms sooner or later do a "dieting show." From early on, sitcoms showed that eating disorders affected men as well as women. In "Ralph's Diet" (a *Honeymooners* "lost episode," April 25, 1953), Ralph starves himself for a day and then succumbs to an eating binge more desperate than comic. In "Archie's Weighty Problem" (*All in the Family*, February 9, 1976), Archie is ready to binge when a ninety-two-year-old woman talks him out of it. Neither Kramden nor Bunker, of course, loses any weight.

8. Darrell Y. Hamamoto, *Nervous Laughter: Television Situation Comedy and Liberal Democratic Ideology* (New York: Praeger, 1989), 22–24.

9. See, for example, Barbara DeGenevieve, "Masculinity and Its Discontents,"

Camerawork 18, nos. 3–4 (1991): 3–5, and Abigail Solomon-Godeau, *Male Trouble: A Crisis in Representation* (New York: Thames and Hudson, 1997).

10. Mildred Klingman, *The Secret Lives of Fat People* (Boston: Houghton Mifflin, 1981), 111.

11. Peter Lehman, *Running Scared: Masculinity and the Representation of the Male Body* (Philadelphia: Temple University Press, 1993), 31. Recent efforts to revitalize American masculinity have struggled to make allowances for the postfeminist "sensitive male" without compromising the hard ideal. The cinematic hard body—most notably the spectacularized, overdetermined body of Arnold Schwarzenegger, who has alternated between "hard" action roles and "soft" comedies—was the focus of one such effort whose self-consciousness frequently bordered on parody. See Yvonne Tasker, *Spectacular Bodies: Gender, Genre, and the Action Cinema* (New York: Routledge, 1993), and Susan Jeffords, *Hard Bodies: Hollywood Masculinity in the Reagan Era* (New Brunswick, N.J.: Rutgers University Press, 1994). Another effort involved the search for the "inner warrior" advocated by the men's movement guru Robert Bly, who bemoaned the prevalence of soft males in America, noting "the lack of energy in them. They are life-preserving but not life-giving. Ironically, you often see these men with strong women" (*Iron John: A Book about Men* [Reading, Mass.: Addison-Wesley, 1990], 3).

12. Laura Kipnis, *Bound and Gagged: Pornography and the Politics of Fantasy in America* (New York: Grove, 1996), 110.

13. Ella Shohat and Robert Stam, *Unthinking Eurocentrism: Multiculturalism and the Media* (London: Routledge, 1994), 198.

14. Ibid., 214.

15. William Conrad, quoted in Anthony Davis, *TV's Greatest Hits* (London: Boxtree, 1988), 37.

16. Advertisement, quoted in Richard Meyers, *TV Detectives* (San Diego: A. S. Barnes; London: Tantivy, 1981), 162.

17. William Conrad, quoted in Dick Adler, "'How Old Bill Conrad?' Old Bill Conrad Fine—and Fat," *TV Guide,* March 3, 1973, 18–20.

18. The male action hero's frequent use of cars and guns as "penile extenders" can be seen as an attempt to close the gap between the penis and symbolic phallus—between insecure male performativity and the imaginary ideal of masculinity. See John Fiske, *Television Culture* (New York: Routledge, 1987), 210–11.

19. Marcia Millman, *Such a Pretty Face: Being Fat in America* (New York: Norton, 1980), 195.

20. Tasker, *Spectacular Bodies,* 6.

21. Adler, "'How Old Bill Conrad?'" 18.

22. J. Fred MacDonald, *Blacks and White TV: African Americans in Television Since 1948,* 2nd ed. (Chicago: Nelson-Hall, 1992), 186.

23. "Returning Network TV Programs," *Variety,* September 27, 1978, n.p.; Ralph Schoenstein, "Review: *What's Happening!!*" *TV Guide,* February 19, 1977, 36.

24. The show's producer, Bud Yorkin, told *TV Guide:* "The time has come when we don't have to put a color on what's funny. We're more sophisticated than that" (quoted in Al and Joanne Martinez, "Instant Rerun," *TV Guide,* April 2, 1977, 11).

25. Charles Ramírez Berg, "Bordertown, the Assimilation Narrative, and the Chicano Social Problem Film," in *Chicanos and Film: Representation and Resistance,* ed. Chon A. Noriega (Minneapolis: University of Minnesota Press, 1992), 37.

26. "Returning Network TV Programs," n.p.

27. See Mikhail Bakhtin, *Rabelais and His World,* trans. Hélène Iswolsky (1968; reprint, Bloomington: Indiana University Press, 1984).

28. Wexman, "Returning from the Moon," 24.

29. Ibid., 27.

30. Mark Christensen and Cameron Stauth, "Everybody Knows Their Names," *American Film* 10 (1984): 52.

31. The classical ideal encourages fat people to indulge in secret eating, which Mildred Klingman calls "the secret to staying fat. It is one of the ways in which fat people can go on a diet and still succeed in not losing any weight" (*The Secret Lives of Fat People,* 8).

32. See Raymond Chen, *Normisms,* 1996, <http://s9000.furman.edu/ejorgens/cheers/archives/normisms.html> (accessed April 15, 1998).

33. A successor to Norm Peterson is Drew Carey, star of *The Drew Carey Show* (1995–), a frustrated assistant personnel director in a Cleveland department store who takes hedonistic refuge in food and drink.

34. Richard Dyer, *Heavenly Bodies: Film Stars and Society* (London: BFI, 1987), 12.

35. Jean Baudrillard, *Fatal Strategies,* ed. Jim Fleming, trans. Philip Beitchman and W. G. J. Niesluchowski (New York: Semiotext(e); London: Pluto, 1990), 28. Like *Cheers'* Cliff Claven, postal carrier Newman, the surly fat man on *Seinfeld* (1990–98), continually complains about the overwhelming burden of processing a never-ending stream of junk mail.

36. Television delivers audiences to advertisers by glorifying consumption in both commercials and shows. But explanations of fat as merely a result of overconsumption are simplistic and reductive, as demonstrated in Baudrillard's problematic characterization of obesity as "deformity by excess of conformity" (*Fatal Strategies,* 27).

37. Hillel Schwartz, *Never Satisfied: A Cultural History of Diets, Fantasies, and Fat* (New York: Free Press, 1986), 307.

38. Kathleen Rowe, *The Unruly Woman: Gender and the Genres of Laughter* (Austin: University of Texas Press, 1995), 50–91.

39. John Goodman, quoted in Peter de Jonge, "Being the Big Guy," *New York Times Magazine,* February 10, 1991, 44.

40. As John Caldwell notes in *Televisuality: Style, Crisis, and Authority in American Television* ([New Brunswick, N.J.: Rutgers University Press, 1995], 44), *All in the Family* and other Lear-Yorkin shows "still had a political axe to grind, still believed in a recognizable package of progressive causes" and thus did not have "the blankness of intent" that characterizes recent dysfunctional family sitcoms such as *Roseanne, Married with Children* (1987–97), and *The Simpsons* (1989–).

41. Goodman claims the show's producers considered casting Audrey Meadows, who played Alice Kramden on *The Honeymooners,* as Dan's mother. See David Rensin, "Breakfast and Heartburn with John Goodman," *TV Guide,* December 28, 1991, 6.

42. John Goodman, quoted in de Jonge, "Being the Fat Guy," 49.

43. Lewis Cole, "Roseanne," *Nation,* June 21, 1993, 878.

44. Ibid.

45. WhaleRider, *Home Page for WhaleRider,* August 6, 1997 (updated September 18, 2000), <http://users.aol.com/whalerider/private/mainmenu.html> (accessed April 15, 1998).

46. See A. Steadham, *Lovin' Large: Women Who Love Big Handsome Men,* 1997, <http://www.eden.com/crusader/lovebhms.html> (accessed April 15, 1998; site now defunct).

47. Bob Donahue and Jeff Stoner, "The Natural Bears Classification System: A Classification System for Bears and Bearlike Men" (v1.10), in *The Bear Book: Readings in the History and Evolution of a Gay Male Subculture,* ed. Les K. Wright (Binghamton, N.Y.: Harrington Park/Haworth, 1997), 149–56. See also *The Natural Bears Classification System: A Classification System for Bears and Bearlike Men,* May 7, 1996 (updated April 21, 2000), <http://www.resourcesforbears.com/NBCS/> (accessed April 15, 1998). Donahue and Stoner also maintain a list of bears in the media; see *Bears in Movies,* April 1994 (updated September 4, 2000), <http://www.resourcesforbears.com/MOVIES/> (accessed April 15, 1998).

48. Henry Jenkins, *Textual Poachers: Television Fans and Participatory Culture* (New York: Routledge, 1992), 23.

49. Fiske, *Television Culture,* 228. See also Roland Barthes, *The Pleasure of the Text,* trans. Richard Miller (New York: Hill and Wang, 1975).

50. For example, *The Big List: The Original Big Man Movie Site* (1998) proclaimed that its purpose was "to catalog all existing nude scenes done by heavyset male actors" <http://www.chubnet2.com/biglist/> (accessed April 15, 1998; site now defunct).

51. Fiske, *Television Culture,* 229.

52. Jenkins, *Textual Poachers,* 12.

53. WhaleRider, *David Anthony Higgins' Page for WhaleRider,* 1997 (updated January 1, 1999), <http://users.aol.com/whalerider/private/higgins.html> (accessed April 15, 1998).

54. de Jonge, "Being the Big Guy," 49.

55. Alexander Doty, *Making Things Perfectly Queer: Interpreting Mass Culture* (Minneapolis: University of Minnesota Press, 1993), 107 n. 7.

56. Jenkins, *Textual Poachers,* 185–222.

57. Ibid., 186.

58. Millman, *Such a Pretty Face,* 245.

59. Les Wright, "Introduction: Theoretical Bears," in Wright, *The Bear Book,* 4.

60. Kipnis, *Bound and Gagged,* 121.

REFERENCES

Adler, Dick. "'How Old Bill Conrad?' Old Bill Conrad Fine—and Fat." *TV Guide,* March 3, 1973, 18–20.

Bakhtin, Mikhail. *Rabelais and His World.* Translated by Hélène Iswolsky. 1968. Reprint, Bloomington: Indiana University Press, 1984.

Barthes, Roland. *The Pleasure of the Text.* Translated by Richard Miller. New York: Hill and Wang, 1975.

Baudrillard, Jean. *Fatal Strategies.* Edited by Jim Fleming. Translated by Philip Beitchman and W. G. J. Niesluchowski. New York: Semiotext(e); London: Pluto, 1990.

Berg, Charles Ramírez. "*Bordertown,* the Assimilation Narrative, and the Chicano Social Problem Film." In *Chicanos and Film: Representation and Resistance,* edited by Chon A. Noriega, 29–46. Minneapolis: University of Minnesota Press, 1992.

The Big List: The Original Big Man Movie Site. 1998. <http://www.chubnet2.com/biglist/> (accessed April 15, 1998; site now defunct).

Bly, Robert. *Iron John: A Book about Men*. Reading, Mass.: Addison-Wesley, 1990.

Butler, Judith. "Critically Queer." *GLQ* 1, no. 1 (1993): 17–32.

Caldwell, John Thornton. *Televisuality: Style, Crisis, and Authority in American Television*. New Brunswick, N.J.: Rutgers University Press, 1995.

Chen, Raymond. *Normisms*. 1996. <http://s9000.furman.edu/ejorgens/cheers/archives/normisms.html> (accessed April 15, 1998).

Christensen Mark, and Cameron Stauth. "Everybody Knows Their Names." *American Film* 10 (1984): 48–52.

Cole, Lewis. "Roseanne." *Nation*, June 21, 1993, 878–80.

Davis, Anthony. *TV's Greatest Hits*. London: Boxtree, 1988.

DeGenevieve, Barbara. "Masculinity and Its Discontents." *Camerawork* 18, nos. 3–4 (1991): 3–5.

de Jonge, Peter. "Being the Big Guy." *New York Times Magazine*, February 10, 1991, 54.

Donahue, Bob, and Jeff Stoner. *Bears in Movies*. April 1994 (updated September 4, 2000). <http://www.resourcesforbears.com/MOVIES/> (accessed April 15, 1998).

———. *The Natural Bears Classification System: A Classification System for Bears and Bearlike Men* (v1.10). May 7, 1996 (updated April 21, 2000). <http://www.resourcesforbears.com/NBCS/> (accessed April 15, 1998).

———. "The Natural Bears Classification System: A Classification System for Bears and Bearlike Men" (v1.10). In *The Bear Book: Readings in the History and Evolution of a Gay Male Subculture*, edited by Les K. Wright, 149–56. Binghamton, N.Y.: Harrington Park/Haworth, 1997.

Doty, Alexander. *Making Things Perfectly Queer: Interpreting Mass Culture*. Minneapolis: University of Minnesota Press, 1993.

Dyer, Richard. *Heavenly Bodies: Film Stars and Society*. London: BFI, 1987.

Entertainment Weekly. *The 100 Greatest TV Shows of All Time*. New York: Entertainment Weekly Books, 1998.

Fiske, John. *Television Culture*. New York: Routledge, 1987.

Francis, Paul. "On the Grapevine: Weight Watchers." *TV Guide*, June 18, 1988, A-2.

Hamamoto, Darrell Y. *Nervous Laughter: Television Situation Comedy and Liberal Democratic Ideology*. New York: Praeger, 1989.

Jeffords, Susan. *Hard Bodies: Hollywood Masculinity in the Reagan Era*. New Brunswick, N.J.: Rutgers University Press, 1994.

Jenkins, Henry. *Textual Poachers: Television Fans and Participatory Culture*. New York: Routledge, 1992.

Kipnis, Laura. *Bound and Gagged: Pornography and the Politics of Fantasy in America*. New York: Grove, 1996.

Klingman, Mildred. *The Secret Lives of Fat People*. Boston: Houghton Mifflin, 1981.

Lehman, Peter. *Running Scared: Masculinity and the Representation of the Male Body*. Philadelphia: Temple University Press, 1993.

MacDonald, J. Fred. *Blacks and White TV: African Americans in Television Since 1948*. 2nd ed. Chicago: Nelson-Hall, 1992.

Marc, David. *Demographic Vistas: Television in American Culture*. Philadelphia: University of Pennsylvania Press, 1984.

Martinez, Al, and Joanne Martinez. "Instant Rerun." *TV Guide*, April 2, 1977, 11.

Meyers, Richard. *TV Detectives*. San Diego: A. S. Barnes; London: Tantivy, 1981.

Millman, Marcia. *Such a Pretty Face: Being Fat in America*. New York: Norton, 1980.

Orbach, Susie. *Fat Is a Feminist Issue: The Anti-Diet Guide to Permanent Weight Loss*. New York: Berkley, 1978.

Rensin, David. "Breakfast and Heartburn with John Goodman." *TV Guide*, December 28, 1991, 4–7.

Rowe, Kathleen. *The Unruly Woman: Gender and the Genres of Laughter*. Austin: University of Texas Press, 1995.

Schoenstein, Ralph. "Review: *What's Happening!!*" *TV Guide*, February 19, 1977, 36.

Schwartz, Hillel. *Never Satisfied: A Cultural History of Diets, Fantasies, and Fat*. New York: Free Press, 1986.

Shohat, Ella, and Robert Stam. *Unthinking Eurocentrism: Multiculturalism and the Media*. London: Routledge, 1994.

Solomon-Godeau, Abigail. *Male Trouble: A Crisis in Representation*. New York: Thames and Hudson, 1997.

Steadham, A. *Lovin' Large: Women Who Love Big Handsome Men*. 1997. <http://www.eden.com/crusader/lovebhms.html> (accessed April 15, 1998; site now defunct).

Tasker, Yvonne. *Spectacular Bodies: Gender, Genre, and the Action Cinema*. New York: Routledge, 1993.

Wexman, Virginia Wright. "Returning from the Moon: Jackie Gleason, the Carnivalesque, and Television Comedy." *Journal of Film and Video* 42, no. 4 (1990): 20–32.

WhaleRider (WhaleRider@aol.com). *David Anthony Higgins' Page for WhaleRider*. 1997 (updated January 1, 1999). <http://users.aol.com/whalerider/private/higgins.html> (accessed April 15, 1998).

——— *Home Page for WhaleRider*. August 6, 1997 (updated September 18, 2000). <http://users.aol.com/whalerider/private/mainmenu.html> (accessed April 15, 1998).

Wright, Les K. "Introduction: Theoretical Bears." In *The Bear Book: Readings in the History and Evolution of a Gay Male Subculture*, edited by Wright, 1–17. Binghamton, N.Y.: Harrington Park/Haworth, 1997.

PART IV

Deconstructing the Carnivalesque, Grotesque, and Other Configurations of Corpulence

10 "It's not over until the fat lady sings"

Comedy, the Carnivalesque, and Body Politics

ANGELA STUKATOR

In *The Muppet Movie* (dir. James Frawley, 1979), Kermit the frog and his companions find themselves at a county fair, witnesses to the crowning of the Bogen Beauty Queen. She is the picture of classical beauty: dressed in a white satin gown accented with a simple strand of pearls, her long blonde hair falling into soft, full curls. But the image is troubled. The Beauty Queen is a pig, literally; her physical features are dominated by a large snout, small pointed ears, and an ample girth. On the one hand, Miss Piggy can be read as consistent with one of the dominant paradigms of the representation of women in contemporary mainstream cinema. Large, audacious women are often constructed as comic spectacles, the target of our laughter and the butt of the joke. The link between woman and pig serves to specify the crux of the mockery, a link that can be traced to antiquity, when the Latin slang "little pig," *piorcus* or *porcellus,* was used to describe female genitalia.[1] Images of fat women in the mass media have tended to exploit the derogatory and often violent connotations of this connection, while extending and ascribing them to aspects of fat women's physical, psychological, and emotional disposition.

On the other hand, the energy expended on constructing Miss Piggy as a joke can be read symptomatically. From a feminist perspective we might examine Miss Piggy as an unruly woman who acquires oppositional power from her ambivalence: she is the object of disgust and desire, being both repellent and attractive, strong and delicate, friendly and hostile, and, most significantly, woman and animal. As an anthropomorphized pig, she accentuates the masquerade of femininity and exposes the contradictions in the ideology of "true femininity." Her performance as the passive object of desire, for example, is counterbalanced by her performance of virile masculinity; indeed, on numerous occasions Miss Piggy out-masculinizes Kermit, who out-feminizes her.

This essay examines films that use comedy as a weapon for and against female subjugation and fat oppression. I begin by sketching the stakes in theorizing female obesity and its representation in contemporary film. Fat women are, as Mary Russo observes in her analysis of the grotesque, "always and already transgressive";[2] consequently, what is at issue are the aesthetic and political strategies of representation. As I suggest below, the paradigm of woman as comic spectacle is one way in which the threats posed by the unruly fat woman are contained. This strategy is linked to the tradition of the carnivalesque and the grotesque body, which is redeployed in mainstream comedies to comply with dominant misogynist attitudes toward female obesity.

But other comedies also draw on the subversive force of the carnivalesque; prime examples in this category are *She-Devil* (dir. Susan Seidelman, 1989) and *Hairspray* (dir. John Waters, 1988). Aesthetically, these films reject classical verisimilitude in favor of the sensibility of camp: they revel in style, artifice, and spectacle. Moreover, though they appear to be mediocre parodies with simplistic politics, closer analysis reveals that the comedies are in fact radical and, at times, utopic. Most notably, the obese female character functions as an unruly woman who is able to lay claim to her desire and pleasure. In so doing, she releases the "laugh of the Medusa," breaking down the institutionalized hierarchies and conceptual categories by which social identities are ordered and defined.[3]

WHAT'S SO FUNNY ABOUT THE FAT LADY?

Nowhere is the ideology of true femininity more forcefully expressed than through the "cult of thinness" whereby, as the media critic Kathleen Rowe explains, "patriarchy inscribes itself insidiously and viciously on female bodies."[4] Since the 1950s, we have witnessed a shift from the neo-Victorian, hourglass figure of woman to what has been called the "tyranny of slenderness."[5] The hourglass figure (large breasts and full hips) was, of course, itself a patriarchal inscription on female bodies: women in postwar America were relocated from factory to home and coerced into the ideology of maternal, domestic femininity. This image, rejected in the 1960s, was succeeded by the boyish slenderness and androgynous look popularized by Twiggy. As Naomi Wolf notes in *The Beauty Myth,* the thin woman has a contradictory status: she "has the freedom from the constraints of reproduction of the earlier generation while reassuring men with her suggestion of female weakness, asexuality, and hunger."[6] The obese body, with its soft, loose, excessive flesh, has come to signal resistance to this cultural norm. And as Marcia Millman documents in *Such a Pretty Face,* resistance is met with extreme hostility and disgust: the "obese" are often viewed in terms that suggest an infant sucking hungrily, unconsciously at its mother's breast—greedy, self-absorbed, and lazy, without self-control or will power.[7]

For these reasons, the obese woman is an unruly woman, a paragon of outrageousness and transgression. Rowe observes that unruliness "reverberates whenever bodies, especially women's bodies, are considered excessive—too fat, too mouthy, too old, too dirty, too pregnant, too sexual (or not sexual enough) for the norms of gender representation."[8] Such a definition gives unruliness an implicit oppositional power: woman as defiant, wild, rebellious, undisciplined, trouble. Yet this radical quality is balanced by the various ways in which the unruly woman sanctions traditional structures and categories. She is a product of the bourgeois imagination and the politics of patriarchal relations. Within a network of interrelating and dependent hierarchies, unruliness gains its meaning from that which it is not: ordered, rule-bound, and restrained, attributes associated with normative masculinity and femininity. In short, the transgressions of the unruly are neither intrinsically radical nor conservative; instead, they are contradictory, conflicting, and paradoxical.[9]

But contemporary mainstream films, almost without exception, disavow the radical and subversive potential of the unruly fat woman in favor of exploiting her "otherness." With her generous bulges and flabby flesh, the obese woman violates the cultural ideal of femininity and is therefore represented as an object of fear, pity, or ridicule. She is also represented as threatening, because hunger has always been a cultural metaphor for female sexuality, desire, and power.[10] The slender woman signals the repression of autonomous female sexuality, whereas the obese woman functions as a metaphor for uncontrolled hunger, unbridled impulses, and uninhibited desire. Rendering the unruly fat woman as comic spectacle is one common strategy for designating her doubly marginal status—as woman and as fat woman—and ridiculing her aberrant body. As a genre, comedy is progressive, for it has the capacity to demystify the world, to expose oppressive hierarchies, and to express utopian desires. Yet comedy is also inherently conservative, for it involves the use of cultural stereotypes and archetypes. Moreover, comedy's tendency toward the reflexive

(most notably in parody) is an additional sign of its conservative bent, since reflexivity stays within the conventions of the genre and is not (necessarily) a subversive strategy.[11]

Feminist critics have noted that film comedy, like other classic genres, has used and abused women; the comic (patriarchal) tradition is distinguished by the subjugation (if not absence) of women.[12] In her work on women in television situation comedies of the 1950s and 1960s, Patricia Mellencamp asserts that the fundamental problematic is "women's simulated liberation through comic containment."[13] Arguably, women find themselves in the same bind in classic and contemporary film comedies. The female protagonist is often shown to challenge patriarchal "truths" and assumptions through her words or actions. However, her unruliness merely marks the need for her transformation, which becomes the basis of the comedy. The narrative traces the conversion of the female protagonist, which is complete when she accepts the confinement and patience mandated by patriarchal authority.

Fat women, because of their position within comic discourse, follow a slightly different pattern. They are rarely featured in film comedies, appearing rather as secondary and exceedingly stereotypical characters: mother/mammy, spinster, cultural other, or female buddy. Sometimes obesity is represented as a temporary, physical manifestation of the female protagonist's emotional disposition. In any case, the fat woman is made into a spectacle for our amusement. While the laughter she evokes may or may not be bound to her wit, a narrative gag, or prank, it invariably pertains to her physical body.

The fate of women in comedy can be and has been explained by Freud's theory of the joke and the comic.[14] He establishes how women function as the object of the joke and, in the case of smut, how women's elision is essential to the comic process. The comic, as distinct from the joke, offers women the hope of a more positive role: it is a two-way process and it is not gender-defined. We laugh empathetically at the person who is pitted against the harsh world. In Freud's account, the principal comparison that structures the comic is between the adult and child: the adult reduced to a child, or the adult discovering the child in him- or herself.[15] The globular fat woman is particularly effective in rousing "pleasurable empathy," since her body reinforces her association with the child—specifically, the child's ignorance of moderation and restraint, its self-absorption, and its evocation of auto-eroticism.

Freud's account of jokes and the comic is valuable in suggesting how film comedy adheres to patriarchal constructs of women as Other, and it also sheds light on the specularization of the fat woman and the techniques that structure her into the "joke work." But his theory is both too sweeping and too provisional to account for the cultural, historical, and political meanings and implications of the unruly fat woman in film comedy. A more productive avenue of analysis is suggested by the discourse of the carnival and theories of the carnivalesque.

Comedy, it should be understood, is not synonymous with *carnival.* As theorized by the Russian linguist Mikhail Bakhtin, carnival includes three forms, only one of which—comic and parodic verbal and oral compositions—is comedy. The other two are ritual spectacles (feasts, pageants) and various versions of billingsgate (curses, oaths, profanations).[16] Carnival culture is thus a heterogeneous form. Indeed, carnival is fundamentally defined by its rejection of homogeneity. The carnivalesque abolishes hierarchies, prohibitions, and regulations in favor of a view of the world from below, a view that privileges the marginal and excluded over that which is considered sacred and authoritative. It thus seems, like comedy, to be a progressive critical category. But the carnival is no more intrinsically radical than is comedy. Carnival culture can be appropriated to sustain marginality or it can be used to subvert and challenge the dominant official culture and its representations. As the film theorist Robert Stam suggests, we need to ask "who is carnivalizing whom, for what reasons, by which means and in what circumstances."[17]

The relationship between cinema and carnival culture has been noted by critics and historians. According to Stam, the link between carnival and American cinema "is both metonymic and metaphoric: metonymic in that cinema grew up, as it were, in the shadow of the side show, as an entertainment quite literally situated near the fairground and the penny arcade and metaphoric in the sense that countless films cite the regressive pleasures of commercial carnivals to analogize those of the cinema itself."[18] The genre of film comedy has a particularly intimate association with the carnivalesque. Past and present, many comedies have been set at fairgrounds and amusement parks: *The Circus* (dir. Charlie Chaplin, 1928), *Big Top Pee-Wee* (dir. Randal Kleiser, 1988), and *Shadows and Fog* (dir. Woody Allen, 1992) are just three random examples. There are also filmmakers who consistently evoke the carnival spirit: the Marx brothers, Lina Wertmuller, Robert Altman, and Ethan and Joel Cohen, among others. Finally, film comedy is distinguished by its cast of carnival characters: dwarfs, transvestites, hermaphrodites, freaks, monsters, and, of course, fat women.

In theorizing the carnivalesque, Bakhtin places particular emphasis on the grotesque body, which he conceives of as a symbolic representation of a utopian social collectivity. Examining the grotesque body therefore provides insight into the inherent ambivalence of tropes of the carnivalesque. We can then identify how that ambivalence is inscribed on mainstream images of fat women. Bakhtin uses the material body to represent the dispersion and multiplicity of a model social system: the grotesque body is multiple, bulging, open, the body becoming, the body in process. While his grotesque body is not related to an individuated ego, it has an uncanny affinity with women, particularly fat, pregnant, and old women. Indeed, Bakhtin finds his concept of the grotesque embodied in the Kerch terracotta figurines of pregnant hags. The image, Bakhtin suggests, is ambivalent in that it simultaneously evokes birth and death. Yet as Mary Russo accurately notes, it is more than ambivalent: "it is loaded with all of the connotations of fear and loathing associated with the biological processes of reproduction and aging."[19]

In contemporary mainstream comedy, the spectacle of the fat woman epitomizes Bakhtin's grotesque body and its functions as a symbol of ambivalence. She is constructed as disgusting and delightful, attractive and repulsive, normal and deviant. Yet that initial ambivalence is invariably replaced and resolved by hegemonic certainties. Her power is aborted or neutralized by privileging the pervasive (patriarchal) discourse of female denial: of hunger, desire, indeed of a socially sanctioned subjectivity.

Death Becomes Her (dir. Robert Zemeckis, 1992) offers an exceedingly rich and relevant example of the female grotesque and fat oppression. The film is about women's fear of aging, particularly as it is manifest in the degeneration of the body. It is also a film about female rivalry: Hel[en] Sharp (Goldie Hawn) is a dowdy, frumpy, would-be writer who is set against Mad[elaine] Ashton (Meryl Streep), a Broadway superstar. Helen's mediocre life goes from bad to worse when Madelaine steals Helen's fiancé (Bruce Willis); though Helen's dull equivalent, he is redeemed by his superior moral character. To mark Helen's romantic ruin, a title signals the passing of six months, after which we see Helen physically transformed: she is ugly and fat. Moreover, she is disgusting and pathetic, eating ice cream out of the container with her fingers, watching TV, and surrounded by filth. Her function as the grotesque, comic spectacle is marked physically and stylistically. The first image of the transformed Helen is a close-up of her buttocks as she leans over to pick something off the floor. This view is repeated in the next scene when, in jail for failing to pay her rent, she is forced to attend group therapy. The camera is positioned behind her, focused on her buttocks as they spill off the small, wooden chair. There are also numerous low angles of Helen that magnify her bloated and freakish body. Finally, fat, the measure of Helen's failure, becomes the basis for the joke of her death: Madelaine shoots Helen at close range, ripping out her stomach. The gaping hole left behind functions as an apt and poignant metaphor for the requisite repression of female hunger. The humor of Helen's descent and death thus relies entirely on rendering her a grotesque spectacle and tapping into cultural intolerance of obese bodies.

The representation of Helen as an unruly fat woman is only one of the film's manifestations of the grotesque. A number of others in *Death Becomes Her* can be expressed as a series of binaries: closed and open, life and death, youth and age, beauty and revulsion, ego and other. Helen and Madelaine are women mourning the loss of the first terms of each and moving inevitably downward toward the earth. From a vampiristic woman (Angelica Huston) they purchase a potion that is meant to stop the aging process and to make eternal what Bakhtin labels the "classical body" (as distinguished from the grotesque body)—the body as static, monumental, infinite.[20] But impelled by jealousy (of men, beauty, and power), Helen and Madelaine kill each other; consequently, they are forced back into a struggle with the grotesque body, this time exaggerated as processes of death: their skin loosens and loses its color, their bones break, and their facial features slide. Their grotesque bodies become a genuine nightmare, the price paid for defying the natural process of aging. Moreover, the women's antagonism is replaced by mutual dependency; they mend each other's fragile limbs and rapidly changing features. Men, by contrast, are allowed to grow old gracefully, without the narcissistic torment suffered by women. Indeed, the film's conceit is to address women's anxiety about aging. This feminist concern is ultimately elided in favor of reviving a valid but insipid moral: eternal life can be achieved only through procreation and good deeds.

Death Becomes Her, like most mainstream films that feature unruly women, is distinguished by reactionary body politics. It redeploys the grotesque to affirm and exaggerate the taboos associated with women's bodies. It thus can be understood as a "licensed affair"—a term borrowed from the Marxist critic Terry Eagleton, who has argued that there are cultural events and rituals that function as "permissible ruptures of hegemony, contained, popular blow offs."[21] Because the discourse of the unruly fat woman in *Death Becomes Her* functions as a form of social control of the marginal, it is complicit with the official culture that it only apparently opposes. The physical unruliness of the specularized women, which is the basis of the comedy in the film, is not about them; it is about what they mean to us. How then might a feminist appropriation of the radical power of unruly fat women take place? What would it look like? How might it challenge the boundaries of patriarchal hierarchies and categories? And how might it lay claim to female desire and subjectivity? In the following sections, I take up these questions in an analysis of films that employ the aesthetic and political strategies of subversive carnivalesque art.

RECLAIMING THE UNRULY FAT LADY

The Muppet Movie and especially Miss Piggy herself suggest a preliminary link between a feminist body politics and the carnivalesque. In their illuminating study of social hierarchies, *The Politics and Poetics of Transgression,* Peter Stallybrass and Allon White propose a "social semiotic of the pig." They interpret the pig as a creature who, in medieval times, was on "the threshold": it resembled a baby, lived next to and with humans, and ate similar food, yet was marked as "not-man" by virtue of its status as a greedy scavenger fit only to be devoured.[22] The symbolic meaning of the pig within Western culture has since been transformed because of a number of social and economic changes, most notably urbanization, after which the pig became a hated object of disgust lacking any appeal.

Arguably, Miss Piggy can be understood as a determined appropriation of the rural pig as a symbol of ambivalence—a symbol given full expression within the carnival spirit of *The Muppet Movie.*[23] As already noted, Miss Piggy possesses the physical and psychological attributes of an animal *and* a woman. Thus, she affirms the union between woman and nature, albeit a nature that has become alienated and hostile. In addition, the symbolic polarities embodied by Miss Piggy are shown to be conflicting yet also mutually constitutive. Finally, Miss Piggy signals the radical potential of the unruly fat woman to produce *herself* as spectacle: she puts on femininity with a vengeance that hints at the masquerade's ability to "act out" the dilemmas of femininity.[24]

While Miss Piggy's unruliness is more evocative and utopian than are most conventional representations, her unruliness is ultimately arrested by the film's overall commitment to gender stereotypes and to a conventional narrative trajectory. The film satirizes sexual roles only to hold those roles in place. It is, at best, a gentle parody of romantic comedy wherein Miss Piggy's deviant, disorderly conduct is rendered idiosyncratic rather than subversive. What is lacking in *The Muppet Movie* are formal strategies that would release rather than contain the disruptive power of the unruly fat woman. To put the problem more precisely, neither *The Muppet Movie* nor *Death Becomes Her* forges a link between thematic and formal transgressions, the link characteristic of the tradition of carnivalesque irreverence.

When the carnival, as a real social ritual, ceased to occupy a significant place within European culture, it was displaced onto the avant-garde; according to Stam, revolutionary carnivalesque strategies are evident in movements such as expressionism, dadaism, and surrealism.[25] These strategies also exist in American underground cinema—the films of Kenneth Anger, Paul Morrissey, and John Waters, among others—and much of women's cinema. They are distinguished by their marginality to the dominant mode of film production. Indeed, at their most radical, marginal discourses oppose the hierarchical discursive practices that characterize the official patriarchal culture. In so doing, they correspond to the anthropologist Barbara Babcock's notion of symbolic inversion: "any act of expressive behavior which inverts, contradicts, abrogates or in some fashion presents an alternative to commonly held cultural codes, values or norms be they linguistic, literary or artistic, religious social and political."[26] Marginal discourses can function as privileged sites of inversion when they negate or deform social, aesthetic, and narrative conventions.

IS SHE THE DEVIL IN DISGUISE?

Susan Seidelman's *She-Devil* provides an interesting although not entirely successful example of a subversive parody of romantic comedies and melodrama. In their study of film and television, Steve Neale and Frank Krutnik note that melodrama turns on the narcissistic eroticism of the female protagonist whereas romantic comedy is concerned with the marital union of the heterosexual couple.[27] In *She-Devil,* Ruth (Roseanne Arnold) is the protagonist, defined not by narcissistic eroticism but its opposite: she is a woman of humble repulsion. Ruth's story is that of a woman whose mundane yet comfortable American dream is destroyed by the myth of beauty and heterosexual romance.

The credit sequence establishes Ruth as an unruly woman: she is fat and ugly (an unsightly mole dominates her face). The futility of Ruth's efforts to mask her physical "abnormalities" is established by the stunning women who surround her and by Ruth's voice-over narration: "Some women are born beautiful, some have to put an effort into it, and some need all the help they can get." Ruth cannot get enough help, and the film suggests that her husband, Bob (Ed Begley, Jr.), is justified in leaving her for the classically beautiful and hopelessly romantic Mary Fisher (Meryl Streep). The film then becomes a conventional revenge narrative. Ruth systematically destroys Bob's "assets": his home (she blows it up), his family (she gives Bob sole custody of their two children), and his career and freedom (she frames him for fraud and embezzlement, crimes for which he is ultimately sent to prison). The love affair between Mary and Bob, unable to withstand the pressure of external forces, degenerates into a "normal," destructive relationship. The film parodies the mythic paradigm of heterosexual romantic love, and it also satirizes our need for such romanticism.

Yet *She-Devil* is less about female oppression within the paradigm of heterosexual romantic love than it is about female antagonism. The film pits the two women in a struggle between two archetypes. Mary represents idyllic femininity; she is the incarnation of the fantastic, melodramatic heroines she writes about. Ruth, in contrast, is the she-devil, woman as grotesque monster. As in her highly acclaimed film *Desperately Seeking Susan* (1985), Susan Seidelman seeks to dissolve the distinction between the archetypes by tracing the disintegration of social identities. Mary loses control of her fantasy world and becomes a neurotic hysteric; when Bob and his children leave, she takes control again and ascends to the position of a successful feminist author. Ruth also descends to the depth of despair, though she maintains control throughout. She chooses to work at the Golden Twilight nursing home, where she constructs a new identity. She changes her name to Vesta Rose and transforms her appearance—significantly, she chooses to exaggerate her physical ugliness: she lets her mustache grow in; she wears heavy, black-rimmed glasses; and she ties her hair back in a tight ponytail. Her ascent is equally dramatic, as she becomes the head of an employment agency for "unloved and unwanted women." And she scrupulously appropriates the symbols and sources of Mary's power: the accoutrements of proper femininity (e.g., a gentle hairstyle, delicate makeup that effectively conceals her mole, feminine clothing), roses, the color pink, and media attention.

In the end, both women's accomplishments are suspect. Mary has simply assumed a more politically correct trope of femininity—she has becomes a nonthreatening, white, upper-middle-class feminist—while Ruth succeeds in cleverly disguising herself as an angel. The final image is a high-angle shot of Ruth walking down a busy Manhattan street, dressed in a flowing white dress and smiling victoriously; appropriately, it is accompanied by Elvis Presley's "Devil in Disguise." The image has the same unsettling resonance as Hannibal Lecter merging with the crowd in the final image of Jonathan Demme's *Silence of the Lambs* (1991). Yet Ruth's masquerade of normality is quite distinct from Hannibal Lecter's. The source of its disruptive power is Ruth's ambivalence; she is constructed to elicit disgust and fascination, empathy and humor. The casting of Roseanne Arnold reinforces the effect.[28] Kathleen Rowe, in an insightful article titled "Roseanne: Unruly Woman as Domestic Goddess," examines the unruly qualities of excess and looseness—qualities that mark Roseanne in opposition to bourgeois and feminine standards of decorum.[29] In *She-Devil* these qualities are both employed and repressed. Ruth/Roseanne's body is exploited for its affinity with the grotesque body of Bakhtin, which is set against Mary/Meryl Streep's classical body. Moreover, the affinity between the unruly fat woman's body and Bakhtin's notion of the grotesque body is heightened by the ways in which Ruth's body "speaks" social relations and values. Ruth's initial status as middle-class wife and mother is represented as a downscale version of the fantasy life of Mary. Mary lives in a decadent pink estate, whereas Ruth lives in a nondescript suburb called Palace Manor; Mary is surrounded by servants from exotic countries, whereas Ruth interacts with marginal, carnivalesque figures, most notably Nurse Hooper (Linda Hunt). Hooper is a dwarf whose sexual identity is rendered ambiguous by her masculine features and mannerisms. The women's friendship and alliance inevitably follow; as Ruth tells her, "Women like us should stick together." The two team up to create the Vesta Rose Temp Service for women of color, older women, and women with no skill or work experience (read "mothers" and "housewives"). Collectively the clients become Ruth's "army," strategically placed in patriarchal institutions and called on to participate in Ruth's attack on Bob's sanctioned power.

She-Devil suggests the possibility of redeploying culture and pleasure by representing the unrepresented within a familiar and popular paradigm. Ruth exposes the ideological restrictions within which women are contained, and she delights in countering female passivity, obedience, and patriarchal authority. Yet the work of narrativizing Ruth's unruliness also suggests a problem inherent in inverting representational norms. Formal strategies may be altered in conceiving of a different social subject; but if they rely on inversion, they ultimately reinforce and maintain the existing conceptual categories that are crucial to the process by which social identities are fixed. Thus, in the film's resolution, Ruth's association with marginal figures and her violation of codes of feminine posture and conduct are repressed and replaced by their opposite: ties to the socially acceptable and compliance with nonthreatening codes.

OUTRAGEOUS BODIES

Hairspray, a utopic, parodic musical, offers a much more radical representation of the unruly fat woman and the oppressive structures that define her social identity. The film centers on Tracy Turnblad (Ricki Lake), a fat teenager who dreams of becoming a regular dancer on the *Corny Collins Show*. Her success coincides with the rise of racial unrest in Baltimore. The climactic scene of the film takes place at the Tilted Acres Amusement Park, as several narrative lines reach their crisis point: a black teenager named Seaweed and his friends break into the fairground and instigate a race riot, and Tracy is arrested for supporting the blacks. These events lead Tracy's mother, Edna (Divine), to confess that it makes her "embarrassed to be white," and she heralds the changing of the times: "Something," she says, "is blowin' in the wind." Meanwhile Tracy's best friend, Penny Pingleton, is locked in her room while a doctor (John Waters) attempts to exorcise her desire for Seaweed. Amber Von Tussle takes the title of Miss Auto Queen 1963 by default but is dethroned when Tracy is pardoned by the governor and shows up at the award ceremony. Wearing a gown patterned with cockroaches (specially designed by the owner of Hefty Hideaway, Mr. Pinky), Tracy shouts the final line of dialogue: "Let's dance!"

These scenes suggest the possibility of going beyond inversion to a merging of seemingly irreconcilable elements: male and female, human and insect, black and white, reality and fantasy, narrative and spectacle. Stallybrass and White label this merger *hybridization*, a form that produces new combinations and strange instabilities in a given semiotic system. It thereby generates the possibility of shifting "the very terms of the system itself" as it erases and interrogates the relationships that constitute it.[30] While *Hairspray* explores a number of symbolic social domains—law, government, carnival, media, and family—my focus is on the body and the social engendering of identity.

Tracy's coming-of-age narrative is unique because her grotesque body is coupled with racial unruliness. The style of dancing that wins Tracy fame expresses her incongruous racial mix: she dances as if she had a "black soul." The black-white harmony is visually manifest in her two-tone, blond-brunette hair and in her Miss Auto Queen gown—black roaches on white satin. Ruth in *She-Devil* and Miss Piggy in *The Muppet Movie* are allied with a diverse cast of marginal figures, but Tracy seems herself to have ingested "otherness." She is the manifestation of the film's gender and racial politics: "segregation never, integration now."

Yet the film's transgressive representations are found not just in Tracy but also in Edna Turnblad and Arvin Hodgepile (the president of the television network), both played by the renowned transvestite Divine. Divine, weighing more than 300 pounds, exemplifies the *grotesque,* particularly as defined by Stallybrass and White: "a mobile and hybrid creature, disproportionate, exorbitant, outgrowing all limits, obscenely decentered and off-centered, a figural and symbolic resource for parodic exaggeration and inversion."[31] While the two characters share Divine's grotesque body, they cannot and should not be conflated: in Edna, Divine is required to impersonate an unruly woman; in Arvin, she reveals herself as a biological male.

The tradition of transvestism in film comedy is well-documented, and a variety of theories have been put forward on its significance.[32] The important point here is that in her long-term collaboration with John Waters, Divine has consistently made a spectacle of herself rather than being made *into* a comic spectacle. She flaunts the masquerade of both normative masculinity and femininity in her gross, excessive physical appearance and her outrageous performances of archetypes. In *Hairspray* she satirizes the myth of femininity, in particular the symbolic representation of motherhood marked by its repression of desire. And in her depiction of Arvin, a neofascist media mogul, she ridicules patriarchal authority, exposing its obsessive and maniacal nature. In so doing, she puts into question the social and cultural construction of gender difference, going beyond a critique that returns to the categories of male and female and toward a new and mobile notion of gender identity.

Significantly, the transgressions of the unruly fat women in *Hairspray* are given full representation through a number of carnivalesque strategies, most notably the spectacle of the musical comedy as a display of utopic collectivity. For example, on the *Corny Collins Show,* dances such as "The Madison," "The Roach," and "The Mashed Potato" are not expressions of individuality but choreographed group performances. Tracy's "physical abnormality" disappears precisely because she is able to blend into the rhythm of the collective, to dance just as well as (or better than) the other kids. Thus the oppressive prejudices against fat are transcended by music: the integration of blacks on the television show follows in turn. Ironically, in the process, Amber and her parents (Debbie Harry and Sonny Bono), who represent the status quo, become marginalized. Their increasingly hysterical, neurotic, and dangerous actions—verbal and physical—render *them* freakish, monstrous, and comic.

Another key carnivalesque strategy in *Hairspray* is its use of camp style, which functions as an anticlassical aesthetic to demystify cinematic realism. Camp has the same function in *She-Devil,* as the archetypal characters are reflected and reinforced by the stylistic excesses of Ruth's and Mary's worlds. However, in Waters's film the artifice and spectacle of the mise-en-scène are taken to extremes. Each setting is distinguished by exaggerated decor that functions hypersymbolically to satirize racist and sexist stereotypes. In one scene, Tracy and her boyfriend Link Lark, along with Seaweed and Penny, visit the black neighborhood. After a highly erotic dance number, the couples retreat from the hall to the back alley to act on their passion. The stereotype of the black ghetto as a hellhole is manifest in the rats that scurry around their feet; and the assumption that all blacks are musically talented is conveyed through the appearance of a bum who staggers past the lovers, singing the same song as the black performer in the dance hall and with equal proficiency. In contrast, WASPs are represented along a spectrum of oppression. Penny suffers from sexual and moral tyranny—the windows in her room have bars to keep her in and Seaweed out. The Turnblads are lower-middle-class, and their burden is evident in the endless piles of laundry that Edna takes in to pay the bills. And the Von Tussles, who exemplify capitalist success, suffocate themselves in the excesses of material property to secure their power.

In *Hairspray,* and to a lesser extent in *She-Devil,* the subversive potential of the unruly fat woman is unleashed through formal and thematic strategies of irreverent carnivalesque art. In the process, these films generate Medusian laughter that, like Bakhtin's carnivalesque laughter, is "gay, triumphant, and at the same time mocking, deriding."[33] In *She-Devil,* the laughter is literally and figuratively represented: Ruth's face in close-up, laughing devilishly, punctuates her transgressions and her liberation. These specularized moments rupture narrative continuity; moreover, they displace the isolated and integrated comic moments of conventional film comedy with a laughter that is directed at the spectator. *Hairspray,* as I have argued, employs the ideas and tropes of carnival to effect a symbolic revolt on several levels, each of which incarnates Bakhtin's "culture of laughter." The film dislocates the conventions of bourgeois realism by appropriating the sensibilities of camp, making the world of *Hairspray* function as a poignant resistance to the rigidity of official life and style and providing a topsy-turvy view that delights in the unexpected and bizarre. The film also refuses to privilege an individual agent and instead claims the community and the passion of the social collective. A giddy, jubilant laughter is evoked by the characters' rejection or, conversely, acceptance of the burdens and inhibitions of gendered categories and hierarchies. Specifically, Tracy and Edna, as unruly fat women, are positioned within this utopic world in which all barriers, all norms, and all social taboos are suspended. I do not minimize their specific function within the derisive carnivalesque spirit that defines the film: indeed, as I have suggested, the film's most radical and progressive quality is bound to Tracy's and Edna's aberrant bodies. Waters exploits their excessive, outrageous, rebellious female bodies as discursive terms by which to articulate a revolutionary cultural politics, one that releases the body from the restrictions of socially sanctioned gendered, racial, and sexual roles.

NOTES

1. Peter Stallybrass and Allon White, *The Politics and Poetics of Transgression* (Ithaca, N.Y.: Cornell University Press, 1986), 44–45.

2. Mary Russo, "Female Grotesques: Carnival and Theory," in *Feminist Studies/Critical Studies,* ed. Teresa de Lauretis (Bloomington: Indiana University Press, 1986), 217.

3. The term *laugh of the Medusa* is borrowed from Hélène Cixous, "The Laugh of the Medusa," trans. Keith Cohen and Paula Cohen, in *New French Feminisms,* ed. Elaine Marks and Isabelle de Courtivon (Amherst: University of Massachusetts Press, 1980), 245–64.

4. Kathleen Rowe, "Roseanne: Unruly Woman as Domestic Goddess," *Screen* 31, no. 4 (1990): 413.

5. See Kim Chernin, *The Obsession: Reflections on the Tyranny of Slenderness* (New York: Harper and Row, 1981).

6. Naomi Wolf, *The Beauty Myth: How Images of Beauty Are Used against Women* (Toronto: Random House, 1990), 184.

7. Marcia Millman's observations in *Such a Pretty Face* (New York: Norton, 1980) are succinctly reviewed by Susan Bordo, *Unbearable Weight: Feminism, Western Culture, and the Body* (Berkeley: University of California Press, 1993), 99.

8. Rowe, "Roseanne," 410–11.

9. For further discussion of the complex workings of unruliness, see Natalie Zemon Davis's argument in *Society and Culture in Early Modern France* (Stanford: Stanford University Press, 1975) that the unruly woman's power is "multivalent" (130). Unruliness and disorderliness do not always function to affirm hierarchies; they can also undermine them (131–51). See also Rowe, "Roseanne," 408–19.

10. Bordo, *Unbearable Weight,* 101.

11. Steven Neale and Frank Xrutnik, *Popular Film and Television Comedy* (London: Routledge, 1990), 82.

12. Patricia Mellencamp analyzes the subjugation of women in comedy in "Situation Comedy, Feminism, and Freud," in *Studies in Entertainment: Critical Approaches to Mass Culture,* ed. Tania Modleski (Bloomington: Indiana University Press, 1986), 80–95. Lucy Fischer theorizes the absence of women in traditional comedy in "'Sometimes I feel like a motherless child': Comedy and Matricide," *Comedy/Cinema/Theory,* ed. Andrew Horton (Berkeley: University of California Press, 1991), 60–78.

13. Mellencamp, "Situation Comedy, Feminism, and Freud," 94.

14. Sigmund Freud, *Jokes and Their Relation to the Unconscious,* trans. and ed. James Strachey (London: Routledge and Kegan Paul, 1960). See also Mellencamp's summary of Freud's account of the comic and humor ("Situation Comedy, Feminism, and Freud," 91–95). Mary Ann Doane has a relevant study of how woman functions as the "butt of a [dirty] joke" in "Film and Masquerade: Theorising the Female Spectator," *Screen* 23, nos. 3–4 (1982): 82–87.

15. Freud, *Jokes and Their Relation to the Unconscious,* 290.

16. Mikhail Bakhtin, *Rabelais and His World,* trans. Hélène Iswolsky (1968; reprint, Bloomington: Indiana University Press, 1984), 8.

17. Robert Stam, *Subversive Pleasures: Bakhtin, Cultural Criticism, and Film* (Baltimore: Johns Hopkins University Press, 1989), 95.

18. Ibid., 113.

19. Russo, "Female Grotesques," 219; see Bakhtin, *Rabelais and His World,* 25–26.

20. Bakhtin, *Rabelais and His World,* 21.

21. Terry Eagleton, *Walter Benjamin: Towards a Revolutionary Criticism* (London: Verso, 1981), 148; quoted in Stallybrass and White, *The Politics and Poetics of Transgression,* 13. Umberto Eco makes the same argument in his contribution to *Carnival!,* edited by Thomas Sebeok (New York: Mouton, 1984), discussed in Stam, *Subversive Pleasures,* 91.

22. Stallybrass and White, *The Politics and Poetics of Transgression,* 44, 47.

23. Walt Disney's work has also been discussed in terms of a nostalgia for rural simplicity. It would be interesting to consider the ambivalent power of the "three little pigs" or the rodent Mickey Mouse.

24. On the power of masquerade, see Russo, "Female Grotesques," 225.

25. Stam, *Subversive Pleasures,* 98.

26. Barbara Babcock, *The Reversible World: Symbolic Inversion in Art and Society* (Ithaca, N.Y.: Cornell University Press, 1978), 14.

27. Neale and Xrutnik, *Popular Film and Television Comedy,* 139.

28. The casting of Meryl Streep as an angel—the classical body—is, of course, equally ingenious, but a detailed consideration of her persona falls outside the scope of this essay.

29. Rowe, "Roseanne," 413.

30. Stallybrass and White, *The Politics and Poetics of Transgression,* 58.

31. Ibid., 9.

32. In "Sometimes I Feel like a Motherless Child," Fischer argues that transvestism erases women from film comedy while finding women in men (62). Annette Kuhn, in *The Power of the Images: Essays on Representation and Sexuality* (London: Routledge and Kegan Paul, 1985), demonstrates how representations of transvestites conventionally function to affirm that men make better women than women (73). And Doane asserts that "male transvestism is an occasion for laughter, female transvestism only another occasion for desire" ("Film and Masquerade," 82).

33. Stallybrass and White, *The Politics and Poetics of Transgression,* 8.

REFERENCES

Babcock, Barbara. *The Reversible World: Symbolic Inversion in Art and Society.* Ithaca, N.Y.: Cornell University Press, 1978.

Bakhtin, Mikhail. *Rabelais and His World.* Translated by Hélène Iswolsky. 1968. Reprint, Bloomington: Indiana University Press, 1984.

Bordo, Susan. *Unbearable Weight: Feminism, Western Culture, and the Body.* Berkeley: University of California Press, 1993.

Chernin, Kim. *The Obsession: Reflections on the Tyranny of Slenderness.* New York: Harper and Row, 1981.

Cixous, Hélène. "The Laugh of the Medusa," translated by Keith Cohen and Paula Cohen. In *New French Feminisms,* edited by Elaine Marks and Isabelle de Courtivon, 245–64. Amherst: University of Massachusetts Press, 1980.

Davis, Natalie Z. *Society and Culture in Early Modern France.* Stanford: Stanford University Press, 1975.

Doane, Mary Ann. "Film and Masquerade: Theorising the Female Spectator." *Screen* 23, nos. 3–4 (1982): 82–87.

Erens, Patricia, ed. *Issues in Feminist Film Criticism.* Bloomington: Indiana University Press, 1990.

Fischer, Lucy. "'Sometimes I feel like a motherless child': Comedy and Matricide." In *Comedy/Cinema/Theory,* edited by Andrew Horton, 60–78. Berkeley: University of California Press, 1991.

Freud, Sigmund. *Jokes and Their Relation to the Unconscious.* Translated and edited by James Strachey. London: Routledge and Kegan Paul, 1960.

Garber, Marjorie. *Vested Interests: Cross-Dressing and Cultural Anxiety.* New York: Routledge, Chapman, and Hall, 1993.

Kuhn, Annette. *The Power of the Image: Essays on Representation and Sexuality.* London: Routledge and Kegan Paul, 1985.

Mellencamp, Patricia. "Situation Comedy, Feminism, and Freud." In *Studies in Entertainment: Critical Approaches to Mass Culture,* edited by Tania Modleski, 80–95. Bloomington: Indiana University Press, 1986.

Millman, Marcia. *Such a Pretty Face: Being Fat in America.* New York: Norton, 1980.

Neale, Steven, and Frank Xrutnik. *Popular Film and Television Comedy.* London: Routledge, 1990.

Rowe, Kathleen. "Roseanne: Unruly Woman as Domestic Goddess." *Screen* 31, no. 4 (1990): 408–19.

Russo, Mary. "Female Grotesques: Carnival and Theory." In *Feminist Studies/Critical Studies,* edited by Teresa de Lauretis, 213–29. Bloomington: Indiana University Press, 1986.

Stallybrass, Peter, and Allon White. *The Politics and Poetics of Transgression.* Ithaca, N.Y.: Cornell University Press, 1986.

Stam, Robert. *Subversive Pleasures: Bakhtin, Cultural Criticism, and Film.* Baltimore: Johns Hopkins University Press, 1989.

Wolf, Naomi. *The Beauty Myth: How Images of Beauty Are Used against Women.* Toronto: Random House, 1990.

13

uring Women

eality and Autonomy in Fiction
omen Since the 1960s

SARAH SHIEFF

This paper has two connected starting points. My interest in novels about physically extraordinary women dates back to the early 1980s. Around then, I'd been on a Weight Watchers diet, lost weight, felt smug, then gained back all the weight I'd lost, and more. My disappointment lead me to the "self-help" shelves in the university bookstore, where I discovered Susie Orbach's *Fat Is a Feminist Issue* (1978).[1] In turn, this book pointed me toward other feminist-oriented nonfiction about weight control.[2] These works suggested that the recidivism I had experienced was entirely to be expected, as it was part of what keeps the diet industry booming; that the imperative toward thinness may well be a response to women's increasing economic and political power; and that compulsive eating was a futile attempt to satisfy needs that had nothing to do with physical hunger. It was a road to Damascus experience for me: where I had once seen a simple failure of the will, I now saw the web of signification in which women's bodies have always been entangled. About the same time, I stumbled on Margaret Atwood's *Lady Oracle* (1976).[3] Although similar in key to the nonfiction I'd been reading, this novel struck rather a different chord: it put human flesh on the bones of the nonfiction, animating the anguish that Orbach and others had only gestured toward, despite their well-intentioned and sensitive case histories. *Lady Oracle* became the first addition to my collection of novels about women whose bodies were in some way "out of the ordinary."

I decided to convert this personal interest into a more sustained inquiry and offered a graduate seminar in English titled "The Fat Lady Sings: Women, Food, and Fiction Since the 1960s." In many ways it was the culmination of my own casual reading about the relationship between women, food, and writing, yet it soon brought to light a surprisingly large and previously unidentified fictional genre.[4] Students showed a gratifying level of interest in the novels, all of which had "grotesque" females as protagonists; the course was well attended, being itself out of the ordinary in terms of my department's graduate offerings.

This teaching experience crystallized some important questions about the genre. In relation to eating disorders and corporeality, what different responses do fiction and nonfiction promote? Why are the characters in these novels so talkative? Why are mother-figures treated so harshly in these books? Is it significant that a high proportion are first novels? This essay addresses some of these issues. I begin by surveying some ways of reading corporeality in fiction: after considering some insights derived from analogies with nonfictional accounts of eating disorders, I review two recent analyses that interrogate the grotesque female body. From these observations, I develop a hypothesis about fiction and female authorship, elaborated in relation to the grotesque, maternity, writing, and eating.

THE BANALITY OF SELF-HELP

Having decided to shape a course around these novels, I faced several problems. The first related to the possibility of a perceived "authority differential" between fiction dealing with body image and nonfictional analyses of eating disorders: if a person is interested in body image, food, and obsession, why should she read fiction at all? Further, what reasons might we have for reading these books—some arguably of dubious "literary merit"—in an English department, rather than in a department of psychology, say, or of women's studies? This brought up another, related, question: how might we read this fiction *as* fiction and not as fake case histories, with the protagonists offering themselves up for amateur therapy?

Why, then, should we read these novels at all, given the huge quantity of professional and self-help literature about eating disorders? The nonfiction is striking for its inability to produce a consensus even regarding the definition of the disorders, let alone their causes and treatment: Abigail Bray notes that anorexia nervosa has been described as everything from "a rejection of the role of adult femininity and a retreat into the asexual body of a child" to "an obsessive-compulsive disorder best treated with benzodiazepines, haloperidol, . . . trazodone, . . . bilateral ECT or, if all else fails, a stereotactic limbic leucotomy (aka lobotomy)."[5] Clearly the nonfiction represents a tremendous range of positions—medical, surgical, psychiatric, psychological, sociological, new age. A professional journal is devoted to the problem: the *International Journal of Eating Disorders* was founded in 1981 "to digest the growing literature."[6] An equally diverse and sometimes overlapping range of feminist analyses bulks out the genre even further.[7]

The mysteriously intractable and polymorphous nature of the disorders means that although the analyses are variously insightful, and offer a range of possible solutions, none appears to offer a full answer or a wholly reliable treatment. Novelists may not gather data by the same methods, but fiction and nonfiction can be mutually enlightening in approaching these insidious and pervasive problems: looking across the genres it is possible to see their connection through a relatively consistent range of preoccupations. For example, both may explore women's emotional needs in the context of their socially ordained nurturing function. What happens when a woman's needs for love, food, fulfillment, are subsumed under the demands of her partner and family? Fay Weldon's *Fat Woman's Joke* (1967) and Susan Sussman's *Dieter* (1989) have central characters who turn to food in lieu of emotionally sustaining relationships, and Marian MacAlpin, the central character in Margaret Atwood's *Edible Woman* (1969), narrowly escapes the trap of marriage and maternity when her body rebels on her behalf. At first Marian is unable to see her fiancé as a predator, but her body progressively refuses food as a gesture of solidarity with other prey, until she realizes that she is about to become another victim sacrificed to domesticity.

Psychotherapists and novelists alike analyze how the preparation, consumption, and refusal of food can structure the relationship between mother and daughter.[8] Similarly, writers in both genres note the ways in which women turn to food when sexual relationships go wrong—either as consolation, revenge, compensation for denial, or self-punishment.[9] Susie Orbach, Kim Chernin, and more recently Susan Faludi have argued that the imperative toward thinness—and the resultant obsession with diet and body size—is a backlash against women's increasing economic power and visibility; while there are few real-life examples of large, powerful women, there are at least some fictional examples of women whose great power matches their size.[10]

Recourse to this thematic overlap can be helpful in reading fiction, but it can also lead to interpretive banalities. It becomes too easy to glibly psychologize the texts: one might suggest, for example, that in *Lady Oracle* the protagonist, Joan Foster, "uses" her fat to resist her mother's attempts to shape her in her own image. Weldon's *Fat Woman's Joke* is similarly open to facile observations. The joke—such as it is—involves the central character pulling the rug from under the feet of her complacent and selfish friends and family. Esther Sussman runs away from home and eats all she wants to revenge herself on the dreadful diet that drove her husband into the arms of his secretary. Even though Esther comes to understand her behavior, she is powerless to change the situation that precipitated it: she must return to her family, as her identity is entirely contingent on her position within it.

Although the self-help literature related to eating disorders might facilitate insights such as these, a critical reader needs to be more than a talk-show psychologist to these fictional characters. How, then, might one approach these books without turning to pop psychology?

HUNGRY BODIES

Mary Russo suggests some productive ways of reading the inordinate female body in *The Female Grotesque: Risk, Excess, and Modernity* (1994). Whereas feminist nonfiction generally regards the grotesque body as a painful by-product of psychological dis-ease, Russo's book valorizes the grotesque in order to explore its subversive potential. Her subjects are all outside the bounds of normalcy: they are female aviators, acrobats, Siamese twins, and "freaks." Russo's stated aim is to revise what she calls normality-based constructions of feminism, placing feminism instead within the realms of the ordinary. In distinguishing between the normal and the ordinary, she contends that to make any headway at all within the mainstream, feminism has had to conform to correct, conventional behaviors and identities—that is, to give the appearance of a nonthreatening normality. A circumscribed and static *normal* feminism, she suggests, is easily recognized, and therefore easily marginalized and disavowed. On the other hand, an *ordinary* feminism would be "heterogeneous, strange, polychromatic, ragged, conflictual, incomplete, in motion."[11] This ordinary feminism would be difficult to pin down, flexible, encompassing, resistant, mercurial, and vital. It would be inherently unstable and hence risky.

Russo's ordinary feminism draws on the discursive formations of carnival and the uncanny in order to extend itself to the grotesque, subversive margins of femininity. After Mikhail Bakhtin, she defines the female grotesque in opposition to the monumental classical, static, self-contained male body. The grotesque female body is an "open, protruding, extended, secreting body. [It is] the body of becoming, process and change."[12] This positive valuation of the grotesque female form, which nevertheless lies within the compass of the ordinarily feminine, suggests a possible way into the fiction of body image: it permits the reading of literary fat ladies not as abject and self-destructive victims of their psychology and circumstance, but as risk takers and trailblazers who transcend and destabilize the normal, though they may well pay huge personal prices for their resistance. Russo turns Bakhtin's description of the grotesque, embodied in the Kerch terra-cotta figurines, into a potent image for the subversive laughter of the fat (abject) woman: "This is typical and very strongly expressed grotesque. It is ambivalent. It is pregnant death, a death that gives birth. There is nothing completed, nothing calm and stable in the bodies of these old hags. They combine senile, decaying and deformed flesh with the flesh of new life, conceived but as yet unformed. . . . Moreover, the old hags are laughing."[13]

The hag's monstrous laughter is clearly audible in Jeanette Winterson's *Sexing the Cherry* (1989). Of the books so far mentioned, I believe this is the only one that manages a positive valuation of the inordinate female form. The protagonist of the book is the so-called Dog-Woman, who lives in Cromwell's London. She is called the Dog-Woman because she breeds dogs, not because she looks like one, although she is vastly ugly and proud of it. She is a Rabelaisian grotesque: huge, scarred and pitted, vigorous. She loves her dogs and her adoptive son Jordan with a mountainous passion, and she is the nemesis of the hypocritical Puritans who condemn sensual pleasure from the pulpit and indulge their bestiality in secret. Her effectiveness as a scourge is a function of her prodigious size—she likes a fight better than anything, and kills one man by smothering him against her gargantuan breasts. She later dispatches several Puritans who have violated her home and threatened her son:

> I ran straight at the guards, broke the arms of the first, ruptured the second and gave the third a kick in the head that knocked him out at once. The other five came at me, and when I had dispatched two for an early judgement another took his musket and fired me straight in the chest. I fell over, killing the man who was poised behind me, and plucked the musket ball from my cleavage. I was in a rage then.
>
> "You are no gentlemen to spoil a poor woman's dress, and my best dress at that."[14]

The Dog-Woman is strong in another way as well. She throws her huge shadow into the future, seeming to occupy the body of a young female scientist who lives in the present. This modern woman was a fat child—not because she ate too much, but "because I wanted to be bigger than all the things that were bigger than me. All the things that had power over me. It was a battle I intended to win."[15] The young woman loses weight when she goes to university, gaining through knowledge the power she once felt through her size. But she starts to notice something odd once she has become slim: "When the weight had gone I found out something strange: that the weight persisted in my mind. I had an *alter ego* who was huge and powerful, a woman whose only morality was her own and whose loyalties were fierce and few. She was my patron saint, the one I called on when I felt myself dwindling away through cracks in the floor or slowly fading in the street. Whenever I called on her I felt my muscles swell and laughter fill up my throat."[16]

The fat woman within is the source of this young woman's power. They share a hatred of hypocrisy, yet the young woman no longer needs to be fat in order to resist the things that have power over her: she doesn't need a large body in order to be able to throw her weight around. Although she is not very powerful in the larger scheme of things—she conducts a lonely protest vigil outside a chemical factory that is contaminating local waterways—she *is* making a spectacle of herself as a thorn in the side of the multinational company. This slender but unruly young woman is protected by the residue of her fat and the echo of the Dog-Woman's laugh.

Whereas Russo's book suggests productive, positive ways of reading the female grotesque, Maud Ellmann's *Hunger Artists: Starving, Writing, and Imprisonment* (1993) offers other, bleaker possibilities. Ellmann's book is not about fat women—the opposite, in fact. *The Hunger Artists* is a thoroughgoing psychoanalytic account of self-starvation in which Ellmann draws together the parallel but distinct discourses of anorexia and the hunger strike. Kafka's story "A Hunger Artist" (1938) and Richardson's *Clarissa* (1747–48) are her main literary examples of self-starvation; her nonfictional narratives of disembodiment encompass, among others, Jane Fonda's obsessive exercise rituals and Simone Weil's account of anorexia. Her hunger strikers are the suffragists and the ten Irish Republicans who starved themselves to death in Long Kesh jail for the right to be held as political prisoners rather than common criminals. In linking these imaginative and historical experiences, Ellmann argues that exploring the realm of fantasy will provide access to the experience of lived starvation.

Ellmann suggests that eating disorders dramatize fundamental, prelinguistic conflicts and privations, and that the subject rejects food because she lacks access to any other medium through which to articulate its discontents. The body is the text in which these discontents become encoded. Although the observation that the anorectic is literally starving for attention seems like common sense, Ellmann acknowledges that common sense breaks down in the face of the sufferer's apparently contradictory desire for death: this death drive suggests that "attention" is not quite the same as what the anorectic wants. As the linguist Gillian Brown points out in her examination of nineteenth-century America,[17] the anorectic's fundamental desire is *not* to desire. In practical terms, this means she must master her desire to consume: her just desserts are starvation and death. To accomplish her aim, she must keep inviolate her body, the private and personal space from which she can deny the existence of anything exterior at all. Her diminishing body itself encodes these denials. In refusing food, she rejects the multiple meanings of its circulation. Her wasting body denies the past stored up in its tissues. She becomes "inebriate of air,"[18] rejecting any attempt to bring her back to herself, so intent is she on terminating the desiring self and the loathed, demanding corporeality in which it is housed. By rejecting the body she hates for its reminder of the desire to consume, the anorectic finally triumphs over desire: "They always say they're concerned about me, about my health, when all they want is to control me. They want to pin me down and force-feed me: with lies, with what they call love. Like prisoners everywhere—like the suffragists, even—all I have left is the power to refuse."[19]

But excessive consumption can endow an agency just as efficacious. While the anorectic's refusal to ingest is synonymous with the refusal of her subjectivity, the compulsive eater's refusal to distinguish between what she needs and what she doesn't need may be equally devastating.

Claude Tardat's *Sweet Death* (1989) is about a young woman's concerted and successful attempt to eat herself to death. The book takes the form of a journal, which records the unnamed protagonist's expansion and disintegration: "My neck is swelling, a sponge saturated with lemonade and strawberry punch. I'm filling myself up, overflowing, spilling onto the chipped enamel of lavatories; I'm decomposing."[20] Her grossness is a reproach to an absent and preoccupied mother who withheld her love, imparting to her small daughter only her own love of literature and occasional sweetmeats. Embodying Freud's observation that girls reproach their mothers for not giving them enough milk,[21] the now-adolescent girl sets about gorging herself on vicarious mother love. Insatiably hungry, she stuffs herself with all the sweet food she can devour, taking perverse pride in her expanding bulk. But becoming huge is not only a way of reproaching her slender and elegant mother: it is also a way of attracting her attention. The mother makes occasional guilty trips to Paris to tisk over her gross daughter, leaving behind gifts of bathroom scales.

However, if her hunger for love and revenge can be so clearly inscribed in her grotesque form, why should the girl further desire death? Like Josie, the anorexic protagonist of Jenefer Shute's *Life-Size* (1992), the young woman in *Sweet Death* appears to make two contradictory announcements, saying "look at me" and "I am undeserving." Both the anorectic and the fat girl are equally desperate not to be; but unlike the anorectic who desires not to consume, the woman in *Sweet Death* can't get enough. Her desire, however, is only partly for the love embodied in surrogate mother's milk; her more profound hunger is for the breast itself, where there is no boundary between the eater and the edible. She desires to be indistinguishable from the object, but she is nevertheless constantly aware of its lack. The awareness—of the absence of wholeness, or of desire—can manifest as hunger, but it is a hunger that can never be satisfied, because what is desired is not food but the other. In her last diary entry she writes, "To be so heavy, and yet so empty" (126). In longing for union she longs for stasis, for a time before desire or the consciousness of self—in effect, she longs for death. By engulfing the body she desires, she finally triumphs over its lack.

Yet the girl's excessive form also embodies Russo's female grotesque. She is quite consciously "making an exhibition of herself" (50). She goes on a bus trip, ostensibly to renew her supplies of sugary food, but mostly to be stared at. On the bus trip the normal and the ordinary collide head-on. She's observed getting onto the bus by a little girl:

> "Hey, Mama, the lady's going to tip the bus over!" exclaimed a little girl, eyes wide with astonishment as I got on a Number 138, selected at random. Craning her neck, she sat proudly in her seat like a little princess, swinging legs too short to reach the ground. Patent leather shoes, clean ankle socks, Sunday dress, nicely combed bangs. . . . Next to her, the mother glued her nose to the window without a word, as if she hadn't heard a thing.
>
> Me, the lady who doesn't deserve such a title, I laughed good-naturedly, very loudly, and the little girl began to laugh with me, relieved to notice that my outlandish weight wasn't preventing the bus from continuing on its way.
>
> I sat down across from her. Pulling out a handful of Cracker Jacks, I offered her some while her mother looked on suspiciously. A game sprang up between us. At first it was tacitly understood that we would crunch the sweetened popcorn in the same rhythm before swallowing it with an exaggerated expression of pleasure. Then the child decided to turn the game into a real dialogue of clowns. We pummelled our cheeks, puffed out as far as they would go, using our fists instead of our teeth to grind up the popcorn inside. The little girl pretended to be choking and pressed her lips tightly together to keep from bursting with laughter. She was funny. Myself, grotesque.

> But I know it. And this experience gives me a certain feeling of euphoria. No one suspects this: I find it amusing to be the object of awkward glances that would rather avoid me altogether. Hiding behind their newspapers, the travellers sought shelter in an uneasy and hypocritical silence that we filled with our laughter. A child's laughter is often contagious. But a monster who dares to have fun—that's inconvenient, that keeps people from letting go and enjoying themselves. That freezes laughter into a grimace on the lips. (51–52)

This female grotesque is clever and sassy and she dares to indulge her wild appetites shamelessly and in public. She enjoys shocking people. Her image is as ambivalent as that of Bakhtin's laughing, senile terra-cotta hag.

It seems, then, that Russo and Ellmann may both be helpful in reading these novels. But their approaches are at once too specific and not specific enough. Russo's paradigm validating the grotesque might tempt one to overlook the anguish of the grotesque heroine. And Ellmann's finely nuanced analysis of extreme self-starvation doesn't adequately encompass less pathological, less overtly political states. The women in these fictions are subject to much more everyday hungers. Their overeating often begins as compensation for a diet that results not in slimness so much as in sustained and stored-up hunger. But once the dam is breached, they cram in food in an effort to allay other hungers that are inevitably misrecognitions of equally clamorous psychic lacks. There are no somatic signals for these hungers, and food can never satisfy them. The compulsive eater is never replete, as food can never satisfy her hunger for love, words, connection, independence—for whatever it is that causes the black hole at her center.

These approaches may offer the reader a partial purchase on the grotesque fictional subject; more might be added by examining the genre's metaphors in relation to our impression of the author herself. Apart from their physically extraordinary protagonists, these novels have several other commonalities. Many of their main characters suffer from some form of logorrhea: along with their obsessive consumption or denial of food, they talk or write compulsively. Many of them have overbearing, controlling mothers. And many of the books are first novels. This fictional yoking of corporeality, food, maternity, and writing highlights some of the fundamental anxieties of female authorship.

DEVOURING WOMEN

Eating and writing (or talking) are related activities in *The Fat Woman's Joke, The Dieter,* and *Life-Size*—all first novels. Each of their protagonists has a female friend to whom they tell their story. Not simply textual correlates of the reader, these narratees also have an important "therapeutic" function: by auditing the narrative, they help their friends effect a "talking cure" by unstopping mouths previously jammed shut, or jammed with food. If, as Ellmann and Brown suggest, the anorexic/obese body encodes the subject's suffering, then the body may be released from this signifying burden by finding the right conditions under which to articulate its discontent.

However, for the woman in *Sweet Death*—also a first novel—writing serves a rather different purpose. Although her diary is her "perfect friend; a patient and sympathetic ear" (104), the woman is not interested in recovery. She is intent on suicide-by-gluttony. Eating and writing are her joint compulsions, and each is meaningless without the other. With her death, and the precise means of its execution, the woman perfects a punishment for her cold and beautiful mother: "Her mink was soft and sweet-smelling, my mother brittle and imperious within its folds. When she stroked my cheek absent-mindedly, checking her reflection in the cheval glass, there were icy needles in her kid gloves" (15). Without her diary, the woman's revenge might remain unrecognized, or worse, misinterpreted: her death from overeating could easily be misconstrued as the result of a "mere" eating disorder. "I write above all to be able to verify that someone calling herself *me*—will be able to retire from the field at the right moment, at the height of her sweet glory, faithful to her promise to have done with the sorry comedy of life" (65–66). But her suicide is a both a triumph and a capitulation. Believing that she is punishing her mother and exercising her own autonomy, she is also returning to a time before desire, when mother and daughter were one.

Writing and eating daughters aren't always so bent on self-destruction. Writing can also mean at least partial liberation from an overbearing mother. Although *Lady Oracle* is not a first novel, in it writing has much structural and thematic significance. Joan Foster maintains a degree of financial independence by writing Gothic romances; but despite her success, she is unable to break out of a deadlock with her domineering and disenfranchised mother. During her mother's lifetime Joan's body is the battleground,[22] and the struggle for ascendancy extends beyond the grave. Joan has frequent visitations from her mother's shade, dressed in a navy-blue suit with a white collar. Mascara runs from her eyes in black tears. Joan asks her what she wants, but she doesn't answer. "She stretched out her arms to me, she wanted me to come with her; she wanted us to be together."[23]

The mothers in these novels become monstrous in their very powerlessness.[24] With their domains extending only as far as their kitchens, control of food substitutes for any real agency; food becomes the daughter's logical weapon in her struggle for autonomy. Ironically, the focus on food locks the combatants even more tightly together; the daughter can claim a degree of independence only after escaping from the domestic space and its suffocating denizen. But mother's shadow is long, and the combat mortal. In willing their own deaths, Josie and the woman in *Sweet Death* reject their mothers through their denunciation of the economy of the kitchen, whose usual job is to give life. Rejecting the kitchen, the women also reject the future that their mothers embody. Their own secondary sexual characteristics are effaced in starvation and obesity:

> She was not a pretty sight, my mother, oily and unwashed in a shapeless floral housecoat. "Josie, I don't want to hear any more of this nonsense. You're a growing girl. You are not fat: you're just developing."
>
> Into what?
>
> Into you?[25]

Female subject-formation is represented in these novels first by a control of the body independent from maternal control and later by language's displacement of food as the primary instrument of the autonomous self: whereas the child or adolescent defines her self by putting things into her mouth (or by refusing to put things into her mouth), the adult self is defined by things that come *out* of her mouth. Domestic spaces are the arena for this drama.

It is possibly not surprising that grotesque mother-figures feature in these domestic bildungsromans. Perhaps of more interest is that many of these books are themselves first novels.[26] Although Marian McAlpin's own mother doesn't feature in *The Edible Woman* (written when Atwood was twenty-four), the lives of her closest friends are absorbed and depersonalized by their maternal functions. Marian's friend Clara marries before finishing her degree, and is now constantly and monstrously pregnant. Her body is "so thin that her pregnancies are always bulgingly obvious, and now in her seventh month she looked like a boa-constrictor that has swallowed a watermelon. Her head, with its aureole of pale hair, was made to seem smaller and even more fragile by the contrast."[27] Marian's roommate Ainsley also falls victim to biology-as-destiny thinking; between them they embody the maternal antirole that Marian only narrowly escapes.

Why do these mother-figures command the early and fascinated attention of so many beginning writers? If talking endows some of their creations with agency outside the domestic, might writing function similarly for their creators? If so, what specific anxieties do these grotesque mothers embody for women who want to write? How might writing help them escape these specters of circumscribed femininity?

The question suggests a range of possible answers. As the literary critics Sandra Gilbert and Susan Gubar have noted, the models available to women who want to write have historically been limited.[28] Poised at the juncture of the familiar (domesticity, motherhood) and the unfamiliar (writing), the women who invent these hobbled and destructive characters may feel a need to demonize the domesticity that has engulfed the creative energy of so many other women, thereby warding off the danger of suffering a similar fate themselves. Locating the mouth as the site of the body/world interface (taking things in, spitting things out), they dramatize their own transition from the private and the domestic to the public. Asserting their autonomy as writing subjects, writing daughters spit the mother out, claiming new spaces for themselves, avoiding the catastrophic sinking of self into other. Luce Irigaray makes the terms of rejection clear: "Once more you're assimilated into nourishment. We've again disappeared into this act of eating each other. Hardly do I glimpse you and walk toward you, when you metamorphose into a baby nurse. Again you want to fill my mouth, my belly, to make yourself into a plenitude for mouth and belly. . . . I want no more of this stuffed, sealed up, immobilized body. No, I want air. . . . Farewell, mother, I shall never become your likeness. . . . I'll live my life, my story."[29] In their novels about monstrous mothers and rebellious, talkative daughters, young writers externalize the fear of being trapped in a single function; purging themselves of at least one of their anxieties about writing and femininity, they clear the way for other work.

Having exorcised the monstrous mother-figure in her first book, *Oranges Are Not the Only Fruit* (1985),[30] Jeanette Winterson produces the Dog-Woman from a position of authorial security. This character's energy is not sapped by the demands of the nuclear family, so she is able to defend her adoptive son to the limit of her strength while encouraging him on his own journeys; her bulky ghost is her spiritual daughter's enabling genius. Although the Dog-Woman is grotesque, she takes pride in her physicality and has no need of the domestic battles through which other fictional mothers attempt to exercise their will to power. This makes her an important exception in a genre that anatomizes the distress of corporeality. This distress seems general; that physically grotesque mother-figures should be antitypes for many writing women indicates the extent of their anxiety.

FICTION OF AGENCY

The women in these novels rage and cry; they eat and talk incessantly. Their excesses brand them as grotesque—either grotesquely large, or emaciated, or fantastically and magically misshapen. If "normal" equates with moderation in consumption, physical standardization, and emotional equilibrium, then these women are not normal. But they are ordinary, resisting the normal in specific ways. While their methods of resistance differ, many of them have in common an insatiable, unruly hunger. Although this hunger has multiple causes, it produces a common effect: grotesque bodies, which are a sign of at least subconscious resistance to the normal. But normalcy exerts its inevitable pressure, making these bodies obscene to their very owners. The resultant self-loathing perpetuates a vicious cycle.

The size of this fictional genre attests to the scale and ubiquity of women's self-disgust. Although this is obviously not "just" a woman's problem, the stakes are perhaps higher for women. Textualizing the imperatives of corporeality, fiction's strength lies in its capacity to dramatize and interrogate such lived alienation. While these novels do not promise a "better body" for women crushed by dieting and exhausted by social and media pressure, they do offer examples of what it might be like to possess the requisite agency; for some readers, they generate paradigmatic scenarios on which to draw in forming their own lines of resistance.[31] Beginning writers, themselves working in (and through) the genre, demonstrate fiction's enabling potential. Their monstrous mothers are not symptoms of a widespread matrophobia. Rather, they are the inhabitants of social spaces (maternity, the kitchen, the obligation to nurture) that some women feel they must circumscribe before they can take up their own positions. These novels offer writers and readers not only the opportunity to interrogate lived alienation but also the chance to rehearse in imagination their own ways of being.

NOTES

1. Susie Orbach, *Fat Is a Feminist Issue: The Anti-Diet Guide to Permanent Weight Loss* (New York: Paddington, 1978).

2. For example, Kim Chernin, *Womansize: The Tyranny of Slenderness* (London: New Woman's Press, 1983); Ramona Koval, *Eating Your Heart Out* (Ring-

wood, Vic.: Penguin, 1986); Jasbindar Singh, *No Body's Perfect: A Self-Help Manual for Women Who Have Problems with Food* (Auckland: New Women's Press, 1989).

3. Margaret Atwood, *Lady Oracle* (1976; reprint, London: Virago, 1982).

4. The following list is representative but not exhaustive: Patricia Angadi, *Sins of the Mothers* (London: Black Swan, 1989); Margaret Atwood, *The Edible Woman* (1969; reprint, London: Virago, 1980) and *Lady Oracle;* Angela Carter, *The Passion of New Eve* (London: Virago, 1982) and *Nights at the Circus* (London: Chatto and Windus, 1984); Mavis Cheek, *Janice Gentle Gets Sexy* (London: Hamilton, 1993); Jacqueline Deval, *Reckless Appetites* (Toronto: Burgher, 1993); Cathie Dunsford, *The Journey Home* (Melbourne, Vic.: Spinifex, 1997); Lucy Ellmann, *Sweet Desserts* (Harmondsworth: Penguin, 1988); Laura Esquivel, *Like Water for Chocolate* (London: Black Swan, 1989); Mary Gordon, *Final Payments* (London: Hamilton, 1978); Stephanie Grant, *The Passion of Alice* (London: Sceptre, 1995); Dorothy Hewitt, *The Toucher* (South Yarra, Vic.: McPhee Gribble, 1993); Margaret Laurence, *The Diviners* (Toronto: McClelland and Stewart, 1974); Toni Morrison, *Beloved* (New York: Knopf, 1987); Sara Paretsky, *A Taste of Life* (Harmondsworth: Penguin 60s, 1995); Rosie Scott, *Glory Days* (Auckland: Penguin, 1988); Jenefer Shute, *Life-Size* (London: Minerva, 1992); Susan Sussman, *The Dieter* (London: Headline, 1989); Claude Tardat, *Sweet Death* (London: Pandora, 1989); Minette Walters, *The Sculptress* (London: Pan, 1993); Fay Weldon, *The Fat Woman's Joke* (1967; reprint, London: Coronet, 1982) and *Life and Loves of a She-Devil* (London: Houghton and Stoughton, 1983); Jeanette Winterson, *Sexing the Cherry* (London: Vintage, 1989).

5. Abigail Bray, "The Anorexic Body: Reading Disorders," *Cultural Studies* 10 (1996): 413–14.

6. Maud Ellmann, *The Hunger Artists: Starving, Writing, and Imprisonment* (Cambridge, Mass.: Harvard University Press, 1993), 23.

7. See, for example, Naomi Wolf, *The Beauty Myth: How Images of Beauty Are Used against Women* (London: Chatto and Windus, 1990); Susan Faludi, *Backlash: The Undeclared War against Women* (London: Vintage, 1992); Geneen Roth, *Feeding the Hungry Heart: The Experience of Compulsive Eating* (Harmondsworth: Plume, 1993); Kim Chernin, *The Hungry Self: Women, Eating, and Identity* (New York: HarperPerennial, 1994); and Patricia Fallon, Melanie A. Katzman, and Susan C. Wooley, eds., *Feminist Perspectives on Eating Disorders* (New York: Guilford, 1994).

8. For example, Chernin, *The Hungry Self,* 41–77; Orbach, *Fat Is a Feminist Issue,* 112–13; Atwood, *Lady Oracle;* Tardat, *Sweet Death;* Shute, *Life-Size;* and Paretsky, *A Taste of Life.*

9. For example, Geneen Roth, *Feeding the Hungry Heart,* Weldon, *The Fat Woman's Joke;* Sussman, *The Dieter;* Shute, *Life-Size;* and Paretsky, *A Taste of Life.*

10. Orbach, *Fat Is a Feminist Issue,* 36–38; Chernin, *Womansize,* 96–110; Faludi, *Backlash,* 237–55; for fictional examples, see Scott, *Glory Days,* and Winterson, *Sexing the Cherry.*

11. Mary Russo, *The Female Grotesque: Risk, Excess, and Modernity* (New York: Routledge, 1994), vii.

12. Ibid., 62.

13. Mikhail Bakhtin, *Rabelais and His World,* trans. Hélène Iswolsky (1965; reprint, Bloomington: Indiana University Press, 1984), 25–26; quoted in ibid., 63.

14. Winterson, *Sexing the Cherry,* 66.

15. Ibid., 124.

16. Ibid., 125.

17. Gillian Brown, "The Empire of Agoraphobia," in *Domestic Individualism: Imagining Self in Nineteenth-Century America* (Berkeley: University of California Press, 1990), 189–95.

18. Ellmann, *The Hunger Artists,* 2; the phrase is Emily Dickinson's (J. 214).

19. Shute, *Life-Size,* 50.

20. Tardat, *Sweet Death,* 60; quotations from this work are hereafter cited parenthetically in the text.

21. Ellmann, *The Hunger Artists,* 43; she points to an aside in Freud's "Female Sexuality" (1931).

22. Atwood, *Lady Oracle,* 69.

23. Ibid., 329.

24. Adrienne Rich writes, "Powerless women have always used mothering as a channel—narrow but deep—for their own human will to power, their need to return upon the world what it has visited on them. The child dragged by the arm across the room to be washed, the child cajoled, bullied, and bribed into taking 'one more bite' of a detested food, is more than just a child which must be reared according to cultural traditions of 'good mothering.' S/he is a piece of reality, of the world, which can be acted on, even modified, by a woman restricted from acting on anything else except inert materials like dust and food" (*Of Woman Born: Motherhood as Experience and Institution* [New York: Norton, 1976], 38).

25. Shute, *Life-Size,* 107.

26. First novels include Atwood, *The Edible Woman;* Esquivel, *Like Water for Chocolate;* Gordon, *Final Payments;* Shute, *Life-Size;* Tardat, *Sweet Death;* and Weldon, *The Fat Woman's Joke.* Questions about the relationship between these fictional mothers and the authors' "real" mothers are beside the point of this inquiry, but the following hypothesis does address the concern of my older students that mothers are treated very badly in many of these novels.

27. Atwood, *Edible Woman,* 31.

28. See Sandra M. Gilbert and Susan Gubar, "Infection in the Sentence: The Woman Writer and the Anxiety of Influence," in *The Madwoman in the Attic: The Woman Writer and the Nineteenth-Century Literary Imagination* (New Haven: Yale University Press, 1979), 45–92.

29. Luce Irigaray, "And the One Doesn't Stir without the Other," trans. Hélène Vivienne Wenzel, *Signs: Journal of Women in Culture and Society* 7 (1981): 62–63.

30. Jeanette Winterson, *Oranges Are Not the Only Fruit* (Boston: Pandora, 1985).

31. Cf. Steven Knapp, *Literary Interest: The Limits of Anti-Formalism* (Cambridge, Mass.: Harvard University Press, 1993), 84–85.

REFERENCES

Angadi, Patricia. *Sins of the Mothers.* London: Black Swan, 1989.

Atwood, Margaret. *The Edible Woman.* 1969. Reprint, London: Virago, 1980.

———. *Lady Oracle.* 1976. London: Virago, 1982.

Bray, Abigail. "The Anorexic Body: Reading Disorders." *Cultural Studies* 10 (1996): 413–29.

Brown, Gillian. *Domestic Individualism: Imagining Self in Nineteenth-Century America.* Berkeley: University of California Press, 1990.

Carter, Angela. *Nights at the Circus.* London: Chatto and Windus, 1984.
———. *The Passion of New Eve.* London: Virago, 1982.
Cheek, Mavis. *Janice Gentle Gets Sexy.* London: Hamilton, 1993.
Chernin, Kim. *The Hungry Self: Women, Eating, and Identity.* New York: HarperPerennial, 1985, 1994.
———. *Womansize: The Tyranny of Slenderness.* London: Women's Press, 1983. First published in 1981 as *The Obsession: Reflections on the Tyranny of Slenderness.*
Creed, Barbara. *The Monstrous-Feminine: Film, Feminism, Psychoanalysis.* London: Routledge, 1993.
Deval, Jacqueline. *Reckless Appetites.* Toronto: Burgher, 1993.
Dunsford, Cathie. *The Journey Home.* Melbourne, Vic.: Spinifex, 1997.
Ellmann, Lucy. *Sweet Desserts.* Harmondsworth: Penguin, 1988.
Ellmann, Maud. *The Hunger Artists: Starving, Writing, and Imprisonment.* Cambridge, Mass.: Harvard University Press, 1993.
Esquivel, Laura. *Like Water for Chocolate.* London: Black Swan, 1989.
Fallon, Patricia, Melanie A. Katzman, and Susan C. Woolley, eds. *Feminist Perspectives on Eating Disorders.* New York: Guilford, 1994.
Faludi, Susan. *Backlash: The Undeclared War against Women.* London: Vintage, 1992.
Gilbert, Sandra M., and Susan Gubar. *The Madwoman in the Attic: The Woman Writer and the Nineteenth-Century Literary Imagination.* New Haven: Yale University Press, 1979.
Gordon, Mary. *Final Payments.* London: Hamilton, 1978.
Grant, Stephanie. *The Passion of Alice.* London: Sceptre, 1995.
Hewitt, Dorothy. *The Toucher.* South Yarra, Vic.: McPhee Gribble, 1993.
Irigaray, Luce. "And the One Doesn't Stir without the Other," translated by Hélène Vivienne Wenzel. *Signs: Journal of Women in Culture and Society* 7 (1981): 60–67.
Knapp, Steven. *Literary Interest: The Limits of Anti-Formalism.* Cambridge, Mass.: Harvard University Press, 1993.
Koval, Ramona. *Eating Your Heart Out.* Ringwood, Vic.: Penguin, 1986.
Laurence, Margaret. *The Diviners.* Toronto: McClelland and Stewart, 1974.
Morrison, Toni. *Beloved.* New York: Knopf, 1987.
Orbach, Susie. *Fat Is a Feminist Issue: The Anti-Diet Guide to Permanent Weight Loss.* New York: Paddington, 1978.
Paretsky, Sara. *A Taste of Life.* Harmondsworth: Penguin 60s, 1995.
Rich, Adrienne. *Of Woman Born: Motherhood as Experience and Institution.* New York: Norton, 1976.
Roth, Geneen. *Feeding the Hungry Heart: The Experience of Compulsive Eating.* Harmondsworth: Plume, 1993.
Russo, Mary. *The Female Grotesque: Risk, Excess, and Modernity.* New York: Routledge, 1994.
Scott, Rosie. *Glory Days.* Auckland: Penguin, 1988.
Shute, Jenefer. *Life-Size.* London: Minerva, 1992.
Singh, Jasbindar. *No Body's Perfect: A Self-Help Manual for Women Who Have Problems with Food.* Auckland: New Women's Press, 1989.

Sussman, Susan. *The Dieter.* London: Headline, 1989.
Tardat, Claude. *Sweet Death.* London: Pandora, 1989.
Walters, Minette. *The Sculptress.* London: Pan, 1993.
Weldon, Fay. *The Fat Woman's Joke.* 1967. Reprint, London: Coronet, 1982.
———. *Life and Loves of a She-Devil.* London: Hodder and Stoughton, 1983.
Winterson, Jeanette. *Oranges Are Not the Only Fruit.* Boston: Pandora, 1985.
———. *Sexing the Cherry.* London: Vintage, 1989.
Wolf, Naomi. *The Beauty Myth: How Images of Beauty Are Used against Women.* London: Chatto and Windus, 1990.

12 Sex and Fat Chics

Deterritorializing the Fat Female Body

JANA EVANS BRAZIEL

Sex and fat chics. Sexy fat chics. Fat chics. Sex. For many, the juxtaposition of these words probably seems unnatural. That is an idea I hope to challenge. This essay analyzes the sexual and social representations of the fat female body. I use the singular deliberately because the rigidity of this construction, as defined in mainstream media, erases the multiplicity of differences manifest in fat embodiment. However, the construction of the fat female body is also marked by a fundamental ambivalence. I contend, in fact, that this body has been the site of two diametrically opposed sexual definitions—the first marked by a dearth of sexual signification (thus the purportedly benign asexuality of the fat body), the second reflecting an oversignification of sexual meaning (thus the fat female body as saturated with sexual masquerade). These two poles of definition render the representation of that body ambivalent.[1]

I isolate examples that illustrate this double paradigm of sexual definition and representation, both addressing the ambiguity of the fat body and speculating about the reasons for that construction. My primary sources include media representations of such various and publicly defined "corpulences" as Elizabeth Taylor, Roseanne Barr, and Oprah Winfrey; a multifarious excess of magazine and television advertisements and articles; and copious postcards of fat women in "drag" (so designated because my research affirms that the fat female, when presented as sexual—at least in mainstream media—is delineated as participating in sexual masquerade). The paucity of sexual signification, which results in the determination of asexuality as one pole, is itself scarcely represented; therefore, I seek to make visible the absences, fissures, and lacunae in this *lack* of representation of fat women. Ironically, the absence in this lack does constitute a necessary presence (as the double negative suggests), because it establishes the necessary subtending representation. What is erased subtends what is visible; what is absent *must* be absent for what is present to have meaning. As Judith Butler contends, "every oppositional discourse will produce its outside, an outside that risks becoming installed as its nonsignifying inscriptional space."[2] In the analysis that follows I intend to give this abstract idea concrete meaning, thereby making visible the erasure of corpulence and corpulent sexuality.

Underlying this ambivalent space (the liminal territory between the *corps/chora* of the sexually carnival-burlesque[3] and the benignly asexual) is the social delineation of the fat female body as perilously diseased and (de)formed. I thus attempt to ground philosophically and theoretically *why* fat female bodies are so problematic. As we will see, fat female bodies undermine the stability of Western metaphysical and dualistic thought: they topple philosophical binarisms in which the female is subordinated to the male, the body subordinated to the soul, and materiality to form. In arguing this point, I examine the Western constructions of the body, especially within Platonic and Aristotelian thought, although I briefly trace the entry of these ideas into modern metaphysics through Christian ideology and Cartesianism. Corpulence as *excessive feminine* (to use Butler's term) catalyzes insubordination to the binaristic thought of Western, patriarchal knowledges and discourses.[4]

Moreover, I conjecture that this proliferation of materiality disrupts and deconstructs subjectivity as metaphysically constructed (initiated within Platonic reason that denies the body, and culminating in the Cartesian *cogito, ergo sum*—"I think, therefore I am"). A nomadic, pluralistic, and destabilized subjectivity ensues, as corpulent bodies present a limitless cartography of intensities, to evoke the language of Gilles Deleuze and Félix Guatarri, for remapping desire. I analyze texts that iconoclastically treat fat female bodies as sites at which subjectivity and signification proliferate, subversive sites of visual and linguistic impropriety. Combining the schizoanalytic work of Deleuze and Guattari in *Mille plateaux* with the feminist theoretical explorations of materiality in Elizabeth Grosz's *Volatile Bodies*, I outline an immanent zone for heterogeneous mappings of desire.[5]

THE CORPOREAL MARK OF ABSENCE AND SEXUAL MASQUERADE: LOCATING THE FAT FEMALE BODY

The mainstream definitions of the fat female body fall under two predominant rubrics: first, the fat female body is defined by a benign asexuality that is marked by a paucity of representation and exists as the unrepresentable, or near-representable (that which is located on the margins of representability), because of an exclusion that I term the *corporeal mark of absence;* second, the fat female body is defined as a site of sexual masquerade—conveying both an excessive salaciousness and a hyperbolic derision of that prurience.

The first definition of the fat female body is difficult to grasp, because it renders visible what does not appear to be present at all. However, the *corporeal mark of absence* cannot *not* be present, as it is a corporeal entity and constitutes the *corps* that sustains the representation. Consider one exemplary representation of a present absence. In perusing the magazine rack in a local grocer (the time and place are irrelevant), the observer can readily establish the paradigms for this genre: the thin, photogenic cover girl; the headline regarding the "newest, medically researched diet plan" that promises to help the reader lose twenty pounds in just three weeks; and a glut of ultrarich chocolate desert recipes. Given the pervasiveness of these magazines, one might assume that their target audience is an overweight woman, but she is nowhere in sight. The corpulent woman constitutes the absence that is evoked as outside the frame of signification and representation, while remaining structurally present as a subtending absence. In this configuration, the fat female is often metonymically signified by representations of food—signifiers that allude both to her excessive fatness that cannot be shown and to her massive materiality that is best represented through inanimate matter—or words that allude to her presence by signifying food, diets, weight loss.

Additionally, food pervades women's magazines (from cover to cover). In four magazines that I examined—*First: For Women, Ladies' Home Journal, Good Housekeeping,* and *Woman's Day*—such advertisements are located on 243 of 851 total pages, constituting nearly 30 percent of the published texts. The individual breakdowns are, respectively, 41 pages, or 33 percent; 61 pages, or 23 percent; 81 pages, or 31 percent; and 60 pages, or 35 percent. The perpetual affiliation of the female with food is a polysemic representation. It also suggests, as Ann Ferguson astutely notes, the domestic sexual division of labor that makes women largely responsible for grocery shopping and food preparation.[6] In this sense, it evokes the "female body" (as construct). However, it also seems to evoke that body's excess, the "fat female body" (as construct). The ever-*present* food advertisements parallel the *absent* body-in-excess: an all-consuming, uncontrollable monstrosity that can be represented only by what she consumes. Food, then, is a metonym that effectively obscures the grotesqueness of what cannot be depicted. This corporeal mark of absence that is the female body—and more excessively, the fat female body—reiterates the archetypal theme that the material world does not exist, or is privative in nature. It thereby constitutes the negative pole of what exists, or what *is* (ontologically speaking), precisely because it *is* incorporeal: in other words, the form, the soul, and the idea all have *being* precisely because they are *not* corporeal.

In "The Anorexic Body," Elspeth Probyn explores the historical construction of *anorexia nervosa,* tracing its transformation from a Christian definition as the *inedia miraculosa* to the medicalized hystericization of the female body.[7] The prevalence of anorexia in the Middle Ages within the Catholic Church, and later as a field of medical and psychoanalytic discourse in the Victorian era, is unsurprising: both periods were overly preoccupied with the body, the first (and perhaps both) marked by an exaggerated desire to eradicate the prison house of corporeity. But Probyn rejects psychoanalytic interpretations of the eating disorder, preferring a Foucauldian analysis for this *technology of the self* as she attempts "to explore anorexia as an embodied moment of negotiation: as a site which shows up the articulations of discourse, the female body and power."[8] I appreciate Probyn's efforts to restore agency to female subjects, and her ideas are potentially subversive. Indeed, her analysis does offer one way out of the self-abnegation related to anorexia, as does Deleuze's, discussed below; but I believe that anorexia usually, and lamentably, manifests a societally imposed and self-interpellated dictum to *not be* that plays out in the diminution of the self through a process of dissolution, a death drive propelled toward nonexistence. An anorexic woman interviewed on the November 16, 1995, episode of CBS's *48 Hours* made a statement that seems to exemplify this interpellation of female nonexistence (though of course she does not speak for all anorectics): "I won't be happy if I weigh five pounds—I won't *be*—because there'll still be those five pounds" (emphasis added).

Before the Victorian era, lasciviousness and corpulence were frequently conjoined, as equally rooted in the essence of corporeity—uncontainable, excessive. After it (concurrent with a Freudian definition of woman as "lack"),[9] sexual eroticism was split from corpulence; in this paradigm shift, carnal desire was inscribed onto the thin female body. Artistic images of beauty suggest such a shift: compare the exemplarily fleshly women in *Le bain turc* (1862) by Ingres—already excessive in its orientalizing mask, its plethora of nude female bodies—with the waif-like Kate Moss, portraying perhaps a sort of opulence but certainly not bodily exorbitance.

A recent study brings this ontological ideal onto the plane of medicalized discourse. Researchers at Harvard Medical School and Boston's Brigham and Women's Hospital "found that women weighing at least 15 percent *less* than average were the least likely to die prematurely, and that death rates rose steadily with increasing heft—even in women who weren't officially obese."[10] Even without the *Newsweek* reporters' emphases ("women weighing *at least,*" "the *least* likely," "death rates *rose* steadily with *increasing heft*"), the implicit message is that *least is best.* The established binarism opposes a contained to an intractable, transgressive, and unbound corporeality that will (through its very excess) induce illness and death. And the pole of the *contained* is the body that weighs less than 120 pounds (given a 5'5" frame)—anything beyond this limit constitutes the body unbound, or out of bounds. One could question the presuppositions motivating such a research project, but the circular logic that propels researchers in the name of Science need not be deconstructed here. However, equally suggestive is the article's pictorial accompaniment: on the left, Kate Moss stands slender in her CK midriff-baring T-shirt, juxtaposed to a sweatsuit-clad Oprah (who despite her weight loss and improved fitness, the findings imply, still faces an early demise, because she is not slightly underweight); and framing this whole material affair, on the far right (farthest from the "threshold of 'fat' "), the even more portly Roseanne.

The second definition of the fat female body is almost directly opposed to the first: the corpulent woman is depicted in full regalia, ornamented and flamboyantly arrayed; she is licentiously saturated with sexual masquerade. Her excess is both jocund and rotund; her body is the site of performative excess—she is the unbound carnality of hypercorporeity. The pornographic magazine *Plumpers and Big Women,* touted as a cornucopia of corpulence *for the men* who love it (and thus hardly woman-centered), is nonetheless an arguably fat-positive and fat-sexy medium.[11] The magazine, moreover, seems either to celebrate or satirize the language of corpulence with such feature titles as "Big and Dominant Women: Part I," "P(l)umping Up," "Bulk Rate," "Excess," "The Big Picture," and "Maximum Exposure."

The female bodies in *Plumpers* range from the extremely thin (since most of the advertisements in the magazine are for phone sex lines whose ads feature models exhibiting traditional standards of beauty and body size); to the slightly chubby, heartily Rubenesque or voluptuous body; to the more fleshily corpulent models of 500+ pounds. Yet here even the thin pornographic models bear the mark of corporeal excess, because most of the photos are of women-on-women: a compounding of the corporeality already constructed on the materiality of the female body. One advertisement in particular features three women in black lingerie posing above a mirror, so that the image is automatically doubled, excessively autoproliferating.

The December 1995 issue of *Plumpers* contains an interview with Teighlor, a fat pornography model who also poses for a greeting card company called *Rockshots*, described by the interviewer—in a huge understatement—as a corporation that creates "greeting cards with big women in wild outfits."[12] Although the pictorials in *Plumpers* are largely standard pornographic delineations, the photographs taken for *Rockshots* border on the carnivalesque. In one *Rockshots* Christmas card featuring Teighlor, she is standing in front of a bright red backdrop that matches her artificially colored and ringleted hair, adorned with a brilliant royal blue flower. Loosely suspended along the axis of her body, but hardly concealing it, hangs a yellow beach towel with the cartoon eye of Betty Boop gazing from its center. Teighlor's face is also an artifact—masked in garish makeup and a maniacal simper. The card opens, and as the paper unfolds, the layers of Teighlor's corpulence cascade; the rolls of flesh move centrifugally, escaping the axis, the bounds of the *contained* body.[13] Another *Rockshots* Christmas card that features a different model provides an even more farcical delineation of the fat female body. The model is dressed in a green-and-red tutu, holding a bouquet of poinsettias that match the two flowers attached to her nipples; as if parodying the "big hair" of many pornographic models, but of course hyperbolically, she has bright red hair that has been teased out, Phyllis Diller–style; she is masquerading in a gold-sequined mask, framed by green Christmas-ornaments-turned-earrings and by a beaded necklace that dangles between her drooping poinsettias. From top to bottom, she is the carnivalesque inscribed on the body of the fat female, grounded in her red Converse All-Stars.

The two definitions of the fat female body—*corporeal absence* and site of *sexual masquerade*—merge in a Foster Grant ad that ran in a 1995 issue of *People Magazine*.[14] The ad shows two young, thin women pedestaled on a washing machine, donning sunglasses. The caption below the picture reads: "We wear Foster Grants to avoid contact with the lady folding the incredibly huge panties." The sunglass lenses simultaneously cut off the gaze and block out the body of the fat lady. This prohibited gaze, and the resultant erasure of corpulence, establishes a discursive boundary that demarcates bodies—thin and fat, beautiful and (presumably) not, present and absent. Though "the lady folding the incredibly huge panties" does not appear in this ad, she exists as the corporeal mark of absence that allows the structural coherence of the advertisement; her "huge panties" are the synecdochal markers of her absent presence, signifying her logical and even corporeal necessity, yet suggesting the transgressive corporeity that cannot be imaged. The fat female, who thus marks the *unseen* and the *unrepresentable,* also constitutes the space of marketed derision, spectacle, and ridicule. But though the laughter of the beautiful, thin models is structurally founded on her fatness, they clearly must avoid contact with this dissolute and polluting, if carnivalesque, corpulence.

In a similar advertisement for Fox's *Melrose Place* that ran in several national magazines, including *TV Guide,* a photograph of the crew's bombshell beauties is juxtaposed to a picture of two antiquated, stodgy—and yes, fat—women in swimming caps and old-fashioned bathing suits. Above them are two separate captions: "Cool like them" runs above the fat women, "Cool like us" above the actresses. At the bottom of the page, a third caption declares: "You are what you watch" (recalling the adage "You are what you eat"), providing not only an advertisement for *Melrose Place* but another prohibition against gazing on the fat female body, as if making a teasing threat. The fat female body again constitutes that which should not be seen, perhaps that which should not *be* at all.

This ontological prohibition against corpulence, like our contemporary dis-ease with corpulence, stems from a metaphysical proscription against corporality itself, historically rooted in the Platonic tradition of discomfort with the body. In the next section, I outline the Western perceptions of the body and, more negatively, fat bodies or bodies out of bounds.

WESTERN PERCEPTIONS OF THE BODY AND BODIES OUT OF BOUNDS

Richard Klein writes in his scandalously wonderful and mantric book *Eat Fat,* "Hippocrates, the father of Greek medicine, considered fat a disease." Klein remarks on a Greek ambivalence toward fatness, noting both the aesthetic balance (of angles and curves) in Greek statues and the tendency of medical and philosophical discourses to denounce fatness. After all, he observes, "Socrates danced every morning as a way of controlling his weight."[15] Klein focuses on the aesthetic "landscape of the human body" within Greek culture in order to expose a more fat-friendly time;[16] however, it is the Greek philosophical conception of fat, rather than any aesthetic appreciation of flesh, that has most indelibly left its mark on Western thought.

Indeed, Hippocrates considered fat not only a disease but also a largely gendered affliction. Even today, fatness in men marks them as "effeminate," "emasculated," and "soft." For both the male and the female, health depends on a homeostatic balance, but the porous nature of the female—in her capacity to retain moisture, as well as exude it—renders her particularly vulnerable, in Hippocrates' view, to fluctuation and imbalance.[17]

For Plato and Aristotle, corporeality and its excess, corpulence, are also gendered categories. According to Elizabeth Grosz, "since the inception of philosophy as a separate and self-contained discipline in ancient Greece, philosophy has established itself on the foundations of a profound somatophobia." She points to the etymological association made in Plato's *Cratylus:* "Plato claims that the word *body* (*sōma*) was introduced by Orphic priests, who believed that man was a spiritual or noncorporeal being trapped in the body as in a dungeon (*sēma*)."[18] And some dungeons are worse than others: in the *Timaeus,* Timaeus states that if man "lived a good life throughout the due course of his time, he would at the end return to his dwelling place in his companion star, to live a life of happiness that agreed with his character"; however, "if he failed this, he would be born a second time, now as a woman" (42b2–4).[19] As a man, without any constitutional "flaw" (or "corrupt condition," 86e) and with "proper nurture to supplement his education, he'll turn out perfectly whole and healthy, and will have escaped the most grievous of illnesses" (44b6–c10).

This "most grievous of illnesses" is a process of deformation in which "all the bodily processes are made to flow backwards" (84c11–12) and the "process of generation that led to the formation of these structures is reversed" (82c5–6). Under normal conditions, according to Timaeus, fibrous matter prevents this liquefaction, and the "the body resists dissolution" (85e21–22): "These fibers act to preserve a balance of thinness and thickness, i.e., to prevent . . . the blood from getting *so liquid, due to the body's heat, that it oozes out from the body's pores*" (85c7–8, emphasis added). The hyperbolic descriptions of this state in certain passages of the *Timaeus* reveal a metaphysical hydrophobia:

> For when flesh that is wasting away passes its wastes back into the veins, the veins will contain . . . agents of destruction. . . . [And they wage] war against the constituents of the body that have stayed intact and kept to their posts, corrupting and dissolving them. (82e16–83a8)

> The flesh, which collapses with it away from its roots, leaves the sinews bare and full of brine. And the flesh itself succumbs back into the bloodstream, where it works to aggravate the previously mentioned diseases. (84a19–b2)

> [As it] flows in, it overpowers the fibers with its own heat. It boils over and shakes them up into utter confusion. And if it proves capable of sustaining its power to the end, it penetrates to the marrow and burns it up, thereby loosening the cables that hold the soul there, like a ship, and setting the soul free. (85e17–21)

These pathological fluids attack all other elements on contact; and although these organs resist dissolution and attempt to stand firm and "keep to their posts," in the end they suffer putrefaction, decomposition, liquefaction. It is precisely this lack of fixity—the vulnerability to flux, fluctuation, and Becoming—that renders fluidity so problematic for Timaeus; the somatic dissolution (from flesh to fiber to blood to bile) caused by disease is a process of deformation, rather than an alteration in substance.

As I argue below, *fat is pollution.*

Moreover, fat—an excessive corporeality—which has been historically affiliated with the female body (posited within the Western metaphysical tradition as inherently material and intrinsically devoid of form, rationality, and soul), is also associated with disease, with the polluting dissolution of the body manifest in an oozing liquidity. The *Timaeus* suggests that for Plato, the female is a pathological liquefaction of the male, a dissolution of Form; this purely privative and diseased state must be eradicated through restoration of the fe/male to maleness—the ideal and positive Form.

For Timaeus, decomposition further indicates a correlation between corporeity and the female—indeed, between corpulence and the female—by isolating body parts where women store more fat: "thighs and calves, the area around the hips, arms (both upper and lower), and all other bodily parts where there are no joints as well as all the internal bones, are all fully provided with flesh. It is because they have only small amounts of soul in their marrow, and so are devoid of intelligence" (75a15–19). The excessive liquidity and compositional porosity of the female, as noted earlier, is distinctly Hippocratic in origin.

This Timaean premise precedes but also anticipates the Aristotelian association between physical softness and moral weakness, a link that is further related to the female: "self-indulgence is a kind of softness," declares Aristotle, and "the female is distinguished [by softness] from the male" (*Nicomachean Ethics* 7.7, 1150b3, 16).[20] A correlation between softness (*malakia*), frequently interpreted metaphorically, and intemperance (*asōphrosunē*) or, more explicitly, incontinence (*akrasia*), is outlined in the *Nicomachean Ethics.* Aristotle repeats this correlation frequently in the treatise, always emphasizing the baseness of these characteristics: "Trying to avoid burdens is softness" (3.7, 1116a14–15); "Incontinence and softness seem to be base and blameworthy conditions" (7.1, 1145b9–10); "The person who is prone to be overcome by pleasures is incontinent; the one who overcomes is continent; the one overcome by pains is soft; and the one who overcomes them is resistant" (7.6, 1150a13–15); "The continent person is opposed to the incontinent, and the resistant to the soft" (1150a33); "Someone who is deficient in withstanding what most people withstand, and are capable of withstanding, is soft and self-indulgent; for self-indulgence is a kind of softness" (7.7, 1150b1–3).

The mantra, for Aristotle, is *softness equals baseness.*

As in the *Timaeus,* this state of softness (*malakia*) is gendered. Aristotle also writes that "the female is distinguished [by softness] from the male" (7.7, 1150b16). This association suggests a physiological cause for incontinence, if we take the term *malakia* not metaphorically but literally—as a physical softness of the body (an interpretation that seems appropriate, given that, according to book 2 of the *Generation of Animals* [see especially 726b–766b], female inferiority has an anatomical basis). Moreover, in the *History of Animals* Aristotle delineates the female body as *malako*-corporeal, fleshy and porous—a distinctly Hippocratic description—further supporting the contention that softness is a morphological condition: "the female is less muscular and less compactly jointed . . . more flaccid in texture of flesh" (538a23–b11).[21] Deborah Modrak, a feminist philosopher, also interprets *malakia* as a corporeal attribute: she writes that "the ultimate explanation for moral weakness is, Aristotle claims, physiological."[22]

Corporeality = softness = moral weakness
Corpulence = excessive softness = excessive moral weakness

Thus we have the Western conception of fatness, as shaped by Aristotle—a stereotype that still persists, as the medical discourses of obesity and psychological discourses of pathological fatness reveal.

Aristotle's paradigm—the female principle as corporeal and inferior, the male principle as incorporeal and superior—is adopted by subsequent generations of thinkers, and his views fully inform the early Christian writers who not only equate woman with corporeity but further affiliate this materiality with carnality.[23] As these ideas become further moralized within Christian thought, there begins at least one strain of the Western problematic of consumption and bodies. The female, as agent culpable for the fall of mankind, manifests both irrationality and sensuality and thereby entices the more reasonable male with the wiles of her tainted flesh. In contrast, the male is regarded as bearing the divine image of God; thus he is capable of rational reflection, although his postlapsarian reason is also limited. The two main results of the Fall are incontinence (a corruption of the created body) and mental opacity (a corruption of man's reason, limiting his capacity to comprehend divine Being): according to the church fathers, the female more fully bears the former, corporeal fate, and the male suffers from the latter, mental consequence, precisely because the female is believed to lack a reason that could have been corrupted. In Aristotelian fashion, the female was determined to be responsible for the material, the male for the immaterial. Many of the church fathers, displaying the dualistic thought characteristic of early Christianity, even believed sensuality and promiscuity to be the defining nature of original sin. The carnality of woman seduces man, leading him astray morally, just as Eve seductively deceived Adam into tasting the forbidden fruit. Ironically, the first transgression is an act of eating.

Austerity and asceticism, not plenitude or indulgence, defined the limits of the body. Klein notes, "In early Christian times, one aspired . . . to the anorexic skeleton of the anchorite, or hermit, who retreated from the material world, from all its delicious pleasures. For Christians, appetite is a lure that ensnares the soul and perverts its pious impulses."[24] In the early Christian era, according to Grosz, "the matter/form distinction is refigured in terms of the distinction between substance and accident and between a God-given soul and a mortal, lustful, sinful carnality. Within the Christian tradition, the separation of mind and body was correlated with the distinction between what is immortal and what is mortal."[25]

Notably, what persists into the Christian era is the gendered mark of corporeality, and the femininity of materiality is hyperbolized in corpulence.

Fat is feminine.

These ancient and medieval ideas about materiality and embodiment culminate perhaps most fully in Descartes's thought—as Cartesian dualism "establishes an unbridgeable gulf between mind and matter" and ultimately "succeeded in linking the mind/body opposition to the foundations of knowledge itself." Grosz continues, "the Cartesian tradition has been more influential than any other tradition in establishing the agenda for philosophical reflection and in defining the terrain, either negatively or positively, for later concepts of subjectivity and knowledge."[26]

NOMADIC TRAJECTORIES, METAPHYSICAL DECONSTRUCTION, AND REVALUATIONS OF MATERIALITY

Many feminist, poststructuralist, and queer theorists have been instrumental in deconstructing the structural binarisms inherent within metaphysics. In this section, I sketch out some of their ideas, which offer a theoretical frame for deconstructing the singular (and delimiting) construction of the "fat female body" and suggest ways of rethinking the pluralities of fat embodiment, and indeed all embodiment.

In terms strikingly similar to those employed in Plato's *Timaeus*, Elizabeth Grosz finds parallels for the classical gendered paradigm lingering into our postmodern era. Using Julia Kristeva's *Powers of Horror: An Essay on Abjection* and Mary Douglas's *Purity and Danger*, Grosz articulates the disquieting and uncontainable nature of fluidity, maintaining that body fluids "attest to a certain irreducible 'dirt' or disgust, a horror of the unknown or the unspecifiable that permeates, lurks, lingers, and at times leaks out of the body."[27]

In the chapter of *Speculum of the Other Woman* titled "Volume-Fluidity," Luce Irigaray also isolates fluidity as defining the male construct *femininité*.[28] All liquids seem to take the shape of a container, remaining malleable; the male therefore can funnel female liquidity into whatever space necessary within discourse. She thus can be made to serve as the essential outside of his thought. Yet all liquids also threaten to elude containment entirely. This fluidity, whether it gives rise to an actual hydrophobia or spurs a more abstract fear of what is uncontainable—undesignatable, unascertainable, or inherently unfixed—is en-gendered by the male categorically as an opposed and perilous Other: the female body, which threatens male authority. My main point here is that these constructed binarisms will collapse if overburdened—and ultimately they will be.

Grosz clarifies Irigaray's deconstructive reading of the Western metaphysical tradition by explaining that for Irigaray, the philosophical "disquiet about the fluid, the viscous, the half-formed, or the indeterminate has to do with the cultural unrepresentability of fluids." Grosz further notes the association of fluidity "with femininity, with maternity, with the corporeal, all elements subordinated to the privilege of the self-identical, the one, the unified, the solid."[29] Fluidity, like materiality, threatens to disrupt the metaphysical ideal of immutability by its very potential for flux, flow, dissolution, and alteration. Within this metaphysical economy, the female is seen to incarnate (and fluidly, malleably disincarnate) that which disrupts and subverts thought itself. Intimating that this affiliation of materiality, femininity, and fluidity is "contemporary," Grosz asks: "Can it be that in the West, in our time, the female body has been constructed not only as a lack or absence but with more complexity, as a leaking, uncontrollable, seeping liquid; as formless flow; as viscosity, entrapping, secreting; as lacking not so much or simply the phallus but self-containment—not a cracked or porous vessel, like a leaking ship, but a formlessness that engulfs all form, a disorder that threatens all order? I am not suggesting that this is how women *are*, that it is their ontological status. Instead, my hypothesis is that women's corporeality is inscribed as a mode of seepage."[30] This inscription of *feminine* corporeality, though contemporary, has roots extending back for centuries within Western thought, as the earlier examination of fluidity in Hippocratic and Platonic thought demonstrates. Unsurprisingly, one of the most pervasive representations of fat in contemporary culture is as a "diseased" material—bilious, humorous, gelatinous, lethargic, insalubriously asalacious, and markedly asexual, if not utterly revolting. To use Kristeva's word, it is the abject.[31]

A postcard photograph by Michael Huhn titled the *Slime Lady* vividly displays the association of corporeity with fluidity—indeed, a polluting, contaminating, and viscous liquidity—in an artifact of popular culture.[32] In female corpulence—to a more exaggerated degree than in female bodies that are thin—this fluidity (posited as noxious, venomous, and virulent) manifests the body-in-excess. As such, it actively exceeds the boundaries of solids; it melts and dissolves into a scrofulous and pustulant exudate that cannot be contained, that is both deforming and threatening to deform. Therein lies the perilousness of the corporeal (defined as intrinsically *female* in the metaphysical tradition) for the male: its liquescent capacity for eroding the ideal form—solidity—of the male, for transgressively deconstructing "masculinist" discourse through its purportedly essential flow and flux, and for subverting the one, the unified, the solid, the phallic. The visual and grotesque representation of the *Slime Lady* captures this quintessentially (according to masculinist logic) deforming and abortifacient corpulence: covered with green and yellow slime, she is squatting on a trash can on the sidewalk of an urban street, manifesting *en corps* an act of auto-deformation, as if aborting herself. This disfiguring liquidity of female corpulence parallels almost exactly the ancient Platonic and Aristotelian associations of the female body with a degenerative, dissolute materiality.

Flux, and the fluctuations of the material, has always been problematic for metaphysical theories that seek to transcend the body and find solidity, fixity, and stasis in abstract ideals. If the body is already viewed as manifesting the tenuousness of flux and fluctuation, then the *in*-flux, *out*-flux, *up*-flux, *down*-flux of the fat body heighten that tenuousness (also suggestive is the *re*-flux of the bulimic body, though that falls outside the scope of this essay). Thus, in the next section I structure my readings of the corpulent bodies of Roseanne and Liz Taylor around the topoi of *flux* and fluctuation, amorphousness and malleability—as opposed to the metaphysical ideas of immutability, stasis, and solid resistance to transformation.

The theories most persistently anti-Platonic are perhaps those formulated by Gilles Deleuze and Félix Guattari, who propose a radical materialism in constant creative flux within a field of immanence. They thereby reject such Platonic premises as the rationality of the soul and the fixity and immutability of Being in a transcendent realm. The Deleuzo-Guattarian "body without organs," the BwO, promises an affective, not teleologically effective, field for the reinscription of bodies and desires:

> The BwO is made in such a way that it can be occupied, populated, only by intensities. Only intensities pass and circulate. Still, the BwO is a scene, a place, or even a support upon which something comes to pass. It has nothing to do with phantasy, there is nothing to interpret. The BwO causes intensities to pass: it produces and distributes them in a *spatium* that is itself intensive, lacking extension. It is not a space nor is it in space; it is matter that occupies space to a given degree—to the degree corresponding to the intensities produced. It is nonstratified, unformed, intense matter. The matrix of intensity, intensity = 0.[33]

The BwO enables the cartography of desire, the mapping of intensities and their traversal on this immanent matrix; the BwO is "the *field of immanence* of desire, the *plane of consistency* specific to desire (with desire defined as a process of production without reference to any exterior agency, whether it be a lack that hollows it out or a pleasure that fills it)."[34] Deleuze and Guattari thus offer in their body without organs a model for rethinking materiality and the body in anti-essentialist and antifoundationalist ways.

The body without organs is a materiality stripped of deterministic, biologistic limitations; the BwO is materiality as mapped by energy, intensities, desires, and the affects of those energies and desires. Deleuze and Claire Parnet declare: "Bodies without organs—this is desire. There are many kinds, but they are definable by what occurs on them and in them:

continuums of intensity, blocs of becoming, emissions of particles, combinations of fluxes."[35] The BwO therefore offers a model for thinking about corporeality, and thus corpulent bodies, that resists the metaphysical subordination of body to soul, matter to form. The body without organs is always that which desire assembles. In the case of bulimia, they write, "It is a question of food fluxes." The bulimic body "consists of a body without organs with voids and fullnesses. The alternation of stuffing and emptying: anorexic feasts . . . void and fullness are like two demarcations of intensity; the point is always to float in one's own body."[36] This reading of the bulimic body does not idealize it: all BwO are constituted by the desires and intensities passing through them. Like Probyn's reading of anorexia as self-technology, Deleuze and Parnet's reading of bulimia offers a way out of a self-abnegating discourse/disease by providing a space in which the corpulent body can be redefined. For just like the anorexic or bulimic body, the corpulent body *is* a desiring machine—a spatium in *flux* through which intensities flow, energies pass. The corpulent body without organs becomes as a spatium defined by the desires and intensities traversing it: all its food fluxes, rippling affects, and fleshly intensities.

Ironically, Deleuze and Guattari maintain that the way to make oneself a BwO is by entering a process of "becoming" initiated first by "becoming-woman" (*devenir-femme*): "She never ceases to roam upon a body without organs. She is the abstract line, or a line of flight." For these postmodern theorists, "although all becomings are already molecular, including becoming-woman, it must be said that all becomings begin with and pass through becoming-woman. It is the key to all other becomings."[37] I read this "becoming-woman" as a deliberate reversal of the Platonic/Timaean argument about the wayward man "becoming woman" in his next life if he behaves too lasciviously in this one. Thus, the process of "becoming" inaugurated by the "becoming-woman" is also a reversal of Platonic form (the immutable base of the soul's subjectivity) that is then disrupted by deliberate retreat into matter: the excessive feminine in her endless flux and the multiplicity manifests the quintessence of that materiality—as posited by Plato.

The excessive feminine—because the female is historically postulated as the corporeal pole of human existence, or even by some metaphysicians as that which is *essentially* nonexistent—confounds definitions of the self based on the oppositions body/soul and interiority/exteriority. The excessive feminine simultaneously burdens the confines of containment, "the demarcation of limit," and overflows into "the sign of excess":[38] thus, the excessive feminine always already threatens the limits of containment and confinement. In this context, fat female bodies can only hyperbolize "incarnate" excess, threatening to overflow the parameters of metaphysical thought and metaphysical constructs; the intensities and desires of fat, transgressive bodies without organs cannot be contained. I do not mean to argue an essentialist position; on the contrary, my point is that the male economy (in its dichotomous constructions of gender, etc.) cannot support a logical outgrowth of its own constructions. The system thus falls into disarray.

I turn now to alternative (even anomalous) representations of female corporeity—and, more excessively, female corpulence or sexy fat chics—that unsettle the dualistic ideals of the Western metaphysical tradition. Perhaps overdetermining, burdening, and loading (gorging, gormandizing, and saturating) the traditionally devalorized pole within this bipolar paradigm will cause it to collapse under the weight of its own divisive premises. In the next section, I adopt some of the theoretical language of the two poststructuralist models outlined above. Specifically, I borrow Grosz's conception of *flux,* as defined in her retheorizations of corporeality in *Volatile Bodies,* and Deleuze and Guattari's terms *desire, intensities,* and *bodies without organs* from *Mille plateaux.*

CORPOREAL SITES OF SUBVERSION AND THE "BECOMING-MULTIPLICITOUS" OF THE FAT FEMALE BODY

As if satirizing, parodying—or perhaps even embracing—the association of female corpulence with fluidity and pollution, Roseanne poses with now ex-husband Tom Arnold in a playful and interpretively loaded photographic image by Annie Leibowitz.[39] The lovers are mire-spattered, lying in watery mud: Roseanne's body—in all its glorious corpulence—surrounds the male body of Tom Arnold. This smothering embrace reveals, I believe, one of the elements implicit within the metaphysical tradition: fear of being dominated by an indomitable materiality that eludes containment, that overwhelms, and confuses male control. By deliberately embodying the corpulent female Other in all her carnal, lascivious, dissolute materiality, Roseanne also embodies a masculinist fear of the unbound. Transgressing containment, proliferating multiplicitously into corpulence, her body is truly one of *flux.* As such, it is defined by the intensities and desires—the mud, the muck, the mounds of fluid flesh, the embrace—traversing it.

Not only does Roseanne transgressively embody corpulence, she also shifts like a chameleon, constantly fluctuating in appearance, temperament, mood, and personality. After Roseanne married Ben Thomas, Carrie Fisher captured her malleable subjectivity in a profile in *Vanity Fair:* "Full of different things at all times (alternately, for example, she might be full of fun, beans, the dickens, mischief, shit or foreboding), Roseanne emanates mainly life," adding, "Ben has dragged this Sumerian fertility goddess by her ragged brown hair screaming and laughing all the way back to their spacious Brentwood love cave."[40] Fisher's words illustrate the polymorphic personality (and perversity?) of Roseanne—at once, *this;* suddenly, *that.* Fisher playfully alludes to traditional representations of corporeity—ludicly, the fat female body (here, Roseanne's) is both carnal and irrational—while also confounding such corporeal archetypes: the fat female is swollen not exclusively with the fullness of "beans" and "shit," but also with "fun," "the dickens," "mischief," and "foreboding." This carnality, ambivalently tinged with sadomasochistic desire (perhaps a parody of the submissive and subordinate female, which Roseanne is obviously not!), also displays the fecundity of a "Sumerian fertility goddess." Her shifting subjectivity seems self-crafted, elusively (and yet ironically) self-defined, as revealed in the opening clip to her TV sitcom *Roseanne:* a rapid montage that blurs various images of Roseanne over the years, making her appear to be mal- or transforming before the viewer's gaze. In flux. Laurel Fishman also notes this shifting subjectivity in an article titled "Big Beautiful Women of the 90s," which appropriately introduces Roseanne as "Actress. Comedienne. Producer. Screenwriter. Entrepreneur. Restaurateur. Author. Multimillionaire. Iconoclast. Feminist. Mother. Former maid, dishwasher, window dresser, waitress and prostitute."[41] The first, seemingly stable elements are valorized syntactically, distinctly separated by periods (and marked by affluence and prestige). The elements in the last fragment enter a metonymic, fluid slide signaled punctuationally, rendered indistinct and indeterminate by commas. By its structure, the description emphasizes how working-class jobs (indeed poverty and the poor) blur indistinguishably for the affluent. The audience, the readers, her viewers are reminded of Roseanne's own (paradoxical?) fluid distinction/indistinction in relation to issues of class. This metonymic, fluid slide seems to constitute that enigmatic and ever-shifting self called Roseanne. *Flux. Desire.*

Elizabeth Taylor has also occupied the public imagination, for nearly fifty years—moving in and out of the media's dissecting eyes; in and out of tragedy, scandal, and success; and, more mundanely, in and out of rehabilitation clinics, dress sizes, and marriages. She too has incarnated a shifting site of subjectivity, constantly traversing the ever-metamorphosing trajectories of her unstable self. As with Roseanne, Liz's corpulence (and the flux that it sets in motion) is central to this shifting subjectivity. In a 1996 documentary on Elizabeth Taylor's life, written by David Ansen and produced by Ellen M. Krass and Bruce Bailey for PBS, the actress very aptly states her excessively nomadic subjectivity, ever-changing in several sections of the documentary as well as in phases of her life: "I have had everything, I've been back and forth like a yo-yo." She later adds, " 'The more the better' has always been my motto," and the narrator, Constance McCashin, describes her as "a chameleon who changed *our* colors." Although the fluid bodily shifts of Liz Taylor may seem to more closely resemble the out-of-control body without organs than the desirous, subversive corpulence of Roseanne, Taylor's body-in-flux, like that of her younger colleague, overburdens the body/soul divide.

In an exciting essay that probes the limits of beauty in relation to corpulence, " 'I embrace the difference': Elizabeth Taylor and the Closet," Melissa Jane Hardie discusses the vacillation between thinness and fatness of this popular, public icon. Hardie argues that "recent representations of Taylor's body as unattractively abundant, as perilous and physically uncontainable—as having over-stepped the mark" are inextricably grounded "in her historic sex appeal," and explores the semiotic coding of Taylor's corpulent corporeality, the very codification of her fat: "Taylor's positionality is cemented in and by her body. It is stretched across the conundrum of feminine corporeality as both expanse and circumference, the demarcation of limit and the sign of excess. . . . To resemble 'a woman who has everything' offers Taylor's look as a vulgar excess matched materially by her dress; to have herself—her body—is already to have too much."[42] As Taylor's weight and body size continually shift, "these deliberations offer her body as grotesque, a characteristic apparent as much in its ability to shed as to gain weight." Hardie further connects this oscillatory facet of Taylor with her oft-repeated positioning of herself as wife: "As Taylor's body has been depicted as waxing and waning, her sheer capacity has been troped through her marriages as a symptom of excessive plurality."[43] For Hardie, Taylor's writing is also associated with her body *as* text, reflecting her "tactic of making visible in writing the question of the visibility and invisibility afforded by the body"—for as Taylor herself declares in *Elizabeth Takes Off*, "I had taken my image and scratched it with graffiti."[44]

By recognizing a ludic interplay between delimitation and augmentation, reduction and expansion, and loss and gain in Taylor's body and in her construction of identity, Hardie emphasizes the role in Taylor's book of the rhetorical trope that she calls *dilation,* which she defines as "rhetorical expansion, dilation and deferral, a figure traditionally associated with the fat woman, and signaling also a concern with walls, or partitions, and with the control of excess and deferral as constitutive textual features."[45] In describing its rhetorical, textual functioning, Hardie relies on the analysis of Patricia Parker in *Literary Fat Ladies:* "To dilate means variously to expand and to adumbrate, to defer and to generate; the rhetorical figure of *dilation* reads the text organically to diagnose texts which go on: for their 'amplified textuality and dilated middles' (Parker 1987:15). . . . *Dilation* is also interested in the ways in which texts are partitioned, in the 'dividing of a discourse': '*Dilation* . . . is always something to be kept within the horizon of an ending, mastery and control, and the "matter" is always to be varied within certain formal guidelines or rules' (Parker 1987:14)."[46] Hardie's use of Parker's model is fascinating: in reading the vacillating body as a trope for the textual style that marks Taylor's autobiography, she effectively employs a strategy of "writing the body" that includes a textual reading of the body as well: "If she is always a visual text, always a 'take off,' her text operates a radical containment, and, like her weight gain *and* weight loss, as writing on top of the movie still."[47] Taylor's capacity to lose/gain, to constantly traverse the bounds of corporeity, to shift the significance of the body that she variously inhabits—as fat, thin, pudgy, and every possibility along such a continuum—enacts forms of rhetorical dilation; yet even in her dilations, control is never finalized. Thus, her body-in-flux manages to elude the fixity of signification and unchanging subjectification.

I am interested in Taylor's persona, her image, her public body without organs, and the intensities of our own conflicting desires that pass through that body image. Even if not always in control of her body-in-flux, Taylor still nomadically embodies an alter-corporeality that subverts the idealized thin body. In her fluctuating body images, Taylor subverts (for us, perhaps?) the dominant paradigm of thin beauty, by both embodying this ideal and embodying that which is other. In this sense, she radically incarnates (and disincarnates) a nomadic subjectivity. Liz Taylor *as* Liz Taylor clearly has a "public" body and a "private" body—*Liz* as "image" and as person. Hardie notes that "the public body, being, like all bodies, in the world, but also in the *limelight,* is also the body that betrayed her private habits (overeating)."[48] However, in a Deleuzo-Guattarian reading, her "public" body constitutes a spatium, a "body without organs" for the traversal and movement of social desire, intensities, and energies, both those of pleasure and those of conflict.

In this final section, I have traced the trajectories of fat deterritorialization in the textual bodies of Roseanne and Liz Taylor, as they perform the spectacle of their bodies-in-flux, their bodies-in-excess. As women whose representations, even within mainstream media, defy the reductive and singular depictions of the "fat female body," Roseanne and Liz have opened new doors for representing fat beauty and fat sexualities.

In alternative media, Teighlor's pornographic photographs (in *Plumpers* and elsewhere) challenge traditional notions of beauty grounded in thinness and explicitly redefine fat bodies and sexualities, even if her *Rockshots* poses regrettably (in my mind) reinforce corpulence as carnivalesque. Other venues such as *FaT GiRL* (a pornographic dyke zine that is, regrettably, now no longer being published), eloquently discussed by Le'a Kent in this volume, also have created alternative, provocative, and sexy possibilities for fat lesbian, bisexual and trans-identified women. Even in mainstream media, the last couple of years have marked a subtle, but notable shift (or at least a ripple in the oceanic immensity of idealized thin beauty). Actress Camryn Manheim of *The Practice* and Star Jones, talk show co-host of *The View,* force prime-time and day-time television viewers to rethink the boundaries of corpulence, beauty, and sexuality (if less graphically than the pornographic media do). Manheim's memoir, *Wake Up, I'm Fat!,* features Camryn on the cover as a bathing-suited beauty queen, crowned in the pageant as "Miss Understood."

Sex and fat chics? Sexy fat chics? Yes! Or, as Manheim playfully writes in the closing lines of her book, "this fat lady is singing . . . and the celebration has just begun."[49]

NOTES

1. In her careful and thoughtful reading of this manuscript, Ann Ferguson noted that these two poles fail to represent the positioning of the maternal body, which may be represented as sexual and positively "full." Her point is important; however, the topos of the "maternal" body bears a specificity that does not necessarily parallel the construct of the "fat female body," which is by default *non-productive.* In other words, it seems to me that the "fat" body must be explicitly productive—i.e., pregnant or maternal (a literal testament to its possibility for sexuality?)—to attain sexual representation not defined along the poles I have suggested. To be sure, counterhegemonic or transgressive sexual representations of fatness do exist: e.g., the sexual representations of the fat lesbian body in *FaT GiRL,* touted as a "zine for fat dykes and the women who want them" (see Le'a Kent, "Fighting Abjection: Representing Fat Women," chapter 7 of this volume). Ann also expressed reservations about my reading of Elizabeth Taylor as "subversive." Because I speak less to Taylor's personal experiences of fat-thin than to her public persona and the public's gaze, which regards her body-in-flux, I maintain

that Taylor does subvert the dominant paradigm of thin beauty by at once embodying this ideal and also embodying (at times) something that is other. It is in this sense that I call Taylor the "chameleon who changed our colors." I am grateful to Ann for her suggestions, as I am for her friendship and continual support. For reading early drafts of this paper, I am immensely grateful to Neil Hartlen. I am equally indebted to Lisa Henderson for her personal encouragement and pedagogical insight.

2. Judith Butler, *Bodies That Matter: On the Discursive Limits of "Sex"* (New York: Routledge, 1993), 52.

3. See Mary Russo, *The Female Grotesque: Risk, Excess, and Modernity* (New York: Routledge, 1994).

4. See Butler, *Bodies That Matter,* 39.

5. Gilles Deleuze and Félix Guattari, *A Thousand Plateaus: Capitalism and Schizophrenia,* trans. Brian Massumi (Minneapolis: University of Minnesota Press, 1987), and Elizabeth Grosz, *Volatile Bodies: Toward a Corporeal Feminism* (Bloomington: Indiana University Press, 1994).

6. Ann Ferguson, personal correspondence with author, May 1998.

7. Elspeth Probyn, "The Anorexic Body," in *Body Invaders: Panic Sex in America,* ed. Arthur and Marilouise Kroker (New York: St. Martin's, 1987), 201–12.

8. Ibid., 202.

9. While I understand that Freudian "lack" defines women as "not having" the penis/phallus, and not as "not being" the penis/phallus, I follow Luce Irigaray's interpretation of this lack as not merely psychological (Freud) or symbolic (Lacan), but also ontological. Irigaray argues that the association of woman with negativity reifies her sociosymbolic position as an ineluctable absolute, thus, she cannot *be.* See the opening section of Luce Irigaray, *Speculum de l'autre femme* (Paris: Minuit, 1974); translated by Gillian C. Gill as *Speculum of the Other Woman* (Ithaca, N.Y.: Cornell University Press, 1985). Also insightful is "Così Fan Tutti," in *Ce sexe qui n'en est pas un* (Paris: Minuit, 1977), 83–101; translated by Catherine Porter with Carolyn Burke in *This Sex Which Is Not One* (Ithaca, N.Y.: Cornell University Press, 1985), 86–105.

10. Geoffrey Cowley and Karen Springen, "Critical Mass. Health: A New Study Lowers the Threshold of 'Fat,'" *Newsweek,* September 25, 1995, 66.

11. For an excellent analysis of fat as pornographic, see Laura Kipnis, "Life in the Fat Lane," in *Bound and Gagged: Pornography and the Politics of Fantasy in America* (New York: Grove, 1996), 93–121.

12. Jack Nixon, "The Wide Angle: Teighlor: A Big Person," *Plumpers and Big Women* 3, no. 8 (1995): 27–31.

13. My reading of the *Rockshots* cards as sites of the carnivalesque does not rule them out as places of autonomy or self-technologizations for the models posing for the shots. The cards are hybrid—contradictory and ambivalent discursive spaces for representations of fat.

14. Foster Grant advertisement, *People Magazine,* May 22, 1995, 5.

15. Richard Klein, *Eat Fat* (New York: Pantheon, 1996), 123 [see chapter 1 of this volume].

16. Ibid., 127.

17. See the Hippocratic treatise *Diseases of Women I,* trans. Ann Hanson, in *Women in Greece and Rome,* ed. Mary F. Lefkowitz and Maureen Fant (Toronto: Samuel-Stevens, 1977), 65–69.

18. Grosz, *Volatile Bodies,* 5.

19. Plato, *Timaeus,* trans. Donald J. Zeyl, in *Complete Works,* ed. John M.

Cooper with D. S. Hutchinson (Indianapolis: Hackett, 1997), 1224–91; all subsequent quotations from the *Timaeus* are from this translation.

20. Aristotle, *Nicomachean Ethics,* trans. Terence Irwin (Indianapolis: Hackett, 1985); all subsequent quotations from the *Nicomachean Ethics* are from this translation.

21. Aristotle, quoted by Nancy Tuana in *Woman and the History of Philosophy* (New York: Paragon House, 1992), 24.

22. Deborah Modrak, "Women, Deliberation, and Nature," in *Engendering Origins: Critical Feminist Readings in Plato and Aristotle,* ed. Bat-Ami Bar On (Albany: State University of New York Press, 1993), 215.

23. The moral works of Tertullian, Jerome, and even Augustine are prime examples of writings that link female materiality with carnality. For an overview, see Rosemary R. Ruether, "Misogynism and Virginal Feminism in the Fathers of the Church," in *Religion and Sexism: Images of Woman in the Jewish and Christian Traditions,* ed. Ruether (New York: Simon and Schuster, 1974), 150–83.

24. Klein, *Eat Fat,* 128.

25. Grosz, *Volatile Bodies,* 5.

26. Ibid., 7, 6, 10.

27. Ibid., 194.

28. Irigaray, *Speculum of the Other Woman,* 227–40.

29. Grosz, *Volatile Bodies,* 195.

30. Ibid., 203.

31. On the abject, see Julia Kristeva, *Powers of Horror: An Essay in Abjection,* trans. Leon S. Roudiez and Alice Jardine (New York: Columbia University Press, 1982). See Kent's excellent discussion of fat as "abject" in "Fighting Abjection."

32. Michael Huhn, *Slime Lady* (n.d.), © The American Postcard Co., Inc.

33. Deleuze and Guattari, *A Thousand Plateaus,* 153.

34. Ibid., 154.

35. Gilles Deleuze and Claire Parnet, "Dead Psychoanalysis: Analyse," in *Dialogues,* trans. Hugh Tomlinson and Barbara Habberjam (New York: Columbia University Press, 1987), 105.

36. Ibid., 109, 110.

37. Deleuze and Guattari, *A Thousand Plateaus,* 277.

38. Melissa Jane Hardie, "'I embrace the difference': Elizabeth Taylor and the Closet," in *Sexy Bodies: The Strange Carnalities of Feminism,* ed. Elizabeth Grosz and Elspeth Probyn (London: Routledge, 1995), 159.

39. *Roseanne Barr & Tom Arnold* (1990), © Annie Leibowitz, James Danziger Gallery, New York. For excellent analyses of Roseanne as "carnivalesque," see Kathleen Rowe, "Roseanne: Unruly Woman as Domestic Goddess," *Screen* 31, no. 4 (winter 1990): 408–19, and *The Unruly Woman: Gender and the Genres of Laughter* (Austin: University of Texas Press, 1995), 54–55; and Angela Stukator, "'It's not over until the fat lady sings': Comedy, Carnivalesque, and Body Politics" (see chapter 10 of this volume).

40. Carrie Fisher, "Roseanne's Fifth," *Vanity Fair,* September 1995, 164–65.

41. Laurel Fishman, "Big Beautiful Women of the 90s," *Big Beautiful Women* 16, no. 7 (1995): 61.

42. Hardie, "'I embrace the difference,'" 159.

43. Ibid., 163.

44. Elizabeth Taylor, *Elizabeth Takes Off: On Weight Gain, Weight Loss, Self-Image, and Self-Esteem* (New York: Putnam's, 1987), 48; quoted in ibid., 167.

45. Hardie, "'I embrace the difference,'" 165.

46. Ibid., 167; see Patricia Parker, *Literary Fat Ladies: Rhetoric, Gender, Property* (London: Methuen, 1987).

47. Hardie, "'I embrace the difference,'" 167.

48. Ibid.

49. Camryn Manheim, *Wake Up, I'm Fat!* (New York: Broadway Books, 1999), 289.

REFERENCES

Aristotle. *The Generation of Animals.* Translated by A. L. Peck. Rev. ed. Loeb Classical Library. Cambridge, Mass.: Harvard University Press, 1953.

———. *Nicomachean Ethics.* Translated by Terence Irwin. Indianapolis: Hackett, 1985.

Braidotti, Rosi. *Nomadic Subjects: Embodiment and Sexual Difference in Contemporary Feminist Theory.* New York: Columbia University Press, 1994.

———. *Patterns of Dissonance: A Study of Women in Contemporary Philosophy.* Translated by Elizabeth Guild. New York: Routledge, 1991.

Butler, Judith. *Bodies That Matter: On the Discursive Limits of "Sex."* New York: Routledge, 1993.

Cowley, Geoffrey, and Springen, Karen. "Critical Mass. Health: A New Study Lowers the Threshold of 'Fat.'" *Newsweek,* September 25, 1995, 66.

Deleuze, Gilles, and Félix Guattari. *A Thousand Plateaus: Capitalism and Schizophrenia.* [*Mille plateaux.*] Translated by Brian Massumi. Minneapolis: University of Minnesota Press, 1987.

Deleuze, Gilles, and Claire Parnet. "Dead Psychoanalysis: Analyse." In *Dialogues,* translated by Hugh Tomlinson and Barbara Habberjam, 77–123. New York: Columbia University Press, 1987.

duBois, Page. "The Platonic Appropriation of Reproduction." In *Sowing the Body: Psychoanalysis and Ancient Representations of Women,* 163–83. Chicago: University of Chicago Press, 1988.

Fisher, Carrie. "Roseanne's Fifth." *Vanity Fair,* September 1995, 164–65.

Fishman, Laurel. "Big Beautiful Women of the 90s." *Big Beautiful Women* 16, no. 7 (1995): 61–64.

Grosz, Elizabeth. *Volatile Bodies: Toward a Corporeal Feminism.* Bloomington: Indiana University Press, 1994.

Hardie, Melissa Jane. "'I embrace the difference': Elizabeth Taylor and the Closet." In *Sexy Bodies: The Strange Carnalities of Feminism,* edited by Elizabeth Grosz and Elspeth Probyn, 151–71. London: Routledge, 1995.

Hippocrates. *Diseases of Women I,* translated by Ann Hanson. In *Women in Greece and Rome,* edited by Mary F. Lefkowitz and Maureen Fant, 65–69. Toronto: Samuel-Stevens, 1977.

Irigaray, Luce. *Ce sexe qui n'en est pas un.* Paris: Minuit, 1977.

———. *Speculum de l'autre femme.* Paris: Minuit, 1974.

———. *Speculum of the Other Woman.* Translated by Gillian C. Gill. Ithaca, N.Y.: Cornell University Press, 1985.

———. *This Sex Which Is Not One.* Translated by Catherine Porter with Carolyn Burke. Ithaca, N.Y.: Cornell University Press, 1985.

Kipnis, Laura. "Life in the Fat Lane." In *Bound and Gagged*: Pornography and the Politics of Fantasy in America, 93–121. New York: Grove, 1996.

Klein, Richard. *Eat Fat.* New York: Pantheon, 1996.

Kristeva, Julia. *Powers of Horror.* Translated by Leon S. Roudiez and Alice Jardine. New York: Columbia University Press, 1982.

Manheim, Camryn. *Wake Up, I'm Fat!* New York: Broadway Books, 1999.

Modrak, Deborah. "Women, Deliberation, and Nature." In *Engendering Origins: Critical Feminist Readings in Plato and Aristotle,* edited by Bat-Ami Bar On, 207–22. Albany: State University of New York Press, 1993.

Nixon, Jack. "The Wide Angle: Teighlor: A Big Person." *Plumpers and Big Women* 3, no. 8 (1995): 27–31.

Plato. *Timaeus,* translated by Donald J. Zeyl. In *Complete Works,* 1224–91. Edited by John M. Cooper with D. S. Hutchinson. Indianapolis: Hackett, 1997.

Probyn, Elspeth. "The Anorexic Body." In *Body Invaders: Panic Sex in America,* edited by Arthur and Marilouise Kroker, 201–12. New York: St. Martin's, 1987.

Rowe, Kathleen. "Roseanne: Unruly Woman as Domestic Goddess." *Screen* 31, no. 4 (1990): 408–19.

———. *The Unruly Woman: Gender and the Genres of Laughter.* Austin: University of Texas Press, 1995.

Ruether, Rosemary R. "Misogynism and Virginal Feminism in the Fathers of the Church." In *Religion and Sexism: Images of Woman in the Jewish and Christian Traditions,* edited by Ruether, 150–83. New York: Simon and Schuster, 1974.

Russo, Mary. *The Female Grotesque: Risk, Excess, and Modernity.* New York: Routledge, 1994.

Tuana, Nancy. *Woman and the History of Philosophy.* New York: Paragon House, 1992.

PART V

Bodies in Motion

Corpulence and Performativity

"I'm an appetite outlaw. With wild ways and a bad attitude." Katy Dierlam as Helen Melon at Coney Island's Sideshows by the Seashore. (Photo: Sharon Mazer)

13 "She's so fat . . ."

Facing the Fat Lady at Coney Island's Sideshows by the Seashore

SHARON MAZER

She's so fat . . . it takes four men to hug her, and a boxcar to lug her.

Sideshow bally[1]

Hi there. I'm Helen Melon and I'm fat. Take a good long look. It's all here. Just for you. Five hundred pounds of fat female. You know, all fat ladies are different. Some fat ladies are big up here [touches her breasts]. Some of us are big down here [touches her belly and hips]. And some of us are big in the rear [turns and shimmies at audience]. Take a good *look.*

Katy Dierlam as Helen Melon[2]

When Katy Dierlam took the stage as "Helen Melon" during the 1992 summer season at Coney Island's Sideshows by the Seashore, what spectators faced was far more than "[f]ive hundred pounds of fat female." Dierlam's appearance as Helen Melon superficially acknowledged the clichés of the sideshow Fat Lady: a smiling, fleshy woman in a baby-doll costume. But her evocation of the traditional Fat Lady was only the starting point for a play of identification in which Dierlam modeled and discarded a wide range of roles from "appetite outlaw" and sexual provocateur to sideshow historian, contented wife, and cabaret singer. Each role, in turn, became an opportunity to challenge onlookers to look beyond her appearance as a sideshow Fat Lady. By mapping her psyche as well as her body, she problematized the relationship between who she is and what she looks like. From her opening salvo—"Hi there. I'm Helen Melon and I'm fat."—Dierlam progressively revealed aspects of her own personality, history, and desires in a series of narrativistic shifts designed to make her "self" as visible as her body. Yet as Dierlam toyed with the differences between what we could see for ourselves and what she told us about herself, her "identity" ultimately remained beyond us.

Dierlam's text was created from a multiplicity of contemporary discourses on women and the body, including the work of performance artists (most prominently, Annie Sprinkle and Karen Finley)[3] and of feminist researchers on overeating and anorexia (notably Susie Orbach and Kim Chernin).[4] Its theatricalism was rooted in carnival, drama, and satire: in earlier sideshow spectacles, to be sure, but also in the defiantly corpulent figure of Falstaff and the grotesque giants of Rabelais and Swift.[5] At the same time, the act of exposing her body "[j]ust for you" mimicked both seduction and, given that the performance was a part of a dollars-for-looking transaction, burlesque. That is, its commodification of fleshy excess mocked the erotic exchange between male spectator and female stripper or topless dancer.[6] In the contemporary social vernacular, her soft body, vulnerable to our gaze and judgment, was easily recognizable as a common sign of personal dysfunction, of overeating.[7] Yet this same body also represented transgressive female appetites, conflating the gastronomic with the psychosexual.[8] That body, as an exaggerated sign for what is life-embracing—the drive to survive by consuming and reproducing—also carried, in performance, the signs of something monstrous, at once cannibal and *vagina dentata.* The interactions between what was signaled by her body's appearance and by her discursive referents served to create an extraordinarily complex and, at certain points, contradictory performance.

Underlying the multiple threads of Melon/Dierlam's performance was the tension between visible body and spoken word. The text of her performance—what she said, what we were to hear—was a series of interlocking narratives that simultaneously acknowledged and denied her appearance as a Fat Lady—what we saw. While we looked *at* her body we were asked to look *through* that body to the individual within, to see her body and to see the person at the same time. As such, the material body was to become transparent, visible but balanced against the ephemeral inner life as selectively revealed in Dierlam's script. But more questions were provoked than resolved by this Fat Lady's juxtapositioning of spectacle and text. Is what we see what we ultimately get? Can such a body, female and fat, be embraced and our response to it shaped by the spoken word? Must this body be effaced in order for the woman within to be revealed? Does the body prevail? Do dominant cultural readings of the body, especially the female and fat body, inevitably supersede the individual's narrative, her (counter)presentation of her subjective "self"?[9] The sideshow necessarily teeters at the edge of tricks and illusions. Its "talkers" (the term literally marks the distinction between those who speak and those who are looked at) turn bystanders into audiences by promising astonishment: we will see here what we cannot see elsewhere. Many times the payoff is no more revelatory than the realization of having been conned out of an extra fifty cents. The blade box leaves plenty of room for the young woman trapped therein, while the video of an early-twentieth-century electrocution at Coney Island features Topsy, a particularly destructive elephant and not a human being as implied in the tease. At other times, the performances are manifestly "real." Men and women eat fire and glass, dance with snakes, put nails up their noses and through their tongues, reveal tattoos, and perform magic tricks. Moreover, the spectacle of physical abnormality—"freaks, wonders, and curiosities"—is, of course, the sideshow's most familiar stock-in-trade: the Fat Lady, the Thin Man, the Siamese twins, the three-armed man, and so on.[10] Indeed, elsewhere at Coney Island during the summer of 1992 one could pay a dollar to see a "two-headed baby," a preserved fetus that was presented as a warning against prenatal abuses, as well as the "giant rat."

At Coney Island we were an accidental audience, passersby momentarily enticed from the seedy pleasures of the boardwalk—from the rides, games, junk food, beach, and beer—by the promise that our prurient curiosity would be satisfied. The hour's entertainment we were given in exchange for purchasing tickets costing between $1 and $3 included the chance to stare at an overweight woman's body, its excesses something men are trained to shun, women to fear in themselves. At least superficially, then, Melon/Dierlam's performance, her "trick" was manifestly herself. Her personal, private history of overeating, what Weight Watchers and its ilk would term a woeful lack of control and self-discipline, was made public in the display of her body for onlookers. By her own estimate, Dierlam weighed over 500 pounds that summer; in the hyperbole of Coney Island's talkers her weight was usually represented as 550 pounds. The sideshow's clichés preceded and followed her performance, establishing an additional discursive frame into which her appearance, as well as her own narrative, was set. The question, "How fat is she?" was always quickly followed with the refrain, "She's so fat . . ."—as in, "She's so fat, she was born on July first, second, and third" and "She's so fat, she's got more chins than a Chinese phonebook." What outside talkers offered ticket buyers was a chance to see a woman whose actual body, rather than any bizarre skill (e.g., eating glass) or facility with illusion, distinguished her as a grotesque, a "freak."

In fact, at seeing this body more revealed than concealed by a light, brightly colored baby-doll dress, her arms and legs fully exposed, the spectators frequently gasped, then hooted and snickered. We had been promised a Fat Lady fatter than any woman we'd ever seen, and at the moment of her entrance, we got our money's worth. Elsewhere we might covertly watch such a woman making her way down the sidewalk, observe her willing herself to be invisible to gawking passersby and impervious to unwanted jeers and advice. Here at the Coney Island sideshow we paid our money for the opportunity to "take a *good* look."[11]

But this Fat Lady also looked back at us. "Oh, I know what you're all thinking," she would invariably lead off:

> I've heard it all before. All right. Let's get it over with. Come on. Come on. Let's get it over with: "Oh my god, look at her." "Yo, there's a girl for you, Leroy." [Into the microphone, she mimics the mockery that her footsteps hitting the sidewalk can provoke.] "Baboom baboom baboom baboom baboom." "Thar she blows!" "She should be ashamed of herself." Or my mother-in-law's favorite, "I just worry about your health, dear." I've heard it all.

By mimicking and mocking the stock phrases of ridicule and pity generally left to behind-the-hand snickerings, Melon/Dierlam appears to demand that we reconsider what it means to be both human and female in a world where appearance frequently supersedes and, indeed, effaces presence. Moreover, by telling us she has "heard it all before" and articulating the shrieks, taunts, and condescension her appearance regularly provokes, she not only preempts our responses, she also reverses the lens of her performance. Our reactions to her become transparent as clichés, our positions as spectators characterized as cultural stereotypes. Her character is no longer in question; ours might be. The anticipated exchange—spectators free to stare (even jeer) at a passive Fat Lady—is abrogated and a question left in its place. Will we now be affected by her performance or will we continue to hold to our expectations, rooted in what has been said and heard before, ourselves remaining stock characters rather than full-bodied individuals?

Further, with the spotlight turned against the spectators, the roles offered to us are limited: we can become the hostile "Other" in the terms she presents, or we might begin to align with her against the "others," perhaps by acknowledging our own anxieties about being looked at and judged in the same way. I must confess that seated in the bleachers, I never failed to take a quick inventory of my own body: How much heavier, really, is she than I? How does the loose flesh on my own upper arms, belly, and thighs compare with hers? How much does she have to eat to sustain her weight? How much would I? Isn't her appearance mine somehow? Or could she represent a fate that I am even now avoiding only through my own "greater" discipline, my dietary willpower? How can a woman so obviously smart and talented have lost control to such an extent, jeopardizing both her social and her physical well-being? What could possibly justify the emotional risk she was taking at the sideshow? How could she face the taunts and bear the implicit shame of exposing herself to gawking strangers as often as ten times a day? And why am I looking?

In her sideshow monologue and in a series of personal interviews, Katy Dierlam made it clear that her decision to step into the role of sideshow Fat Lady was both deeply personal and profoundly political. Performing as Helen Melon was a new phase in her ongoing struggle toward renewed social self-confidence as well as a way of directly confronting the prejudice with which her "disability" (as she frequently terms it) is greeted in her daily life. To perform the Fat Lady was to refuse to hide behind either walls or words. By giving herself a sideshow name Dierlam both entered into the tradition of Fat Ladies such as Baby Ruth Pontico, Jolly Trixie, and Dolly Dimples and converted it to suit her own agenda. "Helen Melon" implies size and sexuality rather than diminution and girlishness, a ripe, desirable woman, as in Helen of Troy and "how 'bout them melons," rather than a smiling doll. For Dierlam, taking a character maintained her integrity as a stage performer at the same time that it liberated her from her mundane self. Where Katy Dierlam might suffer inhibitions or limitations because of her weight, Helen Melon could re-present her body as a sign of social and erotic power. What might generally be perceived as a liability in life could become an asset at the sideshow.[12]

It is as Helen Melon, therefore, that Dierlam can reject the euphemisms that one might employ to describe her:

> You know, people ask me, they say "Helen?" They call me Helen. "Helen, how did you get to be so . . . ah . . . so ah . . . heavyset?" [Pause. Scans the audience.] FAT! Please. The word is fat. F-A-T. A perfectly good word. It means what it says. It's very descriptive. No, I was not a fat baby. And it's not glandular, either. It seldom is. No, I weighed five pounds six ounces when I was born.

Implying that our response to her appearance is far from original, she declares her refusal to employ nice words or sentimentality in her exchange with us. Our curiosity, which she tells us is common rather than unique, is to be satisfied. The questions we could not ask her elsewhere will be answered. We are to hear the plain truth, without denials or evasions. But given the obvious fiction of her character's name and her place in the sideshow itself, might what she tells us also be suspect? If Helen Melon exists only on the sideshow stage in five-minute units, then how are we to apprehend the presentation of her personal history? Is Dierlam telling us about an invented, fictional character, in the same way that she might elaborate upon an imagined history for the character of Masha in Chekhov's *Seagull*? Or is she telling us about her "real" self, exposing the identity that lurks behind the mask of Helen Melon?

Her stance should put us on alert. The truth about who this woman *is* is to remain less visible than her appearance as "five hundred pounds of fat female." (And in the context of the con artistry of the sideshow, even the "five hundred pounds" is questionable.) What her discourse does make visible is that whatever she tells us must be understood to be constructed as much as it is "natural"; she is acting as much as she is "being." However much is to be revealed, more remains concealed, a mystery locked in the space between performance and identity.

Dierlam told me privately that, in truth, she was a small baby. As a girl she did battle with the scales through childhood and early adulthood, alternately rebelling against the constraints of calorie counting and then once again subjecting herself to the rigors of dieting. While in college she dieted herself down to a socially respectable 135 pounds, and for most of her life, her weight hovered in the 200-pound range, until a series of crises, including a period of alcohol dependency complicated by severe agoraphobia, led her to her current weight. Dierlam is a pretty woman, who dresses with an elegant flair as much as any other downtown artist might. In the Style section of the Sunday *New York Times*, interviewer Bob Morris describes Dierlam as she changes back into street clothes backstage at the Ridiculous Theatrical Company: "With all her makeup off and her soft, reddish hair brushed back from her pretty face, Ms. Dierlam slipped on a sea-green turtleneck sweater that matched her startling clear eyes."[13]

Outside the narrative of her entry into extreme obesity, Dierlam's story is not much different from that of anyone else. Raised in an intellectual household—her father taught college theater, her mother was a librarian—Dierlam's love for the history, literature, and practice of theater led her first to Bennington College and then to New York City, where she settled into the thriving performance scene of the late 1960s. In past decades, she collaborated with Charles Ludlam and Ethyl Eichelberger, most notably in her appearance as Hanno, an obese androgyne, in Ludlam's *Salammbo* at the Ridiculous Theatrical Company and as Elektra in Eichelberger's *Klytemnestra* at PS 122. In recent years, she has appeared in television programs and films as diverse as *The Feverman* (for the *Monsters* TV series) and Woody Allen's *Shadows and Fog*. More recently, she appeared at the Ridiculous in *How to Write a Play* as Natalie, a role Ludlam created for her in 1984. In addition, Dierlam writes; she has performed in her own one-woman show and cabaret act. She is married to an artist with whom she negotiates the trials of a one-room, fifth-floor walk-up apartment, filled with cats and clutter, in Greenwich Village. Ironically, she supplements her income by performing phone sex, substituting verbal imagery for the fact of her body to paint herself into the fantasies of male callers.

Having seen Dierlam in a number of performances at the Ridiculous Theatrical Company as well as at other downtown venues over the years, Dick Zigun, artistic director at the Coney Island Sideshow, made several unsuccessful attempts to coax Dierlam into the Fat Lady role before she finally, and with understandable trepidation, accepted his offer and the challenge. The terms were quite simple: he gave her the fragments of information about other Fat Ladies he had managed to collect and the freedom to invent both her persona and her performance. Armed with Zigun's research, with what little she could garner from New York City's Library of the Performing Arts, and with her husband's own long-treasured copy of the autobiography of Dolly Dimples, Dierlam began to build a contemporary version of the Fat Lady. Her script was designed to provoke rather than to reassure spectators; her strategy centered on the act of animating the customary spectacle of a cheery but primarily passive body exposed to gawkers who would move toward and past her as part of the traditional sideshow promenade.

At the same time, she attempted to disrupt a series of assumptions about the fat female body and the person within, moving beyond the types of performers described by Robert Bogdan as "[h]uge women [who] wore dainty, little girl's outfits, danced a soft shoe, and chuckled"[14] and taking on Leslie Fiedler, who insists: "Indeed, though not immune to real sorrow, circus Fat Ladies have apparently proved as cheerful and amiable in private as they are presented as being in public."[15] By juxtapositioning her personal narrative against the clichés framing her appearance she hoped to make her complex humanity as fully present, as visible and material, as her overweight body.

Moreover, Dierlam resisted representing her obesity as a source of shame. Instead of allowing her body to stand silently as a sign of physical and psychological ill-health, a sign of dysfunction to be cured by diets and therapy, she reinvented herself as a Rabelaisian hero, gleefully gargantuan, unbounded by the constraints imposed by contemporary dietary propriety.[16] Dierlam might refer to her obesity as a "disability" in private, but in her performance as Helen Melon her size became a verifiable asset, a sign of her inclusion in a privileged group of women, highly valued both as performers and as wives/lovers. Unlike Katy Dierlam, Helen Melon rejects societal pressures to consume "all those fat-free products in the supermarket . . . Ultra Slim-bleaaaaach," daring spectators to regard her condition as desirable:

> Fat is the dirtiest word in the English language. Yeah. Fat people are ugly and stupid and lazy and probably smelly too. And if you believe that, you'd better stay away from me. I have to be on constant guard against dwindling. And I am, folks.[17]

To say that certain people are not attracted to the Fat Lady's body is to imply that *some* people are.[18] Thus "to be on constant guard against dwindling" explicitly reverses the values associated with the effort to create and maintain a slender body, the demand of diets that one not only perpetually resist the nourishment that food so obviously represents but also constrain all distasteful, unfeminine manifestations of appetite.

Melon/Dierlam proposes the desirability of the fat body both for herself as the wearer of that body and for onlookers, whose desire to see her body is the first focus of her narrative. She is not the victim of some obscure body chemistry. Rather, she *wants* to be fat. She has chosen her body. Her obesity is the visible sign of her self-willed attainment of her own desires. Moreover, by our presence we act as markers for her body's desirability, which her narrative represents as our envy for her obvious satiation, her rebellion against restraint. We've paid to see her. As spectators, she frequently reminds us, we must reaffirm our wish to see her perform. And in order to continue to look at her we must listen to what she says. Her assertion thus inscribes a kind of totalizing, dialogic boundary: spectators who are unwilling to surrender their stereotypes of fat people had "better stay away." Those who remain, from her perspective, must in some way share her values.

Further, by introjecting the language of desire into her representation of obesity, Dierlam's use of the word "fat" comes to echo other "dirty words" which refer not just to the body but also to sexuality and the erotic. "Fat Lady," like "foxy lady," indicates a person whose metaphysical attributes (beauty, intellect, industry, grace) have been effaced by the physical, particularly enlarged and/or fetishized parts of the body (the breasts, hips, buttocks, and so on). Like the stripper or the topless dancer, the appearance of the Fat Lady's body is presented as a provocation to the imaginative life of the (presumably male) spectator. If she remains silent, this spectator is free to develop an erotic scenario in which he can incorporate what he sees and what he desires. One such spectator, albeit from a scholarly remove, Leslie Fiedler in *Freaks* reminds us that Dolly Dimples was on occasion promoted as the "It Girl" of Fat Ladies, and he declares unequivocally: "Fat Ladies are, in short, the most erotically appealing of all Freaks, with the possible exception of male Dwarfs."[19] He explains the sex appeal of Dolly Dimples in particular and fat ladies in general:

> Even in the United States, where skinny women are accounted especially attractive, she—and her sisters in size—had no difficulty finding admirers, lovers, and husbands. . . . All of us have memories of having once been cuddled against the buxom breast and folded into the ample arms of a warm, soft Giantess, whose bulk—to our 8-pound, 21-inch infant selves—must have seemed as mountainous as any 600-pound Fat Lady to our adult selves. And to rediscover in our later loves the superabundance of fat female flesh which we remember from our first is surely a satisfaction we all project in dreams, though we may be unwilling to confess it once we are awake.[20]

Although Fiedler's Freudian desire for the Fat Lady may or may not be the cultural norm, his rapture recalls again the erotic element encoded into all displays of the female body. At the same time, this notion that the fat woman is a manifestation of exaggerated femininity, encoded with ambivalence about mothers and mothering, can also be located in much of the writing on women and the body, particularly in discussions of anorexia wherein the hyperslender body is seen as an adolescent rejection of the woman's curves.[21] It is this conflating of the soft body with the sexual body that Melon/Dierlam seems simultaneously to promote and to mock in her use of sexual language to refer to her body.

Thus, while Dierlam's performance of the sideshow Fat Lady masquerades as a disquisition on the pleasures of overeating and obesity, it also seems designed to ignite underlying anxieties associated with femininity and sexuality, what has been termed by Barbara Creed the "monstrous-feminine."[22] Helen Melon begins to reminisce:

> I'll tell you a secret. One of my earliest memories was waiting for the ice cream man's truck to come onto our block. With pennies stolen from my mother's purse. Oh Mama, she taught me right from wrong. Just like your mamas did, I'm sure. [Skeptical, she scans the audience as if to verify.] But, no, I went my own way. Let that be a lesson to you. I'm an appetite outlaw. With wild wild ways and a bad attitude.

In this, she echoes woman-centered discussions of eating disorders, which generally promote the twin, and paradoxical, theories that anorectics are rejecting the markers of femininity (soft breasts, belly, and hips) by starving themselves into boyish bodies, and that, at the same time, fat women are rebels whose large bodies mark their confrontation with cultural ideas of femininity. In Susie Orbach's words: "[F]at expresses a rebellion against the powerlessness of the woman, against the pressure to look and act in a certain way and against being evaluated on her ability to create an image of herself."[23] Jane Hirschmann and Carol Munter reiterate this sentiment even more forcefully, speaking directly to the reader: "But you the rebel are a success. You break the rules and assert your right to eat what you want and look as you do."[24]

Substituting the eating of ice cream for sexual (mis)adventure, Melon/Dierlam mimics the archetypal tale of the "girl gone wrong," the moment in B movies and bad fiction when the whore unburdens herself to the sympathetic hero. Superficially, she plays the role of penitent, warning that spectators who stray from the moral path as she has could end up as she is. But contrary to the whore's plea for absolution, with its concurrent affirmation of mundane definitions of right and wrong, Melon/Dierlam valorizes herself as an "outlaw" who refuses to submit to everyday morality. Her body is the sign that she stands outside the rules; like Madonna, she is a victorious rebel against the ordinary limitations imposed on desire and attainment, someone to be envied for her success rather than pitied or condemned by conventional bourgeois values.

From stealing pennies and eating forbidden sweets, Melon/Dierlam moves into a more explicitly menacing stance. Like a modern, female Gargantua, she threatens, literally, to consume the spectators:

> I love almost anything to eat and drink in large quantities. I'm passionate about cream and sugar and butter. As a matter of fact . . . [Pause. Scanning the audience.] You all look so good out there today, I could eat you up with a spoon. Hi there, little sweetie [to a small child in the front row]. You look awfully cute over there. Yes. Could I have you for dinner tonight? [Long pause.]

Embracing the stereotype of the voracious woman, Melon/Dierlam proposes to violate one of our most confirmed cultural taboos, that against cannibalism. The specifics with which she toys—that is, whether to make her target the main course or dessert—make the danger of the encounter vivid. More important, the dream of the embracing mother, the "warm, soft Giantess" of Fiedler's imagination, is converted (or perverted) into the equally Freudian nightmare of the all-powerful mother confronting, and threatening to consume, the diminished and powerless child.[25] Instead of embracing with "ample arms" and nourishing with a "buxom breast," or for that matter remaining passively positioned as a fetish, compliant with the spectator's erotic imagination, this Fat Lady appears, at least momentarily, to violate the rules of engagement.

Then too, the woman whose fat body exceeds the feminine ideal must be seen as overstepping the boundaries of heterosexual accommodation, a threat to male sexuality. Because "to eat you up" clearly resonates as sexual slang, the threat she poses conflates one kind of "hungry mouth" with another, the *vagina dentata*. Maggie Kilgour, in *From Communion to Cannibalism*, acknowledges the proximity between "kissing and eating," adding that "at an extreme level of intensity the erotic and aggressive sides of incorporation cannot be differentiated, so that it becomes difficult to tell at what point the desire for consummation turns into the desire for consumption."[26] As Susan Bordo notes in *Unbearable Weight:* "In the figure of the man-eater, the metaphor of the devouring woman reveals its deep psychological underpinnings. Eating is not really a metaphor for the sexual act; rather, the sexual act, when initiated and desired by a woman, is imagined as itself an act of eating, of incorporation and destruction of the object of desire. Thus, women's sexual appetites must be curtailed and controlled, because they threaten to deplete and consume the body and soul of the male."[27] Unchecked eating is unchecked sexual appetite. By implication, to violate the social constraints against gluttony imperils the provisions against voracious sexuality as well. Melon/Dierlam's threat to "eat you up with a spoon" is a pun directed at male spectators, in particular, and designed to provoke primal anxieties even as it plays with spectators' assumptions about women's hunger(s).

In fact, Melon/Dierlam's pointed display of aggression regularly activated audience response. The small child in question would turn shy and shrink against the nearest adult, while adult spectators would shriek in what may or may not have been mock horror and derision. That spectators easily recognized the double entendres and the conflation of appetites in Melon/Dierlam's threat was certain. At one performance, several rowdy men in the audience loudly urged her to take them on—"Eat me! Eat me!"—to which, after a lengthy display of consideration, she replied, "No, he's too big, too big and too ugly," provoking a round of laughter and backslapping among the men. Yet it is this very invective against the hostile male spectators (and they were often hostile) that ultimately seems calculated to reassure rather than to continue to agitate: no matter how big this Fat Lady may be, these men were too big for her to swallow, too unsweet, too much man for her. In the end, the Fat Lady did not "get" anyone; she remained on the stage well within the frame of the performance. The danger was no more than that of the roller coaster or the haunted house, titillating to be sure but nonetheless a safe ride guaranteed, in the end, to release spectators intact.

From this highly charged exchange with the audience and the anxiety it seems to have unleashed, Dierlam's script quickly shifts to safer ground: a historical narrative which leads to personal revelation. The memory of other, earlier sideshow Fat Ladies (in particular, Dolly Dimples, who, like Helen Melon, once appeared at Coney Island) is recalled to locate Dierlam's Helen Melon within the context of a very specific category of performance history. Thus Helen Melon speaks of her sideshow foremothers:

> There have been Fat Ladies at the sideshow for a long time. The most famous Fat Lady was Dolly Dimples. Now, she was about my size. And there were bigger Fat Ladies, for example, Baby Ruth Pontico who worked for Ringling Brothers. She weighed 815 pounds at her top weight. She was about the biggest Fat Lady I know of in America. But Dolly Dimples, she was the most famous Fat Lady. You see, back in the thirties and forties when Dolly was famous, there was no TV, and people went to the circus and the sideshow for entertainment. Dolly was famous from coast to coast. She went up in an airplane back when anybody who went up in an airplane was a big deal. She even worked out here at Coney Island, with the Wagner Brothers' World Circus Sideshow.[28]

By contextualizing and canonizing her performance as a sideshow Fat Lady, Melon/Dierlam does more than simply offer us a bit of odd trivia. She both legitimizes her appearance at today's Coney Island and repositions herself as a potential star. She's not inventing her performance out of whole cloth. Rather, she's following in a time-honored performance tradition; its stars were as important to the culture then (read "famous") as television stars are today. Baby Ruth Pontico and Dolly Dimples were the celebrities of the carnival circuits in the recent past. Helen Melon is also a famous celebrity. Spectators should therefore recognize how privileged they are to see her in person and up close at this sideshow, when authentic Fat Ladies are rare, and other types of stars far more remote.

In addition, Melon/Dierlam's emphasis on the mobility of other Fat Ladies implies her own: If Dolly Dimples can go up in an airplane "back when anybody who went up in an airplane was a big deal," then so can this woman in front of us. What she has presented as our assumptions about a 500-pound woman's limitations are imaginatively exploded. The image of the passive, sedentary woman incapable of occupying the same space as everyone else is displaced by the provocative image of an adventurous, very fat woman much like the woman facing us in the cockpit of a two-seater, complete with leather jacket, white scarf, and goggles.

The point at which Melon/Dierlam's recitation of sideshow history converges with Dierlam's personal, domestic history again signals Dierlam's ongoing campaign to jolt, or at least coax, spectators into looking beyond her body to her person. Again the discourse shifts. In place of the aggressive giantess and the Fat Lady celebrity now stands a married woman whose husband desires her both because he is attracted to fat women and because he shares other affinities of mind and spirit with her:

> But, you know folks, Dolly retired from the sideshow, gave it up, went on a diet and weighed 123 pounds for the rest of her life. She even wrote a book about her experiences. Yeah. My husband, when he was 10 years old, he read Dolly Dimples' book. And he fell in love with all those pictures of Dolly. He spent a lot of his life looking for a lady as fat and as pretty as Dolly Dimples was . . . and sure enough he found me, because there are a lot of us out there. Of course I was suspicious. I knew what a "chubby-chaser" was, and I didn't want to be anybody's fetish. I said, what do you want a fat lady like me for? Well, folks, I'm not going to tell you what he said, because this is a family show.

The prescription is simple: spectators should view Melon/Dierlam as her husband views her. In addition to reiterating that she is desirable *because* rather than in spite of her weight, her personal feelings are presented as potential points of contact with the lives of people in the audience. That she is married becomes a sign of her membership in the familiar domestic world. That she wants to be loved for herself rather than as a "fetish" is no more than any of us might desire. That there are "a lot of us out there" further implies a kind of normalcy, a nonfreak status for the fat woman. That this is a "family show," with implied limits upon what can be said, she well understands because she, like us, belongs to a family.

This textual slide from sideshow history to personal history seems calculated to make the "real" Katy Dierlam visible from within the "performance" of Helen Melon. The specifics of Melon/Dierlam's personal narrative resist a superficial reading of her body and attempt to force recognition of her subjective individuality. The sly discontinuation of the personal revelations—"I'm not going to tell you what he said"—

(re)presents Melon/Dierlam's narrative as both private and provisional. We have been offered a look at her inner, true self, the self masked by the freak show presentation of obesity. Yes, the personal narrative affirms, this Fat Lady does have sex, intimate relations with one designated man and, possibly, others. But it also reminds us of her autonomy: her body may be the object presented in the Fat Lady performance, but she nonetheless retains a private self, hidden from public view. Just as she has chosen to display her body, she can choose to reveal her inner life, or not. She is, in other words, a real person like us, an autonomous individual with the same claim to subjective perspective and right to privacy, and with the freedom to choose her confidants, to expose or shield her "real" self according to her own inclinations.

As her performance nears its end, Melon/Dierlam again shifts the role she is playing, this time to cabaret singer, a mode of performance which literally displaces the display of her body with that of her voice. Mocking the clichés once more, she announces, "But you know, it ain't over until the fat lady sings." Instead of continuing the mockery, however, she sings a blues song a cappella in a serious and straightforward manner. The joke of waiting "until the fat lady sings" is on us, it seems. If we initially paid our dollars to see her perform her obesity and, consequently, became the target of her narrative, at this point we must pay another kind of price for our voyeurism if we wish to see her performance through to the end. By shifting the mode of performance, Melon/Dierlam again reconfigures the rules of engagement and recasts both herself and us. In the place of a confrontational exchange about her body and what it means, and supplanting the narrative of alignment with our own family values, is a performance in which we are to listen attentively to her song, to its poetic and romantic imagery, and applaud the grace of the singing and the talent of the performer at its conclusion.

With the end of the song comes an abrupt return to Helen Melon, sideshow Fat Lady:

> There are many more delicious acts to come, so you stay put. And when you do go out there on that boardwalk today, you have yourselves some cotton candy, hot dogs and ice cream and fries, if that's your pleasure. Enjoy your lives. But . . . aaaah . . . save a little bit for me.

Dierlam thus simultaneously recloaks herself as Helen Melon and reminds us that the figure before us does not exist solely as a character or performance. The Fat Lady we see at the sideshow is also a real person in the outside world. Although not all of us weigh 500-plus pounds, we do eventually occupy the same turf. We will leave the sideshow, as she will leave. And we will turn to food, much as she does: for satiation of hunger and satisfaction of a particular desire for pleasure.

Given the specific strategies with which Dierlam orchestrated her confrontation with spectators, it is tempting to speculate about her effectiveness in challenging prejudice and forcing recognition of the humanity masked by her body. Yet whatever Dierlam said and did as Helen Melon that summer, what her audiences apparently responded to was still what they had expected to see: a Fat Lady. Indeed, after seeing Katy Dierlam perform as Helen Melon for the first time, I walked out onto the boardwalk with my own mother-in-law, who unconsciously echoed Melon/Dierlam's opening salvo: "She has such a pretty face. It's a shame she's so fat. Doesn't she know she's killing herself by not going on a diet?" Later that summer, a scout for a cable comedy show accidentally left behind his report, which listed the various acts, including his response to Helen Melon: "There's a really gargantuan thousand pound lady who sings. I don't get it." Other reviewers translated Helen Melon's aggression into feminism and referred to Dierlam's performance as the "feminist fat lady," a label which appears to conflate assumptions about fat women with those about feminists.[29] For myself, every time I see Dierlam perform, I am thrown into a reverie about my own struggles with weight and body, while friends who have accompanied me to her performances invariably insist on beginning diets (together) immediately.

The Fat Lady performance, then, appears to function much as a reflection in the funhouse mirror. That is, it ultimately fails to be about her and becomes instead about us, about our lapses and failures as we attempt to measure up (or down) to the dominant ideal. The appearance of this 500-pound woman standing on the stage seems, in the end, resistant to didactic exchange, her body effectively more visible, more affective, than her words. The complex reworking of Fat Lady clichés—from carnival and literature, from psychoanalytic and feminist writings about the body, as well as from performance history and personal revelation—may be provocative, but in the final analysis it is probably less evocative of this particular woman's identity than of the general assumptions with which we approach her.

The sideshow, with its spectacle of "freaks, wonders, and curiosities," may provide a carnival context for potential challenges to, and subversions of, social norms. But the transgression appears to remain fixed in the act of looking, rather than in reconsidering or transforming. To look where one is not ordinarily permitted may indeed be a radical act, but to change in response to what has been seen and heard remains more problematic. No matter what Helen Melon (or Katy Dierlam) says or does, no matter how wide-ranging her narratival or theatrical strategies, her performance is still locked inside the talkers' rhetoric, defined by the dominant culture, and framed by the question that begins with "How fat is she?" and is answered with "She's so fat . . ."

NOTES

This essay originally appeared in *Theatre Annual: A Journal of Performance Studies* 47 (1994).

1. A bally, or ballyhoo, is the come-on used by the "talkers" at a sideshow; "outside talkers" stand on a platform at the entrance promoting the sideshow to passersby, while "inside talkers" sell extras, from whoopee cushions to a closer look at the woman in the blade box. For a discussion of the 1989 Coney Island sideshow, see Fred Siegel, "Theatre of Guts: An Exploration of the Sideshow Aesthetic," *TDR: The Drama Review* T132 (winter 1991): 107–24. For the autobiography of Dolly Dimples, one of the best-known Fat Ladies of this century, see Celesta "Dolly Dimples" Geyer, *The Greatest Diet in the World,* originally *Diet or Die* (Orlando, Fla.: Chateau, 1968). For more general explorations of the sideshow genre, see Robert Bogdan, *Freak Show: Presenting Human Oddities for Amusement and Profit* (Chicago: University of Chicago Press, 1988); Leslie Fiedler, *Freaks: Myths and Images of the Secret Self* (New York: Anchor, 1978); and Ricky Jay, *Learned Pigs and Fireproof Women: A History of Unique, Eccentric, and Amazing Entertainers* (London: Robert Hale, 1986).

2. All Helen Melon quotations are from a composite transcript of her performances throughout the summer 1992 season. Katy Dierlam developed her own script, which varied from appearance to appearance. A version of this script appears in *Facing Forward: One-Act Plays and Monologs by Contemporary American Women at the Crest of the Twenty-first Century,* ed. Leah D. Frank (New York: Broadway Play Publishing, 1995), 209–13. I owe a tremendous debt to Katy Dierlam for sharing her sideshow performance and personal history with me. This essay properly belongs to her. Dick Zigun, Coney Island's sideshow impresario, has also been an invaluable informant. In addition, Carol Martin, Donna Heiland, and Leah Frank have generously reviewed this work as it evolved.

3. In particular, Dierlam's invitation to "take a good look" is clearly borrowed from the performance art of Annie Sprinkle, performances derived from the strip show and pornography in which she invited spectators to place their faces against her breasts, to examine her vagina with a speculum, and to otherwise look, touch, and smell her body as closely as desired. For a thoughtful reading of the body-centered performances of Sprinkle, Karen Finley, and others, see Elinor Fuchs, "Staging the Obscene Body," *TDR: The Drama Review* T121 (spring 1989): 33–58.

4. Susie Orbach, *Fat Is a Feminist Issue: The Anti-Diet Guide to Permanent Weight Loss* (New York: Berkley Books, 1978), and Kim Chernin, *The Obsession: Reflections on the Tyranny of Slenderness* (New York: Harper and Row, 1981). See also Jane R. Hirschmann and Carol H. Munter, *Overcoming Overeating* (New York: Fawcett Columbine, 1988). Ironically, much of this literature is presented as a way to "break out of the diet/binge cycle and lose weight naturally" (from the

cover of *Overcoming Overeating*). Moreover, these writers assume an average-weight, anorexic, or bulimic reader rather than one who is overweight. See, for example, Chernin, 35.

5. Note that the name of Rabelais's most (in)famous hero, Gargantua, is associated both with size (giant) and appetite (gluttony), while Gulliver's description of the Brobdingnagian wet nurse conflates the grotesque with the overlarge: "I must confess no object ever disgusted me so much as the sight of her monstrous breast, which I cannot tell what to compare with, so as to give the curious reader an idea of its bulk, shape and colour. It stood prominent six foot, and could not be less than sixteen in circumference. The nipple was about half the bigness of my head, and the hue both of that and the dug so varied with spots, pimples and freckles, that nothing could appear more nauseous: for I had a near sight of her, she sitting down the more conveniently to give suck, and I standing on the table" (Jonathan Swift, *Gulliver's Travels and Other Writings* [New York: Bantam, 1962], 99).

6. It is possible, of course, to conceive of all exchanges in which the performer is female and the assumed spectator is male as erotic by definition. See Laura Mulvey, "Visual Pleasure and Narrative Cinema" (1975), in *Visual and Other Pleasures* (Bloomington: Indiana University Press, 1989), 19. See also Elin Diamond, "Brechtian Theory/Feminist Theory: Towards a Gestic Feminist Criticism," *TDR: The Drama Review* T117 (spring 1988): 89.

7. Even Marcia Millman, whose argument is aimed at redressing prejudice against fat women, admits: "Indeed, it is difficult to listen to overweight people without concluding that obesity, especially in an extreme form, is indeed often a symptom of unconscious conflicts or disturbances" (*Such a Pretty Face: Being Fat in America* [New York: Norton, 1980], 87).

8. Susan Bordo recognizes overeating as a "furtive, shameful, illicit act" and adds: "Food is not the real issue here, of course; rather the control of female appetite for food is merely the most concrete expression of the general rule governing the construction of femininity . . ." ("The Body and the Reproduction of Femininity: A Feminist Appropriation of Foucault" in *Gender/Body/Knowledge: Feminist Reconstructions of Being and Knowing*, ed. Alison M. Jaggar and Bordo [New Brunswick, N.J.: Rutgers University Press, 1989], 18). Consider, too, Maggie Kilgour's discussion of the female body as "transgressive, a naturally grotesque body that is always exceeding itself" (*From Communion to Cannibalism: An Anatomy of Metaphors of Incorporation* [Princeton: Princeton University Press, 1990], 243). See also Chernin, *The Obsession*, 56–61.

9. For a provocative examination of the relationship between the "visible" and the "real," see Peggy Phelan, *Unmarked: The Politics of Performance* (London: Routledge, 1993), esp. 69. The idea of looking through the body to some sort of authentic "self" is problematized by Phelan, who recognizes that "[i]dentity cannot, then, reside in the name you say or the body you can see" (13), as well as by such writers as Jean Baudrillard, who, in *Fatal Strategies*, considers the obese body as specter, "at once saturated and empty" (ed. Jim Fleming, trans. Philip Beitchman and W. G. J. Neisluchowski [New York: Semiotext(e); London: Pluto, 1990], 27). See also Kilgour, *From Communion to Cannibalism*, 4.

10. Robert Bogdan offers this definition: "By 'freak show' I mean the formally organized exhibition of people with alleged and real physical, mental, or behavioral anomalies for amusement and profit" (*Freak Show*, 10). But Leslie Fiedler notes that "the Fats also seem different from other Freaks, since they, too, begin not with an irreversible fate, but a tendency, a possibility of attaining monstrous size, which they can fight or feed or merely endure" (*Freaks*, 125). See also Yoram

Carmeli, "Wee Pea: The Total Play of the Dwarf in the Circus," *TDR: The Drama Review* T124 (winter 1989): 128–45.

11. See Mary Russo, "Female Grotesques: Carnival and Theory," in *Feminist Studies/Critical Studies,* ed. Teresa de Lauretis (Bloomington: Indiana University Press, 1984), 213–29, and Chernin, *The Obsession,* 143–44.

12. For Celesta Geyer, performing Dolly Dimples also appears to have allowed her to confront scoffers directly—at least in her accounts of her improvisations: "I was a 555-pound freak, the side-show fat lady. Curiosity seekers came from all around to see me and to poke fun at me. Most of them refused to believe what they saw. A woman in Pittsburgh once asked me if my beefy legs were really mine. With my tongue in cheek I told her that they were phony, that I had an intake valve on my big toe and each morning I was inflated just to look that way" (*The Greatest Diet in the World,* 13).

13. Bob Morris, "The Enormity of It All: A Quarter-Ton Actress and Her New Year's Resolution . . . ," *New York Times,* January 2, 1994, sec. 9, p. 3.

14. Bogdan, *Freak Show,* 114.

15. Fiedler, *Freaks,* 129–30.

16. Orbach (*Fat Is a Feminist Issue*), Chernin (*The Obsession*), Hirschmann and Munter (*Overcoming Obesity*), Millman (*Such a Pretty Face*), and Susan Bordo all struggle with the notion that the overweight (or underweight) female body appears as a sign of psychological and/or social dysfunction. Of these, Bordo is perhaps most successful in *Unbearable Weight: Feminism, Western Culture, and the Body* (Berkeley: University of California Press, 1993), noting that "[f]at (that is to say, becoming *all* body) is associated with the taint of matter and flesh, 'wantonness,' mental stupor and mental decay" (148). Consider, too, Baudrillard's reading of obesity as a metaphor for cultural obscenity in *Fatal Strategies* (esp. 28).

17. In contrast to this bit of bravado, however, in her *New York Times* interview with Bob Morris, Dierlam admits: ". . . I can't believe I'm saying this because it's such a cliché . . . but I'm going to start a new diet right after New Year's" ("The Enormity of It All," 3).

18. That the relationship between a woman's weight and her attractiveness to men shifts radically from culture to culture is explored in detail in Anne Scott Beller's *Fat and Thin: A Natural History of Obesity* (New York: Farrar, Straus, and Giroux, 1977). Moreover, Marcia Millman opens her study of women and weight in America with a series of descriptions of the male "fat admirers" who attend dances sponsored by the National Association to Advance Fat Acceptance (NAAFA) in order to meet and seduce hyperfat women (*Such a Pretty Face,* 3–25).

19. Fiedler, *Freaks,* 131–32.

20. Ibid., 131.

21. For example, in *The Obsession,* Kim Chernin posits that "anorexics are afraid of becoming, not adults, not teenagers, but women" (64). See also Millman, *Such a Pretty Face,* 105–11.

22. Consider, for example, Laura Mulvey's assertion that "the woman as icon, displayed for the gaze and enjoyment of men, the active controllers of the look, always threatens to evoke the [castration] anxiety it originally signified" ("Visual Pleasure and Narrative Cinema," 21). Susan Bordo, for her part, notes that "female hunger as sexuality is represented by Western culture in misogynist images permeated with terror and loathing rather than affection or admiration" (*Unbearable Weight,* 116–17). See also Barbara Creed's psychoanalytic discussion of the rep-

resentation of women in horror films in *The Monstrous-Feminine: Film, Feminism, Psychoanalysis* (London: Routledge, 1993).

23. Orbach, *Fat Is a Feminist Issue,* 9.

24. Hirshmann and Munter, *Overcoming Overeating,* 49.

25. For a parallel, albeit heavily Freudian, exploration of the terror evoked by the image of the all-powerful mother in popular film, particularly in the "Alien" movies, see Creed, *The Monstrous-Feminine.* See also Chernin, *The Obsession,* 117.

26. Kilgour, *From Communion to Cannibalism,* 8.

27. Bordo, *Unbearable Weight,* 117. See also Chernin, *The Obsession,* 117.

28. This narrative uses the autobiography of Celesta "Dolly Dimples" Geyer as its primary source. See also Fiedler, *Freaks,* 125–26.

29. For example, in an *American Theatre* report on the sideshow, the name "Helen Melon" does not appear; instead, Dierlam is referred to only as the "Feminist Fat Lady" (Janice Paran, "Dick Zigun: He's the Self-Appointed Custodian of Coney Island's Faded Glory," *American Theatre* 9, no. 6 [1992]: 34–36).

REFERENCES

Baudrillard, Jean. *Fatal Strategies.* Edited by Jim Fleming. Translated by Philip Beitchman and W. G. J. Neisluchowski. New York: Semiotext(e); London: Pluto, 1990.

Beller, Anne Scott. *Fat and Thin: A Natural History of Obesity.* New York: Farrar, Straus, and Giroux, 1977.

Bogdan, Robert. *Freak Show: Presenting Human Oddities for Amusement and Profit.* Chicago: University of Chicago Press, 1988.

Bordo, Susan. "The Body and the Reproduction of Femininity: A Feminist Appropriation of Foucault." In *Gender/Body/Knowledge: Feminist Reconstructions of Being and Knowing,* edited by Alison M. Jaggar and Bordo, 13–33. New Brunswick, N.J.: Rutgers University Press, 1989.

———. *Unbearable Weight: Feminism, Western Culture, and the Body.* Berkeley: University of California Press, 1993.

Carmeli, Yoram. "Wee Pea: The Total Play of the Dwarf in the Circus." *TDR: The Drama Review* T124 (winter 1989): 128–45.

Chernin, Kim. *The Obsession: Reflections on the Tyranny of Slenderness.* New York: Harper and Row, 1981.

Creed, Barbara. *The Monstrous-Feminine: Film, Feminism, Psychoanalysis.* London: Routledge, 1993.

Diamond, Elin. "Brechtian Theory/Feminist Theory: Towards a Gestic Feminist Criticism." *TDR: The Drama Review* T117 (spring 1988): 82–94.

Dierlam, Katy. Script for "Fat Lady" performance. In *Facing Forward: One-Act Plays and Monologs by Contemporary American Women at the Crest of the Twenty-first Century,* edited by Leah D. Frank, 209–13. New York: Broadway Play Publishing, 1995.

Fiedler, Leslie. *Freaks: Myths and Images of the Secret Self.* New York: Anchor, 1978.

Fuchs, Elinor. "Staging the Obscene Body." *TDR: The Drama Review* T121 (spring 1989): 33–58.

Geyer, Celesta "Dolly Dimples." *The Greatest Diet in the World* [originally titled *Diet or Die*]. Orlando, Fla.: Chateau, 1968.

Hirschmann, Jane R., and Carol H. Munter. *Overcoming Overeating*. New York: Fawcett Columbine, 1988.

Jay, Ricky. *Learned Pigs and Fireproof Women: A History of Unique, Eccentric, and Amazing Entertainers.* London: Robert Hale, 1986.

Kilgour, Maggie. *From Communion to Cannibalism: An Anatomy of Metaphors of Incorporation.* Princeton: Princeton University Press, 1990.

Millman, Marcia. *Such a Pretty Face: Being Fat in America.* New York: Norton, 1980.

Mulvey, Laura. "Visual Pleasure and Narrative Cinema" (1975). In *Visual and Other Pleasures,* 14–26. Bloomington: Indiana University Press, 1989.

Orbach, Susie. *Fat Is a Feminist Issue: The Anti-Diet Guide to Permanent Weight Loss.* New York: Berkley, 1978.

Paran, Janice. "Dick Zigun: He's the Self-Appointed Custodian of Coney Island's Faded Glory." *American Theatre* 9, no. 6 (1992): 34–36.

Phelan, Peggy. *Unmarked: The Politics of Performance.* London: Routledge, 1993.

Russo, Mary. "Female Grotesques: Carnival and Theory." In *Feminist Studies/Critical Studies,* edited by Teresa de Lauretis, 213–29. Bloomington: Indiana University Press, 1984.

Siegel, Fred. "Theatre of Guts: An Exploration of the Sideshow Aesthetic." *TDR: The Drama Review* T132 (winter 1991): 107–24.

Swift, Jonathan. *Gulliver's Travels and Other Writings.* New York: Bantam, 1962.

14 Fatties on Stage

Feminist Performances

PETRA KUPPERS

> The cover of the December 1990 issue of *Vanity Fair*—headlined "Roseanne on Top"—shows Arnold holding the wrists of her husband Tom Arnold to pin him beneath her. Her mouth is open in what appears to be a laugh. She is wearing a low-cut red dress, a strawberry-blonde wig, diamonds, and a white fox fur, a look that parodically recalls the blonde bombshell and gold diggers of early classical Hollywood film. The photograph . . . centers on Arnold's massive cleavage. Tom Arnold's face . . . is upside down.
>
> The words and images of the cover suggest that Arnold wields power in multiple dimensions—power over men, financial power, celebrity power, sexual power.[1]

In introducing Roseanne Arnold's image, Kathleen Rowe focuses on one aspect of her chosen photograph—the accumulation of power. Another aspect of the photo is relegated to the margins, is not analyzed: the power of discourse that abstracts Roseanne into the ultimate fat pig. A slightly less optimistic reading of the same cover photo would read a stereotypical presentation of the grotesque woman, her boundaries (the mouth, the cleavage) opened up and ravenous; her animalistic nature underlined by the fox fur and the unruly, unkempt hair; her fat straining at the seams of femininity. In this reading, the woman on top is a shapeless blob, out of control, outside the social, a monster, a grotesque, threatening the male order. And although we can celebrate the image for being transgressive, its political potential is heavily curtailed by its reinforcement of the main stereotyped feature of fat women: their excess.

So how can we as women of size present ourselves, perform our specific and subjective identity in a world in which our bodies are read against our will? One of the major obstacles to allowing women of size a voice of their own is the connotation of fat in contemporary society. As it splits away agency and subjectivity, fat takes away the voice and acquires its own vocabulary. And that vocabulary of the fat female body tells not of agency but of loss of control. The feminist philosopher Susan Bordo paraphrases Foucault when she claims that aristocratic Greek culture, itself the root of Western culture, made a science of the regulation of food intake in the service of attaining self-mastery and moderation.[2]

Body regulation, regulating the connection between mind and body, is at the heart of the Western problem with fat. The link between body and meaning is deeply embedded in our cultural vocabulary. Thus Patricia Parker can connect discourse and embodiment in her discussions of literary topoi, giving striking examples of how the physical becomes the literal in the body politics of concepts; in particular, the "tradition of rhetorical *dilatio*—with its references to the 'swelling' style or its relation to the verbal 'interlarding' produced through an excessive application of the principle of 'increase'—provides its own links between fat bodies and discoursing 'at large,' between the size of a discourse and the question of body size."[3] If we apply this topos to performance, we see that for the fat body, all communication is removed from the speaking or showing subject once the sign of the "extra" is acquired. Instead of standing for itself as a direct expression of the performer's wish to communicate, the act of communication, whether oral or visual, stands for the performer's loss of control. Thus, speaking from a large body is always already arrested—the spoken word, the performance, the gesture all become sucked into the sign of excessiveness that fat connotes.

Most performers who started to explore the large female body as an arena of cultural politics seem caught in this labeling of loss of control and in the literality of their bodies. They are too easily read—to twist discourse away from their size proves nearly impossible. Their size is already performance, prior to any staging of it; as one cultural critic explains, "there remains one true physical freak in modern culture: the obese person."[4] If their performances try to reclaim the "body out of control" as site of transgression and empowerment without attempting to question these very assumptions of fertility, grossness, carnival, and the grotesque, their work can easily fall back into the stereotype, still allowing no space for inscriptions of subjectivity. Instead of showing the problems with the essentialist account of fat, they embrace the large woman as caught up in her (culturally determined) fat.

Rowe's analysis of Roseanne Arnold's star persona is a case in point. Roseanne's persona is framed and interpellated with her personal story, a story that surely is larger than life. Her second HBO special, *Roseanne Barr: Live from Trump Castle* (1991), included a direct challenge to the comedian Arsenio Hall, who had made her the butt of fat jokes:

> Excuse me, Arse. I'm thirty-seven years old. I got four kids. I'm Jewish and I was raised in Salt Lake City, Utah. My Dad sold crucifixes door-to-door to Mexicans. When I was seven I fell down, tore off my whole lip, had to have it sewed back on. When I was sixteen I was hit by a car [and] my head was impaled on the hood ornament . . . I got pregnant the first time I had sex. My parents made me give her up for adoption. I found her eighteen years later when her face was splashed across the cover of the National Enquirer. I spent eight months in a state institution, a mental institution. I hitchhiked three times across the country by myself, with hepatitis. I lived in a car, a cabin, a cave. I married a guy just because he had a fucking bathtub. I had three more kids. He treated me like shit every day for sixteen years, and when I finally got the guts to dump the sonofabitch, I have to pay him half the money I make for the rest of my goddam life, Arsenio. *FUCK WITH ME*![5]

Rowe comments that one of the effects of this monologue is that it "transforms a potential narrative of *victimization* into one of power."[6] For me, a feminist performance artist, writer, and woman of size, it is an amazing piece of testimonial, melodrama, and psychological cliché and a framing device of fat. It closely mirrors early feminist attempts to reclaim fat by pointing to it as a survival mechanism—the barrier that holds at bay all the grief of being a woman in a man's world. I do not find this soul baring, the conflation of private and public persona, empowering. Instead, it guides me back to narratives about women's lives being determined by their bodies, or their bodies determined by their lives.

The main argument that Rowe puts forward in the first two chapters of her book about female comedians is that going for the "other" of rule and control opens up the field of *liminality,* Victor Turner's term for the space of transformation and play, for the social moments "when a culture explores the 'subjunctive' rather than the 'indicative' mode of its being—the 'what might be,' rather than the 'what is.' In such moments, a culture reflects on its codes."[7] Rowe is not interested in arguing for or against the liberating force of the grotesque and the carnivalesque; she instead sees the "feminist potential of (the unruly women's) image in its copiousness, or fatness, if you will—citing a chain of associations leading to Mae West, and from West to other vamps and female impersonators."[8] Proliferating discourses, stereotypes, images, and roles are invoked as the unruly, loud, fat, gross woman appears on stage. The possibilities that lie in her fatness can be revalued, wrested back from patriarchal discourse, and made into a trope for female empowerment.

Yet such a claim is essentialist: it inverts the values of contemporary culture while accepting the structures underlying them. Instead, we must find a way to talk about women and acknowledge their culturally devalued difference (here, size) without reducing them to the pool of images available within our culture to express that difference (here, nature out of control, grossness, excess). This is the dilemma that confronts a feminist performance artist of size—how to break out of the image presented at first glance by one's body without denying that body or turning against it. My essay, using the theoretical framework of feminist performance theory, explores two female performers who both address these issues in their performance work.

SQUEEZED OUT

Only a small, clearly demarcated pool of images is available for representations of identity. Each is held in a rigid grid of binary oppositions: madonna/whore, straight/gay, normal/other, and so on. Size, like sexual orientation, class, race, or disability, has clear connotations of value. Size, fat, and their concomitant attributes slide toward the black hole of the abject. The fat body is the body without the rule of the mind: the body let loose, animalistic, instinctive, out of control. Thus, sexual voraciousness, stupidity, and helplessness are all associated with the fat body. The fat body becomes the enemy. We live in a culture in which a young girl has to speak about the split between controlling mind and loose body, about her constant fear of becoming fat: "My body can turn on me at any moment; it is an out-of-control mass of flesh."[9]

Images themselves cannot escape these connotations; they are always already bound into the system of communication that structures understanding by assigning value. But artists engaged in stretching our visual language of images have never been satisfied with these narrow boundaries. Because escape is impossible, they have had to find another approach. A wide area of feminist performance politics can be subsumed under Djuna Barnes's description of the work of the image: "an image is a stop the mind makes between uncertainties."[10] How can we break into the uncertainties that hide between and behind the images, and what does that entrance mean for a fat performance artist?

Feminist performers, in particular lesbian women, have keenly felt the need to claim uncertainties. They contend with a pervasive invisibility—no social discourse is given to the lesbian woman (a point discussed in more detail later in this chapter). Her representation in popular discourse conventionally relies on overdetermination: too masculine, too fat, too thin, too loud. The feminist is always already a caricature in representation. The fat woman has equally needed uncertainties; in her case, the body leaves no possibility of other identity. The fat woman is fat, and this sign rules all her other aspects.

Feminist performance aesthetics developed to address the problem of ill-fitting images. Split Britches is one of the most visible of the theater groups developing alternative strategies of representation. Rejecting both "positive images" and essentialism, their theater has relied on distanced pleasure. Performers move fluently from one gender stereotype to the next, or from one material, historical image of woman to another, always confounding the search for their "true character." The feminist critic Sue-Ellen Case sees the aim of camp lesbian performances of groups like the Split Britches as "not to conflict reality with another reality, but to abandon the notion of reality through roles and their seductive atmosphere and lightly manipulated appearances."[11] Because they destabilize gender and body expectations, the spectator is forced to examine her own categories in order to make sense of the performance. Easy recognition is denied. The feminist theorist Elin Diamond sums up the effect on audiences: "Feminist practice that seeks to expose or mock the strictures of gender usually uses some version of the Brechtian A-effect. That is, by alienating (not simply rejecting) iconicity, by foregrounding the expectations of resemblance the ideology of gender is exposed and thrown back to the spectator."[12] Thus, categories of the "natural" explode. There is no "truth" presented about the women on stage—these feminist performances show only the uncertainty of our socially accepted version of reality.

One problem with the Brechtian strategy for women of size is their inability to escape. While the lesbian performer can play with the "not-sure" by taking the position of the femme, or can dress up in male clothes to subvert heterosexist behavior patterns, the fat performer does not escape her physicality. Since her sign of difference is overpowering, she is in the same position as the woman of color—she cannot jump from discourse to discourse, from passing to being. Her "essence" is always already embodied on stage. She can utilize the techniques of alienation—she can move from power woman in a dark suit to aerobic instructor in leotards, from working-class mother to diva. But the physicality of the fat woman's presence doesn't allow the skip between straight, femme, and butch that the performers of Split Britches can exploit to destabilize their images as "weak women." The fat woman remains, in all her guises, the fat woman. There seems no way out of this body, no matter how it is dressed up—fat seems to work as the master sign that determines the body and rules all discourses. The alienation and distance that Brechtian politics demand cannot be achieved. Fat's association with the grotesque enables every action, every dressing up to be reclaimed as carnivalesque masquerade. Each performance becomes just another sign of the excessive nature of the fat body. Since mobility (that is, the ability to invade everything and incorporate it) is already part of the sign of the grotesque fat body, the mobility that feminist performance politics relies on to destabilize the status quo cannot free the fat performer from her stereotype. Instead, it reinforces it.

One way in which performers have appropriated feminist performance techniques is by putting into question the content of the category *fat.* Rather than exploring the deconstructive potential of the category *carnival,* they play by inserting the carnivalesque and grotesque connotations of their embodied selves into other discourses. By so doing, they can make their presentation truly deviant—instead of reinforcing the image of fat as all-embracing category of masquerade and discursive excess (the rich, spreading text imagined by Parker), they reduce their bodies without denying them. Their bodies come back to the smaller discourses of lived reality, of a specific subject, rather than being spread out across connotations of the grotesque and boundaryless.

In my analysis of two performances, I demonstrate how women of size have reclaimed their specificity in the face of a culture that associates their bodies with loss of self and loss of control. Their subject position as individuated women with their own histories, desires, and physicality becomes visible under the mountains of proliferating discourses.

WALKING THE TIGHTROPE

Jo Brand is a highly successful British comedy artist, with her own television series, newspaper articles, audiotapes, and books. She tours the country regularly, playing in front of sell-out audiences. Her performances on TV and on stage usually consist of stand-up comedy—she remains onstage, with the occasional excursion forward into the auditorium, and lets rip. The butt of her jokes is her size, men in general, anything to do with body orifices, food, and sex. Her humor ranges from the crude to the supercrude, and she elicits winces of pain as well as rowdy laughter from her mainly female audiences. Her performances have proved problematic for feminist analysis, as they can be read to reinforce cultural stereotypes of femininity.[13] I want to complicate the negative reading of Brand's self-deprecation in her performance by showing the different addresses at work in it. But before turning to her onstage persona, I will trace the main trajectories of my analysis in the opening sequence of *Through the Cake-hole* (1995–96), her successful Channel 4 TV show. Brand does not actually appear in the sequence, but it brings up two of her main themes: excess and control.

The images we see in this sequence are from a genre associated with femininity, with traditional women's roles, with the kitchen. In a voice-over similar to that of cookery programs, Jo Brand delivers a recipe. We see butter being cut in close-up, sugar sieved over it, three eggs languidly dropped into a bowl. A hand manipulates an oven dial; the oven is high-class, modernist, expensive. All of these images are beautiful, displayed in sexy color against a black background—food is eroticized. The measurements are "normal," fully in keeping with our expectations, and the sexy, detached voice gives no hint of grossness or greed. Instead, the images belong to the genre of food photography—the image of food is distanced, aestheticized.

But the registers of reception soon change. As the voice maintains its controlled, measured delivery, the images start to verge away from the normal routine. Excess begins to appear as the cake is assembled: the voice-over instructs us to "pour over brandy"—a whole bottle's content is nonchalantly emptied over the cake. As we follow the bottle's course over the table, a bowl of cigarette stubs, full to the brim, briefly comes into view. "Put on some cream"—a great big whack of whipped cream drops from a height onto the cake—"Add some more cream"—"and some more"—"Serve with custard, ice cream—and no friends." There follows an image of a chair being wedged under the door handle. The final transgression from modernist aestheticized food to the grotesque occurs in the last instruction: "Garnish with chocolate bars—and a large pork pie." From the image of a pork pie being stuffed into the mountain of cream, we cut to the studio where Jo Brand is taking the stage.

This credit sequence plays with two contrasting attitudes toward food: food as excess and food as aesthetic pleasure. Here food is sexily and secretly brimming over into the other realm of bodily excess, sex, where the same issues about proper behavior, norms, and boundaries are at stake.[14] The binary revolves around control—control is needed to adhere to the measurements given, control is needed to keep the images pure and simple (and to keep one's fingers out of the bowl during the filming). This detachment is signaled in the first half of the sequence. The second half questions or undermines that control. What is seen as female, hysterical, irrational behavior is elevated to the status of instructions, to the right way to do it—putting a chair under the door handle is just as important as breaking the eggs. In the second half, the personal intrudes into the smooth surfaces of the images as the ashtray and a brandy glass become visible. Finally, the excess of large quantities, whole chocolate bars, and the matter-out-of-place of the pork pie make the "perfectly normal" recipe for a cake into a grotesque farce. Throughout the sequence, though, the coolness and detachment of Brand's voice do not change. Her voice portrays no bodily engagement with her presentation—no pleasure, no greed taints its calm edges.

Is this woman slave to her food? Does she lose self-control in the face of a large cream cake? What happens to food obsessions and eating disorders if their "methods" are framed in visual and aural discourses of control and rationality? These are the questions raised for me by Jo Brand's take on fatness and food, on desire and sex, and on gender relations. Hysteria and powerlessness are the discourses most often linked with women's attitudes toward their bodies and their food. Brand barges through these associations by shifting the goalposts of normalcy. Who decides what is "over" in relation to eating? Why does "lonely eating" become "deviant eating"? In destabilizing these connotations through ambiguous laughter, she opens up possibilities of respect for women of size.

Brand's embodied performance of herself mobilizes the same tropes of control and excess, mixing and playing with expectations, that we see in her credit sequence. The television studio decor of her show connotes the sexual, oral, excessive register of the grotesque woman: a pair of huge, open, pink lips stands against a deep purple background. Brand performs against this backdrop in a circle surrounded on three sides by the audience on raised seating. The lighting is in keeping with the plushy, feminine associations of the monstrous lips: dark reds, pinks, and saturated hues of other colors play in the round. These colors can be read as pointers to the liminality of the show. Private and public are mixed, the body opens to display its carnivalesque inside: the threatening *vagina dentata*, the womb space, the monstrous feminine.[15]

Brand's appearance in this highly charged arena is surprisingly mundane—no feathers, no velvet, no cleavage. Her physical performance rejects the readings of the fat body as open, or as a liminal space in which inner and outer surfaces meet. When she takes the stage, she is always dressed in black, with a wide, tuniclike top over black leggings. She reveals only her hands, her calves, and her face. Even her red shoes reject any reading of blood or glamour: they are highly sensible, hard Doc Martens. Without being armored, this body clearly delineates its space and contains the subject. The effect of completion and self-assurance is further stressed by Brand's hairstyle. Her black hair is swept upward, into a pyramid, which closes off her body shape into one satisfying block. No jewelry breaks through the implied lines. Only her big, red mouth echoes the stage design; but here again, the openness one could impute to it is held at a distance—Brand uses a microphone onstage, held firmly in front of her mouth, thereby creating a clear vertical that hardly wavers during her show.

Brand's physical appearance plays with the connotations carried by her clearly big body. Instead of trying to break the associations by heightening them (an effort that is doomed to failure), she holds the associations in tension. Her dress is not weight-negating—never does she attempt to minimize her body, which is the source of many of her verbal jokes, or to write it out of her performance. Instead, she inhabits it comfortably, joyfully, relaxed and with no stiffness, while still maintaining her compact, enclosed space.

A publicity shot for her 1997 tour softens this very hard image of her TV show by allowing some reference to female body stereotypes. Brand wears earrings and is seen on the floor, her head to the camera, her feet up in the air sideways behind her. But even in this comic take on glamourpuss photography (a posture similar to that struck by Roseanne on the *Vanity Fair* cover), Brand denies an expansive reading of her body. Her hair and feet end at the same height in a line, while her knees and the edge of the image create the lower half of a compact rectangle. Brand gazes outward at the spectator, but her head is stopped by the hand on which she rests it. The fleshy but strong elbow is the part of the photo most prominently set before the spectator. Where her cleavage would be in a "normal" glamour shot is the top of a furniture puff, upholstered in flesh-colored jacquard. It blocks out any appropriation of her body.

Brand's visual performance stresses control, closure, and comfort. But the fat body always intrudes—for her to move away from it is impossible, as any reading of her must always fall back on it. Thus, Brand gives it a place: the verbal content of her show abounds with references to size, fat, grossness, genitalia, masturbation (male and female), anti-man jokes of the monstrous woman, food, obsession, fecal matter, farting, spit, and blood. The whole gamut of Bakhtin's carnival explodes on stage, while the audience winces and laughs. Her humor veers from self-deprecating jokes about her inability to get men to severe man bashing: "On the very rare occasions that I do get a bloke in a room on his own, it seems too good an opportunity to miss—just to punch him in the bloody gob" (*Through the Cakehole*). Restraint is not part of Brand's vocabulary—her language is foul and offensive. Her delivery, though, is always measured and controlled. No screaming, no loud laughter, no hysteria impinges on her clear, matter-of-fact style. References to her own history are sparse, and left very general. More often, she refers to the experiences of all women by treating sexual assault, misogyny, and objectification with tough gallows humor.

We never see her own body caught up in the excesses she narrates. Whenever she appears in sketches between the stand-up routines of the TV show, her own body is covered up, even though the narrative calls for sex and nakedness (the men in the scene are exposed). A simulated advertising break is the only occasion on which we see a female body amid abject matter, in a style reminiscent of Cindy Sherman's famous photograph of herself reflected in a mirror in a landscape of bodily waste.[16] "Lardie," Brand's travesty of Barbie, is seen in her accessorized plastic living space—a disgusting kitchen with food stains and decaying matter, a bathroom complete with vomit and shit, a Barbie doll with a fag[17] hanging from her mouth. By allocating the visual space of the abject to the squeaky-clean Barbie, Brand destabilizes the connotations of carnival that her size instantaneously activates. She does not disavow or negate them or create positive images of women of size; instead, she makes the carnival unstable in itself. Carnival erupts in her language and in the content of her show, but it is kept at bay in her physical presence. Brand's doing and being are not separable—acting together as she addresses the audience, they create an image that destabilizes the "loss of control" connoted by fat. By complicating her persona, by inhabiting the world of control and the world of excess simultaneously but separately (unlike a woman using excess to control, as Roseanne does in the *Vanity Fair* cover), Brand creates for me an image of a woman of size at ease, in charge, and on top.

NAKED FLESH

Brand performs the possibility of women of size in control without the help of excess by denying the carnivalesque image of her body. She doesn't corset herself or otherwise deny the physicality of her being—her familiarity with female masturbation, her joy in food, and her pleasure in sex and sleep are constant themes in her show. But her control of the performance might recall Yvonne Rainer's refusal to show the naked female body in her films, fearing that its cultural meanings and connotations of pornography, female submission, and heterosexual dominance might swamp any possibility of female agency. Another female performance artist, Nao Bustamante, presents a different interplay of excess and control. Her show *America the Beautiful,* which ran at the London Institute for Contemporary Art in 1995, presents a woman of size naked on stage.

Bustamante uses the genre of performance art, not comedy, to inscribe her presence onstage. She is therefore framed by an avant-garde discourse, by an aura of respect or attention that the comedian cannot command. Bustamante's performance links her to a feminist aesthetic of masquerade. During the show, she manipulates her body, puts on makeup and a wig, and disrupts the transparency of realism with her control over the staging. She herself operates a turntable to provide her stage music, and she hands her props to a (male) stagehand in full view of the audience.

Conventional images of fat women are sent up—she does portray the "sad blob having a fag at the bar," but she does the image while balancing precariously high up above the stage on a stepladder that she has climbed laboriously on high heels, clad in restrictive cling-film. Throughout the show, the bodily effort and coordination necessary to achieve spectacles of abject femininity and grotesqueness are mercilessly displayed. Instead of just putting shoes on, Bustamante tucks her glamorous long evening gloves under her wig (effectively blinding herself), props up a small stepladder with the shoes on top, and climbs up to step into them. On the way, she falls off the ladder twice.

Repetition and excess are marked in other ways on her body as well: she persistently applies hairspray onto a huge blonde wig, circling her head over and over. She draws out the spectacle of containing her unruly body to uncomfortable lengths, as she winds cling-film tightly about her bulging figure. At the beginning of the show, Bustamante sets up the plunge into the abject. After climbing out of her clothes, she sits on a chair, listening and mouthing to a soundtrack of a male voice encouraging listeners to think about their bodies as a temple for the living spirit. During this sequence, she unpacks the kind of toilet-seat cover available in public rest rooms and drapes it over her head. The realms of the spiritual, of self-control, and of the abject matter of shit and piss—these discourses capture and tear at the large female body that both acts (in stage performance) and is acted on by them.

The highlight of the show is a rendition of the U.S. national anthem on bottles. Having been handed an ironing board on wheels, Bustamante sets up a bottle piano carefully, slowly, and with determination, swigging occasionally. Still wearing the All-American Barbie doll wig, with her flesh trying to squeeze past the rolls of restrictive cling-film, she quotes Roseanne's famous and outrageous performance at a baseball game in San Diego. Literally treating the anthem to a blow job, she goes down on the bottles in gestures that connote obscenities of sex and of excess drink and food. But she also renders the anthem completely and accurately, tuning a bottle with the help of a piano as its note falls flat.

At the beginning of this essay, I criticized those readings of the fat female performance artist that celebrate her disruptive, carnivalesque, and grotesque potential. How can I now read this cringe-inducing, abject performance as empowering? Bustamante laboriously constructs her image, creating the body in abjection through her performance of self. But, as I have shown above, the alienating construct—which foregrounds feminist performance aesthetics—fails to destabilize the fat body with its vocabulary of spreading discourses and multiplicity. How then does Bustamante avoid being a sign of her own oppression?

Bustamante does not negotiate the content of the fat sign as Brand does, though Bustamante does claim her agency at all stages of the show. But through her embodied performance, she shows the pain of discursive existence. Unlike Roseanne, whose rowdy image is in itself relatively coherent, this performer enacts the stitching of the grotesque role onto her own flesh in detail. In doing so, she does not necessarily link with her audience in a prelinguistic, romantic state. Her citation of the body's pain is not the same as theater theorist Antonin Artaud's play with performer's and spectator's bodies, when he writes: "The key to throwing the audience into a magical trance is to know in advance what pressure points must be affected in the body."[18] The magic that opens up for me in Bustamante's spectacle is instead the magic of connection, of presence, of history, and of discourse. Elin Diamond explains this more problematic view of presence, of the interaction between embodiment and representation: "In its signifying operations language splits the speaker from the presence of her own words; at the moment of utterance the signifier is . . . always traveling to another context, arriving from still another. Presence, then, is never simply present. The 'auratic' uniqueness of the performer's body, its apparent 'unity' as logical and experiential home of the subject, is dispersed by its 'own' discourse, the discourse it cannot own."[19] Bustamante vanishes and reappears under the burden of cling-film, images of fat, her control of the stage space, and discourses of objectification: a subject in discourse, interpellated, dispersed, always different and yet so familiar. The tension and violence of the subject attempting to speak while being spoken can become visible, as Diamond makes clear: "The body's emphatic ('live') presence is offered as a momentary habitus of what is not present—the forgotten objects and cultural detritus that constitute a piece of the 'historical experience of women.' "[20] Her pain, the falling, the tortured flesh, my cringing are the emphatic markers that can help me make the connection between the political analysis of fat women's cultural images and my own body, without hardening her or my subjective experience into a unified, linear self.

The search for tactics to speak embodied experience has proved painful. Writing this essay, I have journeyed again through my own practice. I have strutted about in stately Victorian costumes, in revealing satin underwear; I have danced the grotesque waltz of finding my body language. I have directed women of size to play detectives, to parody and appropriate the eye of the spectator. I have had them sitting at the edges of the stage, eating excessive amounts of cake and bananas. I have been in pain; I have laughed; and I have attempted to sit on my image while reading Michel Foucault and Judith Butler. Writing, I re-created these encounters of performers, directors, choreographers, and audiences, suffering again the indignities that I have felt while in even my informed, analyzed, and constructed stances on stage. In our own corporeality, we struggle for possibilities to prove that, in the words of Mary Russo, "The figure of the female transgressor as public spectacle is still powerfully resonant, and the possibilities of redeploying this representation as a demystifying or utopian model have not been exhausted."[21] The end of the journey is not in sight, and that is a good thing, since performance happens only in the act of recalling and vanishing, never in being. This delegation to memory is the final act that all the performers discussed here have achieved—they have all broadened our image of fat women in cultural discourse, touching lives by embodying their negotiated experiences.

NOTES

1. Kathleen Rowe, *The Unruly Woman: Gender and the Genres of Laughter* (Austin: University of Texas Press, 1995), 54–55.
2. Susan Bordo, *Unbearable Weight: Feminism, Western Culture, and the Body* (Berkeley: University of California Press, 1993), 185.
3. Patricia Parker, *Literary Fat Ladies: Rhetoric, Gender, Property* (London: Methuen, 1987), 14.
4. Andrea Stulman Dennett, "The Dime Museum Freak Show Reconfigured as Talk Show," in *Freakery: Cultural Spectacles of the Extraordinary Body,* ed. Rosemary Garland Thomson (New York: New York University Press, 1996), 323.
5. Roseanne Barr, quoted in Rowe, *The Unruly Woman,* 76.
6. Rowe, *The Unruly Woman,* 76.
7. Ibid., 48. See also Victor Turner, "Frame, Flow, and Reflection: Ritual and Drama as Public Liminality," in *Performance in Postmodern Culture,* ed. Michael

Benamon and Charles Caramello (Milwaukee: University of Wisconsin–Milwaukee Press, 1977), 33–55.

8. Rowe, *The Unruly Woman,* 48–49.

9. Dalma Heyn, "Body Vision?" *Mademoiselle,* April 1987, 213; quoted in Bordo, *Unbearable Weight,* 189.

10. Djuna Barnes, quoted in Rosi Braidotti, "Body Images and the Pornography of Representation," *Journal of Gender Studies* 1 (1991): 137.

11. Sue-Ellen Case, "Toward a Butch-Femme Aesthetic," in *Making a Spectacle: Feminist Essays on Contemporary Women's Theatre,* ed. Lynda Hart (Ann Arbor: University of Michigan Press, 1989), 296.

12. Elin Diamond, "Brechtian Theory/Feminist Theory: Toward a Gestic Feminist Criticism," in *A Sourcebook of Feminist Theatre and Performance: On and Beyond the Stage,* ed. Carol Martin (London: Routledge, 1996), 123.

13. See Lizbeth Goodman, "Gender and Humour," in *Imagining Women: Cultural Representations and Gender,* ed. Frances Bonner, Goodman, Richard Allen, Linda Janes, and Catherine King (Cambridge: Polity, 1992), 289–90.

14. Lorraine Gamman and Merja Makinen, *Female Fetishism: A New Look* (London: Lawrence and Wishart, 1994), 145–70.

15. See Barbara Creed, *The Monstrous-Feminine: Film, Feminism, Psychoanalysis* (New York: Routledge, 1993).

16. Cindy Sherman, untitled #175 (1987); for discussion, see Rosemary Betterton, *An Intimate Distance: Women, Artists, and the Body* (New York: Routledge, 1996), 134–36.

17. *Editors' note:* Here and later in the chapter, *fag* has its British meaning of "cigarette."

18. Antonin Artaud, *The Theatre and Its Double,* trans. Victor Corti (1970; reprint, Montreuil: Calder, 1993), 95.

19. Elin Diamond, *Unmaking Mimesis: Essays on Feminism and Theater* (London: Routledge, 1997), 151.

20. Ibid., 150.

21. Mary Russo, *The Female Grotesque: Risk, Excess, and Modernity* (New York: Routledge, 1994), 61.

REFERENCES

Artaud, Antonin. *The Theatre and Its Double.* Translated by Victor Corti. 1970. Reprint, Montreuil: Calder, 1993.

Betterton, Rosemary. *An Intimate Distance: Women, Artists, and the Body.* New York: Routledge, 1996.

Bordo, Susan. *Unbearable Weight: Feminism, Western Culture, and the Body.* Berkeley: University of California Press, 1993.

Braidotti, Rosi. "Body Images and the Pornography of Representation." *Journal of Gender Studies* 1 (1991): 137–51.

Case, Sue-Ellen. "Toward a Butch-Femme Aesthetic." In *Making a Spectacle: Feminist Essays on Contemporary Women's Theatre,* edited by Lynda Hart, 282–99. Ann Arbor: University of Michigan Press, 1989.

Creed, Barbara. *The Monstrous-Feminine: Film, Feminism, Psychoanalysis.* London: Routledge, 1993.

Dennett, Andrea Stulman. "The Dime Museum Freak Show Reconfigured as Talk Show." In *Freakery: Cultural Spectacles of the Extraordinary Body,* edited by

Rosemary Garland Thomson, 315–26. New York: New York University Press, 1996.

Diamond, Elin. "Brechtian Theory/Feminist Theory: Toward a Gestic Feminist Criticism." In *A Sourcebook of Feminist Theatre and Performance: On and Beyond the Stage,* edited by Carol Martin, 120–35. London: Routledge, 1996.

———. *Unmaking Mimesis: Essays on Feminism and Theater.* London: Routledge, 1997.

Gamman, Lorraine, and Merja Makinen. *Female Fetishism: A New Look.* London: Lawrence and Wishart, 1994.

Goodman, Lizbeth. "Gender and Humour." In *Imagining Women: Cultural Representations and Gender,* edited by Frances Bonner, Goodman, Richard Allen, Linda Janes, and Catherine King, 286–300. Cambridge: Polity, 1992.

Parker, Patricia. *Literary Fat Ladies: Rhetoric, Gender, Property.* London: Methuen, 1987.

Rowe, Kathleen. *The Unruly Woman: Gender and the Genres of Laughter.* Austin: University of Texas Press, 1995.

Russo, Mary. *The Female Grotesque: Risk, Excess and Modernity.* New York: Routledge, 1994.

Turner, Victor. "Frame, Flow, and Reflection: Ritual and Drama as Public Liminality." In *Performance in Postmodern Culture,* edited by Michael Benamon and Charles Caramello, 33–55. Milwaukee: University of Wisconsin–Milwaukee Press, 1977.

15 Divinity

A Dossier, a Performance Piece, a Little-Understood Emotion

MICHAEL MOON AND EVE KOSOFSKY SEDGWICK

EKS: This is a dream I had a couple of years ago. I was shopping for clothes for myself at a store that was nominally Bloomingdale's. I was dubious about whether they would have any clothes that would be big enough for me, but a saleswoman said they did, adding that rather than being marked by size numbers, each size-group of clothes was gathered under a graphic symbol: over here, she said, were the clothes that would fit me. "Over here" referred to a cluster of luscious-looking clothes, hung on a rack between two curtained dressing rooms. The graphic symbol that surmounted them was a pink triangle.

I woke up extremely cheerful.

MM: My love of opera as a protogay child growing up in rural Oklahoma in the fifties had at least as much to do with the available "visuals" as it did with the music—opening nights at the Met photographed in living color in *Life* and *Look* and on television, featuring befurred and bejeweled divas, usually fat, radiating authority and pleasure, beaming out at cameras from the midst of tuxedoed groups of what I remember one of the slick newsmagazines of the time calling "hipless" men. I was struck by the strangeness of that locution even when I read it at age eleven or twelve; like so many other bits of knowingly inflected pseudo-information about adults, their bodies, and their mystifying sexualities, all I could figure out about what it meant for a reporter to call an elegant group of men in evening clothes "hipless" is that it must be another bit of code for doing what was called at the time "impugning their masculinity." It was a deep fear of mine as a twelve-year-old boy putting on pubescent weight that after having been a slender child I was at puberty freakishly and unaccountably developing feminine hips and breasts. My anxieties on this count made me a fierce discriminator of the prevailing representational codes of bodies and body parts, but everything about this urgent subject seemed hopelessly confused and confusing. Why was John Wayne's big flabby butt taken as yet another sign of his virility while my aging male piano teacher's very similarly shaped posterior was read as that of a "fat-ass pansy" by some of my nastier age-mates? What was the difference between a hermaphrodite—a figure still presented in freak shows at the local county fair in my childhood—and a male movie star like Victor Mature who was considered hypermasculine despite his overdeveloped and to my and many other childish eyes quite feminine-looking breasts? Was a man supposed to have hips or not? What regimen of diet, exercise, and character-building could possibly produce the apparently unattainable ideal of right-sized and-shaped male hips on my seemingly out-of-control body—a body that was supposed to be neither "hipless," i.e., gay, nor "fat-assed," i.e., gay?

For many gay men, as for such diverse modern avatars of male sexual and social styles as Byron and Wilde and Henry James and Marlon Brando and Elvis, dramatic weight gain and loss have played a highly significant, much remarked but almost completely unanalyzed part in the formation of our identities. One happy aspect of the story of my own and many other gay men's formations of our adolescent and adult body images is that the fat, beaming figure of the diva has never been entirely absent from our *imaginaire* or our fantasies of ideal bodies; besides whatever version or versions of the male "power-body" of the seventies and eighties we may have cathected, fantasized about, developed or not developed, and, in our time, pursued down countless city streets, the diva's body has never lost its representational magnetism for many of us as an alternative body-identity fantasy, resolutely embodying as it does the otherwise almost entirely anachronistic ideal, formed in early nineteenth-century Europe, of the social dignity of corpulence, particularly that of the serenely fat bourgeois matron.

EKS: Catherine Gallagher has written[1] on the complex representational functions of the image of the large human body in political economy after Malthus. By Gallagher's account, Malthus in 1798 inaugurated a representational regime in which the healthy working body both continued, on the one hand, to function—as it had for millennia—as a symbol and prerequisite for the health of the social and economic body as a whole; but at the same time the same substantial and hence procreative individual body began on the other hand, through the newly activated specter of overpopulation, to represent the constitutive and incurable *vitiation from within* of that same economic totality, as well. After Malthus, Gallagher concludes, "a general sense of the body's offensiveness spreads out" from the large body "and permeates the whole realm of organic matter."[2]

The labor of concentrating and representing "a general sense of the body's offensiveness" is not a form of employment that will seem archaic or exotic to large women in modern American society. It permeates the mise-en-scène of my dream, the store where "I was dubious about whether they would have any clothes that would be big enough for me," whose implicit tension and dread must be resonant for almost any fat woman in this culture. The confrontation of the complex labor of representing offense with the female homosocial marketplace of gendered visibility—the materialization of a fat woman in a clothing store—lights up the works of a pinball machine of economic, gender, and racial meanings; at the same time it is likely to register on the steeled body itself as insult, concussion, ejection. To that woman the air of the shadow-box theater of commerce thickens continually with a mostly unspoken sentence, with what becomes, under capitalism, the primal denial to anyone of a stake in the symbolic order: "There's nothing here for you to spend your money on." Like the black family looking to buy a house in the suburbs, the gay couple looking to rent an apartment, the handicapped high school kid visiting a barrier-ridden college in the Ivy League: Who and what you are means that there's nothing here for you; your money is not negotiable in this place. Distinct from the anxiety of never *enough* money, the anxiety that there won't be any roof for my head, food for my hunger, doctor for my illness—the more awful anxieties whose energy, however, at least knows how to be commandeered with a fluency just as awful into the capitalist circulation of meaning—this is instead the precipitation of one's very body as a kind of cul-de-sac blockage or clot in the circulation of economic value. My permeability to offensive meanings in such a situation comes, to follow Gallagher's argument, from the double and contradictory value exacted from my bodily representation. Visible on the one hand, in this scene, as a disruptive *embolism* in the flow of economic circulation, the fat female body functions on the other hand more durably (and through the same etymologic route) as its very emblem.[3] Like the large, dangerous bodies in Malthus, the modern fat female body represents both the efflorescence and the damaging incoherence of a social order, its function sharpened by representational recastings and by the gender specification, class complication, and racial bifurcation that accompanied the shifts from nineteenth-century European to twentieth-century U.S. models. Its consequence: that what I put on to go shopping in is the brittle armor of a membrane-thin defiance whose verso is stained with abjection.

MM: We have for some time been collaboratively compiling a dossier on a feeling or attitude we call "divinity." The presiding figure for these meditations has been, naturally, Divine, the late star of many John Waters films. As a huge man who repeatedly created the role of "the most beautiful woman in the world," Divine seems to offer a powerful condensation of some emotional and identity linkages—historically dense ones—between fat women and gay men. Specifically, a certain interface between abjection and defiance, what Divine referred to as "glamour fits" and which may more broadly be hypothesized to constitute a subjectivity of glamour itself, especially in the age of the celebrity, seems to be related to interlocking histories of stigma, self-constitution, and epistemological complication proper to fat women and gay men in this century. This combination of abjection and defiance often produces a divinity-effect in the subject, a compelling belief that one is a god or a vehicle of divinity.

The subjectivities from which we ourselves are enabled to speak are, it goes without saying, my own experiences of divinity as a fat woman, and Eve's as a gay man.

EKS: John Waters and Divine were a celebrated gay-man-and-diva couple who, until Divine's death in 1987, pursued powerfully mutually enabling careers in film and performance. That Divine, the eponymous diva in question, was not a woman but a biologically male transvestite is important to our project, but so is the way Waters's and Divine's respective body types play themselves out in the representational world of their films, writings, performances, and interviews. Like his mock-sleazy mustache, Waters's body is pencil-thin, what some would call "hipless." Divine's, by contrast, was that of a 300-pound man not trapped in but scandalously and luxuriously corporeally cohabiting with the voluptuous body of a fantasy Mae West or Jayne Mansfield.

MM: In the film and theater of the past two decades, as well as in the body of critical gender theory and performance theory that has arisen during the same period, transvestism has often been trivialized and domesticated into mere "cross-dressing," as if its practice had principally to do with something that can be put on and off as easily as a costume. In fact, influential essays like Elaine Showalter's "Critical Cross-Dressing" have allowed transvestism to become *the* dominant image in feminist theory for the purely discretionary or arbitrary aspects of gender identity.[4] As such, it is sometimes treated as sinister—when men are seen as being empowered by a pretense of femininity they can doff at will, leaving their underlying gender identity and privilege untouched or indeed enhanced. Alternatively, a very similar understanding of transvestism can take on a utopian tinge: as a denaturalizing and defamiliarizing exposure of the constructed character of *all* gender; as a translation of what are often compulsory gender behaviors to a caricatural, exciting, *chosen* plane of arbitrariness and free play.

But the social field in which this universalizing, discretionary "theory" of transvestism gets mobilized is already structured by a very different, overlapping set of transvestite knowledges thereby repressed but by no means deactivated.

EKS: That some people can cross-dress convincingly and others can't.

MM: That some people's bodies make more sense to themselves and others when they're cross-dressed than when they aren't.

EKS: That some people get turned on when they cross-dress and others just feel at home.

MM: That cross-dressing crosses between public and private differently for different people.

EKS: That for some people, cross-dressing signifies their hetero-, and for other people their homo-, sexual identity.

MM: That the embeddedness of cross-dressing in routines, in work, in spectacle, in ritual, in celebration, in self-formation, in bodily habitus, in any sexuality, can vary infinitely from one person to another.

EKS: That some people's cross-dressing is consistently treated as a form of aggression and responded to with violence.

MM: Divine's performances forcibly remind us of what so many treatments of transvestism require that we forget: that "drag" (as Esther Newton has suggested) is inscribed not just in dress and its associated gender codes but in the body itself: in habitual and largely unconscious physical and psychological attitudes, poses, and styles of bodily relation and response—not just on the body's clothed and most socially negotiable and discretionary surfaces. In addition, drag depends on, even as it may perceptually reorganize, the already culturalized physical "givens" of the body, among them ones—size, color, gestural scale—that may have near-ineffaceable associations of power or stigma or both. In stark contrast with the performance style of a relatively "respectable" "female impersonator" like Charles Pierce doing a characteristic turn as Carol Channing or Barbra Streisand in an upscale nightclub, Divine's fiercely aggressive performances do not conceal or disavow what a dangerous act drag can be, onstage and off. Nor do they gloss over how obnoxious many viewers find the act, especially if it is not hedged on all sides with half-truths about why performers "do drag" and why audiences enjoy it—e.g., it's merely a performing skill like any other; it's a classic theatrical tradition; it allows performer and spectator to let off steam without really challenging predominant gender and sex roles for either. Divine's "loud and vulgar" (to use her terms for it) drag style flings the open secrets of drag performance in the faces of her audience: that unsanitized drag disgusts and infuriates many people; and that it is not wearing a wig or skirt or heels that is the primary sign of male drag performance, but rather a way of inhabiting the body with defiant effeminacy; or, the effeminate body itself. And, finally, that it is just this conjunction of effeminacy and defiance in male behavior that can make a man the object of furious punitive energies, of gay-bashing threatened or carried out rather than applause.

EKS: Strangely, in fact, one of the most striking aspects of the current popular and academic mania for language about cross-dressing is its virtual erasure of the connection between transvestism and—dare I utter it—homosexuality. We might take as emblematic an article in the premiere issue of the late Malcolm Forbes's new magazine, *Egg*—which vindicates its claims to chic by featuring an interview with three downtown drag performance artists, an interview in which the word "gay" *is never spoken.* Or again, the business section of a recent *New York Times* ran an article (the front-page teaser headline was "Corporate Cross-Dressers?") about male CEOs of airlines, insurance companies, TV networks, and other established capitalist ventures who dramatize the work of business meetings by appearing in costume—including, as the *New York Times* puts it, "an intriguingly large number of top male executives who turn up in women's clothing."[5] As the subhead explains, corporate drag "can make a point, lighten a mood, or soften bad news." What it apparently cannot do is induce the acknowledgment of so much as the existence of divergent human sexual choice.

We have something of the same sense about most of the current theoretical and critical discussions of transvestism as we have about those uses of a nominally desexualized drag to oil the wheels of corporate business-as-usual. Uncharitably, one might say that gender theory at this moment is talking incessantly about cross-dressing *in order* never to have to talk about homosexuality. (This is the modus operandi of, for instance, the highly popular play *M. Butterfly.*) The usual alibi for segregating discussions of cross-dressing from issues of sexuality is the much-reproduced assertion that "the majority" of cross-dressers "are heterosexual men." We have a lot of trouble with this as an assertion. Survey research is notorious for turning up unexpectedly large concentrations of heterosexual men. Again, why do we suppose empirical research to be capable of telling us what a heterosexual man is, when nobody else can? And frankly, when was the last time any of us was invited to an earring party by a heterosexual man?

We have even more trouble with it as an alibi, however; by the very compartmentalization of cross-dressing between the hetero- and the homo-, it seems both to reduce the almost infinite array of cultural, personal, and contextual meanings cross-dressing can have, and at the same time to repudiate or traduce the profound historical linkages in Western European, English, Euro-American, and African American culture between drag performance and homoerotic identity formation and display. It is like pretending that the ancient music of Druidic rituals provided the roots of rock 'n' roll.

I have used the policial metaphor of the "alibi" to make a polemical point. There is a less accusatory way to put the problem, however, one that is surely nearer the spirit of the critics, some themselves gay and/or gay-loving people, who are busy theorizing transvestism in this odd conceptual vacuum. I think they think they *are* talking about homosexuality. After all, "everyone already knows" that cross-dressing usually at least alludes to homosexuality; "everyone already knows" that the surplus charge of recognition, laughter, glamour, heightened sexiness around this topic comes from its unspecified proximity to an exciting and furiously stigmatized social field. Critics may well feel that the rubric "cross-dressing" gives them, too, a way of tapping into this shared knowingness without having to name its subject; without incurring many of the punitive risks of openly gay enunciation in a homophobic culture; but also—advantageously as far as they can tell—without incurring the *theoretical* risks of essentializing homosexual identity, of presuming a given set of relations between gender identity and sexual object choice, or of ignoring how little coextensive the population of cross-dressers actually may be with the population of gay men or lesbians. But in that case, can't the tactic be innocuous or even useful? *Must* "everyone already knows" be misguided as the structuring strategy of a critical movement or moment? Only if "everyone already knows" is itself *already* the structuring strategy of a homophobic culture: specifically, of the culture's need to revivify itself constantly with the energies of gay experience, while maintaining a semi-plausible deniability about the gay history and sexual specificity of that experience. But that does, of course, describe the status quo exactly. Our culture as a whole might be said to vibrate to the tense cord of "knowingness." Its epistemological economy depends, not on a reserve force of labor, but on a reserve force of information always maintained in readiness to be presumed upon—through jokey allusion, through the semiotic paraphernalia of "sophistication"—and yet poised also in equal readiness to be disappeared at any moment, leaving a suppositionally virginal surface, unsullied by any admitted knowledge, whose purity may be pornographically understood to be violated and violated and violated yet again each time anew, by always the same information in fact possessed and exploited from the start. The "knowingness" most at the heart of this system is the reserve force of information about gay lives, histories, oppressions, cultures, and sexual acts—a copia of lore that our public culture sucks sumptuously at but steadfastly refuses any responsibility to acknowledge.

MM: The most nightmarish versions of this infinitely iterable violation-by-revelation tend to cluster around legal scenes: scenes like the trials of Oscar Wilde, but just as much like the hearings in the U.S. Congress that have led to literally genocidal prohibitions against spending federal funds on AIDS education materials that exhibit any tolerance for the existence of homosexual men. The scenario of these public denudations scarcely varies: they consist simply of the articulation, in so many words, of sex acts, which is to say names of parts of bodies, supposedly unique to or characteristic of gay men. William Dannemeyer's or Jesse Helms's catalogs depend heavily on the mantra word, the ever-new and ever-potent syllables "rectum," for instance (as if this weren't a fairly common thing to have and even to enjoy having). It depends also on the mantra word "homosexual" itself: I am thinking for instance of Dannemeyer's shockingly effective exposé to Congress last summer on the weird facts of gay sexual practice which, he says, "militant homosexuals do not want you to know"—including astounding assertions that the "average homosexual" has "homosexual sex" "two to three times per week," as well as that "other activities *peculiar to homosexuality*" include oral sex (sometimes mutual), anal sex, and the use of sex toys.[6] Two to three times per week! That such a snoozable statistic, when applied to, not sex, but "*homosexual* sex" performed by "*homosexuals,*" would have power to ignite scandal and motivate legislation, is a testimonial to the inexhaustible reserve power of incredulity in our culture. And it is no mere paradox to suppose, as we do, that that reservoir of incredulity represents the invariable concomitant to the reserve of knowingness attached here to the simple adjective "homosexual." A powerful argument, we would say, for placing the project of gay/lesbian theory explicitly at the center of transvestite theory, and hence of gender theory more broadly.

EKS: Recent work by scholars like Marjorie Garber[7] demonstrates very valuably that the relished, taboo omnipresence in our culture of cross-dressing and trans-gender coding may well constitute the very possibility of gender coding at all. What this work does not consider—or at least does not take responsibility for enunciating—is that the rabid frenzies of public deniability are an inextricable part of the same epistemological system as the sophisticated pleasures of public knowingness—pleasures which such work itself richly indulges. The history to which this nominally historicizing analysis appeals (like the history that tacitly undergirds recent, more frankly dehistoricizing, psychoanalytic work on male subjectivity)[8] is never the history of sexuality, of changing and overlapping homo/heterosexual definition, of homophobic oppression and homo-affirmative resistance.

Now the gay specificity omitted from such accounts is undeniably a problematic, perhaps necessarily incoherent, concept—but it has been all the more explosively potent across every space of our culture, for that. Indeed, the economy of "knowingness," far from deconstructing that incoherent concept and its essentialist underpinnings, instead reifies it by silent presumption. Histories, like the one constructed by Garber, of gender play and gender transgression need also to bear explicit relation to explicitly problematized histories of gay specificity, identity, oppression, and struggle. Otherwise, in drawing a surplus value of pleasure and rhetorical force from cultural energies to which it never seems to consider itself directly accountable—in consolidating a community of "knowing" listeners who draw authority and cognitive leverage from allusion to gay communities and resources not always given the stabilizing dignity even of a name—such work risks being, not critical of, but isomorphic with the inflictive and demeaning enunciatory relations of the homophobic culture at large.

MM: When Glenn Milstead was in high school, his body and his effeminate way of inhabiting it infuriated people on sight: he sometimes needed a police escort merely to get to and from school. That he provided, at these moments of identity constitution and enforcement, an apt embodiment of the purely discretionary seems unlikely. When Waters renamed this high school friend of his "Divine," he both recognized Divine's affinity with the abject and apotheosized drag heroine of Genet's *Our Lady of the Flowers* and at the same time set the seal of a name on Divine's dangerous and exciting, though far from arbitrary, course of cultivating and valuing his brazen effeminacy as a primary component of his identity. This involved much more than becoming a "female impersonator"; the name on Divine's passport, we are told, was "Divine." Waters writes that as late as the time they were making *Pink Flamingos* Divine was unable to leave home without attracting violent attention. "His heavy lipstick seemed never to come completely off, so his lips and face were permanently stained a faint pink. Having little interest in his everyday male attire, he wore baggy one-piece white worksuits off the set, giving him the appearance of a demented, rather feminine garbage man," Waters says. "He looked even more bizarre out of drag than he did in."[9] If Glenn Milstead hadn't become Divine, what would he have become? Doesn't it devalue a creativity as deep as the bones and musculature, imperfectly delible as lipstick, and as painful as 300 pounds in high heels, to define it in the inconsequential terms of the free market in genders and identities?

When personal friends talk about Divine, they have a tendency to use the masculine pronoun in discussing the years before he took the name "Divine," the feminine pronoun for periods through about the mid-70s, and the masculine pronoun again for the last decade or so of his life. This is a very rough division; and different people handle their pronoun usage about Divine very differently, not always on a chronological basis.

In any event, Divine in 1981 recollects having been "strange" but not necessarily "effeminate" as a child,[10] but being subject to much-increased gender harassment, by teachers as well as age-mates, in junior high and high school: the bizarre indignity, for example, of being placed in a girls' rather than a boys' gym class. After around age fifteen, new friends, the concept of "drag," and a new aesthetic that interfaced spectacle with filth intervened on Divine's life and identity, apparently feminizing her, declassing her from her comfortable origins, and propelling her toward a subjectivity of glamour. According to Jean Hill, Divine in the early '60s would claim in gay bars actually to have had a sex-change operation; though Divine later suggested she had only distantly considered having one, and only in the early '70s.[11] The last few years of Divine's life, marked by celebrity identity and success, seem also to have been marked by virilization: reflected in Waters's 1981 remark that "his drag fever has almost vanished," while he "lives quietly . . . with his longtime roommate, Phillip."[12]

This history is notable for how little support it gives to a conception of gender as *either* essential and unchanging, *or* free-floating and discretionary. In a person whose native attributes included a potent but very stigmatizable presence, the lack of a consistent lifelong core gender identity seems to have represented both a liability—part of the stigma itself—and a space for certain long-range negotiations and investments of creativity in what Erving Goffman refers to as "the management of spoiled identity." To the degree that Divine could negotiate gender, she used it as a way of hurling her great body across chasms dividing classes, styles, and the ontological levels of privacy, culthood, fictional character, celebrity, and, of course, godhead. Despite Divine's trajectory toward fame, it is not clear that *all* this mobility is best described as upward. It did not, perhaps, either, make her body steadily more intelligible to himself. Moreover, advantageous positionings for one of these ontological levels may well have been debilitating for others. At a certain active level of human creativity, it may be true that the management of spoiled identity simply is where experimental identities, which is to say any consequential ones, come from. To hypostatize these circumstances as either *compelled* or *voluntary,* in terms of either work or play, is, we would suggest, to give in to the available, tendentiously mystified metaphoric alternatives of *the machine* or *the marketplace,* and to do little justice to the exploratory reach of this particular body and the art that at least overlapped it.

EKS: We'd like to say a word at this point about the kind of intervention we are trying to make in the current uses of cross-dressing as a condensed emblem for the whole project of gender and sexual constructivism. Nothing could be further from our intent than to push backward against the constructivist trajectory in the name, or even in the direction, of an essentialism whose killing effects we take to have been amply documented. But we do fear that the choice of cross-dressing *as* emblem for the constructivist project may, along with the real progress it is still enabling (in, for example, the recent work of Judith Butler), also further a dangerous conflation of issues in the current framings of the debate on "constructivism" vs. "essentialism." Briefly, as regards gender and sexual identities, we fear a conflation of the question of what might be called phylogeny with that of individual ontogeny. The origin of this conflation probably has something to do with the double disciplinary genealogy of constructivism itself: on the one hand, through a Foucauldian historicism designed to take the centuries vertiginously in stride; on the other, through an interactional communications theory whose outermost temporal horizon is, in practice, the individual life span. The *phylogenic* question, which asks about the centuries-long processes—linguistic, institutional, intergenerational—by which such identities are or are not invented, manipulated, and altered, gets asked under the rubric of "constructivism" as if it were identical to the *ontogenic* question: the question "how did *such-and-such* a person come to be," shall we say, gay rather than straight.

We see three problems with this tacit devolution from constructivism-as-phylogeny to constructivism-as-ontogeny, a devolution that seems to be facilitated by some current uses of the topos of cross-dressing. The first is simply the cognitive loss, a certain vulgarization involved in the ideational collapse. The second, as we have mentioned, is the frightening ease with which anything that our capitalist/consumer culture does not figure as absolute *compulsion* (e.g., addiction), it instead recasts as absolute *choice* through the irresistible metaphor of the marketplace. One, but only one, terrible effect of this marketplace imagery is the right-wing demand that gays who wish to share in human rights and dignities must (and *can*) make the free-market choice of becoming *ex*-gays—an abuse of the constructivist analysis to which there absolutely must be some response stronger than the currently popular gay politicos' retreat into the abjectly essentialist, "We deserve rights and dignity because *we were born this way and can't help it.*"

Finally, there is reason to be nostalgic for the exhilaration of that founding moment of gay liberation ideology, the moment when the question of gay ontogeny—"What makes Johnny queer?"—got dislinked, seemingly once and for all, from the assertion of the gay subject's claims on the resources and support of the society in which she must exist. The project of gay/lesbian liberation was possible *only* when the fascination, the consequentiality, of the riddle of individual ontogeny had been shattered. So there is a clear (not to say prohibitive) risk in the reviving demand for *any* form of narrative in the ontogenic framework.

MM: In our attention to Divine we are especially interested in the part played in the process of her self-creation by celebrity itself—as a level of culture that refuses to keep its place as merely one level among many; as an ontological status that *dis*articulates the intersections among the person, the artist, the fictional character, and the commodity. Clearly, celebrity was part of what enabled the thereby-constituted Divine to make a certain, new sense of an impossible body.

EKS: What can a celebrity body be if not opaque? And yet what if the whole point of celebrity is the spectacle of people forced to tell transparent lies in public? We have already mentioned what we take to be a central chord in our culture of "knowingness"—the reserve force of information, the reservoir of presumptive, deniable, and unarticulated knowledge in a public that images itself also as a reservoir of ever-violable innocence. The economics of knowingness helps us ask new questions about the transparent lies that constitute celebrity, as well. Why do they have to be lies? And why do they have to be transparent?

MM: I don't diet to look better, I diet to feel better.

EKS: Now I'm sober and back in control of my own life.

MM: Being a mother has made everything meaningful for me.

EKS: I happen to be secure in my masculinity.

MM: Reality is the greatest high.

EKS: I'm taking my time looking for the right part.

MM: I'm taking my time looking for the right woman.

EKS: I think that's why I [act]—to give people hope.[13]

MM: [Now I'm being Bette Midler]: I never explored the baths and I never went anywhere except the dressing room and the stage.[14]

EKS: I took a long look at who I really am, and you know what? I like myself!

MM: I had to spend two months watching people at gay bars to prep for this role.

EKS: I'm feeling better than I've ever felt in my life.

MM: I'm not a transvestite, I'm a character actor.

EKS: In a 1987 interview Divine says, "At this point, I can't help it if others have a lot of misconceptions about what I do, if they're not willing to believe I am a character actor and one of my characters just happens to be a loud, vulgar woman."[15] What needs—whose needs—are served by the construction of divine drag as one more job of work in the free market of the sartorial? And what needs are served when, in the chorus of voices saying and repeating this, no one believes it to be true?

MM: In the same interview, Hal Rubenstein of *Interview* magazine asks the question—obligatory in every celebrity interview—of typecasting. "If you want to be known as a character actor and want to get more male roles, doesn't perpetuating a drag character hinder you from changing the perceptions of ready-to-pigeonhole Hollywood casting people?" And he follows it up: "But is the typecasting all their fault?" And the next question: "Why is it that you are still haunted by your past, long after Goldie Hawn has shed her bimbo image and Raquel has doffed her *1,000,000* B.C. loincloth?" (44).

Divine's rather inspired strategy for dealing with these questions is to persist in pretending to believe that they are all references, not to drag or to sexuality, but to a single, notorious scene in *Pink Flamingos*—the famous final shot, in which Divine, playing a triumphant Babs Johnson, a.k.a. Divine, "the filthiest person in the world," manifests her divinity by eating a mouthful of freshly laid dog shit. "It was designed to shock and make everyone aware of who we were . . . except, talk about having a hard act to follow!"

"Why is it that you are still haunted by your past . . . ?" Divine's final answer: "Because they still want to know if I ate 'it.' It's so old. With everything that's going on in the world, how can that still be on anyone's mind?" (44).

EKS: Divine wants to talk about eating shit instead of about doing drag. A diversionary tactic that self-evidently can't succeed, it dramatizes the overarching premise of the celebrity interview—how it stages the spectacle of divinity eating shit. How it ushers audiences onto an exciting and nauseating scene of creation: the creation of the closet. Public scenes of self-misrecognition are a staple of human relations with the gods; a divinity with self-knowledge, on Olympus, on Sinai, couldn't be expected to have much in the way of world-creating or narrative-inducing powers. But the opacity of gods to themselves used to be a property of their own strength, rage, willfulness, lust, and jealousy. Now, a fascinated, vengeful calculus about who has the power to enforce or exact this spectacle energizes the public in the age of celebrity.

MM: Closet of sexuality, closet of size. But what can it mean—the closet of size? The pink triangle hovering over those big garments in Eve's Bloomingdale's dream? In one sense, in this dream, the relations of knowledge condensed in the pink triangle (a penal marker attached in the first instance by force to a few men from the fear that their desire would otherwise remain subversively indistinguishable from the desire of the many around them) seem to be diametrically different from the relations of knowledge around those large female garments, garments that can only gesture at minimizing a stigma that could never be hidden because it simply *is* the stigma of visibility. But if it is really nonsensical to talk about the fat woman's closet, or if that closet is really destined to remain empty, then why in the dream was this riveting superposition of stigmatic images framed or flanked by the symmetrical pairing of identical, closed cubicles? What kind of secret can the body of a fat woman keep?

Gay people coming out to the people around us report, much more often than encountering a response of simple surprise, experiencing instead the relief that one's associates no longer feel entitled to act from the insolent conviction of knowing something about one that one doesn't oneself know. The closet, that is, seems to function as a closet to the degree that it's a glass closet, the secret to the degree that it's an open one. Nonsensically, fat people now live under the same divisive dispensation; incredibly, in this society everyone who sees a fat woman feels they know something about her that she doesn't herself know. If what they think they know is something as simple as that she eats a lot, it is medicine that lends this notionally self-evident (though, as recent research demonstrates, usually erroneous) reflection the excitement of inside information; it is medicine that, as with homosexuality, transforming difference into etiology, confers on this rudimentary *behavioral* hypothesis the prestige of a privileged narrative understanding of her *will* (she's addicted), her *history* (she's frustrated), her *perception* (she can't see herself as she really looks), her *prognosis* (she's killing herself). The desire to share this privileged information with the one person thought to lack it is more than many otherwise civilized people can withstand.

EKS: It follows from all this, however, that there *is* such a process as *coming out as a fat woman.* Like the other, more materially dangerous kind of coming out, it involves the risk—here, a certainty—of uttering bathetically as a brave declaration that truth which can scarcely in this instance ever have been less than self-evident. Also like the other kind of coming out, however, denomination of oneself as a fat woman is a way in the first place of making clear to the people around one that their cultural meanings will be, and will be heard as, assaultive and diminishing to the degree that they are not fat-affirmative. In the second place and far more importantly, it is a way of staking one's claim to insist on, and participate actively in, a renegotiation of *the representational contract* between one's body and one's world.

MM: In her fascinating essay in speculative history, *Another Mother Tongue: Gay Words, Gay Worlds,* Judy Grahn seems to suggest that gay women and men have, cross-culturally and transhistorically, shared through such roles as that of shaman the liminal and potentially transformative function of representing cultures to themselves.[16] It is hard to pin down, and no doubt quite variable, how discretionary the individual assignment to, or choice of, such ceremonial roles in a given culture may be; what varies even more clearly across economies and cultures are the ideological, material, moral, relational networks of support and reabsorption for these highly volatile and apparently necessary enactments. For instance, in contemporary culture, certainly, gay men since about the 1950s have added to their stereotypical late-nineteenth-century work of representational preservation and renewal (in art, literature, opera, design, couture, etc.) the labor of representing the straight male body to itself: the straight man who looks for the culture's most influential images of him will be looking at Rock Hudson, James Dean, Montgomery Clift, Cary Grant, Marlon Brando, the ephebes or the bodybuilders in *GQ*. Such work is, in our culture, often materially rewarded but at high cost: our puritanical rage against representation itself, manifest in the age of television in a contemptuous orgy of trivialization and in the multiple rubbishing of the lives of our representers, exacts as well from each of these totemic men the mutilating tribute of a public self-misrecognition. The names and images that haunt the straight man in search of his image, at the same time, will be those in which a not altogether dissimilar content of personnel and imagery is explicitly labeled *gay.*

EKS: It is a simpler story but perhaps not an utterly different one when my sister who is deliberately starving herself, under the real or imagined gaze of some man or some other woman, looks in the mirror in the morning and the body that she thinks she sees confronting her is—mine. *No one* would choose the labor of embodying to this woman, to the society that has created this astigmatism in her view, the shame and anxiety of her and their (and my) own economic exploitiveness, physical greed, sexual subjugation, mortality, and unloveliness. No one would choose it, but it is labor—wearing, wasting, perhaps necessary, in any case *exacted* labor, and must be seen and valued as such.

What some women would choose, and do, in particular those of us with the resource of our various lesbian communities: One response—a possible one, but it should not be a compulsory one—to this exaction, is to attempt, acknowledging and sharing the heritages of older women, immigrant women, African American women, to struggle actively with the given bodily code for *material* accumulation until it surrenders, as well, some of its immemorial meanings of the accumulation of spiritual, physical, sexual, and intellectual power. In some of us there is the project, even the necessity, to try to embody this further transformation *in* ourselves and *for* our sisters—and brothers—who, willy-nilly, see their bodies in ours. Again, however, if that is a form of creativity it is also a form of labor, and in this culture a dangerous and fragile one. The support for it, from all of those whose open and covert representational needs it serves, itself requires new forms and new embodiments.

MM: As a form of representational labor, the fat woman's work of emblematizing the circulatory embolisms of a culture might be said to fall into the economic category, not of either production or reproduction, but rather of waste management. The way in which human fat, and especially fat-gendered-female, has represented economic accumulation and waste in post-Enlightenment Western culture is a complicated narrative. Briefly, by the mid–nineteenth century, bourgeois Euro-American women were rigidly subject to a "sphere" ideology that appeared to make their economic position absolutely distinctive, and distinctively that of material consumption, their mercantile husbands' circulatory role manifesting in them as sheer absorption.[17] Thus, when caricatural figures for what Catherine Gallagher refers to as "the fatted body of circulation" would come to be looked for in the bourgeoisie, it was to a very specifically gendered fat body that these meanings were most ineffaceably attached.[18] Dickens is close to the modern nerve with his authentic loathing for the fat female body: the utter and inalterable inability to be forgiven, of precariously middle-class fat women like Flora Finching, seems to suggest a literal-minded *imaginaire* of political economy where the gibbous flesh of such women might be carved directly from the narrow shanks of the smaller bodies—bodies of children, of the poor—in which Dickens saw himself.[19]

EKS: Anne Hollander, in *Seeing Through Clothes,* gives an illuminating account of the aesthetic and material involvements of the shift, after World War I, from a fat to a thin norm for the well-off female body.[20] In an increasingly abstractive economy, the Dickensian revulsion at female size as a phobogenically literal image of exploitive accumulation results, not of course in any revolution in the exploitive economic structures themselves, but in an extravagantly sublimatory semiotic reassignment: not her bodily opulence but her bodily meagerness comes to be the guarantee of the woman of substance. The Duchess of Windsor's gynocidal pronouncement, "You can never be too rich or too thin," marks the absolute boundary of this semiotically ambitious, not to say psychotic, sublimation of use value in exchange value.[21] By contrast, under this economy of radical sublimation, the fleshy female body is catastrophically declassed; so that a large woman of any class or race will now feel more at home among the round faces brown, white, and black of Brooklyn than being stared at over the circumflex cheekbones of Madison Avenue.[22]

Of course, however, there is no such thing in any culture as a simple reversal of meaning. The shift of thinness from being a lower-class to an upper-class female signifier, and vice versa of fatness, had among its mediators one especially powerful discourse—the medical—whose structure of knowledge, at once highly elastic and relentlessly *naturalizing,* ensured that what emerged from the shift of bodily meaning was not a clean and newly inscribed slate of role assignments, but instead a palimpsest of fragmentary meanings, inscribed in a biologistic narrative that can only take itself for the most direct commonsense, but whose actual gaps, overlays, and semi-erasures spell out a much less enabling rebus: a pattern of discreditation and impossibility for the female body of any class and race and of any size. In some of its meanings, the medicalized discourse of fat simply reproduces, in a disguised and hence nonconfrontable form, the direct reading of political economy taken over from Malthus: eating high on the food chain, a diet rich in animal fats or in commodity crops like sugar, spices, and coffee, is ecologically greedy *and in addition* unhealthy; the moral fervor of *Diet for a Small Planet* gets deposited unquestioningly into the account of *The Bloomingdale's EAT™ Healthy Diet*—a transfer enforced by the raging background din, in women's lives, of that further and crazier imperative whose sick-making instruction is, *diet for a small swimsuit.*[23]

MM: Interestingly, it is in the nascent unfolding of a movement much younger than gay/lesbian liberation, namely the fat liberation movement, that the liberatory moment of ontologic *dis*linkage is currently being enacted. New science (much of it being done by gay men scientists) is finally getting around to demonstrating the commonplace—discursively valueless so long as it was spoken only by women, by fat people—that fat people do not actually eat more than thin people. Whether or not *because* of this "scientific development," at any rate, the issue of *being fat* is able to be, even today is being, severed thrillingly (though still with an unstanchable incompleteness) from the moralizing discourses of greed or the medicalizing discourses of "eating disorders"—to be established instead in the assertive, anti-ontogenic space of an emergent identity politics. That the politicized insistence on a willed agnosticism about individual *causes,* the anti-ontogenic crux moment in fat liberation, rhymes so closely with the analogous moment in gay liberation, records a profound and unacknowledged historical debt. It might point as well to the political need for a historicizing, phylogenic, anti-essentialist construction of size indeed already under way in such work as that of Hillel Schwartz as well as in our present work.

EKS: The ontogenic dislinkage of fat is, however, the furthest thing from the obsessive mind of John Waters; indeed, it is his absolute refusal of such a move that makes the center of gravity of his inimitably hefty thematics. In a late-capitalist world economy of consumption, the problematics of waste and residue, hitherto economically marginal, tend increasingly to assume an uncanny centrality. The concept of "ecology" itself, with its profoundly, permanently destabilizing anthropomorphization of the planet as a single living body, emerged in the 1970s much less from the question of how to feed its inhabitants than from that of how to contain or innocuously to recirculate their wastes. At the level of the disciplines surrounding the supposed individual body, the recent strange career of cholesterol in the medical and public imagination suggests that to the conflict between virological and immunological body models, dramatized in discourses around cancer and AIDS,[24] there must be added a muted but potent third term involving not just cardiovascular medicine but the discipline that has come to be called garbology. The issue (in many ways a startlingly new one) of the very viability of our planet has emerged as the need, not merely to limit waste, but—no doubt you'll pick up on the paradox involved—to eliminate it. Which, paradoxically again, can only mean to consume it.

One consequence of these developments has been that the Enlightenment Western fantasy imperative of the hygienic has, not come to an end, but come under increasing and transformative stress. At the moment when Mary Douglas can construct an *anthropology* of hygiene, at least the transcendent self-evidence of the expulsive, projective hygienic project must be nearing its close.[25] If an ecological system includes no "out there" to which the waste product can, in fantasy, be destined, then it makes sense that the meaning-infused, diachronically rich, perhaps inevitably nostalgic chemical, cultural, and material garbage—our own waste—in whose company we are destined to live and die is accruing new forms of interpretive magnetism and new forms, as well, of affective and erotic value.

MM: From his earliest feature-length film, unsurprisingly titled *Mondo Trasho* (1969), onward, John Waters has been the filmmaker who most insistently offers erotic, problematizing images, and performs foregrounded acts, of otherwise taken-for-granted economic processes of consumption, absorption, and waste. Waters is said to claim that his April birthday means he was "born under the sign of Feces"; for that matter, just being named John Waters might conduce to a toilet bowl mentality. Waters's project does not involve any simple, merely paradoxical reassignment of equations between filth and value, although there are moments of his work that could be taken in isolation as doing so. Rather, through a series of metonymies around the body of Divine, he explores one materialized displacement after another: food as clothing, clothing as bodies, bodies as food, bodies as waste, waste as food—and only in these contexts, waste as value.

EKS: *Food as clothing, clothing as bodies*: for only one example, the scene in *Pink Flamingos* in which Divine orders a steak from the butcher, then, after (as the screenplay has it) "carefully survey[ing] the store for detectives, unwraps the steak, and sticks it up her dress and into her crotch. A look of bliss comes over her face when she feels the cold steak against her warm flesh."[26] The bloody steak, diverted from the cash-lubricated path that was to have circulated it as if automatically from living animal to prime cut to dinner to nutrition to waste, instead recovers its materiality as a substitute for the absent panties; as an allusion to the messy, uncomfortable, and fascinating sanitary napkin; as a stimulation to, and representation (as "meat") of, the (absent) female genitals; ditto to and of the impermissibly present male ones, which it also, presumably, veils, bloodies, and comforts; and as a literalization of the fat-phobic fantasy of food that, rather than sublimate and desublimate through the channels of digestion and fat formation, simply applies itself directly to the thighs. By the time the steak is served as dinner, Divine explains that the reason this rag of meaning is so "delicious" is that "I warmed it up when I was downtown today in my own little oven" (TT, 40).

MM: *Bodies as food*: Then there is the delicate matter of occasional outbreaks of cannibalism among the personnel of Waters's Dreamland. Two policemen caught spying on Babs Johnson's birthday party in *Pink Flamingos* get torn limb from limb and snacked upon, while *Desperate Living* ends with the "victory feast" of a huge platter containing the wicked "Queen Carlotta, cooked and garnished" (TT, 177). And hot dogs and marshmallows get roasted over Vera, an unlucky rival-in-filth of Divine's, when she gets torched in the unproduced screenplay *Flamingos Forever.*

EKS: *Bodies as waste:* An intimate, sometimes almost warm Grand Guignol sense of bodies as offal permeates Waters's films. Exemplary moment: a woman in *Desperate Living* (originally supposed to have been played by Divine) gets a penis transplant to surprise her woman lover, but instantly and uncomplainingly cuts it off on finding her grossed out by it instead. According to the screenplay, her lover then "screams, picks up sex-change penis off the dirty floor and throws it out front door. A mangy dog on the street immediately eats it" (TT, 165). A flasher in *Pink Flamingos* supplements his natural endowment with a tied-on turkey neck. Again, the ingenue in *Mondo Trasho* gets her feet cut off by a mad doctor, who replaces them with huge, misshapen feet pulled out of a plastic bag kept in his toilet bowl. For the rest of the film she seems wistfully ashamed of her ugly new feet, but at a dangerous moment they're almost as good as ruby slippers: she clicks her heels together and is transported, magically, from a hog farm in Baltimore to a shopping center in Baltimore.

MM: *Waste as food*: the opening credits of *Desperate Living* probably say it all on this score, "superimposed over an elegant dinner table. A pair of black hands sets the table and pours some wine. Another course is served—this time a boiled rat heavily garnished. A pair of white hands with knife and fork enters the frame, cuts rat, and spears hunks of rat meat. Finally, the fork is set down and a rat bone is placed on center of plate" (TT, 96). The dog shit, whose swallowing in *Pink Flamingos* certifies Divine's divinity, is only the most dramatic synecdoche for Waters's constant deroutinizations of the "ordinary" circulatory relations by which the large body enters, figures, and incorporates the economics of its surround.

EKS: The process by which circulation and signification interrupt each other is generic as much as it is thematic. It is in the genres that he salvages, recycles, or parasitizes to make showcases for the egregious figure of Divine that Waters participates most pointedly in an ongoing gay cultural project as well. The best emblem for this might be *Mondo Trasho*'s momentary *hommage* to Kenneth Anger (as distinct from its format from beginning to end, which parades an indebtedness to the techniques of *Scorpio Rising*). The movie begins with its ingenue, Mary Vivian Pierce, boarding a bus and pulling her reading matter out of her purse: Anger's *Hollywood Babylon*, recognizable as such by the lush cover picture (taken of course before her decapitation in a car crash) of the head and bust of Jayne Mansfield. In his autobiographical book *Shock Value*, Waters says of the film, "I wanted to make real trash this time, and I knew Divine would make the perfect star. We both idolized Jayne Mansfield, and since Divine was getting quite heavy, we agreed she could play the perfect takeoff of a blond bombshell" (54). Divine has, at this moment in the film, yet to make her appearance. But the chiasmus by which the gorgeous, soon-to-be-severed head of the first Hollywood star to make, on her own account, a total profession of celebrity, inverting the supposed hierarchy of product and publicity with an unprecedented candor—the process by which that head stands in for one gay male director being honored by another who trademarks his own films, or figures his own spare off-camera body, with the framed, shamed, celebrated, finally (in this film) disemboweled, irrepressibly overripe body of Divine, uncovers a mise-en-abîme of relations between production and waste—of relations, too, among gender, sexuality, and the ontology of genres.

MM: Waters's films of the '70s (*Multiple Maniacs*, 1970; *Pink Flamingos*, 1972; *Female Trouble*, 1974; *Desperate Living*, 1977) derived from and contributed to a whole range of novel and newly visible social and cultural practices of the time. Gay men and lesbians were often in the vanguard of the development of these practices, many of which were considered grotesque, obscene, perverted, decadent, and/or déclassé by the mainstream. A partial catalog of these practices might include radical drag street theater (the Cockettes, Hot Peaches); glitter or glamour drag as a style of mass performance (Mick Jagger in the film *Performance*, David Bowie, Kiss, etc.); punk subcultures and their sympathy with and frequent enactment of violence, self-mutilation, "bad attitude," hostility to polite hypocrisy and bourgeois social forms in general; "exploitation" films, especially the subgenres of motorcycle, women criminals, women's prison, and low-budget horror; collecting kitsch and spectating related forms of "bad taste" in tacky locales: striptease joints, live sex-show acts, exhibition wrestling, gambling joints, cockfights, pit bull fights; and, perhaps most importantly, various cults of "sleaze"—"anonymous" sex in baths, porn bookstores and theaters, peep shows, backroom bars; enacting "perverse" sexualities, e.g., S&M, exhibitionism, golden showers, and scat; performing, filming, and consuming pornographic films, videos, and magazines.

It is hard to imagine John Waters's films' ever getting made without the occurrence of the Stonewall rebellion in 1969 and the subsequent dissemination of a wide variety of gay identities and "lifestyles" through what soon became an elaborately reticulated network of media representations and leisure markets (urban ones especially but by no means exclusively), representations in the media, and gay political organizing; yet the relation of Waters and his films to recognizably and avowedly gay-affirmative, antihomophobic political and cultural practices is far from simple or straightforward. This is true not only of Waters's work but of that of most of the gay male artists, filmmakers, and performers from whom his work derives and with whom he deserves comparison: Jack Smith, Andy Warhol, Charles Ludlam. Like their work, the spaces in which Waters's films occur comprise a whole series of communicating and interlocking closets—spaces of concealment and disclosure, of avowed, denied, or misrecognized identities of gender, body type, race, class, and sexuality.

EKS: One of the high costs of supporting the systemic series of inversions that Waters performed on bourgeois culture and "sleaze" subcultures is that male-identified gay men, middle-class by definition in Waters's construction of things, can figure only as abject villains in the plots of his films. I'll take *Pink Flamingos* as an example. In that film, Divine plays Babs Johnson, an outrageous woman who, along with her demented son Crackers, her sleazily glamorous "traveling companion" Cotton, and her mother, Edie (Edith Massey), claim [*sic*] to be "the Filthiest People Alive." Connie and Raymond Marble, a greedy, social-climbing, uxorious, and extremely scrawny straight couple, peddle drugs to schoolchildren and run a business kidnapping young women, getting their servant Channing to impregnate them, and selling the babies to lesbian couples. The reliance of the Marbles' raptly infatuated, mutually narcissistic coupledom on the compulsory maternity of enslaved women and on the need of lesbians marks them sufficiently as guardians of the Name of the Family, however they may plot—vainly—to replace Divine and her entourage as "the Filthiest People." Now Waters is a gay man,[27] and so in an important sense was Divine, but neither of them performs that role as such in Waters's films; as the writer and director of his films Waters is the ubiquitous but invisible, and consequently disembodied, source of much of what the films enunciate, and Divine plays not a gay man who does drag performance (as, for instance, Harvey Fierstein does in *Torch Song Trilogy*) but a drag-monster version of an autonomous and obnoxious underclass woman at the center of an experimental family—in short, a female gang leader.

MM: The only character in *Pink Flamingos* who is recognizably a gay man is Channing, servant to the villainous and "assholic" Marbles and hated jailer and inseminator of the young women they hold captive. At first there seems to be almost no difference between employers and servant; Channing seems to be a perfect servant, in every way a mere extension of the will of the Marbles.[28] Channing's distaste for heterosexual intercourse, even as part of his job as the Marbles' lackey, is the first sign the film gives that he is going to be pressed into service as not only the Marbles' but in a sense the film's lackey and its emblematic gay man. The thorough abjection of this only secretly, never openly, defiant character culminates in the scene late in the film when Connie and Raymond Marble return from torching Babs Johnson's trailer house and discover Channing dressed in Connie's clothes playing at impersonating her and Raymond to amuse himself. The scene is structured like an encounter between an abject boy discovered playing in his mother's clothes and his furiously hostile parents. The Marbles pour homophobic contempt on Channing; Connie slaps him repeatedly, and Channing weeps and ineffectually defends his behavior as "just playing" (TT, 49): He says, "Stop hitting me. I didn't do anything to you. I was just here by myself and I start feeling funny when I'm alone. Those girls are down there, don't forget. I can't stand being in the same house with them. I can hear them screaming and crying, and then I get all nervous—then I get these spells. I don't plan it, it just happens, and then, well, I think about my position, my social standing, just like you two do, and I just play. I make believe that I *am* you. I know it isn't reality, I know I'm really me" (TT, 47–48). When Raymond then locks him in a closet and calls him a "closet queen," Channing begs from inside, "Please! Don't lock me in! I'll just stay here and be me while you're gone; I won't even think about being you."

When Babs/Divine and Crackers arrive soon thereafter to put a hex on the Marbles' house, they release Channing from the closet and he guides them downstairs to the pit, where Babs and Crackers free the captive women who take their revenge on Channing by castrating him. In the published version of the script, there is a still from the film of Channing lying on the floor of the pit, dead, eyes and mouth agape, trousers lowered, and "castrated" crotch caked with blood. This photograph is captioned "Channing's Just Deserts." Channing *is* a villain in the economy of the film, but he is also the only character whose recognition and embrace of his own abjection does not "redeem" him. I find the image in the film of the dead and castrated Channing a particularly disturbing one because it images precisely the widespread and violent homophobic fantasy—and, horribly, sometimes the reality—of a gay man's supposed "just deserts," a spectacular scene of total abjection: public castration and death.

In *Desperate Living* the same actor, who actually is named Channing—Channing Wilroy—plays another lackey, a member of the effetely vicious household guard of the wicked Queen Carlotta: versions of the hideously durable homophobic stereotype of the gay man as fascist and Nazi. Here, the fact that the gay guards are massacred as a group in mid-orgy seems to register the pressure of a genocidal wish against gay men, a wish that Eve argues in *Epistemology of the Closet* has been endemic in our culture for the past century, never more than it is today.

Do these films in their theatricalized castrations and executions of their only visibly gay male characters simply mirror this murderous homophobic fantasy? I want to argue that they do not. A second way of reading the image of Channing's castrated body in *Pink Flamingos* is as a figure for Waters's "cutting himself out" of the film as self-aware gay male author, and "cutting out" straightforwardly gay-affirmative representation altogether. Channing's murder and castration is supposedly his "just deserts" for his role of holding women captive *and,* as the Marbles would have it, for "borrowing" their identities, for "playing" them by impersonating them, for being both a drag queen, as Connie calls him, and a closet queen, as Raymond calls him. Such a fate has a strong resemblance to the anxieties Waters himself may have felt and wished apotropaically and symbolically to turn aside, by repeatedly and theatrically "sacrificing" the kinds of roles he casts Channing Wilroy in. Waters, after all, has been a powerful exemplar of the practice he embodies in his films—that of "borrowing" or "trying on" and "playing" with the identities and bodies of abjected groups, particularly highly adversary types of women, gay men, and transvestites. Channing's lackey position suggests that Waters's "lack"—as director rather than star, as male-identified rather than transvestite gay man—is a centrally enabling one for the kind of project Waters's films represent.

EKS: Capture and castration, then, are important markers of Waters's authorial self-insertions/self-excisions in relation to the film-fantasy world over which he invisibly presides. His direct representations of gay men are one major focus for these effects, and his representations of the maternal are another. The Virgin Mary, especially in her role of Stabat Mater, the mother in extremis following her divine son to the scene of his ultimate abjection, is repeatedly a key figure in this process. The "mystery" of the Virgin, according to Christian tradition, is that she was both Mother and Maid. The role of the Virgin and the roles of Mother and Maid, translated into their modern bourgeois forms, mistress and maidservant, housewife and cleaning woman, comprise an unholy trinity of recurrent roles for women in Waters's productions.

Indeed, it seems as if the diminished prestige and visibility there of gay men as such may be systemically related, not only to the apotheosis of Divine, but to an almost explosive multiplication around her of strongly figured female bodies and personalities visibly grappling with the flux of spoiled identity, hovering between mother and maid. These include, in particular, Jean Hill, a 400-pound black woman, and the also huge Edith Massey, a gravel-voiced, gap-toothed, radiantly magnetic, declamatory, and probably retarded older white woman. Massey might seem at first glance to be anything but defiant, exemplifying only the abject side of "divinity," but such an impression fails to register how many of the prohibitions and exclusions constitutive of our culture's representational codes Massey defied by performing, and by allowing Waters to feature her as a "star." Massey's life before her Waters-engineered apotheosis was a typical one for many women of her underclass background: she grew up in an orphanage, passed in and out of prison, subsisted for a long time on the seamier fringes of show business, engaged in casual prostitution and frequently worked as a barmaid in Oklahoma, Chicago, Las Vegas, Florida, and, finally, Baltimore, in the waterfront tavern where she was "discovered"—a place where, according to Waters, writing in his noir mode, "drinks were fifty cents and *any* kind of behavior was tolerated." Waters also says that Massey's first response to his asking her to play both herself—that is, a den mother barmaid in a waterfront den—and the role of the Virgin Mary in "The Stations of the Cross" sequence in *Multiple Maniacs* was to decline because, she claimed, she couldn't act. But Waters disagreed: "After seeing her in the bar, charming every type from drunken sailor to nodding junkie, I knew she was wrong" (*Shock Value*, 180).

Waters perceives what he saw as Massey's characteristic behavior, her potential both as an actress and as a star, as simply "charming" socially intractable and transgressive types of people, but we might look more closely at the uses he himself found for her skill at manipulating, pacifying, and coping with supposedly incorrigible and potentially violent people. After being shot and almost killed in May 1968, Andy Warhol decided to stop cultivating druggies and the other kinds of socially common "psychos" who had frequented the Factory and to make himself unavailable to the very people from whom he claimed to have drawn much of his energy during his most spectacularly productive period in the mid-60s. Isolated by what he came to see as regrettable choice from the "crazy" and "sleazy" people with whom he had formerly surrounded himself, Warhol felt that he had cut himself off from the sources of the disturbing and disruptive perceptions that had enabled his best work. When Warhol met Edith Massey in the early '70s he was impressed and delighted with her, taking Waters aside to implore him, "*Where* did you find her?" Waters, like Warhol, recognized the value of "trash" and "sleaze" as sources of much of the most powerful and engaging representational work of the time. As highly privileged producers of such work, they were probably more aware than most of us can be of how imperiled and potentially lethal (and how perilous to the privileged positions that enable appreciation and expropriation) are the social spaces—the streets, the drug and sex-business subcultures—from which that representational work ultimately derives. Massey's so-called charm, her ability to "cope with" the denizens of these worlds by drawing on hard-earned street smarts and not by invoking class privilege or "calling the cops," might well have looked enviable, if not indeed magical and somehow even divine, to the (in this sense) "lackey" consciousness of the differently situated, and consequently differently vulnerable, Waters and Warhol.

Edith Massey eventually achieved a Waters-influenced celebrity as a performance artist and doyenne of a Baltimore thrift shop called, inevitably, Edith's Shopping Bag. She died after *Polyester* was completed, but her loud, uninflected, achingly kind voice can still be heard on a Rhino Records anthology of the worst recordings ever made, singing, almost unbearably, her theme song, "Big Girls Don't Cry."

MM: This economy of female proliferation results in, among other things, a thematized lesbianism often in the place where a gay-male possibility might have been broached. The climactic victory of the band of lesbian revolutionaries in *Desperate Living,* for example, must be one of the most resoundingly triumphant sexual-political moments of closure in popular representation in the decade after the Stonewall rebellion; as we have suggested, the downside of this moment is that it is underwritten by what is perhaps the most spectacularly self-hating moment in Waters's films, the simultaneous representation of gay men as a fascist goon squad, "deservingly" cut down in mid-orgy.

The prolific spawning of Waters's divas results not only in a thematized lesbianism, but in the almost miraculous absence of male homosocial circulation of any recognizable kind; and most characteristically, in a chunky and funky Mariolatry. For example, Waters's first film narrative of Divine's divinity, the 1969 *Mondo Trasho,* is organized like a medieval saint's life straight out of the *Golden Legend,* crossed with the *National Enquirer.* The film represents Divine on a supposedly typical day, experiencing a series of shocks and disasters and reacting to them with the combination of abjection and defiance that in the course of the narrative render her "divine." The Virgin Mary appears to her three times; first in a laundromat, then in a snake pit insane asylum, and finally in the hog pen where she crawls to die at the end of the film.

EKS: The martyrology *Polyester* is the film that most literalizes the topos of Mother and Maid—and that makes the most of the potential that topos holds for deroutinizing the metaphorics of rubbish, as well. *Polyester* is the only film whose diegesis assumes that Divine's obesity makes her unlovable and powerless rather than magnetically irresistible. In this nightmarish—i.e., naturalistic—frame she is forced, herself, to embody the hygienic imperative, as an abased housewife, Francine Fishpaw, whose impossible dream is a normal and germ-free nuclear family. Through all the stations of her humiliation—her husband abandons her for his skinny secretary, her son is exposed as the psychopathic "foot-stomper" who has been terrorizing Baltimore, her daughter gets pregnant, her glamorous new boyfriend turns out to have been conspiring all along with his lover, Francine's *own* (need I say skinny) *mother*—through it all, her companion, comfort, and faithful friend is Cuddles (Edith Massey).

MM: "Oh, Franciney, *every*thing's gonna be *just fine.*"

EKS: An ex–cleaning woman who has been left a fortune by a grateful client after a lifetime of cleaning toilet bowls, Cuddles is the only one of Massey's roles where she seems to "look retarded," paradoxically because the nouveau riche signs of prepette sportivity are also readable as stigma: the scraped-back-ponytail head as microcephalic, the sweater and hockey kilt as institutional.

Divine's numinous abjection encompasses, more than it diametrically opposes, the hygienic imperative—much as she and her son in *Pink Flamingos* had put a spell on the Marbles' house, inducing the Marbles' own ultrachic furniture to rise up and reject them by coating the chairs and couches with drool. *Polyester* theatergoers were issued "Odorama" cards containing various fragrances and stenches, to be scratch-and-sniffed at appropriate moments of the action (a pizza, a fart, etc.). All the scratching and sniffing puts any viewer, however, in the subject position of Francine Fishpaw herself. Though doomed herself to concentrate and radiate "a general sense of the body's offensiveness" as never before—through her bulk in the claustrophobic, Sirkian domestic space, through her hapless snoring, through the five o'clock shadow that keeps impending over her various chins—the endlessly meek and patient Francine is the most fanatical votary anywhere in Waters's films of Hygiene itself. Like an eight-armed divinity, every arm wielding an aerosol cleaner or deodorant, Francine lives by the projective fantasy of a hygiene that would re-naturalize (as The Family) a space from which production, circulation, excess, predation, and waste were alike evacuated to an outer, unimagined space thereby hypostatized as the vengeful Truth of nature. Accordingly, Francine/Divine, as Every-housewife, is endowed with only one, spectacular talent: a prehensile and almost paranormal receptivity to offensive odor that causes her to spend much of the film darting heavily about her own house trying to catch up with her own flaring nostrils—snuffling noisily at bedclothes and the cracks of doors—wriggling uncontrollably as her nasal antennae tune in to invisible wafts—behaving, in short, like any scratch-and-sniffing animal in the world except *Homo sapiens domesticus nuclearus.*

Surely part of the reason Divine spends much of *Polyester* in olfactory overdrive is that this 1981 film of Waters's was his first to escape an X rating for the more easily bankable and more widely marketable R. Francine Fishpaw's flaring nostrils are a sign of, among other things, the now internalized censor hysterically sniffing out embodiments and enactments of filthy flesh, the primary business of the earlier films. Like them, *Polyester* has the generally paratactic form of a mock Stations of the Cross, a series of excruciating scenes of devoutly cultivated gross-out, but in it, as we have suggested, the gross-outs get domesticated, deodorized, and depilated as they get dematerialized. Of the rankly material circulation of "wasted" humans and—their chief sign—human waste in the earlier films, only a few desultory farts are allowed to linger.

It is by now impossible for many of us who are most interested in studying the joint career of Waters and Divine to make any retrospective assessment of their twenty-year collaboration without registering the pressure of AIDS on our interpretations. In his "Is the Rectum a Grave?" Leo Bersani interrogates Simon Watney's distressed recognition that under the dominant representational regime that has been constructed around AIDS, gay men's rectums have been figuratively posted with a DO NOT ENTER sign—"Premises Off Limits by Order of the Department of Health," as it were.[29] Nineteen eighty-one, the year of *Polyester*'s release, was also the year that many people in and around urban communities in Western Europe and the United States began to register the scope of the threat and reality of AIDS. The rectum, previously the site and source of so much aggressively represented pleasure in Waters's work, *has* almost become a grave in *Polyester.* Characters in the preceding films had eagerly, even frenziedly, pitched their tents in the place of excrement, but no one seems to desire to do so in *Polyester,* least of all the newly hyperhygienic Francine. In *Polyester,* only the liminal appearance of the roseate buttocks of the pizza delivery boy in Francine's wet dream about "ordering out" momentarily suggests the possibility that despite AIDS the rectum may *not* have gotten resituated permanently out of sexual bounds as a site of erotic pleasure of many kinds, including scopic ones.

MM: The most conspicuous textual site for considering the centrality of the anus and the anal, experienced scopically or otherwise, in Waters's and Divine's work must be *Pink Flamingos,* which we hereby rename—or actually merely reaccent—*Pink Flaming O's.* As Naomi Schor does in her work on resituating the clitoris and the clitoral as central and informing rather than marginal detail, anyone interested in making anality a central concern of analysis must counter a pervasive epistemological bias in much psychoanalytic theory (as well of course as in the wider culture) in favor of the phallus and the phallic.[30] On the conventional road map of the body that our culture handily provides us, the anus gets represented as always behind and below, well out of sight under most circumstances, its unquestioned stigmatization a fundamental guarantor of one's individual privacy and one's privatively privatized individuality, as argued by theorists as otherwise different as British cultural materialist Francis Barker and French gay theorist Guy Hocquenghem. In closing, we want briefly to bring to bear on *Pink Flamingos* Bersani's question, "Is the rectum a grave?" as well as the question that D. A. Miller's recent work on Alfred Hitchcock's *Rope* and anality raises, "Is the anus a cut?" or, rather, "How, under what circumstances, and for whom does the anus, especially of the gay male body, get represented as a 'cut,' as a sign of castration? In what other kinds of representational compacts may it figure?"[31] Both questions may call to the mind of the student of the history of sexual representation in the recent past a series of significant moments in film in the time since the making of *Rope* that take up the problem of figuring anal erotics between males in a number of modes, both tender and violent. In this talk, we can only point to a couple of instances. One would be Ken Jacobs's 1963 underground film *Blonde Cobra,* in which at one point Jack Smith presents his bared buttocks to the camera with a butcher knife handle placed to appear to be protruding from his "stabbed" anus while he cries in voice-over, "Sex is a pain in the ass. Sex IS a pain in the ass." The other would be the male-male rape scene which David Lynch is said to have filmed for *Blue Velvet* and then cut sometime before it was released—I have been told at the request of the actor Kyle MacLachlan, who played the character who was to be the victim of the rape, the boy Jeffrey. In the symbolic rape Frank (Dennis Hopper) carries out, he "kisses" lipstick onto Jeffrey's mouth, lip-synchs Roy Orbison's "In Dreams" to him, and then beats him unconscious. I have written elsewhere about how the uncanny effects of this odd ritual permit viewers of the scene to register at some level that a male-male rape is being represented without seeing the rape—or rather, a simulation of it—actually being enacted—a scene which might have been not only too much for Kyle MacLachlan's budding career but also too anxiogenic for many heterosexual-identified male viewers.[32]

EKS: There is nothing of the uncanny about the episode in *Pink Flamingos* that is most closely related to these scenes of real and mock anal rape between males. At Divine's birthday party a boy steps onto the performance platform, doffs his posing strap, lies down on his back, and throws his legs into the air. So far we have the very scene—that of a recumbent gay man with his legs in the air—that Bersani argues in "Is the Rectum a Grave?" is the one that in highly hystericized form unconsciously fuels such homophobic violence against people with AIDS as the notorious attack on three children in the town of Arcadia, Florida, in 1987. But instead of getting fucked as the viewer may expect him to, this young man in *Pink Flamingos* astonishes everyone, once his legs are in the air, by—we hardly have terms for what he does—beginning to "lip-synch" to a record by rapidly flexing his anal sphincter. The scene has a potentially powerfully desublimating effect on many other more conventional scenes of relatively highly sublimated negotiations around the anus of the male body, such as the lip-synching and beating scene in *Blue Velvet* into which anal rape is sublimated. The rectum is demonstrably not a grave nor the anus simply a cut in this representational scheme. This pink, flaming asshole not only makes an impressive show of something we think deserves to be called self-determination, it speaks, and indeed sings.

MM: And what does it say? Interestingly, in Waters's arrangement of things it gets its own song. The other goings-on at Divine's birthday party have taken place to the tune of a 45 that sounds like an inquisitive five year old; the only words to that tune are "Why 'n' why 'n' why?" sung over and over again. When the asshole starts "singing," the song changes to one that goes, "Mau-mau-mau, mau-mau mau-mau-m'mau." What is it saying? Should we be surprised—I suppose not—that it is talking baby talk? It is announcing, I believe, both that it is impersonating the mouth, and that it wants "mau-mau." Who or what, we may ask in response, is the asshole's mother?

Perhaps this anus is naming its mother at the same time it announces the object of its impersonation: the mouth, or "Mau-mau-mau." As it happens, no mouth, maternal or otherwise, appears to answer its call. As if in belated and displaced response to it, a few scenes later, when Divine and her son Crackers break into the Marbles' house to hex it, they cap the hex with an incestuous maternal blow job on the Marbles' couch. As Divine starts to go down on her son, they perform a verbal duet, operatic in its intensity, in which the divinizing effects of the defiant and abject behavior in which they are engaging emerges in explicit terms. Again, it should perhaps not surprise us that as Divine and her son begin to enact their parody transgression "curse," the dialogue waxes increasingly theological:

> CRACKERS: Mama! Mama! ["Mau-mau-mau"] I just thank God above I was lucky enough to be the soul that was placed in my body; the body of Divine's son! The body and blood of another generation of Divinity.
>
> BABS: My only baby, Crackers! My own flesh and blood, my own heritage, my own genes. Let Mama receive you like Communion. Let Mama make a gift to you, a gift so special it will curse this house years after we're gone. Oh, Crackers, a gift of supreme mothergood [misprint for "motherhood"?], a gift of DIVINITY! (TT, 61)

EKS: One of the most refreshing aspects of the representation of fat women in Waters's films (at least until *Polyester,* which in this respect does anticipate the cumulatively compromising effect of Waters's commercial success) is the resistance manifested by Divine and others, male and female, who play fat women in the films to being assimilated to the maternal role, as fat women commonly are in representational schemas of many sorts. When Divine is playing a mother in these early films, she is reliably a terrible one (she kills her grown daughter in *Female Trouble* for becoming a Hare Krishna) when she is not being a monstrous and therefore "divine" one, as she is in the scene just quoted. In these films, organ is represented as yearning for organ, more often than not along forbidden or at least thoroughly involuted paths, but desire that follows the line of familial roles gets ruthlessly inverted and short-circuited; of familial feelings, only incest is respected.

MM: Divine as the Filthiest Woman in the World; Divine as sainted martyr of the dictum Crime Equals Beauty; Divine as phallic Mother and Maid in a world that doesn't envision the joining of Father with Son. If some of these inversions are couched in familiar terms, I hope we have at least suggested how vast is the distance between them and any of the more perfunctory aestheticizations whose claim to a "subversive" political correctness is based on less searching experiments with materiality, identity, economic representation, and the flux of levels of culture.

If Waters's experiments are literal-minded, perhaps there is hardly an alternative way of refusing to take for granted how chunks of literality inject themselves into the circulatory system of symbolic consumption. One of the reasons we are eager to celebrate the literal-mindedness of Waters's early films is because of the dogged (you should pardon the expression) resistance that it seems to offer to a cultural economy of knowingness. If literal-mindedness can never be successful in disambiguating the status of the literal itself, at least it can be stubborn about injecting its emblems and embolisms into the circulatory system of allusive deniability.

We have had especially in our minds the contrast between Waters's sleazily refractory apotheoses, dubious and forever off-key as they are in their refusals and misrecognitions of gay male affirmation, on the one hand; and on the other, the suave and conventional religiosity, the unproblematized access to abstractive cultural authority, of hygienically post-Stonewall gay official culture. A foundational example of the latter might be Andrew Holleran's classic 1978 novel of post-Stonewall gay New York, *Dancer from the Dance,* with the slickly allusive comfort it draws from a whole lexicon of religious metaphor. The habitués of Holleran's discos "glisten with sweat like an idol around which people [kneel] in drugged confusion . . . assuming the pose of supplication at some shrine";[33] they "spraw[l] like martyrs who have given up their soul to Christ" (31); they "pas[s] one another without a word in the elevator, like silent shades in hell, hell-bent on their next look from a handsome stranger" (30); they pantomime "the ecstasy of saints receiving the stigmata" (30–31); they walk through a disco door and are "baptized into a deeper faith, as if brought to life by miraculous immersion" (35); et cetera, et cetera. The unquestioning facility with which these images can be invoked as simply "metaphor"—can be invoked, for that matter, as simply "religious," as they surely could not be in the insistently graphic abjections, scapegoatings, body eatings and blood drinkings, "inspirations" (i.e., blow jobs), transubstantiations, and literal stigmatizations and divinizations of Waters's films—constitutes a virtual orgy of the trivializing but highly legitimating presumption that religion can be stably located, and innocuously exploited, at the sterile distance of "metaphor" from a subculture itself thereby stably located as a securely bounded topos.

We are struck also by Waters's incalculable distance from any authorized account of camp—depending as these have done from Susan Sontag to Andrew Ross on knowing presumptions about the difference between "depth" and "surface," or between levels of culture that in fact mutually constitute, block, circulate, and emblematize one another.

EKS: Each of us, Michael and I, with our different, overlapping, shared, and exchanging hungers, loves, loyalties, and pleasures, with our braidings and leapfroggings from nostalgic to futuristic cultural projects, with the mutual adventures of our spoiled identity, finds a rich supply of things in Waters's and Divine's work of a kind that often seems to be as scarce as it is precious: opulent images and daring performances that suggest the experiment of desires that might withstand the possibility of their fulfillment.

We especially relish—it was the scene, in particular, that finally brought together my own identification with and desire for this impossible, inspiring, ruined and experimental figure—Divine's mirror aria at the end of *Multiple Maniacs,* after murdering her lover, Mr. David, and his new girlfriend:

MM (Divine [to a mirror]): O Divine, you're still beautiful. Nothing that has happened has changed that. . . . I love you so much! And you're still the most beautiful woman in the world! And now you're a maniac! O but what a state of mind that can be!

EKS: (Divine discovers the dead body of her daughter Cookie behind the couch; laments over it and then, extending herself on the couch, begins the following monologue:)

MM: You're finally there, you're finally there, Divine.
You don't ever want to go back now!
Oh, Oh, Divine, you have to go out in the world in your own way now.
You know it's all right!
You know no one can hurt you.
You know no one can even get near you.
You have X-ray eyes now, and you can breathe fire!
You can stamp out shopping centers with one stub of your foot!
You can wipe out entire cities with a single blast of your fiery breath!
You're a *monster* now, and only a monster can feel the fulfillment I'm capable of feeling now!
oh Divine, it's wonderful to feel this far gone!
This far into one's own mania!

I'm a *maniac*! a maniac that cannot be cured!

O Divine, I am Di-*vine*!

EKS: Whereupon a fifteen-foot-long lobster shuffles into the room and attacks Divine.

NOTES

We wrote "Divinity" fully collaboratively, through discussions over a period of about a year. (The listing of the authors' names is alphabetical.) The name attached as the speaker of any given section is seldom in a more than accidental relation to who originally wrote the section. "Divinity" was written for the conference "Discourses of the Emotions," at the Center for Twentieth-Century Studies at the University of Wisconsin, Milwaukee, in April 1990. A few pages of "Divinity" were originally part of a paper, "Labors of Embodiment," that EKS wrote for the MLA national convention in 1986. "Divinity" was first published in *Discourse* 13, no. 1 (winter–fall 1990–91), and then in *Tendencies* by EKS (Durham, N.C.: Duke University Press, 1993).

Jonathan Goldberg and Hal Sedgwick were first among our many unindicted co-collaborators in "Divinity."

1. Catherine Gallagher, "The Body versus the Social Body in the Works of Thomas Malthus and Henry Mayhew," in *The Making of the Modern Body: Sexuality and Society in the Nineteenth Century*, ed. Gallagher and Thomas Laqueur (Berkeley: University of California Press, 1987), 83–106.

2. Ibid., 102.

3. Embolism: cf. embolus: . . . < Gk *embolos* stopper = *em* + *bolos* a throw, akin to *ballein* to throw. Emblem: . . . < Gk something put on = *em* + *blema* something thrown or put, cf. *emballein* to throw in or on. Cf. also abject < L *abjectus* thrown down.

4. Elaine Showalter, "Critical Cross-Dressing: Male Feminists and the Woman of the Year," in *Men in Feminism*, ed. Alice Jardine and Paul Smith (New York: Methuen, 1987), 116–32.

5. *New York Times*, March 25, 1990, 33 (i.e., sec. 3, pt. 2, front page; the teaser headline was on sec. 3, pt. 1, front page).

6. Rick Harding, "Sex Education in Washington, D.C.: Dannemeyer Talks Dirty on the Floor of Congress," *Advocate*, September 26, 1989, 10, quoting from the *Congressional Record*, June 29, 1989; emphasis added.

7. We refer to material in Marjorie Garber's book *Vested Interests: Cross-Dressing and Cultural Anxiety* (New York: Routledge, 1992), on "cross-dressing and cultural anxiety."

8. The "Male Subjectivity" issue of *Differences* (fall 1989) epitomizes such approaches.

9. John Waters, *Shock Value: A Tasteful Book about Bad Taste* (New York: Delta, 1981), 11.

10. Ibid., 146.

11. "John Waters's Issue," *Pandemonium* 3: 23; Waters, *Shock Value*, 154.

12. Waters, *Shock Value*, 146.

13. Interview with John Malkovich, *Interview* 19 (March 1990): 124.

14. Bette Midler, quoted in Hal Rubenstein, "Simply Divine," *Interview* 18 (February 1988): 51.

15. Rubenstein, "Simply Divine," 44; hereafter cited parenthetically in the text.

16. Judy Grahn, *Another Mother Tongue: Gay Words, Gay Worlds* (Boston: Beacon, 1984).

17. By the time of Mayhew and thereafter, in England, an avoirdupois dimorphism of class had come to be the accompaniment of the class-marked differential of gender relations. The reader of Dickens or Trollope would not routinely mistrust a professional or mercantile-class adult man on the sole basis of a certain *embonpoint* or, as it's tellingly called, corporation—while the prodigal baggage allowance of a Mr. Pickwick would look, as Catherine Gallagher's examples show, perfectly depraved on a Sam Weller, or that of a Cheeryble brother on a Newman Noggs or Mortimer Knag, whose proper morphological heritage is the "puny body of production." But whereas for people of the working classes the sexual divisions of labor did not become so marked as to effectually sequester women away from the urban labor marketplace—so that, to go back to *Nicholas Nickleby*, we can be offered the exemplary figures of Miss LaCreevy, Madame Mantalini, and the Infant Phenomenon, seen at their paid labors of miniature painting, dressmaking, or acting, and all as scrawny, as visibly stunted by overwork and undernutrition, as the bantamweight men around them—for the bourgeoisie, the more radically gendered body fantasy increasingly obtained.

18. Lucy Snowe dramatizes this shift in interpretive perspective when, in chap. 19 of *Villette*, she rambunctiously pretends to misperceive a seventeenth-century Rubenesque odalisque as a portrait of conspicuous consumption in a contemporary realist idiom: "It represented a woman, considerably larger, I thought, than life. I calculated that this lady, put into a scale of magnitude suitable for the reception of a commodity of bulk, would infallibly turn from fourteen to sixteen stone. She was, indeed, extremely well fed: very much butcher's meat—to say nothing of bread, vegetables, and liquids—must she have consumed to attain that breadth and height, that wealth of muscle, that affluence of flesh. She lay half-reclined on a couch: why, it would be difficult to say; broad day light blazed round her; she appeared in hearty health, strong enough to do the work of two plain cooks; she could not plead a weak spine; she ought to have been standing, or at least sitting bolt upright. She had no business to lounge away the noon on a sofa. She ought likewise to have worn decent garments: a gown covering her properly, which was not the case: out of abundance of material—seven-and-twenty yards, I should say, of drapery—she managed to make inefficient raiment. Then, for the wretched untidiness surrounding her, there could be no excuse. Pots and pans—perhaps I ought to say vases and goblets—were rolled here and there in the foreground" (Charlotte Brontë, *Villette* [1853; reprint, Edinburgh: John Gray, 1905], 333–34).

19. When the plumpness of a Mrs. Pocket or a Mrs. Jellyby comes actually to verge on the infanticidal, Dickens's fat phobia swims into sudden binocular focus with the hideousness of his marital obsessions: the fat-emblazoned scandal that, in their *sexual* function, they will not cease from productive labor.

20. Anne Hollander, *Seeing Through Clothes* (New York: Viking, 1978).

21. An illustration of the more pluralist aesthetic attaching to use value would be the blues formulation that contrasted women "built for comfort" with the also attractive alternative of those "built for speed."

22. The few large-size clothes that are available for purchase owe to this their penitential meaning for professional-class women: the most portable marker of contemporary class privilege, the wearing of care-intensive natural fibers, is rigorously excluded in the design of all but the most extortionately expensive big garments, so that extent of female body gets manifested in tracts of class stigmatization and cutaneous discomfort, seldom in surfaces expressive of private delight or public display.

23. And the coercive incoherences of this palimpsestic discourse ensure that when, for example, dieting itself begins to be, as it is now being, labeled as a pathological, addictive "disorder" of lifestyle, that damning diagnosis of thinness or of noneating does nothing to budge the damning diagnosis already delivered on fatness and on eating. In a culture where the compulsory may become visible only as a manifestation of the individual will, medicine allows the concept of addiction to play a pivotal role; it ensures that any behavior, any condition of being, is subject to discreditation on the grounds that, while it appears to be an exercise of will, it is, in fact, *compulsive.* (I didn't just make up *The Bloomingdale's EAT™ Healthy Diet*—it's a real book, whose cover explains that the word EAT, not here a real word, is meant to be decomposed and read instead as an acronym—EAT dissolving into the [trademarked] Effective Appetite Training.)

24. See Cindy Patton, *Inventing AIDS* (New York: Routledge, 1990).

25. Mary Douglas, *Purity and Danger* (New York: Praeger, 1967).

26. John Waters, *Trash Trio: Three Screenplays: "Pink Flamingos," "Desperate Living," and "Flamingos Forever"* (New York: Vintage, 1988), 20; hereafter cited parenthetically in the text as TT.

27. In his writing and interviews that we have seen, Waters has not chosen to describe himself in precisely these words, but has also not demurred at others' doing so. For example, when Chris Bull asks him in an interview "What role has being gay played in your development as a filmmaker?" his response is gently to despecify: "I've said this before: I don't think being gay or straight makes one good or bad at all. It definitely makes you accept a little more and see all sides of any question and be more compassionate toward people. I think everyone has what society sees as some neurosis, and everybody has secrets; everybody has things that nobody knows. And I think that's very, very interesting" (Chris Bull, "No More Dirty Waters," *Advocate,* April 24, 1990, 30–35; quotation, 34). But he does tell stories about, for example, taking a male date to a lunch at the White House (John Waters, *Crackpot: The Obsessions of John Waters* [New York: Vintage, 1987], 74–75). Still, "I don't want to ever categorize myself as anything, because then you can't sneak in; you can't mentally creepy-crawl" (quoted in Bull, 35).

28. Significantly, it is in relation to his role as rapist-inseminator that his difference from them begins to emerge. Midway in the film, Channing chauffeurs the Marbles around Baltimore so that they can kidnap another female victim for their "baby ring." In the scene that follows, Channing drags the unconscious woman down into the Marbles' dungeon cellar and announces to the other woman already captive there that he's devised a less disagreeable way of impregnating the new victim. The actor who plays Channing then proceeds to simulate masturbation, and then to simulate artificial insemination with a hypodermic syringe (Waters singles this scene out in his 1988 preface to the published script of *Pink Flamingos* as one that now offends even him; introduction to TT, ix).

29. Leo Bersani, "Is the Rectum a Grave?" in *AIDS: Cultural Analysis, Cultural Activism,* ed. Douglas Crimp (Cambridge, Mass.: MIT Press, 1988), 197–222.

30. Naomi Schor, *Reading in Detail: Aesthetics and the Feminine* (New York: Methuen, 1987).

31. D. A. Miller, "Anal *Rope,*" in *Inside/Out: Lesbian Theories, Gay Theories,* ed. Diana Fuss (New York: Routledge, 1991), 119–41.

32. Michael Moon, "A Small Boy and Others: Sexual Disorientation in Henry James, Kenneth Anger, and David Lynch," in *Comparative American Identities: Race, Sex, and Nationality in the Modern Text,* ed. Hortense J. Spillers (New York: Routledge, 1991), 141–56.

33. Andrew Holleran, *Dancer from the Dance* (New York: Bantam, 1979), 27; hereafter cited parenthetically in the text.

REFERENCES

Bersani, Leo. "Is the Rectum a Grave?" In *AIDS: Cultural Analysis, Cultural Activism*, edited by Douglas Crimp, 197–222. Cambridge, Mass.: MIT Press, 1988.

Brontë, Charlotte. *Villette*. 1853. Reprint, Edinburgh: John Gray, 1905.

Bull, Chris. "No More Dirty Waters." *Advocate*, April 24, 1990, 30–35.

Douglas, Mary. *Purity and Danger*. New York: Praeger, 1967.

Gallagher, Catherine. "The Body versus the Social Body in the Works of Thomas Malthus and Henry Mayhew." In *The Making of the Modern Body: Sexuality and Society in the Nineteenth Century*, edited by Gallagher and Thomas Laqueur, 83–106. Berkeley: University of California Press, 1987.

Garber, Marjorie. *Vested Interests: Cross-Dressing and Cultural Anxiety*. New York: Routledge, 1992.

Grahn, Judy. *Another Mother Tongue: Gay Words, Gay Worlds*. Boston: Beacon, 1984.

Harding, Rick. "Sex Education in Washington, D.C.: Dannemeyer Talks Dirty on the Floor of Congress." *Advocate*, September 26, 1989, 534.

Hollander, Anne. *Seeing Through Clothes*. New York: Viking, 1978.

Holleran, Andrew. *Dancer from the Dance*. New York: Bantam, 1979.

Miller, D. A. "Anal *Rope*." In *Inside/Out: Lesbian Theories, Gay Theories*, edited by Diana Fuss, 119–41. New York: Routledge, 1991.

Moon, Michael. "A Small Boy and Others: Sexual Disorientation in Henry James, Kenneth Anger, and David Lynch." In *Comparative American Identities: Race, Sex, and Nationality in the Modern Text*, edited by Hortense J. Spillers, 141–56. New York: Routledge, 1991.

Patton, Cindy. *Inventing AIDS*. New York: Routledge, 1990.

Rubenstein, Hal. "Simply Divine." *Interview* 18 (February 1988): 51.

Schor, Naomi. *Reading in Detail: Aesthetics and the Feminine*. New York: Methuen, 1987.

Showalter, Elaine. "Critical Cross-Dressing: Male Feminists and the Woman of the Year." In *Men in Feminism*, edited by Alice Jardine and Paul Smith, 116–32. New York: Methuen, 1987.

Waters, John. *Crackpot: The Obsessions of John Waters*. New York: Vintage, 1987.

———. *Shock Value: A Tasteful Book about Bad Taste*. New York: Delta, 1981.

———. *Trash Trio: Three Screenplays: "Pink Flamingos," "Desperate Living," and "Flamingos Forever."* New York: Vintage, 1988.

Contributors

Jana Evans Braziel (English, University of Wisconsin–LaCrosse) holds a Ph.D. in comparative literature and women's studies. Recent publications (in *Journal of North African Studies, Quebec Studies,* and *Tessera: Feminist Interventions in Writing and Culture*) explore the imbrications of ethnicity, nationality, gender, and sexuality in contemporary diasporic and migrant literatures. Her dissertation, "Nomadism, Diaspora, and Deracination in Contemporary Migrant Literatures," explores the nomadic and identity-forming traversals of Algerian, Haitian, and Vietnamese migrant writers in France, Quebec, and the United States. (*And, yes, she's one swank fat chic . . .*).

Marcia Chamberlain (English, Rice University) is a Ph.D. candidate in American literature who is studying the social, economic, and political reasons for the recent boom in "recipe literature." The purpose of her project is to investigate the literary and cultural implications of recipes situated in texts other than cookbooks and to assess the complex impact that these recipes are having on theories about reading and writing. Other recent publications include "Hildegard von Bingen's Causes and Cures: A Radical Feminist Response to the Doctor-Cook Binary," which appeared in *Hildegard von Bingen: A Casebook* (Garland), and "In the Early Mourning," a creative nonfiction piece about Argentina that appeared in the prose journal *Quarter After Eight.*

Cecilia Hartley (English, University of Louisville) is currently completing her Ph.D. in rhetoric and composition. Her research interests include on-line communication in composition classrooms, feminist pedagogies, and women's writing, and she has published in these areas. Most recently, she has coauthored an article with Morgan Gresham, "The Use of Electronic Communication in Facilitating Feminine Modes of Discourse: An Irigaraian Heuristic," in *Feminist Cyberscapes: Essays on Gender in Electronic Spaces,* edited by Pam Takayoshi and Kristine Blair (Ablex, 2000).

Joyce L. Huff (English, George Washington University) is a doctoral candidate and instructor in English at George Washington University. She is currently completing her dissertation, which interrogates the deployment of normative standards for body weight, shape, and size in the construction and gendering of nineteenth-century bodies within social, medical, and literary texts.

Le'a Kent (English, University of Washington) is a doctoral candidate with research and teaching interests in twentieth-century U.S. literature and culture, basic writing, cultural studies, popular culture, feminism, and Marxism. Her dissertation focuses on attempts to represent capitalist systems in literature, and she has also written on lesbian pornography, Cliffs Notes and literary education, male consumerism, and anti-gay legislation such as Oregon's Measure 9. The piece on Measure 9 is published in the electronic journal _*Cultronix*_.

Richard Klein (French, Cornell University) is the author of *Eat Fat* and *Cigarettes Are Sublime.* He lives in Ithaca, New York.

Petra Kuppers (postdoctoral Research Fellow in Performing Arts at Manchester Metropolitan University, United Kingdom) is currently finishing a manuscript on issues of embodiment and representation, and her work on dance and performance has appeared in such journals as *Theatre Topics, New Theatre Quarterly, The Contemporary Theatre Review,* and *Disability Studies Quarterly.* She also works as a community dance and movement artist with disadvantaged people.

Kathleen LeBesco (Communication Arts, Marymount Manhattan College) holds a Ph.D. in communication from the University of Massachusetts–Amherst. Her research interests are in feminist and queer theory, social constructionism, and discourses of the body. Her essays on struggles to redefine fatness have appeared in journals such as *CommOddities* and in several anthologies, and she has presented her work at numerous national and international conferences.

Antonia Losano (English, Middlebury College) has scholarly interests that include Victorian literature, women's studies, literature and visual culture, and art history. She hopes to finish her book on the literary and historical representation of the woman painter next summer, and she is also gathering materials for a project on nineteenth-century elections and their effects on courtship narrative. She has published essays on Marianne North, a Victorian botanist, and on the female double in Victorian fiction.

Sharon Mazer (Theatre and Film Studies, University of Canterbury) is the author of *Professional Wrestling: Sport and Spectacle* (University Press of Mississippi, 1998). Her essays on theater and popular performance have appeared in *TDR: The Drama Review, Theatre Annual, Hop on Pop: The Pleasures and Politics of Popular Culture,* and *Body Show/s: Australian Viewings of Live Performance.*

Michael Moon (English, Duke University) is author of *Disseminating Whitman: Revision and Corporeality in "Leaves of Grass"* (Harvard University Press, 1991) and *A Small Boy and Others: Imitation and Initiation from Henry James to Andy Warhol* (Duke University Press, 1998). Moon has also co-edited *Displacing Homophobia: Gay Male Perspectives in Literature and Culture* with Ronald R. Butters and John M. Clum (Duke University Press, 1989) and *Subjects and Citizens: Nation, Race, and Gender from Oroonoko to Anita Hill* with Cathy N. Davidson (Duke University Press, 1995).

Jerry Mosher (Film and Television, University of California, Los Angeles) is completing his dissertation, "Size Matters: Figuring the Fat Body in American Cinema," which examines how the American film industry has historically constructed and mobilized the perceived deviance of the fat body. He teaches new media technologies at California State University, Los Angeles.

Brenda A. Risch (Comparative Literature, University of North Carolina–Chapel Hill) is currently completing her dissertation on the representation and role of fat women in German and American film, working toward an understanding of the significance of fat in popular culture. Her scholarly interests include women's studies, film and film theory, women and visual culture, body theory, twentieth-century German and American literature, and medical anthropology.

Eve Kosofsky Sedgwick (English, City University of New York) is author of *Between Men: English Literature and Male Homosocial Desire* (Columbia University Press, 1985), *The Coherence of Gothic Conventions* (Methuen, 1986), *Epistemology of the Closet* (University of California Press, 1990), *Tendencies* (Duke University Press, 1993), and *Fat Art, Thin Art* (Duke University Press, 1994). She co-edited *Performativity and Performance* with Andrew Parker (Routledge, 1995) and *Shame and Its Sisters: A Silvan Tomkins Reader* with Adam Frank (Duke University Press, 1995). She has most recently edited *Gary in Your Pocket: Stories and Notebooks of Gary Fisher* (Duke University Press, 1996). Sedgwick's article co-written with Michael Moon, "Divinity: A Dossier, a Performance Piece, a Little-Understood Emotion," is reprinted from *Discourse.*

Sarah Shieff (English, University of Waikato, New Zealand) teaches and researches in the areas of twentieth-century women's writing and New Zealand literature and music. Recent publications include "Gertrude Stein: The Rejection of Closure" (*Antic* 4), "Keri Hulme's *The Bone People*" (*Encyclopedia of the Novel*), "Alfred Hill's *Hinemoa* and Musical Marginality" (*Turnbull Library Record* 28) and "Varieties of Cultural Nationalism: 'Landfall in Unknown Seas,' 1942–1995" (*SPAN* 39). Forthcoming publications include *Talking Music,* a biographical history of classical music in New Zealand, and a collection of essays about corporeality and fiction by women.

Angela Stukator (Film Studies Program, University of Western Ontario) holds a Ph.D. in film from the University of Bristol. She is currently completing a manuscript, "Into the Other: Beyond the Ideal Woman in Film," which examines the representation of female bodies in contemporary narrative cinema. She has published articles on issues of gender representation and identity in the *Canadian Journal of Film Studies* and *Literature/Film Quarterly,* and has presented numerous papers at national and international film conferences.

Neda Ulaby (English, American and Film Studies, University of Chicago) is finishing her dissertation on early-twentieth-century American literature and film. Her academic work has appeared in *Film und Kritik* and *Feminale,* and she reviews film for the *Windy City Times* and on LesBiGay Radio.

Index

Text: 10/13 Aldus
Display: Franklin Gothic Book and Demi
Composition: Binghamton Valley Composition
Printing and binding: Edwards Brothers
Index: Victoria Baker